The Saving Remnant

The Saving Remnant

Religion and the Settling of New England

Cedric B. Cowing

University of Illinois Press   Urbana and Chicago

For Merle Curti

© 1995 by the Board of Trustees of the University of Illinois
Manufactured in the United States of America
1 2 3 4 5 C P 5 4 3 2 1

This book is printed on acid-free paper.

Library of Congress Cataloging-in-Publication Data

Cowing, Cedric B.
    The saving remnant : religion and the settling of New England /
Cedric B. Cowing
        p.   cm.
    Includes index.
    ISBN 0-252-02138-X (alk. paper). — ISBN 0-252-06440-2
(pbk. : alk. paper)
    1. New England—Church history—17th century. 2. New England—
Church history—18th century. 3. England—Church history—17th
century. 4. England—Church history—18th century. I. Title.
BR530.C68 1995
277.4'06—dc20   94-24892
                                                           CIP

Contents

Preface and Acknowledgments

For a long time I have been interested in the development of the American national character. This is an extended essay that reflects that interest, exploring an important aspect of it. I look forward to the reactions and the research that will follow this pioneer effort.

Scholars have cultivated the historical garden of New England with unparalleled intensity, yet because of its vast records, the region is still yielding new information. I have drawn heavily upon recent work in the field and hope I have given full credit wherever it is due.

I would like to thank the following people who have seen or heard excepts from these chapters, mostly in earlier versions: Robert McGlone, James McCutcheon, Mark Bond-Wilson, Kenneth Lockridge, Jonathan Chu, Chadwick Hansen, Robert J. Wilson III, Karen Jolly, Herbert Margulies, Jerry Bentley, Revel Denny, my wife, Sue, and my son, Jim Cowing. It is especially important in this case to make the conventional statement that this interpretation is mine and these helpful persons bear no responsibility for this final version. Very special thanks also go to Everett Wingert of the Geography Department at the University of Hawaii at Manoa for the maps so essential to this work.

I would also like to acknowledge assistance from the American Philosophical Society, the College of Arts and Humanities and the Hamilton Library at the University of Hawaii at Manoa, the Connecticut State Library, the University of Massachusetts–Amherst Library, the Henry E. Huntington Library, and the Sterling Library at Yale University.

The Saving Remnant

And I will gather the remnant of my flock out of all countries whither I have driven them, and will bring them again to their folds; and they will be fruitful and increase. And I will set up shepherds over them which shall feed them: and they shall fear no more, nor be dismayed, neither shall they be lacking, saith the Lord.

—Jeremiah 23:3–4

On the eve of the Great Awakening in the eighteenth century, evangelically inclined clergy—"New Lights"—likened themselves to the biblical saving remnant struggling to keep religion alive in a trough of apathy. For New England, the Saving Remnant has been defined as college-educated ministers active between 1741 and 1744 who supported revivalism, Whitefield, and the New Birth, and for the British Isles, university graduates who supported revivalism, Evangelical or Methodist. Although not as politically astute or economically secure as their opponents, this learned and spiritual elite emerged as a group of effective leaders in a period of religious quickening. They shared the oral culture of the people but had more discipline and consistency in belief. They combined liberal learning and leadership with empathy for evangelism, so their education did not set them too far apart emotionally from their "drowsy" but potentially pious neighbors. And when people face a crisis while they are approaching a peak in a cycle of religiosity, they often turn from priests to prophets, to a more otherwordly cadre offering salvation, charisma, and altruism. The remnant in New England can thus be seen as an outlying segment of a larger group of "mediators" between popular and learned classes in western Europe. They sought reform while maintaining religious vitality and continuity during the transition from orality to print, from the Reformation to the Industrial Revolution.[1]

In the history of Christianity, tension between the orthodox and prophetic (Pauline) traditions has been perennial. Every person, family, town, and region is a mixture of tendencies that represent order and liberty and fluctuate through space and time. The colonial frontier environment, compared with that in the British Isles, has given Pauline forces a larger religious, social, and political influence relative to those of orthodoxy and order. Yet there is a geographical dimension to these two traditions, for in the settlement of the English colonies, priests and prophets have tended to come from different regions and subcultures in their homeland.

Most of the Saving Remnant and others "warmed" by the Great Awakening derived directly from the Northwest, the more pastoral of Britain's two zones, and their forebears were as much pulled by prospects of "westering" in the colonies as pushed by persecution from church and Crown. A smaller group with Northwest surnames who emigrated from the Southeast also contributed significantly to the remnant. The influence of these two groups, however, was for several generations largely overshadowed by the Great Migration that brought so many persecuted Puritans to New England from the market towns of the English Southeast. While those with a Northwest religious tradition shaped by pastoral agriculture were present from the very beginning, they were on the periphery and did not become fully visible or influential at the center until the eighteenth century.

Evangelicals and their ministers came into their own with the Great Awakening. In New England, these New Lights gained more status and power than their British counterparts, the Methodists and Evangelicals, in the parallel revival in the homeland. This major difference in religious sensibility between New Lights and their nonevangelical opponents, the Old Lights and neutrals, shaped and reinforced by geography, has always been present in American life, although it has sometimes lurked below the surface. This religious dimension to order and liberty in the thirteen colonies has been a major fount of American character.

Why did some clergy and laity in New England support the Great Awakening, the major religious phenomenon of the eighteenth century, and others, after hesitation, become opposers? Answers of scholars have varied with time and specialty. Was it the difference in New England between frontier and town, Yale and Harvard, the more and less aesthetic—or more conveniently, for those not interested in religion—

the uneducated and educated, the "lesser sort" and "better sort"? All these explanations, of course, have some validity. After examining many church admission records and contemporary accounts and seeking a more comprehensive and satisfying explanation, I have been drawn back to the first settlers and their origins in the British Isles for answers.[2]

Of the data on the origins of almost three thousand "firstcomers," I have asked a simple question: did the emigrant coming to New England derive from the Northwest of Britain or not? Discrepancies in the parish, town, or, in most instances, even shire of origin are of little consequence for my purposes. The specific alignment of the dividing line between Northwest and Southeast zones, as long as it runs from the Wash to Exeter via Bristol, does not materially affect the outcome either. The results—that more than 70 percent of clerics deriving from Northwest emigrants favored the Great Awakening and a similar percentage not from the Northwest were opposed—are significant, and the magnitude of divergence so large that concern about reliability should be reduced. These findings have guided me in the interpretation that follows and have led me to some new insights, connections, and nuances, although recent scholarship is comprehended. To this reworking I have juxtaposed the parallel developments in the British Isles and added the accounts of John Wesley and George Whitefield.

The findings make apparent the need to modify the longstanding stress on the uniformity and Englishness of the colonial New England population because it does conceal important religious differences. It is true that in the first half century of settlement there were very few African, Scots-Irish, French Huguenot, Dutch, or German settlers in New England and, compared with the Middle Colonies or southern backcountry in the eighteenth century, the region has appeared to be remarkably homogeneous ethnically and culturally. But closer inspection in matters of religion reveals a significant subcultural split.

Some cherished assumptions about settlers and the frontier are also undercut. Since Frederick Jackson Turner first announced his frontier thesis, the consensus has been that while pioneers brought over regional differences, these soon melted away because of the frontier, communality of settlement, intermarriage, and the "free Aire" of the colonies. I have found instead persistence of a religious tendency and have followed this from the beginning not only to the revival of the 1740s, but in some instances beyond, into the nineteenth century. This subcultural difference gives credence to the view that the eighteenth-century revival was not quite general enough in territory or intensity to warrant the label Great Awakening. In New England the awakening was great where Northwest stock set the tone and not really "great," only moderate, transitory, or minimal elsewhere.

The principal task of geographers is to explore areal differentiation in the world and bring out the characteristics of its many regions. To do this, all aspects must be considered, social as well as physical. Social geography has been described as the processes and patterns involved in the understanding of socially defined populations in their spatial setting. Social geographers are interested in broad changes of population structure and distribution. They can move on from this basic demography to several subdivisions; the geography of religion is one of them.

At the turn of the century, geography, like the social sciences in general, was deterministic. The German school, influenced by Marx and Darwin, regarded physical geography alone as "pure," rejecting the social as "unscientific." Although consideration of social aspects was later revived, geographers remained cautious in dealing with immaterial forces bearing on their discipline; they have often felt that these were better left to sociologists.

Geographers describe the geography of religion as a dependent and youthful subfield, recognizable but diffuse. It has been somewhat neglected for several decades because of a preoccupation with developing countries and contemporary urban areas. The discipline has also focused on how religion affects the environment rather than on how the environment shapes religious belief and practice. Most geographers do agree, however, that a dominant religious style, or *mentalité*, affects the values of a whole region, including those of minorities and immigrants.[3]

An early concern of these researchers was the measurement of religious vitality, or religiosity. They wanted to go beyond mere plotting of membership—questionable figures at best—to get some idea of commitment and belief. How could the religiosity of different regions and countries be compared? Using baptisms and attendance statistics, Gabriel Bras tried to measure this for France in 1931. He found that religious vitality seemed to be stronger on the periphery, in Brittany, Flanders, Alsace-Lorraine, Jura, and the Pyrenees, than in the center of France.

After World War II, Michael Fogarty identified a belt of piety running across Europe from the Adriatic to the English Channel that included both Protestants and Catholics, dubbing it the "Christian Heartland." To the north and south religious observance was markedly less. He called pious enclaves he discovered to the south and west—the Pyrenees and Brittany—"outliers" from the Heartland. This is mentioned here simply to suggest that geography—religion and subculture—continue be relevant in assessing religiosity even in western Europe, assumed to be the most secularized part of the world in the twentieth century. The significance of this modern Heartland remains to be explicated, however.[4]

In the United States, what is obviously most American about American religion is the place, according to Martin Marty, although Americans, like Europeans, have emphasized time and neglected space in discussing religion. He has observed that while the country has always been a land of immigrants, their settlement has consecrated it—the Promised Land. The majority of the pious "have regarded their environment as being somehow redemptive and revelatory," where "God himself speaks through the soil, the history, and the people."[5] Yet God seems to do so in a manner that indicates sectional continuity with the British homeland.

Although by Turner's definition the frontier disappeared in 1890, land has remained important and religious competition over land and cityscape continues. While there is much talk of ecumenism and "creative pluralism," sectional competition and conflict remains. The religious system that can best discern specific human needs in a given environment and address them will have satisfied clients, Marty concludes, and can compete in the world of regional American religion.

In American religious history, a major difference between New Lights and Old Lights has been the emphasis of the former on the New Birth, which required a specific date. While New Lights accepted some gradual experiences, they worked for and preferred sudden conversions. Therefore it is useful, and sometimes essential, to distinguish not only New Lights and Old Lights but also the closely related "once-born" and "twice-born."[6] William James, in his classic *Varieties of Religious Experience* (1903), demonstrated the nature of this distinction, although he did not spell out its larger social and political significance.

James, of course, was himself twice-born, and his family history contributed to his insights. Henry, grandfather of William James, was a Scots-Irish immigrant who settled in Albany, New York, in 1789. His son, Henry Jr., suffered a severe crisis before sudden conversion to the Swedenborg religion in 1844 at age thirty-three. He used the Swedenborgian term "vastation" to describe his experience. His son, William, had a similar identity crisis at age thirty. Finally achieving autonomy from his father, he was able to use philosophy and psychology in examining religious phenomena. Because scholarly analyses have used Freud to explain the parental and sibling relationships of the James family, they have naturally tended to downplay this religious ancestry and continuity.

William James's biography indicates a strong antimaterialism, a will to believe, an emphasis on affections, and a preference for sudden conversions. Cushing Strout has noted the striking lack of variety in his *Varieties* and the concentration on one type of experience, the twice-born conversion of the "sick soul." To James "psychical research" was what "remarkable providences" had been to Cotton Mather; he had as little interest in denominational distinctions as George Whitefield. In short, his temperament and interests mark James as a seeker, a late species of New Light, if I may use this term for someone who died in 1910.

He was not alone in his search. With the decline of Calvinistic evangelism in New England, thoughtful persons of a New Light heritage had been drawn to Transcendentalism, Swedenborgianism, Spiritualism, and mind cure groups to satisfy their religious needs. Because of the rise of Darwinism, by 1900 the "warfare of science and religion" was heating up in the United States, with professors on one side and evangelical clergy on the other. James, however, remained sympathetic to religious faith and a seeker open to further light, putting himself at odds with most of his colleagues on the Harvard faculty.[7]

Since James described the twice-born, the idea has been widely acknowledged and refined, but he is still cited. The twice-born are carriers of a religious tradition that comes out of pastoral agriculture. They wait for promptings, leadings, openings, quickenings, or the small, still voice. They trust intuition and expect inspiration in their lives without losing liberty. They feel incomplete and need to be "born again" in young adulthood. Their experience is Pauline, typically leading to a sudden, dramatic climax, a transformation that is lasting and brings personality modifications and career changes. Although literate—sometimes very much so—they have remained residually oral and rely on other senses besides the visual. Of course, postconversion doubts and vacillation occur. Transformation usually comes as a result of hearing the Word from a gifted person, often a visitor or itinerant, but confirming it through group interaction and printed texts. Persons in this pattern could be indifferent to religion, morally lax, or "drowsy saints"—complacent in decent living but without religious vitality until their orality was properly stirred. Transformed, and seeing others they admired similarly affected, converts became more open to social and political changes and were ready to urge them on the unsaved populace. They also longed for "beauty of union," that special feeling that comes from communion of the saved, and for some kind of millennium.

Awakenings, stirrings, "sprinklings," and "downpours" undoubtedly hastened conversion in many cases, bringing persons to earlier and more pronounced crises than otherwise would have been the case. Yet conversions of adult persons from twenty to thirty-five or even forty years of age were conspicuous because they brought major changes in motive and lifestyle. They often came after a moratorium or considerable conflict. William James was reflecting his own experience and his father's as well as case studies when he concluded that these experiences were important and likely to be permanent.

The development of the once-born was smoother although there was adolescent warming and some depressions and epiphanies later in life. They grew into their faith and worldviews without as much concentrated mental and physical anguish as the twice-born. Gradualists in religion, they inclined the same way in social and political affairs, wary of any great leaps forward; their confidence was predicated on incremental progress. Preferring reason over intuition, they were inclined to favor the visual over the other senses. Old Lights in the eighteenth century used law, printed words, and a didactic Plain Style of preaching to restrain passions, not arouse them.

In analyzing "the religious mind" in early America, Alan Heimert found his major theme in the tension between the once-born and the twice-born, between Old Lights and New Lights, a difference that cut across many religious persuasions. He sympathized with New Lights because of their democratic spirit.[8] Studies of popular religion in the twentieth century have made similar distinctions. Gerhard Lenski in *The Religious Factor,* a study of the Detroit area, found it essential to separate peripheral church attenders from faithful adherents because their responses and commitments were so different.[9] More importantly, the psychologist Gordon Allport argued that there are distinct types—"intrinsic" (devotional) and "extrinsic" (orthodox)—within church flocks and that the former were not only more pious but, interestingly, more open and flexible on most social questions, even compared with the general public.[10]

Until recently, social scientists have tended to use pejorative terms to describe those who have experienced religious conversion. They have not only called converts "susceptible" but have sometimes added pathological terms suggesting disease. Even James contributed to this with his famous phrase "sick soul." More recently, some social scientists have adopted more positive language, viewing converts as pilgrims on a quest. Building on Allport's paradigm, they have identified a subgroup among intrinsics, a spiritual elite of "seekers."[11] Seekers yearn for conversion and when it comes, they are led to be creative in developing personal religious views. William James belongs in this seeker elite, and so does the Saving Remnant of the eighteenth century as well as many of the Transcendentalists, Swedenborgians, Spiritualists, and mind cure sympathizers of the nineteenth century. At times of religious controversy and polarization, seekers have tended to sympathize with intrinsic believers in general and defend religious faith.

How important has this cultural and geographical difference in religion—between the more and less otherworldly, twice-born and once-born—been in the United Kingdom and the United States since 1800? And could there be affinities between "burnt-over districts"—so called for their cycles of religious intensity—in Britain and America, between the Bible Belt in the United States and Fogarty's Christian Heartland? My evidence is preliminary and pertains to early New England, but I have tried to keep such questions in mind.

The religious sectionalism in the British Isles in the early seventeenth century is indicated in chapter 1. Chapter 2 compares the geographical origins of two New England towns, Rowley and Hingham, as seedbeds and prototypes of evangelism and orthodoxy, New Light and Old Light. Chapter 3 stresses the continuity of religio-geographic dissent from the beginning, from Hutchinsonians and Quakers to Salem witches and New Lights. Chapters 4 and 5 present the parallel developments in Britain. Chapters 6 and 7 describe the areas of most intense New Light activity during the Great Awakening and the role of the Saving Remnant. Chapters 8 and 9 offer some parallel data for the Old Light and its leaders. The Conclusion suggests the relevance of these findings for the late twentieth century.

Notes

1. Peter Burke, *Popular Culture in Early Modern Europe* (1978), 65–87. "Oral" refers to "folk" culture and not to a "primitive" nonliterate tradition. David Buchan calls the mixture of word-of-mouth and literate influences a "verbal" culture. See *The Ballad and the Folk* (1972), 1–2. I have stayed with the older and more familiar "oral" to designate this blend.

2. Marc Bloch, the French historian, has provided the label "regressive history" for the method of working back from data in one century to gain clues and insights to the previous one where data is less plentiful; it is one of the "oblique approaches" necessary to illuminate popular culture. See Burke, *Popular Culture*, 81–82.

3. James W. Watson, "The Sociological Aspects of Geography," in *Geography in the Twentieth Century*, ed. T. Griffith Taylor (1957), 463–84; Alan R. H. Baker, "Historical Geography: A New Beginning?" in *Historical Geography: A Methodological Portrayal*, ed. D. Brooks Green (1991), 299–304.

4. John D. Gay, *The Geography of Religion in England* (1971), 1–22. Michael P. Fogarty hoped that the postwar Christian Democrat movement emphasizing family and a middle way between laissez-faire and state socialism could expand from this Heartland base. See *Christian Democracy in Western Europe, 1820–1953* (1957), 6–11.

5. Martin E. Marty, *Religion and the Republic: The American Circumstance* (1987), 197–226, quotation from 202.

6. Researchers continue to make direct links between evangelism and sudden conversion. Terry D. Bilhartz does so in his recent study of Baltimore churchgoers, *Urban Religion and the Second Great Awakening: Church and Society in Early National Baltimore* (1986), 83–84.

7. Howard Feinstein, *Becoming William James* (1984), 69–75, 236–50. See also Gerald E. Myers, *William James: His Life and Thought* (1986), chap. 14, especially p. 456, and Cushing Strout, "The Pluralistic Identity of William James: A Psycho-Historical Reading of *The Varieties of Religious Experience*," *American Quarterly* 23 (1971): 136–39. "The hyphenated term 'Scotch-Irish' is an Americanism" and "refers to people of Scottish descent who, having lived for a time in the north of Ireland, migrated in considerable numbers to the American colonies" after 1718. "Perhaps 250,000 of them actually crossed the sea to America, and they bred rapidly." As settlers in northern Ireland they had come into conflict with native Irish Catholics, and this intensified their Protestantism and reinforced their Presbyterianism. James G. Leyburn, "The Scotch-Irish," *American Heritage* 22 (1970): 31. Many of these people today prefer "Scots-Irish," so I have used this term in this work.

8. Alan Heimert, *Religion and the American Mind: From the Great Awakening to the Revolution* (1966). On the other hand, William Hutchison, analyzing biographies of American Protestant religious leaders of the late nine-

teenth century, found the biggest difference between his two categories—"conservatives" and "liberals"—was in the matter of conversion. Two-thirds of the former but very few of the latter had suddenly "got religion," been "born again," and conservatives were three times more likely to come from the South. Otherwise home backgrounds were quite similar—"Anglo-Saxon" and more urban and professional than the general population. He did not attempt to distinguish Scots-Irish or Scottish from the others, however, so perhaps his yardstick was too crude for this clerical group. See Hutchison, "Culture Strain and Protestant Liberalism," *American Historical Review* 76 (1971): 400–410. And statistically minded historians have relied on the distinction between devotionals (pietists) and orthodox (ritualists, liturgicals) in explaining Midwest political culture in the nineteenth century. They have depicted continual tension between right belief and right behavior. Paul Kleppner, in *The Cross of Culture: A Social Analysis of Midwestern Politics, 1850–1890* (1971), found the basic conflicts to be religious, between "pietists" and "ritualists." Local religious and ethnic loyalties contributed heavily to national voting patterns. Richard Jensen, in *The Winning of the Midwest: Social and Political Conflict, 1886–1896* (1971), concluded that forces animating "the electorate were party loyalty and, more fundamentally, religion" (xii). He called his two basic religious types "pietists" and "liturgicals." The categories of Kleppner and Jensen correspond quite closely to the New Light–Old Light comparisons scholars use for the eighteenth century.

9. Gerhard Lenski, *The Religious Factor* (1961). In the wake of the presidential election of 1980, political scientists hurried to reexamine the relationship between religion and politics. They have continued to rely on the simple born-again question, finding it "salient" in measuring evangelical influence at the polls. Charles W. Dunn, ed., *Religion in American Politics* (1989), 147–50.

10. Gordon Allport, "The Religious Context of Prejudice," *Journal for the Scientific Study of Religion* 5 (1966): 447–57. See also Corwin Schmidt, "Evangelicals and the Election of 1984," *American Politics Quarterly* 15 (1987): 419–44.

11. They see the remaining intrinsics as still a bit rigid, not moving far enough beyond new religious tenets acquired with conversion. C. Daniel Batson and W. Larry Ventis, *The Religious Experience: A Social-Psychological Perspective* (1982), 56–96. David A. Snow and Richard Machalek, in "The Sociology of Conversion," *Annual Review of Sociology* 10 (1984): 167–90, review the extensive literature. See also Peter L. Berger, "Some Second Thoughts on the Substantive vs. Functional Definitions of Religion," *Journal for the Scientific Study of Religion* 13 (1974): 125–33.

Chapter One

Southeast and Northwest Britain: Defining Culture and Religion for the Colonies

Frederick Jackson Turner popularized the concept of the American frontier as a melting pot and equalizer, a force for nationalism and democracy. As a corollary, he emphasized the role of sections, not just the North and South before the Civil War, but throughout American history. Although he noted that different "stocks" made for regionalism in culture and religion as well as politics in the new republic, he did not elaborate and failed to recognize just how much sectionalism the pioneers had brought with them across the Atlantic. This was natural, however, because for Turner to have given much notice to cultural or religious differences among the first settlers would have distracted readers from his thesis: a unique American character emerging in the frontier process. Turner was reacting against his professors at Johns Hopkins University who stressed that the "germs" of American democracy came from the forests of Saxony and so could not be expected to consider imported as well as domestic sectionalism.[1]

In England traditional sectionalism had intensified with the Reformation and continued in the seventeenth and eighteenth centuries. The most relevant division for colonial New England is a line setting off Northwest from Southeast, the periphery from the center (see map 1). To separate the two sections, the familiar line from the Wash to Bristol is used throughout this book and is extended in a southwesterly direction to the south coast just west of Exeter. This puts Bristol and

Old Boston just inside the Northwest zone and Exeter east of it. Such a division, although it can be no more than a close approximation, is essential in analyzing the popular religious belief and behavior of the people and those who emigrated to New England from the two sections. In this process, highland and lowland, pastoral and arable, evangelical and orthodox are separated. By tracing the probable seventeenth-century English origins of New England clergy active in the Great Awakening I discovered that this line demarcates not only evangelical and Methodist traditions from the Puritan ones in the home country but also separates those who became New Lights from those who became Old Lights in New England. A Northwest minority living in the Southeast, especially in East Anglia, also carried evangelical and antinomian tendencies.

The Southeast includes East Anglia, the area later called the Home Counties, and half of the West Country and was home to about three-quarters of the English population in 1630. There were wealds, fens, and some hills over a thousand feet, but most land was below four hundred feet elevation and arable. The London metropolis and growing commercial towns were there. This part of England accepted the Reformation more readily than the other part. Christian roots in the archbishopric of Canterbury were Roman without as much admixture of Celtic as in York, the other province. The gentry in rural areas supported parishes of the Church of England that were relatively compact and well endowed. Some could draw well-educated clergy to their churches.

Three-quarters of New England pioneers were from the Southeast, about the same proportion as the English population. The extensive writing about the Great Migration of 1630–40 has therefore concentrated on them. And within the Southeast, East Anglia has been the most significant subregion, both religiously and economically. Calvinism and modifications of it from the Continent reached this area first. In his dissection of the Puritan mind, Perry Miller found East Anglia and Cambridge University dominating his pages, and David Hackett Fischer has gone even further in claiming East Anglian hegemony in New England.[2]

East Anglia

East Anglia was relatively populous and commercial in the sixteenth century, with many ties to the Continent across the English Channel.

Map 1. Southeast and Northwest: The Two Religious Zones

In the cloth towns were a number of workers from abroad—Flemings, Walloons, and the Dutch. Until 1620, religious dissent and separatism were more obvious in East Anglia than elsewhere in the Southeast, and the region had begun to reflect some of the religious diversity of Holland, where toleration was being pioneered.

The geography of East Anglia was conducive to the development of rational religion. The area was fertile with a good mixture of soils. With the growth of metropolitan London and the cloth towns, demand for food mounted. The harbors of East Anglia were small but adequate for shipping down the coast to London and even to the Low Countries. Trade and manufacturing towns were densely populated and growing much more rapidly than the countryside. In Essex the population doubled from 50,000 to 100,000 in the century after the Reformation. The middling gentry rather than the court magnates predominated.

The cloth trade was the most important economic activity. When textile manufacturing came over to England from the Low Countries in the sixteenth century, it arrived in East Anglia first, and even before the Reformation this trade was associated with religious heterodoxy. Workers expected to be read to and would later seek the Word in sermons and lectures. The cloth industry brought income to people who lacked gentry status but had discipline and were upwardly mobile in the burgeoning towns. After the Reformation, "advanced" Protestants gave money for educating clergy, hiring lecturers, and for impropriating—buying up of the right to choose the parish minister. Expanding economic activity facilitated popular education, literacy, and the work ethic as well as the Protestant cause. In England it was these cloth towns that first exemplified the traits Max Weber made famous as auguring "the Spirit of Capitalism." East Anglia was the chief importing area for ideas about business, religion, and politics. These counties were less parochial and more cosmopolitan than any other place except metropolitan London.[3]

East Anglia was the cradle of Puritanism, which emerged at the beginning of Queen Elizabeth's reign in 1558. The Marian exiles, who left the country to avoid the rampant Catholicism of Mary's reign, returned from the Continent reinforced in their Calvinism and determined to complete the Reformation in England. These Puritans first sought to purge the remaining Roman Catholic ceremonies from the Church of England. They also challenged the quality of the established clergy because so many were uneducated and thus incapable of preaching a sermon. Nonpreachers—"dumb dogs"—occupied one-third of the ecclesiastical livings even in prosperous East Anglia. Therefore Puritan benefactors stepped in during the 1560s to support lecturers focusing on the scriptures in parishes where clergy could offer only ritual and sacraments rather than religious instruction. The reformers wanted ministers who were not absentees or pluralists and could preach in the Plain Style. Puritans could be distinguished from other English people by a combination of attitudes: interest in theology and the conversion experience, diligence in a calling, strict observance of the sabbath, as well as preference for the Plain Style. They were sensitive to corruption and luxury and developed a reputation for "tender" consciences. Puritan clerics were expected to be "physicians of the soul" who would encourage introspection and make house calls to the sick, troubled, or corrupt.[4]

When the Church of England adopted its creed of thirty-nine articles in 1571, the language was explicitly Calvinist, part of the reaction to territorial and religious rivalry with Catholic Spain. In mobilizing England against the Spanish threat, Elizabeth I needed Puritan support to counterbalance the still significant number of Roman Catholic sympathizers in the realm. Thus the Puritan faction was tolerated and grew during these years despite the queen's personal distaste for its religious views. Elizabeth sought the middle way for her Church of England, between Catholicism and Calvinism, with the Erastian idea of using the established church to strengthen monarchy and reinforce English nationalism.

The Tudor government was also interested in raising the educational level of the clergy as a means of social control, to create a line of defense against popular religion and the kind of radicalism that had followed the Reformation in Germany. This check was also needed because the major thrust of Protestantism was that people should read the Bible in the vernacular and interpret it for themselves. The Reformation had obviously loosened the social cement uniting the country, and the government was uneasy about the direction and rate of social change. The Crown hoped that by endowing colleges and scholarships and thus raising educational standards for the clergy, religious radicalism could be contained.

Universities moved from joint control by pope and Crown to complete control by the latter and changed rapidly in the second half of the sixteenth century. They retained their seminary character but were educating parish priests for the Church of England instead of regular cler-

gy, whose numbers had been severely reduced by Henry VIII's dissolution of the monasteries. But a university education also became relevant for a larger segment of society, not simply clerks on scholarship.
Student enrollments increased from 150 in 1500 to 600 in 1600 at both
Oxford and Cambridge. During the economic vicissitudes of Elizabeth,
sons of gentry and merchants alike could get an education and even
make careers in the established church. Puritanism came early and was
more pervasive at Cambridge than at Oxford. It was fed by the towns
of East Anglia, which were in turn stimulated by geographical proximity to, and economic connection with, the Continent. Puritanism
took early root here and soon afterward accommodated to a European
rationalistic refinement—Ramism.

Ramism was a modification of scholastic learning particularly suited to a constituency of godly merchants and therefore took hold early
in East Anglia and at Cambridge University among Puritan faculty.
Because it relied more on the Bible and less on the ancients, it was attractive to a rising middle class resentful of the traditional curriculum
and Ciceronian style of the gentry. Ramists claimed to have a new system of learning, replacing Aristotle and scholasticism. In fact the "new"
system was not an entire substitute but rather an abridgement and sim-
plification that deemphasized Aristotle's metaphysics and ethics. It was
easier to visualize, memorize, and retain than the less systematic scheme
of the scholastics. Ramism was a means of instruction that used dichot-
omies and diagrams to make traditional liberal arts accessible and in-
telligible to a large group of the middle class.[5]

The life of its founder, Petrus Ramus (1515–72), also commended
Ramism to Puritans at Cambridge, and its influence cut across colleges to affect the whole university. Ramus was a French pedagogue who
had developed "golden Rules of Art" for logic and later extended them
to religion after converting to Protestantism. When he was murdered
on St. Bartholomew's Day, he became a Protestant martyr.

Ramism claimed to be closer to natural reasoning and actuality than
the "artificial" system of Aristotle. Puritan intellectuals adopted the
Ramistic method while retaining respect for the spoken Word. They
deplored the "dumb reading" of the uneducated among established clergy, who merely pronounced the words without real understanding.
Ramism was consistent with the Puritan emphasis on reducing Catholic vestiges in the church and promoting the Plain Style in sermons,
dress, and art. It democratized learning for the mercantile class but it

also led to a retreat from the orality and spontaneity of English reformers of the first generation following the Reformation.

In the first decades of Elizabeth's reign the Puritans had made much progress. The Calvinism in the church creed was retained despite the queen's effort to steer a middle course between Catholicism and Puritanism, which reflected the slowly changing religious views of her subjects. Puritan scholarship and Ramism took firmer hold at many of Cambridge's colleges, and as their prosperity mounted, more clergy were educated and so gave more sermons. There were more livings and lectureships for them and compensation improved. Puritans also attempted to check bishops' authority and improve efficiency in church government by introducing a presbyterian scheme within the episcopal structure of the church. This effort was most successful in East Anglia because of a history of clerical conferences there.

Expansion of the Puritan party, moreover, was accompanied by signs that Catholic vestiges were declining. Mystery plays, so popular before the Reformation, had virtually disappeared in East Anglia by 1580. The approach of the showdown with Spain no doubt accelerated the decline of overt Catholicism. And Elizabeth's discouragement of prophesying at religious conferences strengthened clergy and presbyterianism at the expense of laity and congregationalism. Even the trickle of Separatists to Holland "without tarrying for anie" must have increased conservative Puritanism a bit. By 1588 when the Spanish Armada was turned back, Puritans were well entrenched in East Anglia despite intermittent efforts by the queen and bishops to circumscribe them. After thirty years, they were ready to move beyond the early Calvinism the Marian exiles had brought back from the Continent.

After leveling off over a generation, Ramism persisted among the Puritans. Neo-scholasticism gained some ground temporarily by reemphasizing natural law. On the Protestant left, some sectarians even attacked Ramist logic in the vernacular as elitist. Ramism actually found more favor with youth bent on action than with mature and philosophical persons. Christopher Hill views the "golden rules of Art" as appealing primarily to the middle class outside the universities who were interested in applied science.[6]

William Ames, England's best-known covenant theologian, was a product of this Ramist influence. Expelled from Cambridge, he went into exile in Holland, joining other nonconformists. There he used his Ramism to combat the lingering influence of Aristotle. Ames perfected Ramism, arguing that "particles" of knowledge could be arranged in a logical order to facilitate learning. While his theology was God-centered and he proved orthodox in defending Calvinism against Arminianism at the Synod of Dort in 1619, his Ramism and practical divinity later led him to be more concerned with method than faith and to develop preparation ideas. He asserted that, despite Adam's fall, people had enough natural ability or free will to prepare themselves, to initiate their own conversion, and should not rely on God to seize their souls suddenly.

A few English clergy had explored preparation in the early years of Puritanism but their ideas remained inchoate with paradoxes unresolved. William Perkins of Warwickshire had been one of the chief initiators of preparation suggestions. He was a mainstream Church of England minister who rejected the Puritan label and appealed to all parties of Anglicans. As an evangelical preacher, Perkins emphasized the conversion experience and sanctified reason as a gift from God. Piety and rationalism were in momentary equilibrium, but after 1600, Puritan thinkers moved beyond Perkins's explanations. Because of their belief in covenant theology, they demanded "a more detailed account about the beginning and growth of grace."[7] The locus of interest in preparation moved to the Southeast and took definite form with the work of two East Anglians, William Ames (b. 1576) and Richard Sibbes (b. 1578).

When Puritan clergy examined their flocks in East Anglia and studied those who had been saved, they refined conceptions of conversion further by defining stages and elaborating on the process. They found a greater role for persons to play before God effectually called them. For their flocks, Lydia's gradual transformation seemed closer to the norm than the sudden and violent experience of Saul on the road to Damascus. In contrast to the revivalists of the eighteenth century, the clergy of East Anglia moved in the direction of baptismal regeneration, gradualism, and growth in the faith.

William Ames taught that people could prepare for salvation without waiting for God to move or seize them. In fact, to be saved, people must renounce their righteousness, evaluate themselves, and pass the checkpoints of conviction, despair, and humiliation before reaching the effectual calling. God did not restrain people and they had much that they "ought" to do before that point.

As a covenant theologian, Ames stressed the importance of baptism as the "very beginning of regeneration." The increase in human beings' natural abilities conferred by baptism removed them from depravity and made them able, susceptible, and obligated to respond to exhortation and acknowledgment of the "promises" of baptism. Covenant theology was beginning to replace the unknowable and arbitrary God of Calvin with "the party of the first part," a more reliable and reasonable God who felt obligated to the contract with humanity. As Perry Miller observed, "To compare the *Institutes* with William Ames's *Medulla* is to perceive at once the difference between the mentality of Calvin and that of the Puritan. Where the *Institutes* has the majestic sweep of untrammeled confidence, the *Medulla,* though no less confident, is meticulously made up of heads and subheads, objections and answers, arguments and demonstration."[8] Ames produced the first complete edition of the *Medulla* (*The Marrow of Sacred Divinity*) in 1627. Two years later, John Winthrop, leader of the Great Migration, urged Ames to come along to New England. Ames promised to follow but wound up in Amsterdam with an English congregation instead. His son spent nine years in New England, graduating from Harvard in 1645 before returning to East Anglia. William Ames's formulation of covenant theology did have a profound impact on East Anglian emigrants, however.[9]

Ames published his major work on practical divinity, *Cases of Conscience,* in 1630, the year Puritans arrived at Massachusetts Bay. In the preceding decade he was still a Calvinist alert to the dangers of Catholicism, but his emphasis was shifting from doctrine to defining the godly life. Puritanism in the Southeast was entering its third generation, and believers wanted specific answers to ethical questions. Ames hoped his *Cases* would meet this need and keep Puritans from resorting to Catholic authorities on ethics. By this time, there was some tendency toward Puritan scholasticism, and opponents, including Archbishop Laud and Charles I, liked to link Puritans with Jesuits on occasion. The combined effects of elaboration of stages of conversion and rules for godly conduct contributed to make Puritans more churchlike and less sectarian, more legalistic and less spontaneous than in earlier decades—the classic evolutionary pattern.[10] "The more minutely we examine their thought, the more it becomes clear that the emotional drive of the piety was . . . already lessening at the time the colonies were founded, and that the colonists thenceforward were progressively more swayed by factors in the intellectual heritage than by hunger of the spirit."[11]

The idea of free will also gained some visibility in England in the

1590s under its old name, Pelagianism. Although Oxford was only brushed by this idea, it took root at Cambridge. Thus Calvinist Puritans not only had to contend with the queen's church and sectarians but also had to refute arguments of a small group who maintained that grace was available to all. Again it was a Continental, Peter Baro, who planted this idea at Cambridge but it soon came to be known as Arminianism after the monk, Arminius, who developed his new version in Holland.

In the debate between Calvinists and Arminians at Dort in 1619, the former had a voting majority but the latter more effectively publicized their views. Afterwards the Remonstrants, as Dutch Arminians were called, continued to argue, publish, and multiply in the commercial towns. Although Ames and other English delegates at Dort supported the Calvinism of the Anglican creed, some influential bishops moved the Church of England in an Arminian direction soon afterward. James I had early Calvinist sympathies but became more pragmatic on the throne; he and his successor, Charles I, moved toward the Arminians, noting that they were respectful of monarchy and therefore good foils for the Puritans.[12]

East Anglian cloth towns, the seedbeds of Puritanism, also felt this drift, following their Dutch counterparts toward Arminianism in theology and, to a lesser extent, presbyterianism in polity. These tendencies would not become obvious, however, until the Civil War. Evangelism and separatism were not absent; they could still be found in some woodland districts and port towns among people who had emigrated from north of the cultural line. But the dominant trend in East Anglia and among its emigrants to New England—despite the atmosphere of persecution and exodus—reflected this tilt away from evangelism.

Yet the Puritans from Southeast England who founded the Massachusetts Bay Colony were consciously retrospective. They sought religious liberty in order to implement the Bible, to restore the covenants and laws of apostolic times. They believed that these were unchanging and were therefore on the alert to oppose "human invention," blaming the Catholics of the Middles Ages for most of the divergences from biblical truths. This backward-looking emphasis made them ascetic and legalistic, suspicious of chiliastic and millennial tendencies.[13] The use of Ramism, congruent with the conservative thrust for law and order, did open the way to some unconscious rationalism.

John Winthrop was leader of the Great Migration to New England that began in 1630. On the *Arbella*, as it crossed the Atlantic, he announced the intention of the pioneers to build a godly community in the wilderness, a city on a hill. As a youth Winthrop had been pious and self-searching. After several years at Cambridge, he gained notice as a lawyer, businessman, and gentleman in his native Suffolk. His conversion in 1618 was the culmination of a long process. By the time of his arrival at Massachusetts Bay, he was forty-two and had begun to reflect some of the currents at work in East Anglia in the 1620s. This became evident six years later when he held office and Anne Hutchinson and her followers challenged the Puritan oligarchy. Winthrop was not a theologian and, according to Edmund Morgan, had to be restrained from committing himself publicly to a refutation of her he had written that was plainly Arminian. His minister saved him from this embarrassment. Winthrop and other political leaders used covenant theology—Ramism—conservatively and maintained that magistrates, although chosen by the people, were accountable to God. Winthrop was elected magistrate many times and thus was able to thwart what he described as "the democratical spirit" that surfaced to oppose magisterial prerogative. Perry Miller was right in depicting Winthrop as the leader of the Puritan elite, who exercised presbyterian godliness and expected the people to be deferential.[14]

The Puritan elite used theology and covenant obligations to channel the conversion experience, maintain order, and restrict subjectivity. The role of conversion in the Puritan movement had changed. In the days of Queen Elizabeth, early Puritans had used the conversion experience to dissent from the Church of England and the religious and social status quo and press for reformation. Later in the Massachusetts Bay Colony, the Puritans made the conversion experience the cornerstone of their religious and political establishment by making the franchise depend on it. Thomas Shepard, pastor of Cambridge, a community of settlers from Southeast England, recorded some fifty-one conversion testimonies, i.e., "confessions" or "public relations," between 1638 and 1644. Under Shepard's guidance, neophytes tended to "dwell more on preparation than on the life of faith," and "not many people openly exalted in profound joy or sublime peace." Meanwhile Anne Hutchinson and those who stressed the Holy Spirit—the antinomians, Quakers, and other sectarians of the English Interregnum—sowed the seeds of revivalism that would supplant Puritanism in the colonies of the eighteenth century.[15]

By the time of the Great Migration to New England, Puritan thinkers had refined their Calvinism and were moving closer to the reformed orthodoxy of the Continent. Ramism had developed and even free grace and the seeds of latitudinarianism were sprouting at Emmanuel College, fount of Puritan theology at Cambridge. When members of the Puritan elite fled East Anglia, they brought some of these tendencies to New England and picked up others in the next decades. Puritans of this sort were present at the Massachusetts Bay and Connecticut colonies in the early years, and they survived and prospered. Continuing on this course would make them natural opponents of the Great Awakening. In this they paralleled the mainline Dissenters of England, who recoiled from the religious chaos of the Civil War, accommodated to the Age of Reason, and did not readily respond to the appeals of George Whitefield and John Wesley in the middle of the eighteenth century.

London

London had much in common with the provincial towns that were emerging in the Southeast at this time, yet there are many reasons for putting the city in a class by itself. In 1630, about a third of a million people, 7 percent of the total population, inhabited London. The next largest town, Norwich, had only 20,000 people. London was the capital and the chief port of England. By 1700 it would surpass Paris and become the largest city in western Europe. Because of its extraordinary growth—especially from 1590 to 1620—all the usual urban problems were magnified. But it grew not by natural increase but by immigration. A great influx was required just to offset the death rate. The mortality rate was highest in the East End among single men who had come to the city for work, but newcomers quickly took the places of those felled by plague, influenza, smallpox, and typhus. Turnover was such that one person in six had spent some time living in the metropolis. One scholar has suggested that before 1640, London was in fact parasitic, actually retarding national economic development by placing so much demand for food and people on the hinterlands.

In the century after the Reformation, London grew not only in numbers but in ideas. It was the center of intellectual ferment and therefore theological innovation. Queen Elizabeth had facilitated this by confining the printing industry to the capital in the hope of censoring it more effectively. The clergy of the Church of England, halved by the Reformation, was recovering slowly in numbers, education, and status but was losing ground relatively because other professions were rising even faster. Puritans predominated among the bourgeoisie, who endowed lectureships in more than a hundred parishes to sustain the gospel in the Plain Style. The incumbents, even in the metropolis, were evidently not educated, moral, or articulate enough to meet Puritan standards. Thus Puritanism and rising literacy were quite visible in London when William Laud became its bishop and conflict between king and Parliament reached a crisis.

While the Puritanism of the Southeast was visible in the capital, other elements were also present. London was a seedbed for Separatism in the late sixteenth century. It attracted young people from farther away than did provincial towns, and many newcomers were only at subsistence level by 1600. The result was social turbulence caused by crowding, disease, and food shortages. From this rural proletariat in the East End came sectarians during the Civil War—Fifth Monarchists and, especially, Levellers.

Positive aspects of immigration to the city should not be overlooked, however. Many younger sons came down from the north to seek their fortunes. Successful ones remembered their roots and sent home money for education and religion. This led to a belated missionary Puritanism in a number of outposts. The Yorkshire contingent designated some 28 percent of its philanthropy for religious purposes. By comparison, Londoners from Norfolk and Buckingham, Southeast counties, gave only 2.3 and 7.5 percent respectively to religion, but more to secular categories of "social rehabilitation" and "municipal betterment." This suggests that those from Yorkshire—and by extension, other Londoners with Northwest antecedents—had retained much of their pastoral piety down to the Civil War. It was just such Londoners who gave not only their money but also themselves to establish the perfectionist colony of New Haven, a later attempt at a city on a hill in New England. These merchants may have become liberalized or secularized compared with folks back home, yet they remained a relatively pious segment of London's bourgeoisie. And regardless of their own religious convictions, their gifts were undoubtedly bent in evangelical-pietistic ways in many instances, given the religious history of the North. These pious philanthropists should be seen as precursors of moral reformers of the early nineteenth century in Britain and the United States.

And finally, because London had such a high population turnover, was so important as an *entrepôt* for people as well as goods, it should be placed close to the middle between the poles of evangelism and nonevangelism. The capital city reflected the rational Puritanism of East Anglia and the Southeast, but this was leavened by many migrants from the Northwest as well as folk from wealds and fens closer to London. For some with pastoral origins, residence in London was simply a prelude to the big jump across the Atlantic to New England. London would supply New England with sectarians as well as Puritans, congregationalists as well as presbyterians in the formative years. But it would be a mistake to exaggerate London's religious role in settling New England. Many members of the London contingent on the *Mayflower*—single non-Pilgrims recruited late—died without issue after arrival in New Plymouth.[16]

Among the 2,885 New England pioneers Charles Banks traced, 732 came from East Anglia but only 203 were from the metropolis. And of course, like Los Angeles in the twentieth century, most of those listed from London had actually come from someplace else first. Approximately 60 percent of immigrants from London appear to have had Southeast origins, with the large minority of 40 percent having roots in the more distant Northwest.[17] In the religious geography of England, countryside was more important than metropolis. The English population was 85 percent rural, and London contributed only modestly to rationalist and evangelical-pietistic streams of New England settlement.

The West Country

The West Country, like East Anglia, contained several areas of advanced textile production and these also proved to be seedbeds of a Puritanism turning rationalistic on the eve of the Civil War. Clergy of this region had attended Oxford and were exposed to Renaissance humanism along with Puritanism.

The cultural dividing line between Southeast and Northwest ran right down the middle of the West Country. An examination of emigrants arriving in New England from Devon and Somerset reveals two divergent streams. The first, originating in the western part, headed for the Piscataqua area or the Plymouth Colony. The second, coming a bit later and from the eastern part, settled chiefly in eastern Massachusetts or Connecticut's three original towns. If a line is drawn through the West Country to maximize the different destinations, it runs south from Bristol, passes east of Taunton, and ends on the coast west of Exeter.

The eastern parts of these two counties were more arable and populous, they contained cloth districts engaged in exporting "New Draperies" to the Continent, and they bore considerable resemblance to East Anglia economically. The western parts, on the other hand, consisted of low-lying cattle country—including the Somerset Levels—or sparsely populated Dartmoor and Exmoor. In geography and culture, these parts had an affinity with Cornwall to the west.

It was eastern Devon and Somerset that should have—and did—generate a rational Calvinism fairly early, after East Anglia but before other places in the Southeast. Emigration from Somerset was split; the large contingent from the eastern part of the county settled in what would be the nonevangelical areas of New England in the eighteenth century. In Devon, westerners had a big majority among newcomers and they settled in what would become evangelical territory. The line separating the divergent streams cut Devon more cleanly than Somerset.[18]

In eastern Devon there was a small cloth district in the hinterland of the cathedral city of Exeter. This ancient community, an outpost of the Romans, obtained status as a county unto itself in the sixteenth century. Soon Exeter was importing high-grade Spanish wool and exporting fine Spanish medley fabrics. Contacts with Spain, France, and especially the Low Countries had belated but similar effects on religion as in East Anglia.

The Exeter district became a Puritan stronghold on the cultural frontier. When Puritan sentiment rose rapidly in the city in the 1590s, a lecturer was hired to give "godly exercises" in the cathedral, and he preached predestination and sin in the vicinity. Fifteen years later Exeter imposed a sabbatarian law on its people. In polity, presbyterianism was popular early, and during the Commonwealth period this district was one of the few places where a presbytery actually operated briefly. This tendency toward presbyterianism can be confirmed by statistics gathered in 1672–73, the year that the Declaration of Indulgences of Charles II was in force. The return of the Exeter diocese showed that among Dissenter congregations, the Presbyterians had 119, the Congregationalists, 32, and the Baptists, 15. We may infer from these post-1641 figures that the presbyterian, rationalist form of Puritanism was percolating here from 1615 to the Civil War.[19]

The major cloth area in the West Country, however, was to the north in western Wiltshire and eastern Somerset along the Gloucester border. Devizes and Frome were centers for the cottage industry that was spread through the countryside. Even the vicinity of Bath, the fashionable spa, had clothiers, fullers, and other textile workers active in their trades. Their fabrics were of high quality, almost equal to the New Draperies of East Anglia. Historians have not sufficiently recognized this West Country cloth area as a source of rationalist religion in New England. While East Anglia was the cradle of Puritanism, the eastern part of the West Country was a nursery and here too there was an early tendency to move beyond Genevan Calvinism.

In fact, this part of the West Country produced most of the best-known advocates of rationalist religion in English history. One was Richard Hooker, born in Heavitree, a suburb of Exeter, in 1554. His grandfather and great-grandfather had been mayors of Exeter. As a very young man he was probably a moderate Puritan like his patron, the bishop of Salisbury, who facilitated his admission to Corpus Christi College, Oxford. But there he was exposed to patristic and Renaissance learning. Later he became master of Temple Church in London, where his hearers were law students from the Inns of Court. He had a brief public controversy with Walter Travers, an intellectual from Nottingham, that caused him to begin work on *Of the Laws of Ecclesiastical Polity*. Major parts of this magnum opus were published in the 1590s. This monumental treatise provided the Church of England, struggling between Catholicism and Puritanism, with a philosophical and logical basis, something it had lacked since its creation. Travers, Thomas Cartwright, and other Puritan controversialists had been claiming since the 1570s that the scriptures required a presbyterian form of government. Hooker's scholarly response was that the form of church government was left to the judgment of the people, and he believed that episcopacy was reasonable, traditional, and convenient and could be traced back through the apostles to Christ himself. Hooker was a convert to this latter doctrine, advanced by Hadrian Saravia, a Dutchman, and several Anglican divines.

It was in theology, however, that Hooker revealed how far he had moved away from the Calvinism of Marian exiles and down the road of rationalist religion. He professed respect for Calvin but believed that the reformer had actually discovered his system of discipline, not in the Bible, but in the social conditions of Geneva. Hooker was irenic in preaching salvation, deliberately showing how close doctrines of the Church of England were to Rome. He suggested that, under certain conditions, even a Catholic could be saved. Travers tagged him as too liberal in interpreting predestination and relying too much on private reason.

Puritans stressed scriptures, but Hooker emphasized natural law. Yet Hooker's rationalism was qualified because he argued that a person could not know God completely because God's knowledge was analogous to, but not identical with, a person's. This position set him apart from rationalists of the eighteenth century who did claim such an identity. He also defended royal supremacy and the concept of an established church. Hooker experts now see him as a late medieval humanist looking back to Aristotle and Aquinas but in a few places seeming to anticipate John Locke.

Hooker passed on his Rational Theology to other Anglican clergy although he was not personally imposing or popular as a preacher. He was weak-sighted and "mean" in stature. He spoke gravely in low tones, avoiding eye contact, and his sermons were short. Evidently he sought to persuade, not arouse, and used no gestures. This kind of Plain Style might seem well-suited to law students of the temple but Hooker compared poorly with Travers, who was methodical but also fluent, graceful, and animated.

Hooker was much more effective in print. While he could use short sentences with "axiomatic force," he most often drew "on a whole flock of several clauses before he came to the close of a sentence" in an unidiomatic, grand, and judicious style.[20] Like a number of scholars of this period, he was equally at home in Latin and English. His elaborate, Ciceronian sentence structure offered opportunity to explore relevant arguments before taking a position. Hooker gave the impression that he was examining all possibilities and inviting readers to reason along with him in reaching a conclusion. Puritans accused him of framing cunning sentences to entangle the simple, but print-oriented readers were reassured by his logic and tone. Hooker's complex sentences were a reflection of the rational process he was advocating.

Because of the disparity between his preaching and writing, Hooker's appeal was mainly restricted to those adjusting to print culture, a minority more numerous in Southeast England. Hooker pioneered Rational Theology and should be seen as the father of latitudinarianism, the rational position that many educated clerics of the Southeast developed in reaction to the sectarians and "enthusiasm" of the Commonwealth years.[21]

The West Country's second contributor to rational religion was John

Hales, a major representative of latitudinarianism before the Civil War. Hales was born at Bath in 1584 and received some schooling at Mells, near Frome. His father came from an old Somerset family and his mother, from Wiltshire. He received his baccalaureate from Corpus Christi College, Oxford, while John Rainolds, a Puritan, was president. Whether the Hales household could be termed Puritan is not clear, but Hales was surely drawn, like Hooker, into the classical and conservative atmosphere of Oxford. He would use natural law and reason in interpreting scripture.

Hales was asked to attend the Synod of Dort and report to the Church of England. Although he went to Holland on behalf of English Calvinists and was presumed to share their views, the Arminian arguments he heard dissolved his faith in the Calvinistic scheme. His distrust of dogma and inclination toward rationality predisposed him toward the latitudinarian course of free inquiry he took after the Synod of Dort.

Hales was a clergyman but did not have a strong voice and avoided accepting a pastorate. Instead he withdrew to Eton and spent the rest of his life with his books. He was good at remembering their contents and enjoyed meeting for conversation with other "Latitude Men" at Great Tew on the Thames. In this setting, Hales could be genial and even witty. The Great Tew Circle was composed of skeptics but the members were also loyal Anglicans and moderate royalists so Archbishop Laud, who was a theological liberal himself, protected them from their critics, although they differed with him on ecclesiastical governance.

Hales was close-mouthed in public and opposed disputation of religious questions because he valued harmony and feared schism. Despite this circumspection, he was charged with Socinianism, a pejorative term reserved for rationalists at that time, for his writings. Most of Hales's work was not published until after his death and indeed did not attract much attention until the Restoration.[22]

Thomas Hobbes, the bane of seventeenth-century philosophy and religion, was also from the West Country; he was born at Westport, now part of Malmesbury in the Wiltshire cloth district, in 1588. He was raised by an uncle, a glover, so his origins were plebian and he retained some of his western dialect. He attended Magdalen, an Oxford hall under Puritan influence, but resisted scholasticism and graduated in 1608.

Hobbes is famous for adapting the scientific insights of Francis Bacon to society and politics. He was bold and lucid but coarse and aggressive in print and showed contempt for the ancients. Personally Hobbes seemed to lack an otherworldly or metaphysical side so it was easy for him to deny the immaterial—ghost, spirit, soul—and argue for outside power, a strong sovereign to restrain the selfish instincts of humanity. He used social contract theory in a conservative way, not to sanction government by consent of the governed as Locke would later do, but rather to bind people together in obedience to the sovereign. This Hobbism, as his system came to be called, drew much polemical opposition. He was so deviant and daring that few thinkers could openly endorse his ideas in his lifetime, but he had much covert influence in the period and region.

Hobbes worked for Bacon in the 1620s and spent time in Paris, imbibing advanced views in philosophy. In England he was friendly with the circle at Great Tew but just before the Civil War, believing he might be persecuted for his heterodox rationalism, fled to France. Safe on the Continent, he turned from his major work to address the English political situation in 1642, but neither king nor Parliament was pleased with his analysis. Like the Great Tew group, he combined rationalism with the royal cause, but much more emphatically. Hobbes reacted to the emergence of sectarianism by suggesting that the Church of England be strengthened and further subordinated to the state in order to restore national tranquility.

While latitudinarians believed in reason in the abstract and among the few, they did not have much confidence in the common sense of the many. Hobbes was probably so reactionary because he wrote about society and politics between 1630 and 1660—*The Leviathan* (1651)—when old authority was in sharp decline and religious enthusiasm became prominent. During the neo-enlightenment of the twentieth century, some scholars critical of capitalism built upon Hobbes's reputation as an individualist and skeptic, depicting him as a pioneer apologist for selfishness in a commercial society, the first modern man. They assumed that his religious speculations were of minor importance, a facade for rank materialism. Actually Hobbes was a transitional figure whose bourgeois tendencies and this-worldly and eccentric religion were still mingled with many aristocratic notions. He signaled the beginning of the divorce between philosophy and religion but hardly as much secularization as some scholars have indicated.[23]

Still another rationalist from the West Country was Ralph Cudworth. The Cambridge Platonist was born at Aller in central Somerset and returned to this region in his last days. While all Platonists saw religion as essentially the same as morality, Cudworth was especially strong on this point and was the least metaphysical of the Cambridge group. Perhaps his proximity to Hobbes caused him to react against any separation or divergence between philosophy and religion and to resist all forms of fatalism that could be found in the works of the philosopher of Malmesbury.[24]

Thus the West Country showed early signs of rational religion. The region produced significant thinkers—Hooker, Hales, Hobbes, and Cudworth—who moved beyond Rational Theology to a still more reasonable latitudinarianism. Late medieval humanism mixed with a shallow Puritanism yielded a religion that was even more rationalist and less metaphysical than the Ramism or Platonism found in East Anglia. This part of the West Country could be dubbed "the cradle of Latitudinarianism." New Englanders from the West Country would reflect their section. In religion this meant a Puritanism or Anglicanism leavened by rationalism, a retreat from evangelism.

Beyond the Line: The Northwest

In the first half of the seventeenth century, when New England was settled, there were many differences setting off the Northwest from the Southeast. This zone had more districts at over four hundred feet elevation, more land that was pastoral than arable. The population, only a quarter of the nation at that time, was sparse and relatively poor, with less than 10 percent of the wealth. Transportation was inadequate and illiteracy higher than in the Southeast. These conditions would not change until the approach of the Industrial Revolution in the next century.

The Reformation took place very slowly here. The transition from Catholicism to Protestantism and the adjustment to the Church of England was uneven and never quite complete, even a century later. Although Henry VIII broke with Rome in 1534, the government had to tolerate the Old Religion, a mixture of Church of England and pre-Reformation beliefs, until Elizabeth came to the throne in 1558. Even with restrictions after that date, people in the Northwest stayed with the old ways, were slow to be weaned from Catholic liturgy and images, and preferred observances linked to the cycle of the week and seasons of the year. As Elizabeth sought greater conformity to the new faith of the Church of England, many of these folk became "church-papists," attending the queen's church only often enough to avoid trouble with authorities. Some gentry, however, withdrew from public life and relied on chaplains who celebrated mass in the seignorial household for family, tenants, and neighbors. They were not organized or antagonistic to the Crown, so their strength is hard to measure. They were religious survivalists, bound to the Old Religion by tradition and sentiment, not conviction.

A small minority became recusants, however, after the Council of Trent and the beginning of the Counter-Reformation. Recusants were those who did feel antagonism toward the Protestant queen and stopped attending services of the Church of England altogether, thereby risking prosecution. They believed that they were acting in good conscience after the pope excommunicated Elizabeth in 1570, absolving Catholics of loyalty to her. Parliament had given Elizabeth a strong anti-witch law in 1563 because the queen's advisors warned of Catholic plots to kill her by witchcraft and put Mary Stuart, a Catholic, on the throne. Witchcraft and the resurgence of Catholicism as a subversive sect were thus linked in the public mind during this period.[25]

The Northwest was also the most Celtic part of the British Isles. Pockets of this influence are obvious in Great Britain to the present day, not only in northern Wales and western Cornwall, but also in many other places from the Devon moors to the Welsh marshes, Yorkshire's West Riding, and the Scottish Highlands. This was the land of Robin Hood, Sherwood Forest, King Arthur, and Camelot. It was the ancestral home of Richard Hakluyt, who mingled religion with geography in his rationalizations of expansion overseas. This was the land of many explorers and colonizers: Calvert, Cook, Drake, Gilbert, Gordon, Hawkins, Hudson, Lawrence, Raleigh, Rhodes, and Captain John Smith. And over time it produced more than its share of romantic poets: Keats, Shelley, Swinburne, Tennyson, Wordsworth, as well as the Metaphysical group. The people retained bardic values and were conservative, joining the Cavaliers in the Civil War and preferring the Stuart monarchy to the uncertainties of Cromwell's Roundhead coalition. In the 1650s, the defeated Northwest, according to a Cromwell commission, was still backward religiously and in need of massive Puritan missionary work. In fact, Puritans of the Southeast compared northern "superstition" to the "heathenism" of American Indians. In 1646, for them the "howling wilderness" referred not only to New England but to the "dark corners" of their own land, such as North Wales. A few itinerants had been active during Elizabeth's reign, but educated clergy could not usually be obtained for these "waste places." Because livings were so poor, itinerant preachers appeared in these regions sporadically; they were generally without "the arts and tongues" and often had antinomian and other radical tendencies.[26] Christopher Hill has shown that bishops and Puritans—fierce opponents—had long agreed about the conditions that made so many places in the Northwest "dark corners of the land."

While much of the Northwest was pastoral, there were some arable districts. In those farthest from East Anglia, Catholicism and the Old Religion hung on stubbornly. In the larger towns with commercial ties to London, however, clerical Puritanism appeared sooner. As noted previously, successful merchants in London often sent money back to their native counties for missionary and educational work, hence the early appearance in Manchester and some other towns of subsidized Puritan ministers. Lay Puritanism, as distinct from the clerical variety, did not really surface until the 1610s, however. On the eve of the Great Migration to New England, Puritanism had only begun to spread out from trading towns. In challenging the Old Religion, Puritanism at this stage was still evangelical and Calvinistic, emphasizing conversion with little emphasis on Ramism and covenant obligations. It would be another century before Wesley, Whitefield, and the Anglican Evangelicals would supplant Catholicism and the Old Religion and follow up on this early Puritanism, carrying Methodism to the Northwest.

The North

Yorkshire is the largest county and contributed the greatest number of New England pioneers from the Northwest. Critics of Yorkshire in the nineteenth century—more concerned with efficiency than poetry and landscape—could be insensitive, characterizing Yorkshire people as stubborn and superstitious. Yorkshire had been the location of the kingdom of Elmet and of a Celtic autonomy that the Middle Ages did not erase. A vestige is the province of York, the separate archbishopric for the North. John Wycliffe, born in the highland district of the North Riding, led the Lollard movement in the fourteenth century. Lollards were precursors of the Reformation because they stressed the English language and individual interpretation of the Bible, trying to break priests' monopoly on Latin and the Word of God. Leadership for the Pilgrimage of Grace, the religio-agrarian uprising of 1536 against dissolution of the monasteries, also came from the North Riding. Two of the most charismatic preachers of the English Reformation, William Tyndale, "the first Puritan," and Miles Coverdale, were from Yorkshire.

Under Elizabeth, the Church of England took hold in the county. Survivalism was strong, however, and Catholicism persisted alongside some reforms, as in other northern counties. The queen had some success in encouraging education and preaching among the clergy. In this adjustment to Elizabeth's religious compromise, early Puritanism had very little impact on the countryside. In Sheffield and the cloth towns of Halifax, Bradford, and Leeds there were a few signs of "advanced" Protestantism, but the percentage of population adjacent to woolen manufacture was less than in East Anglia. Before 1588, Puritanism was therefore largely confined to the clergy and families connected with the cloth towns of the West Riding.

The continuing strength of Roman Catholics in Yorkshire was notable. Among the gentry, sympathizers with Rome outnumbered those with Geneva fifteen to one in 1570, just before the Counter-Reformation. Then Jesuits and seminary priests slipped into the country from the Continent and church-papists were often won back to Rome and became open recusants by not attending church. Authorities had to step up efforts in enforcing conformity to the established church. But in the inaccessible North Riding, Catholic landowners were not seriously challenged.

Puritanism did expand a bit within the urban middle class after 1588. Protestant natives of Yorkshire in London, frugal personally, were generous in sending money north. Grammar schools in Yorkshire established links with Cambridge University and attracted some graduates northward, adding to the Puritan flavor of education.

What distinguished Yorkshire and the Northwest from the Southeast, and especially East Anglia, was this slower development of Puritanism in the face of lingering Catholicism. In the first decade of the seventeenth century, over 90 percent of Puritan clergy were in the Southeast (and the small enclave of Manchester) and less than 10 percent were in the Northwest. Not until the middle of the reign of James I did Puritanism spread out from this small clerical base to the laity. Preachers did increase between 1603 and 1633, but illiteracy remained higher than in the Southeast. Puritan strength in Yorkshire should not be exaggerated. Even in 1642 during the Civil War, there were 163 Catholic but only 138 Puritan families among gentry of the county, and in the correlated matter of loyalty, Cavaliers outnumbered Roundheads two to one in the actual fighting.[27]

More important was the persistence of the Old Religion and the resurgence of a kind of subversive Catholicism, the recusancy that emerged so noticeably after 1588. This challenge, together with the pastoral terrain, kept the Puritan minority evangelical, Calvinistic, and concerned with the Holy Spirit. Ramist tendencies from East Anglia and the Low Countries were weak. Only in a few neighborhoods of the cloth towns could Yorkshire Puritanism approximate the more developed form that was evident in the Southeast.

Therefore, emigrants from Yorkshire arriving in New England were limited religiously to two kinds: nominal members of the Church of England, still following many Catholic ways, or converts to an aggressive sect that preached evangelical Calvinism, maintaining its original otherworldliness because of its frontier position and struggle against the Catholic countryside. This early stage of Puritanism can be termed "frontier," "Spiritual," or even "missionary" because of subsidy from the Southeast. These Yorkshire Puritans sought converts by emphasizing the New Birth, downplaying theological complexities and relying less on the printed word. Yorkshire bore much resemblance to the Northwest in general.

Beyond the West Riding lay Lancashire, a smaller and poorer county that had some similarities with Yorkshire. Many authorities have described Lancashire—especially the north and west—as isolated and backward. Prosperity in the 1480s led to a belated flowering of Catholicism with a renewed interest in images, statuary, and traditional liturgy. Because of this Lancashire felt the Reformation less than any other county in England. Religious practices following the Reformation remained close to the Catholic, therefore churchgoers had little incentive to become open recusants. Fines for nonattendance of church were not collected and prosecutions of recusants were infrequent and ineffective. Catholic landowners employed old Catholic clerics as chaplains and tutors and were joined by young seminarians later. Catholicism was still entrenched in the western arable lands early in the seventeenth century. The countryside was very conservative and persons did not surface as schismatics or heretics until they had left their native Lancashire for London or the Southeast.

As a part of this conservatism, Tudor Lancashire had remained a military society. During Elizabeth's reign wealthy families needed followers for protection because Lancashire folk were inclined to take the law into their own hands. The mob violence was so prevalent that even the clergy were armed, despite their poverty and lack of influence. Leading families used child marriages to cement alliances. Unfortunately, this produced marital instability and adultery, which was ten times more common in Lancashire than in the Southeast.

These conditions, and the threat of Spanish invasion, led Church of England authorities to make Lancashire a special case. They decided to encourage Puritan ministers as an antidote to what they considered irreligion, behavioral laxity, and Catholicism. Puritans from outside were zealous and moralistic missionaries, willing to come into the county to brave these medieval conditions. Manchester became a town prosperous enough to have trade with London and contact with religious ideas of the metropolis. Concerted Puritan effort eventually made Manchester into a frontier base against Catholicism. Among traders of the town, Puritanism there approached the rationalism of the Southeast. In the chapels on the wooded fringe of town, it remained evangelical and sectarian.[28]

The West

In the Far West—that part of the West Country beyond the cultural divide between Northwest and Southeast—the transition from the Middle Ages to the Reformation was also slow. In the small and isolated county of Cornwall, the Cornish language prevailed, and there were few English speakers. When Edwardian reformers changed some church rituals and imposed the Prayer Book in the English language, an uprising, the Western Rebellion, followed. Conservative priests led the folk in resisting Protestant departures from traditional ways; they besieged Exeter and the violence produced ten deaths.

Afterward there was quiet educational progress during Elizabeth's reign. This was achieved despite the dissolution of monasteries and chantries, so important in supplying instruction in this county. Cornwall remained steeped in the Old Religion but some gentry and merchants with maritime interests turned toward Protestantism and the Church of England. Subversive support of Rome was centered in a few families and retainers, who harbored a few Jesuits that were educated at Douai on the Continent. Before the defeat of the Armada, Puritans

were fewer than recusants. Among 160 clergy who held livings in Cornwall in 1586, 32 were nonresident and only 23 offered sermons. A contemporary Puritan authority estimated that only 10 could be classified
as men of "tender conscience" worthy of the Puritan brotherhood.[29]

By the end of Elizabeth's reign, the Church of England had gained
a comfortable hold on Cornwall. The Bible and prayer book were evidently strong forces for anglicanization and the Cornish language was
dying, pushed inland and back toward Land's End. Government was
stubbornly harassing recusants among the gentry, forcing conformity or
family dismemberment. Literacy had improved by the time of the Civil
War, with 28 percent able to sign their names.[30]

The western parts of Devon and Somerset, just east of Cornwall, had
religious and social affinities with their neighbor. In the Middle Ages
this entire Far West area, including Cornwall, comprised the Celtic
kingdom of Dumnonia before it succumbed to the Romans. In this
region that had been Camelot the old ways were accommodated somehow within the established church following the Reformation. Emigrants to New England no doubt retained much of the Cornish version of the Old Religion for there were only a few clerical Puritans and
these were still mainly Calvinistic.[31]

Wales was even more wedded to the Old Religion than Cornwall at
this time. Pagan practices were thoroughly mingled with Catholic, so
the Roman rule held little sway over the people. Welsh fervor before
the Reformation allowed for no spiritual deprivation and little doubt
or heresy. Protestant reformers made little progress and Catholics who
attempted change during the Counter-Reformation encountered the
same obstacles as Protestant reformers: illiteracy and lack of interest in
books or theology. There was no Counter-Reformation in Wales, not
because the people agreed with Catholic dogma or sympathized with
efforts to revive Catholicism, but because the country was still steeped
in the traditions of its Celtic church. Further, Wales had been absorbed
into the English realm in 1536 and loyalty to the Welsh House of Tudor precluded the kind of uprisings that occurred in Cornwall and the
North. The threat of the Spanish Armada found Wales loyally aligned
with Queen Elizabeth.

In attempting to plant the new Church of England in Wales, the
queen made only very moderate progress during her long reign. Her
bishops tried to raise the quality of clergy by improving education for
them. The clergy committed itself to preaching in Welsh and the Bi-

ble was translated into that language. An effort was made to portray the Reformation and the Church of England as representing not only a break with Rome but a return to a Celtic or ancient British church. The gentry, although criticized for acquisitiveness and anglicanization, sought through writing and patronage to foster better religious conditions. By the seventeenth century, Anglicanism was no longer a completely alien faith. The basic belief of reformers and Dissenters, however, that each person should interpret and internalize religious ideas, was far from being realized.

The Church of England was virtually the only vehicle for spreading religion in Wales until the 1650s. When militant Puritanism finally did appear, it sprang from chronic clerical nonresidency rather than opinions about scriptures or church polity. Bishop Laud, later the primate, visited his Welsh diocese only twice in five years, preferring to supervise "from without." There was also a shortage of Welsh clergy despite the publication of a Welsh version of the King James Bible in 1620. It was 1639 before a church was "gathered" in Wales. Its organizers were seeking a deeper spiritual life and may not have intended any schism.

Two persons illustrate the nature of early Puritanism in Wales. Lewis Bayley wrote *The Practice of Piety* while in London early in the seventeenth century. Through its seventy editions, including one in Welsh in 1630, it had an impact on many religious groups in England and its influence spread to the Continent. Because of this book, Bayley became bishop of Bangor in North Wales. He was probably a Welshman but may have been a Scot. He was a great preacher and extreme Puritan in behavior yet continued as bishop, holding and bequeathing many livings. Almost as well known was Rhys Pritchard, an Oxford graduate and pluralist like Bayley, who had been inspired by *The Practice of Piety*. He also supported episcopacy, and when the Civil War came, actually took the king's side. Pritchard was an eloquent preacher of undiluted Calvinism, maintaining that the elect, once God chose them, could not fall from grace. As David Williams has observed, he bore a "close resemblance to the early methodist leaders of the eighteenth century."[32] Thus Pritchard exemplified Welsh Puritanism that was still in the frontier stage—oral and Calvinistic—in the 1620s and 1630s, and had little in common with Ramist Puritans of East Anglia.

During the two decades of the Civil War and Interregnum (1640–60), there was confusion and irreligion here. A Commonwealth commission tried to subsidize preaching in Welsh but efforts were tainted with corruption and fell short. Some Welsh people found themselves paying tithes for sermons never delivered. The Welsh were strongly royalist and favorable to restoration of the Stuart monarchy in 1660 and remained essentially medieval. At the time of the settlement of New England the Welsh people, although accepting the Church of England, had not yet internalized most Protestant ideas, let alone Puritan refinements of them. Their illiteracy and adherence to their traditional ways made them appear to some to be the most backward people in the realm. Despite some Puritan activity during the Interregnum, itinerants and Methodists did not reach the area until early in the eighteenth century.

There are strong indications that the religious sectionalism of Britain in the seventeenth century was imported to New England with the first settlers. The distinction between the evangelical Northwest and the Puritan Southeast was passed down through the descendants of the original colonists. If we look at the religious and social development of two towns, Rowley, up the coast from Boston, and Hingham, down the coast, we can see how the sectionalism of England affected the colonists and their later response to the Great Awakening.

Notes

1. Ray Allen Billington, *The Genesis of the Frontier Thesis: A Study in Historical Creativity* (1971), 26–37, 51, 54, 90–93. In explaining people's behavior and the persistence of sectionalism in the Unites States, Turner wrote, "The influence of the stock from which they sprang, the inherited ideals, the spiritual factors, often triumph over the material interests." See Turner, "Sectionalism and Nation," *Yale Review* 12 (1922): 20.

2. "The English outlook had also much to do with inherited attitudes about land" and was concerned "with monarchy and its pattern of government from the center, which fixed the core of Englishness firmly in the Southeast—where it has remained." David Beers Quinn, *The Elizabethans and the Irish* (1966), 8. Thomas Jefferson Wertenbaker, in *The Puritan Oligarchy* (1947), included Essex with Norfolk and Suffolk in his first chapter, "East Anglia." G. Andrews Moriarty included eastern Hertfordshire in his definition in "Social and Geographical Origins of the Founders of Massachusetts," in *The Commonwealth History of Massachusetts,* Albert B. Hart, ed. (1927), 1:57. More recently, David Hackett Fischer has reemphasized East Anglia as the center of Puritanism in England. See *Albion's Seed: Four British Folkways in America* (1989), 31–36.

3. George C. Homans, "Puritans and the Clothing Industry in England," *New England Quarterly* 13 (1940): 519–29.

4. Like most religious tags, "Puritan" was originally a term of abuse; it is an ambiguous appellation that can refer to a broad stream of religious persons in the population. Patrick Collinson, "A Comment: Concerning the Name Puritan," *Journal of Ecclesiastical History* 31 (1980): 483–88. Therefore English historians, unlike American historians, no longer capitalize "puritan."

5. Walter J. Ong, *Rhetoric, Romance, and Technology* (1971), chap. 7, "Ramist Method and the Commercial Mind." In several works, Ong has stressed the shift from an oral to a visual world that set in with the widespread use of movable type, the print media of the sixteenth century.

6. Christopher Hill, *The Intellectual Origins of the English Revolution* (1965), 133–34, 293–95.

7. In New England also, "pastors like Hooker and Shepard developed the notion with a good deal more refinement of detail and application than found in Perkins." See Ian Breward, ed., *The Work of William Perkins* (1969), 113, quotation from 96.

8. Perry Miller, *The New England Mind: The Seventeenth Century* (1939; rpt., 1954), 96; Miller, "Preparation for Salvation in Seventeenth-Century New England," *Journal of the History of Ideas* 4 (1943): 253–86. The motives pushing out these emigrants to Holland and New England were complex. The religious dimension was important and cannot be disentangled from economic and personal motives. Timothy H. Breen and Stephen Foster, "Moving to the New World," *William and Mary Quarterly* 30 (1973): 189–222.

9. Norman Pettit, *The Heart Prepared: Grace and Conversion in Puritan Spiritual Life* (1966), 79–85; Keith L. Sprunger, *The Learned Doctor William Ames: Dutch Backgrounds of English and American Puritanism* (1972), 50–65, 200, 254–58. Ames's son was one of a talented contingent. Many Harvard students and graduates returned to England between 1640 and 1660. The triumph of Cromwell and the replacement of episcopal clergy created job opportunities there. Some also wanted to obtain more education and become *au courant* with Ramism. Remigration did reduce the ranks of New England's young intellectuals. Of the fourteen ordained clerics from the Southeast who had graduated from Harvard and returned to England, only two went back to New England. Westering was stronger among the Northwest clerics; three of six went back to New England. These three ministers—Nathaniel Brewster, Leonard Hoar, and Increase Mather—were important to developments in New England. The last two would serve as presidents of Harvard after their return. This calculation has been made from Harry S. Stout, "University Men in New England, 1620–1660: A Demographic Analysis," *Journal of Interdisciplinary History* 4 (1974): 375–400. See also Stout, "The Morphology of Remigration: New England University Men and Their Return to England, 1640–1660," *Journal of American Studies* 10 (1976): 151–72; William L. Sachse, "The Migration of New Englanders to England, 1640–1660," *American Historical Review* 53

(1948): 251–78; Andrew Delbanco, "Looking Homeward, Going Home: The Lure of England for the Founders of New England," *New England Quarterly* 59 (1986): 358–86; and Virginia Dejohn Anderson, *New England's Generation: The Great Migration and Formation of Society and Culture in the Seventeenth Century* (1991), 122n.

10. Sprunger, *Ames*, 180–82. Howard Feinstein has noted the similarities between Puritan preparationism and Freudian psychoanalysis. See "The Prepared Heart: A Comparative Study of Puritan Theology and Psychoanalysis," *American Quarterly* 22 (1970): 166–76.

11. Miller, *The New England Mind*, 396.

12. Nicholas Tyacke, *Anti-Calvinists: The Rise of English Arminianism, 1590–1640* (1987), 102–5; Roger Lockyer, *The Early Stuarts: A Political History of England, 1603–1642* (1989), 116–20, 307–13.

13. Theodore Dwight Bozeman, *To Live Ancient Lives: The Primitivist Dimension in Puritanism* (1988), chap. 6.

14. Edmund S. Morgan, *The Puritan Dilemma: The Story of John Winthrop* (1958), 88–95.

15. Jerald C. Brauer, "Conversion: From Puritanism to Revivalism," *Journal of Religion* 58 (1978): 227–43; quotation from Charles L. Cohen, *God's Caress: The Psychology of Puritan Religious Experience* (1986), 212.

16. Peter Clark and Paul Slack, *English Towns in Transition, 1500–1700* (1976), 62–157; Lawrence Stone, "Social Mobility in England, 1500–1700," *Past and Present* 36 (1966): 16–73; E. A. Wrigley, "A Simple Model of London's Importance in Changing English Society and Economy, 1650–1750," *Past and Present* 37 (1967): 44–70.

17. Calculated from Charles E. Banks, *Topographical Dictionary*, ed. E. E. Brownell (1937); Frank Holmes, *Directory of Ancestral Heads of New England Families, 1620–1700* (1964 ed.); and Henry Guppy, *Homes of Family Names in Great Britain* (1890).

18. Calculated from ibid. See also map 1.

19. Wallace T. MacCaffrey, *Exeter, 1540–1640: The Growth of an English Town* (1958), 174–202.

20. George Edelen, "Hooker's Style," in *Studies in Richard Hooker*, ed. W. Speed Hill (1972), 241, 242.

21. Ibid., 241–77; Stanley Archer, *Richard Hooker* (1983), 1–19.

22. James H. Elson, *John Hales of Eton* (1948), 1–108.

23. Richard Peters, *Hobbes* (1956), 13–42, 225–48; Willis B. Glover, "God and Thomas Hobbes," in *Hobbes Studies*, ed. K. C. Brown (1965), 141–68; Peter Geach, "The Religion of Thomas Hobbes," *Religious Studies* 17 (1981): 549–58.

24. Frederick J. Powicke, *The Cambridge Platonists: A Study* (1926; rpt., 1971), 110–29.

25. John Bossy, "The Character of Elizabethan Catholicism," *Past and Present* 21 (1962): 39–59.

26. Christopher Hill, "Puritans and 'the Dark Corners of the Land,'" *Change and Continuity in Seventeenth Century England* (1975), 3–47. See also Hill, *The World Turned Upside Down: Radical Ideas during the English Revolution* (1972), 35–69. In the seventeenth century, very few immigrants to New England came from what Puritans regarded as the darkest corners, such as the Scottish Highlands and North Wales.

27. Roland G. Usher, *Reconstruction of the English Church* (1910), 1:250, 255 (map), 268; John Trevor Cliffe, *The Yorkshire Gentry from the Reformation to the Civil War* (1969), 256–81.

28. For Lancashire, I have consulted Christopher Haigh, *Reformation and Resistance in Tudor Lancashire* (1975), and R. C. Richardson, *Puritanism in North-West England: A Regional Study of the Diocese of Chester to 1642* (1972), 1–22. See also Haigh, "Puritan Evangelism in the Reign of Elizabeth I," *English Historical Review* 42 (1977): 30–58.

29. A. L. Rowse, *Tudor Cornwall: Portrait of a Society* (1969), 253–379, especially 338.

30. H. P. R. Finberg, *West-Country Historical Studies* (1969), 28, 60.

31. Glanmor Williams, comp., *Welsh Reformation Essays* (1967), 11–33.

32. David Williams, *A History of Modern Wales* (rev. ed., 1965), 112.

Chapter Two

Rowley and Hingham: Revivalism and Puritanism in the Massachusetts Bay Colony

Pioneers from the Northwest arriving in New England established at least five major settlements in the seventeenth century: the Isles of Shoals, New Plymouth, Cape Ann, John Davenport's colony at New Haven, and Rowley. The Reverend Ezekiel Rogers and twenty families from the East Riding of Yorkshire founded Rowley in 1639. Although this town, twenty-six miles north of Boston, has been the least noticed of the five, it was important in colonial times as a "hearth" and "hive" on the Massachusetts coast for immigrants from the Northwest. From these places incipient New Light (and Inner Light) would eventually spread to various parts of New England, northward to Canada, westward to upper New York, and beyond.

To illuminate the basic differences in religious sensibility between immigrants from the Northwest and Southeast, Rowley can profitably be compared with several other early towns in the Massachusetts Bay Colony. Considering available data, Hingham, on the shore south of Boston and incorporated in 1635, provides a good contrast with Rowley. Newcomers from Norfolk, East Anglia, arrived there in the middle of the Great Migration and completely engulfed some early settlers from the West Country. A comparison of Rowley and Hingham will throw into bold relief religious differences, not only between Yorkshire and

East Anglia, but Northwest and Southeast, that would later divide New England into New Light and Old Light territory.

Rowley

The economy of new Rowley resembled that of old Rowley on the chalky upland near Hull in Yorkshire, and the similarities between the two increased as the decades passed. Both places had some dairying, but emphasized livestock—cattle, horses, sheep, and swine—with the last two more important in Massachusetts. To the English grains of barley and rye, new Rowley added maize. Clothmaking—from flax, wool, and hemp—contributed to the economy but generally was not anyone's sole occupation. As in later immigration to America, the poorest and richest stayed home so Yorkshire society was replicated but with the extremes absent. These settlers succeeded, despite some differences in terrain, in reproducing the agricultural economy they left behind. In seventeenth-century Yorkshire, the open-field system was still predominant, enclosures had not made much headway, and agriculture was relatively static but still profitable. Therefore Rowley pioneers were not pushed economically as much as they were pulled by prospects of landholding in the colonies. Religiously, however, they were pushed, because church authorities had silenced their minister for nonconformity.

The original land grant to new Rowley was large and irregular, with ten thousand acres of untillable salt marsh. From the beginning, settlement was scattered, not compact. Average landholdings were small—twenty-three acres—with persons holding many parcels and reluctant to consolidate with other landowners. Although a relatively few men owned much of the land, the top 10 percent of the men controlled 44.5 percent of the land, widespread participation was the basis of the open-field system. Disparities in landholding were surprisingly irrelevant to political activity in either Yorkshire or Massachusetts. Town officers had little discretion or power and were chosen to merely carry out the wishes predominating at the town meeting. As in Yorkshire, which was still not very literate, the town form was not fully developed, and overseers of the manorial court enforced bylaws and some customs that were not written down.[1]

The correlation of economic and political life with religious activity in new and old Rowley seems clear enough. Yorkshire was a pastoral society and parishes were large; churchgoers, like inhabitants in general, were spread out. All over the English Northwest, the availability and quality of Church of England clergy was low, and lay Puritanism reached this part of Yorkshire quite late. The people got used to a few seasons of religious quickening when an itinerant preacher passed through. Evangelism was just about the only thing that could overcome bad roads and weather and bring a group to church or a central location. Ezekiel Rogers, minister of old Rowley, adapted to the people of the region, joined them in conventicles, and copied them in prayers. He was tolerant of itinerants, as were most other ministers who would later participate in the Great Awakening. Seventeen years after his arrival in the East Riding, he was finally suspended, like so many other Puritan clerics, for refusing to read the *Book of Sports* to his flock. This was a widely disparaged directive from James I that aimed at thwarting Puritan sabbatarianism by encouraging recreation after church services on Sunday. A refugee from Archbishop Laud, Rogers emigrated to the Massachusetts Bay Colony in 1638, leaving behind a record of nonconformity and successful missionary effort and bringing with him a company of young, faithful followers.

Apparently Rogers retained his popularity as minister in new Rowley until his death in 1661. He was a fervent preacher, emphasizing regeneration and union with Christ. His praying and preaching were "accompanied with strains of oratory which made his ministry very acceptable." Some idea of his orientation can be glimpsed from his sermons. He favored the right of a flock to choose its own pastor and opposed long hair, antinomianism, subscription to a creed, and, after arriving in Massachusetts, reelection of governors. In his will, as so many other missionaries had done, Rogers made gifts to church, town, and young Harvard College.[2]

Rogers apparently helped the settlement of new Rowley on the Massachusetts coast remain stable. More than four-fifths of Rowley's early settlers came from the Northwest, thirty-four compared with only seven from the Southeast, a very rare situation in eastern Massachusetts (see table 2-1).[3] Rogers was able to transplant from Yorkshire a group that formed a cohesive religious community immediately. More than 76 percent of those settling before 1650 decided to stay put for some decades. This was in contrast to the unawakened majority of immigrants from the Northwest who were restless, reflecting their pastoral heritage in England and westering impulses in New England. These settlers

Table 2-1. Rowley's Largest Families in the First Generation of Settlement

Surname	Number of Rowley Residents	Probable Origin
Jewett	566	Yorkshire
Pearson (Pierson)	242	Yorkshire
Todd	215	(Northumberland, 51)
Nelson	202	Yorkshire
Spofford	197	Yorkshire
Pickard	156	Yorkshire
Bailey	154	(Hampshire, 81)
Chaplin	144	Yorkshire
Dresser	142	Yorkshire
Tenney	140	Yorkshire
Palmer	117	Yorkshire
Hopson	115	Yorkshire
Bradstreet	107	Lincolnshire
Wood	107	(Yorkshire, 98)
Brocklebank	105	Yorkshire
Kilbourne	104	Cambridgeshire
Cressy	103	(Lincoln, 29)
Stickney	99	Yorkshire
Dickinson	95	Yorkshire

Sources: George Blodgette, "Early Settlers of Rowley . . . before 1662," *Essex Institute Historical Collections* 19 (1882), 24 (1888); George Blodgette and Amos E. Jewett, *The Early Settlers of Rowley* (1933); Henry Guppy, *Homes of Family Names in Great Britain* (1890).

Note: Surname frequencies per 10,000 from Guppy, *Homes,* appear in parentheses. See appendix A for his methodology.

moved around, but those originally from the Northwest were twice as likely as those from the Southeast to move farther north and west after their initial move to New England. Pastoral heritage, cultural uneasiness, westering, and religious dissent were major reasons for this instability.[4]

The chief religious concern of Massachusetts Bay Puritans in the second half of the century was the decline in conversions. Fewer conversions meant that fewer Puritans could vote, thereby reducing the electorate and endangering the hold that the elect had on the nonelect. Some worried ministers believed that the high standards for church admission set early in the Great Migration, which called for members to submit their testimonies of conversion, or public relations, to receive communion, were too difficult to be sustained in the decades that followed. To expand membership, they proposed the Half-Way Covenant, which called for the church to encourage baptized adults to become half-way members by "owning the covenant," that is, assenting to the creed and discipline of the church, but would not require them to testify to their salvation. This would entitle half-way members to have their children baptized and to vote in local elections but would not allow them to receive communion. The clergy hoped that half-way members would eventually have the saving experience that would make them members in full communion.

Other ministers and many in the congregations were critical of the half-way plan, believing it would undermine the intent of the founders to build a Zion in the wilderness and that they must justify the sacrifices of the first generation of settlers had made to establish these new communities. They argued that merely owning the covenant rather than demanding public relation would be reverting to the corrupt membership standards of the homeland, thereby diluting the power of the saints and further eroding piety. Proponents denied that the half-way formula was a complete reversion to lower English standards of admission and insisted it was a way of retaining high standards for communicants while encouraging half-way members toward preparation. They saw themselves as shoring up the Puritan establishment, pushing through a trough of religious indifference, and advancing down the road to the millennium. In the most prominent and populous areas of Southeast settlement, the plan took hold with relative ease. In the Northwest settlements, however, it spread quite slowly.

The Rowley church, with its Yorkshire heritage, was slow to retreat from the original ways despite what its neighbors did. The high church admission standards had been set in 1631–33, before so many orthodox Southeasterners joined the Great Migration, and Rogers and his Yorkshire company tried to follow them in 1639; over 80 percent of the original settlers were in full communion. In 1690 Rowley finally yielded to the Half-Way Covenant, the last town in the Massachusetts Bay Colony to do so, but the Reverend Edward Payson, the minister at that time, "never recorded how the change was accomplished or how many persons it affected."[5] In this Rowley was showing its kinship with towns of Northwest people in the Plymouth Colony that continued to ignore the covenant compromise until early in the next century.

Rowley also clung to another original plan for New England churches that called for two ministers to guide each flock. In theory, the pastor preached and the teacher catechized. Most churches abandoned this plan because of expense and the shortage of well-educated clerics. Rowley continued the two-minister system until the 1690s, however, despite its rather small size.

The town got long service from its clergy. Samuel Shepard died after less than three years in the pulpit, but the average tenure of Rowley ministers was thirty-three years and there were no dismissals. Piety did ebb a bit after the death in 1661 of Rogers, their inspired pastor, and moral laxity increased, but actually the town fared well in this time of general declension; there were stirrings of the spirit in 1669, 1684, 1695, 1699, 1727, and 1728.[6] When evangelism gathered steam and emerged as the New Light, the torchbearers were the Jewetts, Rowley's most numerous pioneer family.

The Great Awakening reached its peak in Rowley in 1741–42 and met with very little opposition (see table 2-2). For a moment it became excessive. It was here that several zealots irregularly "ordained" Richard Woodbury, an uneducated itinerant. As God's special messenger, he pronounced temporal blessings and curses, cast out devils, and drank healths to "King Jesus." Woodbury's language was blasphemous, his conduct absurd.[7] This was so embarrassing to the evangelical cause that the few New Light clerics in the district condemned his behavior in writing.

Table 2-2. Church Admissions in Rowley

	1735–40	1741–42	1743–44
Male	12	23	8
Female	24	35	6
Total	36	58	14
Average per year	6.0	29.0	7.0
Percent male	33.3	39.7	57.1
Percent male change		+6.4	+17.4

Source: "Admissions to the Rowley Church," *Essex Historical Institute Collections* 34 (1898): 80-103.

Among those censuring Woodbury was Jedidiah Jewett, Rowley's New Light pastor at that time. He had been the colleague of Edward Payson and was elevated to pastor when Payson died in 1732. But Jewett signed the pro-revival testimonial of 1743 and publicly endorsed George Whitefield and his methods two years later when few did. His censure of Woodbury thus must be taken in context, for Jewett and his family were even more evangelical than the community. Jedidiah was the direct descendant of Maximilian Jewett of the West Riding. (This part of Yorkshire has been called "the Burnt-Over District" of England because of its religiosity in the early nineteenth century.) At the height of the Great Awakening in Rowley, eight members of the Jewett family converted in one year, compared with only seven in the previous six years.[8] In 1741–42, the number of converts increased almost fivefold over the previous level and the percentage of male converts increased even more. In this respect Rowley reflected the pattern of most New Light churches.

One of the best indicators of a burgeoning New Light church was the percentage of men admitted to full communion during the Great Awakening. Whether single and without property or married and owning land, such converts revitalized the laity. They participated in church affairs, organized reform societies, and served as missionaries. Converts developed skills in these activities that would later spill over into the political arena. The New Lights arrested the presbyterian drift and strengthened congregationalism. In contrast, Old Light churches generally had smaller admissions and, more importantly, their new members were disproportionately female. Given the relatively low status of women in the eighteenth century, and in Ramistic churches in particular, adding more women to a congregation merely accentuated a tendency already at work and did not raise its evangelical and political influence much. Church responses in New England varied widely, but a good number of converts in the years of the Great Awakening, with 40 percent or more men, and an increased or stable male percentage of the flock were good indicators of a New Light church, even when the minister was opposed to or only mildly inclined toward revivalism.[9]

Georgetown, a western section of Rowley, also reflected this revivalism. James Chandler, the first minister, seemed to echo Ezekiel Rogers in rejecting subscription but insisting on experimental religion in examining ministerial candidates. He signed the pro-revival testimony in 1743 and showed how strong his New Light was by inviting George

Whitefield into his pulpit in 1745. David Jewett, brother of Jedidiah, was persuaded after his graduation from Harvard to move to eastern Connecticut to evangelize the Mohegans. In that hotbed of revivalism, he became the first pastor of the integrated Montville Church. After the revival, Jedidiah Jewett, too, remained devout; in 1747 he wrote the preface for a sermon published by lay evangelist "Baker Dick" Elvins. Jewett led Rowley's "freshening" in 1764-65, and when George Whitefield died suddenly in nearby Newburyport, Jewett was a proud pallbearer. He retired in 1774, and the town was without a settled minister until the end of the American Revolution.

Rowley produced fifteen graduates of Harvard by 1765, and the ministry was their primary calling; 73 percent were ministers. Eight graduates became New Light ministers and there were no Old Lights. Variation from orthodox Congregationalism is noteworthy, however. Thomas Hibbert was dismissed for alcoholism and became a Presbyterian. One resident named Jonathan Searle became a Baptist and another with the same name became an alcoholic. Jacob Bailey later became an Anglican missionary on the Maine frontier. None settled in orthodox eastern Massachusetts.[10] These responses suggest the pressures Rowley clerics, nurtured in the Yorkshire heritage and New Light, faced after the revival. For twenty years afterward, Old Lights gained strength in Southeast areas of settlement while the New Light smoldered among Northwest people in many districts. In Rowley, the New Light may have dimmed a bit but it never disappeared.

The revolutionary era would bring evangelism to the surface again. In discussing the Massachusetts constitution in 1780, Rowley proposed that suffrage be limited to "Protestants" instead of granted to all Christians. This amendment was soundly rejected and set the town apart from others in eastern Massachusetts.[11]

When the Revolution ended, Rowley finally replaced Jedidiah Jewett. After trying out fifty men over eight years, the church passed over graduates from liberal Harvard and moderate Yale to call one from the "log college" in New Jersey (Princeton) that had emerged as the pre-eminent source of New Light ministers. In 1782 the Rowley church settled Ebenezer Bradford, a native of Canterbury in eastern Connecticut. He was a direct descendant of William Bradford, the Pilgrim governor, and maintained and eventually intensified the New Light in Rowley.[12]

Bradford, in reviewing the desirable qualities of a minister in 1785, stressed the New Light prescription for preaching—a plain, simple, "nervous" style. Debt to the "sensationalism" of John Locke and Jonathan Edwards seems evident in his requirement that the preacher's arrangement of words be striking in order to reach the affections; he cited Whitefield as a model for this technique. As a Princeton graduate, Bradford was especially familiar with the work of Edwards, who explained that only the graceful had experimental knowledge, that peculiar taste or discernment of the beauty of God and union. Bradford echoed his Rowley predecessors, Rogers and Chandler, as well as New Lights generally when he warned that ministerial candidates must continue to be examined carefully for signs of free and sovereign grace.[13] This sermon early in his tenure indicates that he was staying in the New Light after the Revolution.

In later sermons, Bradford remained evangelical. He asserted that ministers must be saved themselves and able to preach the particulars of salvation, relying on scripture and not shunning awful truths. God's plan was universal, calling for absolute dependence on Christ. Young ministers were "golden candlesticks" who must study and persevere, not forsake their calling. Bradford himself excelled in preaching and prayer and devoted extra time to preparing young men in religion and for the ministry.[14]

He also reminded the clergy of the importance of "preaching up" the doctrine of human depravity. He began by conceding that in their natural state humans had considerable latitude and power. Such people could, on occasion and through the intervention of providence, promote the glory of God and good of society. Such people could also feel pain and pleasure and were capable of sentiments of sympathy and gratitude. Nevertheless, they were depraved because they had lost their moral image of God and were acting selfishly, motivated by loaves and fishes. Bradford offered a list of reasons for his position. Total depravity explained the continual sinfulness of humanity over centuries and the little headway reform had made. He reasoned that if depravity were less than total, all people would be saved and this would explicitly contradict some passages of scripture. That people in their hearts resisted so stubbornly the Redeemer's scheme of salvation was additional evidence of pervasive sinfulness. The Bible declared in many places that people were evil and drew distinctions between saints and sinners. Finally, he reminded his hearers that the Reformed churches and even the articles of the Church of England endorsed the Calvinist view of total depravity and limited atonement.[15] Total depravity was, of course, a fundamental doctrine of Calvinist churches but evangelical pastors relied on it in particular to produce conviction of sin and explain conversion. In reaffirming it in 1791, Bradford knew he was pushing uphill against a strong Arminian tide in eastern Massachusetts.

When Samuel Langdon, former president of Harvard, attacked Samuel Hopkins's "new divinity," Bradford defended it. Bradford wanted "to militate against the pernicious effects of Langdon's book on some of my less informed friends." He charged Langdon with attempting to frighten readers away from the Hopkins system by labeling it "metaphysical," claiming that the author used the deceitful reasoning of Aristotle that could prove anything, "however false."[16] Bradford suggested that Langdon's latitudinarianism was vague and imprecise, ignored scriptural evidence, and therefore could also be regarded as metaphysical. But metaphysics was a science and the Rowley pastor recommended some reading to his opponent: Watts on ontology, Locke on human understanding, and Bailey and Sheridan on metaphysics.

Bradford supported Hopkins's view of the natures of Christ. He believed it was more reasonable as well as scriptural to assume that Christ had a body and a created soul, that he was one person with two natures "forever," rather than to accept Langdon's theory that Christ's soul was actually the Logos, or uncreated Jehovah. Langdon argued that Hopkins was "overcurious," that his "new divinity" was so complex and speculative that the apostles could never have explained it to the people in biblical times, and true Christianity, in contrast, was simple. Bradford's response was that the apostles did actually consider metaphysical questions—from decrees to regeneration—and were still able to spread the faith.

In steering between antinomianism and Arminianism, Bradford tried to follow Jonathan Edwards, who believed that a convert should show distinterested relish in God's excellency, not merely gratitude for salvation. The holy affections were the substance of religion and at the seat of the heart or will rather than the understanding. Divine sovereignty did not contravene human freedom or abolish a person's activity as a rational, voluntary agent. Bradford claimed that Langdon's Arminian scheme was deterministic in that a person was subject to all, and could not resist any, impressions from the outside.[17]

When Bradford turned from defending Hopkins's Calvinism to attacking Paine's deism, he seemed more effective. He viewed Tom Paine's

Age of Reason as narrow, illiberal, and unreasonable. He also found the style impudent and blasphemous. He said that admirers of Paine's earlier political works, like himself, were very disappointed with this book. He attributed its popularity in the new United States to the author's reputation and the vogue of "reason." What did deists offer, besides astronomy and trigonometry, as substitutes for the Bible? Other religions were incoherent and contradictory, not on a par with Protestant Christianity, and did not reach the ethical level of Christ when he recommended loving one's enemies.

Bradford tried to use his Anglo-American empiricism to warn youth away from deism by attacking its utility. He asked whether converting to deism would humble your pride, make you happy, lead you to love, or fill your empty soul. Of the prominent deists, none, he said, offered a better example of living than Christ and all were uncertain about how to worship the Almighty. Bradford believed that deists were egotistical, yet those rejecting the afterlife put themselves on a par with the ox and horse. Paine's *Age of Reason* was not divinity but natural philosophy. The minister saw this as a consequence of Paine's upbringing as a Quaker who slighted scripture. Reason, unassisted by revelation, did not lead to true religion for the people, Bradford concluded. According to him, the deistic scheme, although temporarily in fashion, failed the empirical test; it could not arouse and reform significant numbers of the populace.[18]

In this time of laissez-faire capitalism, Bradford naturally valued his "experimental" faith and believed he had the truth because, at least among his kind of people, this religion worked. Its efficacy in transforming people was continually being tested and verified in the religious marketplace. He obviously thought that a Calvinistic emphasis was still useful in the 1790s for explaining the phenomenon of evangelism and conversion. Bradford's views are a reminder that liberals and Old Lights did not have a monopoly on reason or the inductive method in this period. Alan Heimert has observed that "America's true Age of Reason unfolded, especially in its post-Revolution phase, more as an affirmative of evangelical principle than its repudiation."[19] This was simultaneously an age of wonders and an age of inquiry. Ebenezer Bradford, New Light and Hopkinsonian, was a good example.

Most clergy in New England endorsed the French Revolution when it broke out in 1789, believing it to be republican, bourgeois, and inspired by the 1776 revolution in their own country. As it moved leftward and was challenged by Great Britain and its allies, however, doubts developed. By the fall of 1794 many ministers were backing away from France and becoming Anglophiles, identifying with the seaboard merchant class and the emerging Federalists. Support for the Jay Treaty, which would improve New England's trade with Britain, was a symbol of the new cause. By this time most clerics no longer compared the French Revolution with the American Revolution; the French movement seemed too libertine, skeptical, and lacking in respect for property. Arminian ministers led the way in this retreat to Federalism, but as the months went by, they were joined by some evangelicals. Yet this reaction of clergy was caused not so much by drastic events in France—execution of the king and queen, the Reign of Terror, and war with Great Britain—as by some sympathetic responses in the United States, i.e., activities of the Democratic-Republican societies and interest in popular deism accompanied by a decline of respect for orthodox ministers and their religion.

Bradford provoked criticism because he continued to proclaim his enthusiasm for the French cause and the democratic societies it spawned in France and the United States. He saw the Revolution as advancing liberty and Jacobin societies as "useful" in promoting democracy; the American and French revolutions should not be condemned because some "pretended patriots" did tyrannical things. He viewed the democratic societies in the United States as analogous to the Sons of Liberty, yet responsible and operating within the law. Bradford argued that Americans should continue to be grateful for the French aid in their revolution. It was the French nation—the people, not the government—that had helped them, and the overthrow of the monarchy did not alter the obligation the United States had to honor its treaties with France. He viewed the destruction of the Roman Catholic Church in France as a defeat for the Anti-Christ and expected true Christianity, evangelical and congregational, to emerge from the ruins.[20]

The Rowley pastor finally attained notoriety for these extreme democratic and Christian opinions and the responses they provoked. To clerical Federalists, Bradford's support of the people smacked of anarchy and they dubbed him "the Vandal of Rowley." Ministers of the Essex County Association ostracized him and demanded a public recantation. Although his was a lonely clerical voice in eastern Massachusetts in 1795, these ministers recognized that evangelical and Jacobin sentiments could come together and be popular in the hinterlands. Most tax-supported churches in eastern Massachusetts were Unitarian in faith by 1800, although legal separation from the orthodox Congregational remainder did not occur until twenty years later.[21]

In religion, Ebenezer Bradford maintained continuity with Rowley's Yorkshire past and the Great Awakening. This descendant of William Bradford held Rowley to Calvinistic evangelism during the rationalist decades of the late eighteenth century. He felt confident and competent enough, moreover, to question in print Tom Paine and answer arguments of a former president of Harvard. Thus the heritage of the Yorkshire pioneers was still evident sixteen decades later. In fact, Rowley reached a religious apogee when the Second Great Awakening arrived. Although Bradford died in 1800 before he could witness the "Republican Millennium"—Thomas Jefferson's regime in the White House—his Massachusetts town was in the forefront of the evangelical order that would become so visible in the United States in the early decades of the nineteenth century. On the eve of the Civil War, it was said of the Rowley church that "its harmony has, in general, been faithfully observed. Its ministry has been marked for intelligence and adherence to gospel truth. In the great defections of New England, this church and its pastors were always true to the faith of the Pilgrims."[22]

Hingham

Immigrants from Southeast England set up a church and formed the town of Hingham twenty-eight miles south of Boston in 1635. By the end of the Great Migration in 1640, Hingham had grown to 131 families. Forty-five of them were from Norfolk, East Anglia, and many others were from Hingham in the homeland. Only five, however, can be directly linked to the Northwest (see table 2-3). Despite the lack of information on the origins of all of the early settlers, it would be conservative to conclude that less than one in five had links with the Northwest and the rest had roots in the Southeast (see table 2-4).

Of these five families, three had left Hingham by 1660, illustrating the tendency of Northwesterners to move out of communities when they were in the minority. John Otis, ancestor of James Otis, a diplomat and legislator during the revolutionary period, had come to Bare Cove, as Hingham was called before the East Anglians arrived in 1635, from Glastonbury in western Somerset. He moved to Weymouth in 1653, and his son to the Plymouth Colony. John Strong, a Welshman, was a

Table 2-3. Probable Origins of Hingham's First Settlers

	Number	Percent
East Anglia	65	61.3
Other Southeast	21	19.8
Southeast, Northwest surnames	15	14.2
Northwest	5	4.7

Sources: David Grayson Allen, *In English Ways: The Movement of Societies and Transferral of English Local Law and Custom to Massachusetts Bay, 1600-1690* (1981). See also Charles E. Banks, *Topographical Dictionary*, ed. E. E. Brownell (1937); Frank Holmes, *Directory of Ancient Heads of New England Families, 1620-1700* (1964 ed.).

Table 2-4. Hingham's Largest Families in the First Generation of Settlement

Surname	Number of Hingham Residents	Probable Origin
Lincoln	177	Norfolk
Cushing	123	Norfolk
Hersey	110	Berkshire
Stoddard	92	(Staffordshire, 10)
Beal	89	Norfolk
Gardner	80	(Warwick, 45)
Wilton	80	(North Hampshire, 30)
Sprague	74	Dorset
Wilder	63	(Berkshire, 12)
Hobart (Hubbard)	53	Norfolk
Tower	53	Norfolk
Loring	46	western Devon
Fearing (Fearin)	45	Cambridge

Sources: George Lincoln, ed., *The Town of Hingham: Genealogies* (1893), vols. 2, 3; Guppy, *Homes.*

Note: Surname frequencies per 10,000 from Guppy, *Homes,* appear in parentheses.

proprietor in Hingham but moved early to Taunton in the Plymouth Colony and later to the upper Connecticut Valley. His descendant, Josiah Strong, was the best-known advocate of Christian missions late in the nineteenth century. Edward Gilman, a good example of Northwestern transience, came from old Hingham to new, went to the Plymouth Colony in 1643, then to Ipswich, and finally "sat down" at Exeter, New Hampshire, in 1652. His grandson, Nicholas Gilman, the pastor of Durham, New Hampshire, was one of the most "enthusiastic" New Light pastors in the Great Awakening.[23]

As in Rowley, residents of new Hingham transplanted their economic activities from their homeland. There was some dairying, livestock raising, and growing of grains. Hingham also exported lumber to Boston. Compared with Rowley, Hingham had more enclosures, fewer open fields, and more even distribution of land, although a greater percentage of assets was invested in land. The higher number of land transactions suggests a more commercial and less communal attitude toward real estate. The people brought this attitude with them overseas, for in old Hingham, as in much of East Anglia, the manor with its bylaws and customs had been superseded by townships and representatives. An emerging modern economic order was more evident in the 1630s in Norfolk than in Yorkshire, and this difference was reflected in the new towns of Hingham and Rowley on the Massachusetts coastline.

Hingham is sometimes remembered for its militia controversy of the 1640s. Town leaders challenged Bay Colony authorities and eventually got the home rule they were seeking. This effort was not really evidence of a democratic spirit because an oligarchy took over rule of the town and fostered presbyterianism in the church, although the power of the magistrates over the town was reduced. Governor John Winthrop criticized the pastor, church, and community for their "presbyterial spirit."[24]

In English Hingham, the electorate put leaders into town office and deferred to them. Certain officers, churchwardens, and overseers of the poor who had money to disburse enhanced corporateness and the town structure. A close connection grew between landholding, social status, and tenure in town office. Officeholding soon became a proprietary right with sons succeeding fathers. In Massachusetts this tendency continued. The Hobarts, Cushings, Beals, and their relatives from old Hingham had the wealth and controlled the new town. By 1680 when the population was estimated at 729, these families dominated. Joshua Hobart served as captain of the trainband from 1652 to 1682 and represented the town in the General Court twenty-five times. Despite their numbers, the families of the Northwest minority—Stoddards, Gardners, Lorings—played only a small role in town affairs. As time passed this trend was reinforced. By 1680 only eighteen families constituted 50 percent of the population. After some "sifting out" of those not from East Anglia, a relatively homogeneous and conservative population remained that was comfortable with a few families in control.[25] After midcentury, new Hingham built on this initial presbyterian tendency, moving steadily toward patriarchy.

From the beginning, Hingham lacked an evangelical disposition. Although religious "quickenings," "freshenings," or "sprinklings" were sometimes reported in the Bay Colony, seldom did revivalism appear in Southeast-dominated towns near the coast. Hingham was religiously tranquil. In 1717 church and congregation, which was virtually the entire town, unanimously called Ebenezer Gay as minister, and this scholarly man spent almost seventy years in this pulpit. Peter Hobart, the original minister who had come over with the early settlers, had "set the ecclesiastical tone"; Gay "inherited a very conservative parish, and a church accustomed to a presbyterian style of governance."[26]

Gay was born in Dedham and went to Harvard after liberals had captured the college from the pious Mather faction. There Enlightenment ideas and attitudes fashionable in England after the Glorious Revolution were gaining ground among students. He graduated in 1714 as the first wave of Arminianism was rising in England. No doubt Gay was affected by these liberal influences. In his early years his theology was elusive, but has been characterized as cautious Arminianism. If he mentioned original sin once in a while, this was offset by hints of the Shaftesbury doctrine that people are innately good. He tried to "improve" upon the "earthquake revival" of 1727 to rejuvenate his own parish, but his efforts met with little effect. As an emerging liberal, Gay believed in private judgment and avoidance of controversy in the pulpit; he did not preach the five points of Calvinism. Yet the people of Hingham offered no indication of their disapproval.

Indeed, on the eve of the Great Awakening, after a quarter of a century in Hingham's pulpit, Gay was a patriarch. His flock compensated him generously, indicating satisfaction with his performance. Perhaps he meshed so well with his congregation because he preferred an inclusive parish church and because his views on church polity were in accord with those of Hingham's founding families. He did, however, have good rapport with south shore ministers who were moderate, nonevangelical Calvinists. Hingham would prove to be a major hive of Old Light sentiment.

Whitefield did not visit the south shore on his first tour in 1740 but persuaded Gilbert Tennent, the Son of Thunder from New Jersey, to itinerate in southeastern Massachusetts. Gay hoped for some spiritual stirring in Hingham and invited Tennent into his pulpit in March 1741. Tennent had developed a searching evangelical style to overcome "the presumptuous Security" of the Scots-Irish in New Jersey, but no report of his immediate impact on Hingham exists.[27] Gay kept the revival that followed under his careful direction, which turned out to be a mild affair that differed markedly from what happened in Rowley and New Light territory generally. Gay's hostility to the Great Awakening soon rose rapidly. He objected to emotionalism, itineracy, and a leveling spirit.

Church statistics reveal the moderate nature of the revival in Hingham (see table 2-5). Admissions for 1741–44 did increase, but more importantly, the percentage of male converts fell noticeably as the awakening continued. Gay's preaching during this period obviously did not attract men and "he would not, and probably could not, embrace the fervent Calvinistic rhetoric of the more successful evangelists" that would attract them. In Hingham this modest stirring meant some new members, but in an old pattern: 73 percent were married and the average age was 31.7, only a small drop from the previous decade. Hingham was relatively prosperous, having grown by 1.7 percent per year for several decades. Although farming was declining and left people without jobs, the expanding mercantile economy absorbed these extra workers. Gay's biographer observes that "Hingham's young men did not need Gay's church as an escape from economic disappointment."[28]

Table 2-5. Church Admissions in Hingham

	1735–40	1741–42	1743–44
Male	42	16	9
Female	57	29	22
Total	99	45	31
Average per year	16.5	22.5	15.5
Percent male	42.4	35.5	29.1
Percent male change		-6.9	-6.4

Source: Calculated from Robert J. Wilson III, *The Benevolent Deity: Ebenezer Gay and the Rise of Rational Religion in New England, 1696–1787* (1984), 92, 93.

Pastor Gay was disturbed by the controversy the revival left in its wake in New England and became more Arminian, putting lip service to Calvinism behind him. When Gay gave the Dudleian lecture at Harvard in 1759, he was ready to mine the rationalist vein of Puritanism. Sometimes invoking Lockean reason and other times a "moral sense," Gay claimed that humans had the power of self-determination. His position was close to that of an Anglican latitudinarian who emphasized virtue and moral duty rather than scripture and faith. Gay was naturally drawn into friendship with some other prominent liberals, such as Charles Chauncy and Jonathan Mayhew. He lagged behind them in assuming a unitarian view, however, so the title Father of Unitarianism, as some have bestowed on him, does not seem appropriate.

Liberals like Gay and evangelicals came together long enough in the 1750s to meet the Catholic threat posed by the French and Indian War. During the revolutionary agitation of the 1760s that followed, however, liberals made early and bold declarations but later became more cautious, noncommittal, and sometimes Tory as they contemplated the social side effects of a popular victory of Patriots over Tories. During the Revolution the liberalism that Gay had done so much to sustain in Hingham served him well. Most people in Hingham respected his right to private judgment and accepted the inoffensive Toryism of their aged pastor. Both Tories and Whigs seemed timid or circumspect in their sentiments. While liberal gentlemen in Hingham might be free to differ on the greatest political question of the time, Gay's Toryism in the pulpit finally strained the tolerance of the community, and the local Committee on Safety felt obliged to visit him although it took no action. His preference for the king set him apart from many Arminian clergy who did support the Patriots, but with trepidations.[29]

Hingham became less tolerant of evangelical, sectarian activity. A town resident followed a Rhode Island itinerant all the way to Abington and invited him to hold a special religious meeting in his house in Hingham. When the preacher arrived, he was greeted by a mob; they set upon him, threw his Bible to the ground, and forcibly escorted him out of town. Ringleaders were a Hingham church member and the houseowner who invited him.[30]

An analysis of Harvard graduates from Hingham confirms the evolving nonevangelism of the town. Harvard College was founded to train a New England–born ministry, but only 40 percent of Hingham graduates chose that calling. From 1724 to 1765 when seven of nine Rowley graduates entered the ministry, not one of the fourteen Hingham graduates did. During Ebenezer Gay's long tenure, few clerics came from Hingham. One who graduated from Harvard was Jonathan Cushing, who was settled at Dover, New Hampshire, in 1717, and married his second cousin, Elizabeth Cushing. He has been described as stout and dignified, as a "sensible, judicious and peaceful gentleman," but was mismatched with the region.[31] New Hampshire, north of Exeter, was New Light territory, but there was no mention of the Great Awakening in Dover or of Cushing's abilities at preaching and prayer. Unlike colleagues in the region, he did not sign the pro-Whitefield testimonial of 1743. When he died in 1769, the town owed him arrears and his estate had to wait fifteen years for payment. This indicates that despite his location, Cushing was a nonevangelical neutral in the revival. Hingham-born clergy were articulate Old Lights or prudent neutrals, but not New Lights who embraced the Great Awakening.

In Hingham, the liberalism Gay had begun continued under his successor, Henry Ware, who was settled in 1787. Ware, an East Anglian and a definite Arminian, was "highly acceptable to his people" but one observer noted that he was "too logical, too sensible, moderate and unimaginative to appeal to all classes in the community." He was characterized as a bashful man of simple tastes who abhorred cant. His premeditation is suggested by the story that he could not sleep on Sunday night until he had made plans for his sermon on the next Sunday.[32]

In his Thanksgiving sermon of 1795 he praised the new constitution and the wisdom of leaders in avoiding foreign war and checking the insurrection of the Whiskey Rebellion. Ware noted that the world envied the United States for its liberty and prosperity but thought that the young republic needed to be on guard; declining morals, like those the French Revolution was spawning, had led to despotism throughout history. He warned against emerging factionalism spurred on by a few speculators trying to arouse passions of the disorderly and discontented. The popular democratic societies that Ebenezer Bradford had defended Ware condemned as "dangerous aristocracies" that usurped power of the people and sought a kind of perpetual revolution. By using certain newspapers for sedition and slander, they were whipping up nationalist sentiment for another war with Britain. He accepted the idea of political opposition but believed it should be moderate, not abusive. For people in "the lower walks of life," Ware recommended cultivation of Ben Franklin's Poor Richard virtues of industry, frugality, and temperance instead of political activism.[33]

In this sermon, Henry Ware showed himself to be typical of Arminians and Unitarians who, more than evangelical Calvinists, used holidays and occasional sermons to shore up the religio-political order in New England. Ware's attempts at maintaining order actually served to undermine it. He was elevated to the Hollis Chair of Divinity in 1805, becoming the first avowed Unitarian to teach theology at Harvard. Calvinists, defeated after uniting to oppose him, founded their own seminary, Andover, three years later.[34]

After Ware's departure religious diversity finally came to Hingham in the second decade of the nineteenth century. Some Baptists from Boston sent missionaries in 1814 but gained few adherents. Methodists organized a class in 1818, and Universalists appeared in 1823. Up to this time Hingham's religious development had been gradual, consistent, and without conflict. The nonevangelical presbyterianism of the founders had moved imperceptibly to Gay's "free and catholic" position and open Unitarianism by the end of the century. As the town historian put it, "For nearly two centuries after the settlement of the town there were no other churches within its original limits, except those which became Unitarian."[35] He explained this monopoly and late arrival of evangelism by suggesting that sons followed their fathers in religion. Thus the original tendency of Hingham—presbyterian polity, nonevangelical theology—easily survived the colonial period and persisted into the nineteenth century.

Once-born Hingham steered a steady course of evolution from covenant Calvinism to Unitarianism before 1800. In contrast, Rowley pioneers practiced a frontier capitalism strongly leavened by pastoralism and evangelism. This initial religious sensibility would lead, after vicissitudes, to a notable reluctance to adapt to materialistic rationalism. Some would later express it evangelically by challenging clerical hierarchy and supporting moral reform; a few, pietistically, would reaffirm pastoralism and mysticism.

From the beginning, Rowley and Hingham were quite different communities religiously, and these differences obviously persisted through the eighteenth century. If they diminished because of some homogenizing effect of the American environment, as other scholars have suggested, there is little sign of it in the colonial period. In Rowley mixed farming declined and grazing expanded, and this was conducive to perpetuating religious pastoralism. Although the towns did become more complex and less self-sufficient as time passed, they retained the religious subcultures they brought over with them from the Northwest and the Southeast.[36]

The differences between Northwestern Rowley and Southeastern Hingham were continual but most discernible and significant at times of spiritual and moral crisis. The most obvious example is the Great Awakening of the eighteenth century, but even before the evangelical-pietistic side won so much ground in that revival, it had challenged the Puritans on several other occasions and had been rebuffed. Roger Williams, Anne Hutchinson, the Quakers, and their sympathizers had been put down early in the seventeenth century, and people sharing this tradition surfaced again during the Salem witchcraft trials of 1692. This colorful and heavily researched episode needs another look in terms of the two kinds of religious sensibility Rowley and Hingham have illustrated.

Notes

1. David Grayson Allen, *In English Ways: The Movement of Societies and Transferral of English Local Law and Custom to Massachusetts Bay, 1600–1690* (1981), 19–54.

2. Cotton Mather, "Life of Ezekiel Rogers," in *Magnalia Christi; or, The Ecclesiastical History of New England* (1820 ed.), 1:369–70. Ezekiel Rogers claimed direct descent from John Rogers (1500–1555), the Protestant martyr. John, born near Birmingham, was a priest that William Tyndale of Yorkshire converted in 1535. He published the Bible in English two years later and was burned to death for heresy. Ezekiel Rogers, converted at age twenty and on a mission from East Anglia to the North, to Rowley in Yorkshire, could therefore be seen as going "home" because Rogers was a Northwest surname. Henry A. Parker, "Paper on Ezekiel Rogers," *Publications of the Colonial Society of Massachusetts* (1911), 48–52. See also Stephen Foster, *The Long Argument: English Puritanism and the Shaping of New England Culture, 1570–1700* (1991), 27–31. In 1618, James I had directed clergy in the established church to read the *Book of Sports* to their flocks to combat Puritanism. Fifteen years later, Charles I reissued the *Book of Sports* order and persecuted clergy who did not comply.

Although there were tensions in Rowley over landholding because of population pressures that arose after Rogers's death, there was little resistance to decentralization and splitting off, according to Patricia Trainor O'Malley. See "Rowley, Massachusetts, 1639–1730: Dissent, Division, and Delimitation in a Colonial Town" (Ph.D. diss., Boston College, 1975), 11–17.

3. This estimate is from the fraction of applicable cases among the 2,885 names Banks cited. See Charles E. Banks, *Topographical Dictionary*, ed. E. E. Brownell (1937), and Virginia Anderson, *New England's Generation: The Great Migration and Formation of Society and Culture in the Seventeenth Century* (1991), 118–21. Rowley was an exception, at least until 1661, because the Northwest majority had been awakened, emigrated as a group, and respected Pastor Rogers. In the next three decades, only a very few families of newcomers had no relations living there. See O'Malley, "Rowley," 117.

4. In the 1920s, Charles Banks used a variety of sources to discover the origins of twenty–five adult males who emigrated to new Rowley; a half-century later, David Grayson Allen, while limiting his research to landholders prior to 1640, confirmed these and added sixteen more. Percentages calculated from Banks, *Topographical*, and Allen, *In English Ways*, 245–49. Frank Holmes added some more persons not mentioned by Banks or Allen who arrived after 1640: from the North, John Crosby (Yorkshire), Leonard Harriman (Yorkshire), William Hopson (Yorkshire), Edward Sawyer (Lincolnshire), and Henry Sewall (Warwickshire); from the West, Anthony Bennett (Wales), Richard Dole (Gloucestershire), and Robert Hazlitt (western Devon); from the Southeast, Isaac Cousins (Wiltshire) and John Gage (Suffolk). See Holmes, *Directory of Ancient Heads of New England Families, 1620–1700* (1964 ed.). Among persons with reported origins, those with no links with the Northwest were scarce: Kilbourne, Prime, Burpee, Wickham, Clark, Cousins, and Gage. The net result, when probable origins, surname frequencies, and in- and out-migration for several decades after 1640 are considered, is that the element with some Northwest connection was probably as high as 85 percent, certainly well over three-quarters of the total population. The East Riding was chiefly represented by old Rowley, Holme, and Cottingham, but many pioneers were from the West Riding. See O'Malley, "Rowley," 30–34.

5. Robert G. Pope, *The Half-Way Covenant: Church Membership in Puritan New England* (1969), 193, 200–201.

6. *An Ecclesiastical History of the Essex North Association* (1860), 367–72.

7. Joseph Tracy, *The Great Awakening: A History of the Revival of Religion in the Time of Edwards and Whitefield* (1842), 336.

8. Clifford Shipton, *Sibley's Harvard Graduates: Biographical Sketches of Those Who Attended Harvard College*, 17 vols. (1933–75), 8:64–69; Richard Carwardine, *Transatlantic Revivalism: Popular Evangelism in Britain and America, 1790–1865* (1978), 82.

9. Mary Marples Dunn found the average percentage of male church members from 1740 to 1749 to be 35, based on forty-six church records in Massachusetts and Connecticut. See Dunn, "Saints and Sisters: Congregational and Quaker Women in the Early Colonial Period," in *Women in American Religion*, ed. Janet James Wilson (1978), 36. In general, if a church gained an average

of ten persons a year from 1741 to 1744 or 1745, if at least 39 percent of those were men, and if that percentage remained stable or increased, it should be considered New Light in response. In a few cases, the presence of two of these three elements seems sufficient. The effectiveness of evangelism in adding members, especially men, and raising church vitality has long been recognized. Recently Terry Bilhartz has shown the success of the Methodists in Baltimore in the first decades of the nineteenth century. Evangelism enabled the Methodists to grow and add men despite the general trend toward a predominantly female membership. In fact, pastors of rival denominations, less comfortable with this emphasis, tried to use it anyway to compete with the Methodists in gaining male converts. See Bilhartz, *Urban Religion and the Second Great Awakening: Church and Society in Early National Baltimore* (1986), 20–21, 83–99.

10. Shipton, *Harvard Graduates*, 8:375–81, 10:43–50, 8:64–69. For a list of Rowley's Harvard graduates to 1765, see appendix B.

11. Ronald T. Tagney, *A County in Revolution: Essex County at the Dawning of Independence* (1976), 280–81; Thomas Gage, *The History of Rowley, Anciently Including Bradford, Boxford, and Georgetown, from the Year 1639 to the Present Time* (1840), 271. The data was compiled from Shipton, *Harvard Graduates*.

12. Richard A. Harrison, ed., *The Princetonians, 1769–1774: A Biographical Dictionary* (1981), 272–76.

13. Ebenezer Bradford, *The Ordination of Israel Day, June 1, 1785* (1785), 1–26.

14. Ebenezer Bradford, *Christ's Presence with His Ministers* (1795), 1–32, sermon delivered at the ordination of Daniel Gould as evangelist at Fairlee, Vermont, October 2, 1795.

15. Ebenezer Bradford, *The Depravity of Human Nature* (1791), 1–24.

16. Ebenezer Bradford, *Strictures on the Remarks of Dr. Samuel Langdon on the Leading Sentiments in the Hopkins System of Doctrines* (1794), 4–5.

17. William Breitenbach, "Piety and Moralism: Edwards and the New Divinity," in *Jonathan Edwards and the American Experience*, ed. Nathan O. Hatch and Harry S. Stout (1988), 181–83; Bradford, *Strictures*, 1–47.

18. Ebenezer Bradford, *An Examination of the Age of Reason* . . . (1795), 17–63. It is noteworthy that John Bradford (1510–55) of Lancashire was a very prominent Protestant martyr, like John Rogers, whose name and fame came down through his religious books, steady sellers in New England. William Bradford (1590–1657) of Yorkshire was the Pilgrim Separatist leader and historian of the Plymouth Colony. Another John Bradford (1750–1805) of Hereford was converted to Calvinism in young adulthood (c. 1770) and became a preacher in Countess Huntingdon's Connexion, a small Evangelical group that split from the Church of England. Ebenezer Bradford of Rowley, more obscure than this trio, was still conforming to this heritage in the 1790s, and his younger brother, William, also a Princeton graduate, served as pastor of the

Canterbury Separate Church in Connecticut early in the nineteenth century. Thus in Anglo-American religion, the Bradford surname continued to be identified with the British Northwest, evangelism, and Calvinism. See *Dictionary of National Biography* (1921–22), 2:1064–72; Harrison, *Princetonians*, 364–65; William B. Sprague, *Annals of the American Pulpit* (1865), 2:373–79.

19. Alan Heimert, *Religion and the American Mind: From the Great Awakening to the Revolution* (1966), 538. He cites many New Light clerics, but not Ebenezer Bradford. Henry F. May mentions him in *The American Enlightenment* (1976), 264. In Central Europe revivalism was the response to religious, ethnic, and political oppression and was an empirical, not a doctrinal or liturgical, reform movement. One authority, Klaus Scholder, has contended that the idea of religion as the way to a better life was the core of the Enlightenment in these parts. In any case, reason and religion, evangelism and science were mixed together there. See W. R. Ward, "The Relationship of the Enlightenment and Religious Revival in Central Europe and the English-speaking World," in *Reform and Reformation: England and the Continent, 1500–1750,* ed. Derek Baker (1979), 281–305.

20. Anson Ely Morse, *The Federalist Party in Massachusetts to the Year 1809* (1909), 131–34; Gary B. Nash, "The American Clergy and the French Revolution," *William and Mary Quarterly* 22 (1965): 392–412.

21. *Ecclesiastical History,* 371–72; Sydney Ahlstrom, *The Religious History of the American People* (1975), 1:489–90. Bradford had a highly visible counterpart in western Massachusetts, Thomas Allen of Pittsfield in the Berkshires. See Richard D. Birdsall, "The Rev. Thomas Allen: Jeffersonian Calvinist," *New England Quarterly* 30 (1957): 147–65.

22. *Ecclesiastical History,* 371–72.

23. Henry Guppy, *Homes of Family Names in Great Britain* (1890), 490. See also John J. Waters, "Hingham, Massachusetts, 1631–1661: An East Anglian Oligarchy in the New World," *Journal of Social History* 1 (1968): 365–66n57; Banks, *Topographical;* and Holmes, *Ancestral Heads.* Charles Banks found the probable English origins of eighty-four of Hingham's first settlers. David Grayson Allen, again limiting himself to the years before 1640, confirmed eighty-one of Banks's cases, but in three instances (R. Jones, G. Knight, J. Phippen), differed as to the county in the Southeast. Allen was able to add probable origins of twenty-two persons. See Allen, *In English Ways,* 250–60. Holmes added five more names. The Gilman surname had a high frequency in Staffordshire (18/10,000) and Derbyshire (13/10,000), but not in the Southeast. No origins were reported for four families prominent in the town, but their Northwest frequencies have been indicated in table 2-4. The net result, when probable origins and surname frequencies are combined, is a Northwest minority of 20 percent in Hingham. See George Lincoln, ed., *The Town of Hingham: The Genealogies* (1893), vols. 2, 3.

24. John Coolidge, "Hingham Builds a Meetinghouse," *New England Quarterly* 34 (1961): 435–43; Waters, "Hingham," 351–70; Robert E. Wall, Jr., *Massachusetts Bay: The Crucial Decade, 1640–1650* (1972), 93–95. The term *presbyterial* meant increased power to pastor and elders and correspondingly less to rank-and-file members. This was the tendency among Puritans in Southeast England, especially East Anglia, which continued in New England. The more familiar term *presbyterian* is used instead of *presbyterial* when referring to England and settlers from there. It is the Scottish form of this church polity that is fully presbyterian.

25. Allen, *In English Ways*, 55–81.

26. Robert J. Wilson III, *The Benevolent Deity: Ebenezer Gay and the Rise of Rational Religion in New England, 1696–1787* (1984), 37. Ebenezer's grandfather, John Gay, arrived in New England in 1630. From Watertown he moved to Dedham and later became its wealthiest inhabitant. The surname was most prominent in Wiltshire (31) and Hampshire (17) in the region labeled the cradle of Latitudinarianism. See Guppy, *Homes*, 489. The *National Encyclopedia of Biography* describes the Gays as of "Norman descent" and lists Kent as the home county (1909), 11:296, (1939), 27:36. Wilson, *Benevolent Deity*, 5, 242n6; see also Robert C. Anderson, "A Note on the Gay-Borden Families in Early New England," *New England Historical and Genealogical Register* 130 (1976): 35–39.

27. Wilson, *Benevolent Deity*, 88.

28. Ibid., 11–79, 91–94, quotations from 92 and 54–56.

29. Ibid., 224–25.

30. The mob, faced with legal proceedings, settled out of court. See Isaac Backus, *A History of New England with a Particular Reference to the Denomination of Baptists* (1784; rpt., 1969), 2:273–74.

31. Shipton, *Harvard Graduates*, 5:334–37, 634–35, quotation from 635. For Harvard graduates from Hingham, see appendix B.

32. Harris E. Starr, "Henry Ware," *Dictionary of American Biography* (1936), 10:447–48.

33. Henry Ware, *The Continuance of Peace and Increasing Prosperity, a Source of Consolation and Just Cause for Gratitude to the Inhabitants of the United States* (1795).

34. Conrad Wright, *Beginnings of Unitarianism* (1955), 274–80.

35. Lincoln, *Hingham*, 1:44–68, quotation from 68.

36. These two towns were in many respects typical of their religious subcultures rather than extreme examples. There were some towns with more New Light than Rowley, and some with more Old Light than Hingham. These two were extreme in some respects, however. Rowley was extreme with its high concentration of Yorkshire settlers, and Hingham was extreme with its high concentration of East Anglians and Tory pastor. Early demographic studies of New

England towns—Sudbury, Andover, Dedham—did not focus primarily on religion and religiosity and treated communities that tilted toward the Old Light. More recently, some extended studies of towns with New Light activity have appeared—see Christopher M. Jedrey, *The World of John Cleaveland: Family and Community in Eighteenth-Century New England* (1979), for Chebacco, and Christine Heyrman, *Commerce and Culture: The Maritime Communities of Colonial Massachusetts, 1690–1750* (1984), for Gloucester.

It is interesting that the most prominent Americans of the nineteenth century with Rowley roots were William Lloyd Garrison, the abolitionist, and Luther Burbank, the mystical horticulturalist known as the "plant wizard." Garrison's paternal grandmother, Mary Palmer Garrison, was born in Rowley but in 1764 moved north to Nova Scotia to spread revivalism. The Burbanks were one of the original families in Rowley. Luther moved west from Massachusetts to California in 1875, joining his brothers. Hingham's counterparts came from its two most numerous pioneer families and were better known. They were both lawyers and political leaders, but very different in personality: Abraham Lincoln of Illinois and Caleb Cushing of Massachusetts. The criterion for prominence used here is the length of the biographical essays in the *Dictionary of American Biography* (1927–), 2:265–70, 623–30, 4:168–72, 6:242–59.

Chapter Three

Witchcraft Executions in Salem: Southeast and Northwest Collide

At the time of the witchcraft trials in 1692, Salem was a thriving town. It had become a legal port in 1683 and was second only to Boston in size. After three decades of fairly rapid economic development, Salem dominated shipbuilding in New England and its ships sailed the world. The shadow of Boston as a mercantile rival was only beginning to circumscribe the independence of Salem merchants. At first glance, the hinterlands of Maine or Carolina, near the "heathen" American Indians, would seem to have been a more likely site for accusations of witchcraft than this prosperous port.[1] While other Bay Colony towns were slowly moving from the Puritan ideal of communal orthodoxy to religious pluralism, Salem's reaction to this transition was spectacular. It is logical to examine the town's early history to explain this unusual development.

The first English settlers of Naumkeag, as the American Indians called this place, came from nearby Cape Ann after the trading post of the Dorchester Company was disbanded in 1626. This small group chose this site because of the peninsula jutting into the large harbor and the proximity of open land. Roger Conant, who had been governor on the cape, was their leader. He had arrived in the Plymouth Colony in 1623 "on his own particular," that is, as an individual without company obligations. He disagreed with some aspects of Pilgrim Separatism and soon moved on to Wessegamett and Cape Ann.

Most Old Planters, as the Salem pioneers are called, had come from the West Country in the Southeast at the behest of English entrepreneurs who were promoting commercial agriculture as a means to supplement fishing and trade. In Limington in eastern Somerset, farmers cultivated their own land rather than participating in the open-field system. In 1628 the New England Company sent over sixty people, including women and children, from this district, more than doubling the number of settlers. This company had chosen John Endecott as governor of the expedition, which meant friction with Conant and his followers. A compromise was soon reached, and in 1628 they named the town Salem, indicating the hope for peaceful coexistence.

In their religious beliefs and behavior, Old Planters were nonseparating Puritans somewhere in the middle between Separatist Puritans and Laudian Anglicans of the established church. The community was stable with no hint of evangelical fervor, and church membership was relatively inclusive. These substantial landholders sought a middle way between religious zeal and ritual.

Between 1633 and 1638 the Great Migration brought many newcomers to Salem including some from East Anglia, the stream that had transformed the locality of Bare Cove into the town of Hingham. Newcomers resented the landed status of Old Planters and scrambled to catch up. They followed the open-field system, working strips of land close to the town that was forming on the peninsula. Their experience in East Anglia made them ready to mix mercantile with agricultural interests. By 1640, they had gained enough status to elect more than one member to the town board.

East Anglians brought a more aggressive and theological Puritanism to Salem. While not subscribing to Separatism, and in fact reacting to it strongly in their home communities, they nevertheless sought to winnow church admissions and set high and explicit standards for new members. Their numbers allowed them to quickly gain church offices, which improved their status relative to other settlers.[2] Along with this more legalistic Puritanism came divisiveness. In the 1640s, geographical separation became evident. East Anglians stayed close to the wharves on the peninsula while Old Planters went to small harbors at the far corners of the township. The result was that three new towns—Wenham, Manchester, and Marblehead—split off. But many of the Old Planter faction also settled down on the Cape Ann side of the Bass River in what became the town of Beverly in 1668.

The presence of Old Planters and East Anglians made for an unusually large upper class, but it took some time for the latter to surpass the former in wealth and status. Old Planters were destined to fall behind in the competition for voters because of their smaller numbers, yet they did gain some political allies in other settlers from the Southeast during the late 1630s and early 1640s, notably William Hathorne of Berkshire and Edmond Batter of Wiltshire. Although they were divided geographically, both groups represented nonevangelical, deferential Puritanism and were amenable to the idea of a Half-Way Covenant broached here as early as 1652. Salem adopted it soon after a Massachusetts synod endorsed it in 1662.

These two groups of Puritans comprised over two-thirds of the Salem population. The remainder were immigrants from the Northwest or had Northwest surnames. As in Hingham, this group was more inclined to move than the Southeast majority. Of the 38 emigrants to Salem from the Northwest up to 1660, only 58 percent stayed. In contrast, nearly 80 percent of the 174 Southeast migrants chose to remain in the town.[3]

This minority played a conspicuous part in Salem's early religious history, however. In this group were dissidents and seekers who would not—or could not—adapt to the orthodox Puritanism that was setting in. They caused what Kai Erikson has called "crime waves" in New England, periods of excitement when magistrates publicized challenges to their authority that justified severe punishment. Roger Williams, Anne Hutchinson, Quakers, and "witches" fell victim to such punishment during these crime waves.[4]

Anne Marbury Hutchinson came with her family from Lincoln to New England in 1634. She was responding to a revelation and following her pastor, John Cotton, a refugee from Laud's conformity, who had left Old Boston for the new one at Massachusetts Bay. Anne was a mother, midwife, and daughter of a minister and well versed in theology. She began her religious work by explicating Cotton's sermons to younger women in her parlor but, according to the authorities, these sessions grew to include men from Cotton's flock, other Bostonians, and some who neglected sermons in church and relied solely on her exegesis. In the course of this work, she was convinced that most Bay ministers were preaching works, not grace, and that after only six years, the "city on a hill," and the Reformation itself, were being undermined by formalism and legalism that took the heart out of religion.

Her views led to what became known as the Antinomian Controversy. Antinomians claimed that a person could be passive in the conversion process because the Trinity seized and dwelt in—possessed or "godded"—an individual. This possession constituted conversion and included sanctification. True conversion was sudden and could be perceived immediately, not discerned later as the orthodox preferred to have it. Thus the struggle to pass through the various stages, the "morphology of conversion" that Puritans emphasized, could be obviated or much compressed. Human efforts to internalize complex law-gospel tensions of the Protestant Reformed faith, something that folk from the Northwest found hard to do on their own, were diminished and reliance was placed on indwelling Holy Spirit. Orthodox Puritans would naturally resent this short-cut to Heaven that minimized human volition and left the hard work to God. If it were not popery, they thought, it must be satanism; obviously it was heresy beyond the bounds of "the New England way." Massachusetts ministers and magistrates in the mainstream of Reformed theology charged Anne and her followers with seeking "A Faire and Easie Way to Heaven."[5]

These ministers and magistrates labeled Hutchinson a fanatic, imposter, liar, and "familist." The last term carried the implication of sexual libertinism, although there was no evidence of any. These charges would later become common among those accused of witchcraft, and in Hutchinson's case were an occupational hazard of a midwife who entered many households and learned family secrets while assisting in childbirth. The General Court examined Anne Hutchinson and, after fencing with the magistrates, she finally made her heresy explicit by admitting she believed in direct revelation. For this heresy, the court banished her from the Bay Colony. She moved with her family to Rhode Island and on to Long Island, where they were all killed by American Indians. Today most scholars perceive her as brave and charismatic, brilliant and self-possessed rather than God-possessed.

Anne Hutchinson was a natural representative of the oral Northwest because she heard sermons and remembered spoken words better than she read scriptures. Driven by her piety, she bent scriptures to suit her feelings, as did others from her part of the world. The Puritan clerics who heard her testimony wanted to believe in only one literal interpretation of the Bible and thus considered her deviations from that interpretation to be lies. They had not been able, however, to impose this standard even on the more religious of the colony's population.[6]

John Cotton, Anne's mentor, shared her bias toward the oral tradition. He had come from Derby to matriculate at Emmanuel College, Cambridge, the center of Puritan ideas. Emerging as a learned but cautious man, he was able to disagree on some points of conformity, yet remain within the Church of England establishment. In preaching, however, he was distinctly evangelical despite the uneasiness of church authorities. He had been influenced by William Perkins of Warwickshire, an outstanding preacher who emphasized the plain over the elegant style. Cotton had great success with this method, first in old, then in new Boston and, like Whitefield, his words were much more effective spoken than read.[7] The spontaneity and boldness of Hutchinson, his disciple, however, finally involved him in a controversy with clerical colleagues and drew attention to his difference with the majority over the role of the Spirit in conversion.[8]

The group that responded to Hutchinson's mysticism, who were often drawn to her parlor, were those in the Boston congregation from the Northwest, especially from her home county of Lincoln, the vicinity of Alford, or old Boston where Cotton had been pastor. These persons seemed to have accepted Anne's views as an extension of Cotton's teachings. They were inclined to believe that the Holy Spirit could suddenly bestow grace and, by indwelling, free them from sin and obligation to merely human laws. Anne believed that among clerics in the area, only her mentor, John Cotton, and her brother-in-law, John Wheelwright, met her standard for grace. Only they were truly sustaining the holy experiment begun in New England.[9]

The geographical origins of the Hutchinsonians are relevant here. Emery Battis explored the movement at its center, and furnished data for a large fraction of the Boston male population. He divided male Hutchinsonians, about a quarter of the men in Boston, into three groups according to their public involvement. Core members were heavily involved in promoting Hutchinson's beliefs. Supporters quietly participated in the movement. Most in the peripheral group were not church members or voters and may not have shared Anne Hutchinson's particular religious doctrines but found her movement an outlet for discontent with the accumulating power of ministers and magistrates. Those without documented origins were not prominent in Boston, were more likely to be latecomers and nonchurch members, and were not involved, except for a few in the peripheral group. Calculating from Battis's data and separating these numbers by geography produces some interesting results (see table 3-1). While it was natural for Hutchinson

Table 3-1. Probable Origins of Boston Hutchinsonians, circa 1637

	Core	Support	Total Core and Support	Total Males Boston	Percent Core and Support
Lincoln County	8	7	15	23	65.2
Other Northwest counties	3	6	9	12	75.0
Northwest zone total	11	13	24	35	68.6
Southeast counties	7	15	22	71	31.0
London					
Northwest surname	2	2	4	6	66.7
Other	1	1	2	8	25.0
Southeast zone total	10	18	28	85	32.9
Unknown origins	3	7	10	237	4.2
Grand Total	24	38	62	357	17.4

Sources: Calculated from Emery Battis, *Saints and Sectaries: Anne Hutchinson and the Antinomian Controversy in Massachusetts Bay Colony* (1962), 329–44; Northwest surnames from London calculated from Henry Guppy, *Homes of Family Names in Great Britain* (1890).

Note: Battis supplied no origins for Richard Cooke or Isaac Grosse. Holmes, however, listed Cooke, a support member, from Gloucestershire, and Grosse, a core member, from Cornwall, where the surname has a high frequency. Cooke and Grosse are therefore included in the Other Northwest counties category. See Frank Holmes, *Directory of Ancient Heads of New England Families, 1620–1700* (1964 ed.), cii, lvi; Guppy, *Homes,* 108, 494.

to receive her strongest support from Lincoln, her home county, the rest of the Northwest also showed significant sympathy.[10]

In this crisis the major issue was how God affected the heart or soul. Did God gradually restore a person or did the Holy Spirit come suddenly to dwell in the heart? Those with roots in the Northwest, a minority in Boston and Salem, were predisposed to believe, because of their traditions, that they could know the immediacy of the other world, that is, they could feel, taste, and savor God's presence. They believed that those from the Southeast, especially clerical leaders, did not have the same sensibility and were "falling out of the light" after the exodus to New England. "Antinomians" and "familists," as these Northwesterners were sometimes called, were catchall terms covering a variety of radical spiritists who believed in a New Light at work in and through them. This belief led to others—prophecy, continuing revelation, spir-

itual equality, congregationalism, anticlericalism, opposition to the war
with the Pequots—that put them at odds with orthodox Puritan leaders from Southeast England. People accused of heretical opinions were
inclined to obfuscate or only admit "misunderstandings" to avoid punishment. The extent of these views in New England in 1637 is hard to
estimate. On the basis of geography and culture, perhaps as many as
four in ten of Boston's inhabitants had the potential to sympathize with
the types of piety the Hutchinsonians represented.

Prominent sympathizers came from the Northwest. From Lancashire came Samuel Gorton, later a sect leader in Rhode Island, and William Aspinwall, political leader of the Hutchinsonians. From Warwick
came Captain John Underhill, Boston's outstanding soldier. From Wales
came Marmaduke Mathews to serve as pastor in Malden; when his
antinomianism became known, he returned to the principality. From
Wales also came Nicholas Easton, a Newbury tanner who followed the
Hutchinsons to Rhode Island and became a lay preacher and link with
the Quaker movement. In 1638 Hanserd Knollys of Lincoln arrived in
Boston and, finding his antinomian views very untimely, moved to
Dover on the New Hampshire frontier, afterward becoming a leader of
the Particular (Calvinistic) Baptists in England. These well-known
spiritists prefigured the Ranters, Levellers, and Quakers of the Interregnum, and they came from the seedbed of sectarianism and mysticism, the English Northwest. Thus the New England population of the
1630s reflected contemporary religious radicalism in England on the eve
of the Civil War.

With the banishment of Anne Hutchinson, the influence of the
Northwest sectarians was reduced at the center, Boston, but reinforced
in Rhode Island and elsewhere on the periphery. Bay Puritans, already
suspicious of "strangers" or "sojourners," in 1637 tightened immigration regulations because they feared an influx of English antinomians,
especially Grindletonian familists from Yorkshire. No doubt Puritan
authorities were right in claiming that religious confusion and political anarchy had been nipped in the bud, that their version of a city on
a hill had been preserved. The price of this, however, was an increase
in formalism and conformity that was unsatisfying to a vocal minority
in Boston and the Bay Colony.

The Hutchinson crisis was in Boston, but it did have some impact
in Salem. William Alford was in the core, William Comins was a supporter, and seven others in Salem were in the peripheral group. After

Hutchinson's trial, two men left and four were disarmed. Some Salem women also kept dissent alive. Mary Oliver from Norwich in Norfolk was the most persistent "heretic" of the time. She shared Samuel Gorton's spiritist views and remained outside the Salem church although her husband acquired some property and joined. In Norwich, she had refused to bow to the name of Jesus and later resisted authority in New England. She saw ministers as "bloodthirsty men" and tried to return that violence. Speaking of William Hathorne, a magistrate, she said, "I do hope to live to tear his flesh in pieces, and all such as he."[11] For this remark she was put in the stocks. Her threats and grumbles sounded "witchlike" to the orthodox and she was indicted for living apart from her husband, among other things. In 1651 she was finally ordered back to England. Such dissidents were ripe for Quaker ideas when they arrived in the 1650s.[12]

The second crime wave began in 1656 when some Quakers landed in Boston and were imprisoned. The Friends decided that Salem was a likely place for Quaker witness because of earlier signs of religious dissatisfaction and deviation there, and apparently they were right. John Copeland of Cumberland and Christopher Holder of Gloucestershire met with "almost instantaneous success." When Holder rose to speak after a Salem church service, someone put a glove in his mouth, but Samuel Shattuck pulled it out. Nicholas Phelps opened his home to traveling Friends and invited Shattuck and other interested persons over to hear their witness. Phelps's house was in Salem Woods five miles from the peninsula and near the border of Lynn. The result of the meeting was that more than half a dozen were converted—"convinced," to use the Quaker term—and soon after, this part of Salem became the seedbed for Quakerism in the Bay Colony.[13]

In England before the mid-1660s, Quakerism drew most of its support from farmers and artisans in the Northwest, especially Cumberland, Westmorland, Yorkshire's West Riding, Lancashire, and the Far West, and sent out missionaries from these parts. Quakerism in New England attracted settlers from the Northwest, so it was in the Salem Woods section of the township that the sect first found favor. This small circle of converts was willing to defy authorities and the law, reject Puritanism and the elect, and embrace a larger spiritual community held together by belief in the Inner Light and higher law. No doubt these few represented merely the boldest and most alienated among those from the Northwest.

Puritan authorities in Massachusetts reacted to the Quaker "invasion" of 1656 in an almost military fashion. Although arriving Quakers were of both sexes and modestly attired, magistrates saw them as part of a conspiracy against the "Chosen People," a Devil's army bent on subverting the wilderness Zion. Experience with Anne Hutchinson in the 1630s and other dissidents in the 1640s made them aware of the potential for confusion, schism, and anarchy such people could pose. Puritans linked the Quaker Inner Light, their concept of direct revelation, with Satan, not God, and "quaking" with possession.[14] While they rejected Quaker theological notions, it was the euphoric intensity with which Quakers denied authority that provoked draconian penalties. Only in this light can the extreme reaction to and severe punishment of these humble "Publishers of the Truth" make sense. Friends were willing to die witnessing for the truth, and Puritan magistrates were willing to maim and kill them in resisting it. Quakers in England supported their missionaries and so this threat to orthodoxy seemed better organized than that of the Hutchinsonians. The greater Quaker sufferings were in Massachusetts, the more Friends wanted to martyr themselves witnessing there. Magistrates were frustrated by this attraction of opposites; laws against this "cursed sect" were not working and grisly penalties—public whipping, ear cropping, banishment, and execution—served only to generate some sympathy and doubt among the orthodox rank and file. This Puritan dilemma was finally solved when the restored Charles II personally ordered Massachusetts to stop persecuting his Quaker subjects there in 1661. After the king's order arrived, the second crime wave in Massachusetts gradually subsided. Pluralism then made quiet headway and the small circle of Friends in Salem grew.[15]

A number of people, especially women, were still reluctant to attend religious services that did not touch their hearts. The way for Quakerism had been prepared not only by Anne Hutchinson's emphasis on grace over works, but also by Roger Williams's legacy of prophesying in Salem's church. This democratic practice of sharing insights and feelings gave women a role in church affairs, but could also be carried on in private meetings. Salem had been at the edge of the Antinomian Controversy, but became a Quaker center later in part because prophecy was maintained. Then Quaker sponsorship of travel, as well as sectarian belief in the priesthood of all believers, gave women an opportunity to become traveling Friends. Thus women traveled unescorted, defying convention and respectability to preach the truth. Their willingness to suffer publicly for "soul liberty" gave visibility and notoriety to the Friends. Quakerism offered the possibility of some organized resistance to Puritan orthodoxy that had settled in after the Great Migration, and women were a conspicuous part of it.[16]

Salem residents attracted to Quakerism, like the radical spiritists that preceded them, derived from the Northwest.[17] This was true of traveling Friends from England also. Quakerism grew in Salem until almost 9 percent of the adult population were convinced. After the crisis years of 1656–61, they gained gradual acceptance. "Sufferings" became merely fines for nonattendance at church, amounting to about what Quakers would have had to contribute to the minister's salary in Salem had they not opposed a "hireling" ministry. They were exempted from paying the minister's rate in 1667.

Quakers in New England, like those in England, moved beyond the prophetic stage in the 1660s. George Fox, their leader, gave his followers a presbyterianlike organizational structure, and as quietism replaced evangelism, Quakers gained some respect and social mobility. Membership included merchants and shopkeepers, adding diversity to the agricultural sect. In Salem Town, Thomas Maule, a Quaker, emerged as a successful merchant and critic of the witch proceedings in 1692.[18]

Town Leaders

Until 1692, a relatively few men from the Southeast majority—Old Planters and East Anglians—dominated Salem's public life. They were reelected quite regularly to high offices, as grand jurors, selectmen, deputies, and, occasionally, assistants to the Bay Colony government. Salem was another example of a Massachusetts town based on Puritan social theory where voters naturally deferred to and elected men who combined church membership with wealth in property. Within these old families some differences about covenants and politics would be continual but there was a religious consensus against emotionalism and sectarians that the crime waves reinforced. After the king's intervention in 1661, town leaders moved grudgingly toward toleration but continued to worry about the sectarian threat to "good order" in the community. After 1670, more persons without pre-1640 roots gained some visibility, and with the decline of the communal ideal, Puritan leaders relied on old families to maintain social order (see table 3-2).

Roger Conant and John Endecott were representatives of the Old Planter faction. Edmond Batter and William Hathorne emerged as

Table 3-2. Salem Leaders

Name	Arrival in Salem	Probable Origin
Conant, Roger	1626	eastern Devon
Endecott, John	1628	eastern Devon
Putnam, John	1630	Buckinghamshire
Bartholomew, Henry	1635	Oxfordshire
Batter, Edmond	1635	Wiltshire
Browne, William	1635	Suffolk
Hathorne, William	1636	Berkshire
Gardner, Thomas	1637	eastern Somerset
Corwin (Curwen), George	1638	Cumberland
Gedney, James	1638	Norfolk
Porter, John	1644	Dorset

Sources: Richard M. Gildrie, *Salem, Massachusetts: A Covenant Community* (1975), 1, 6, 35, 37, 61, 104, 119; Holmes, *Ancestral Heads*, xxxiv, xcii.

leaders in the late 1630s. Henry Bartholomew spent sixteen terms as selectman and nineteen as deputy to the General Court. The Porters were large landowners with commercial ties. George Corwin was the only leader of Northwest origins and a nonchurch member before 1670, although his wife belonged. James Gedney's son, Bartholomew, became a major officeholder. Batter, John Porter, and Corwin together held sixty-two terms as representatives. But William Hathorne was the individual champion with thirty-three, and his influence covered more years than the others. His son, John, was elected to the town board several years after he stepped down. The Putnams expanded their original grant through purchase and became influential belatedly in 1665, representing the rural precinct of Salem Village. The leading families had come largely from the area between London and Exeter, from Buckingham to eastern Devon. While these were the chief actors in Salem's early history, there were supporting players: for the Old Planters, the Balch, Palfrey, and Trask families, and for the East Anglians, the Holgraves and Rucks.

The Northwest minority were, of course, less prominent in officeholding. Jeffrey Massey served on the town board early before moving to the periphery. Nicholas Manning, a gunsmith who arrived long after the first settlers, had one term. Noteworthy on two counts was Joseph Boyce; he was a small farmer and Quaker. His election during the persecution of the Quakers disturbed authorities.[19]

Commercial transformation came early to Salem because it was a port; commerce surpassed agriculture during the 1650s and 1660s. Wealth and, to a lesser extent, population began to concentrate near the harbor on the peninsula in Salem Town instead of in the North and South Fields, Salem Woods, Salem Farms (including Salem Village), and the Cape Ann side of the Bass River that became Beverly. The whole town benefited from this expansion, but did so disproportionately. Merchants and shipowners broke parity with large landowners by tripling their wealth. They became preoccupied with lucrative particular callings and neglected communal obligations. They lost touch with agricultural sections not on the peninsula or near its base. In reaction, farmers moved, with some success, to restrict decisions of these wealthy representatives in matters affecting them. While the commercial class did not intend to subvert communalism and religious orthodoxy and often sought to bridge gaps, their emergence did have social and religious consequences.

In the new atmosphere of commercial hegemony, church membership was not an absolute prerequisite for social mobility, respectability, or public office. Most merchants from Salem families, therefore, joined the church late to seal the success they had already achieved in business or even after a first election to office. By the mid-1660s, merchants from the Salem Town section dominated the board although other sections always had some representation. In the Farms district, Salem Village gained its own church and became the rallying point for orthodoxy. In the village, 28 percent of the population belonged to the church, compared with 18 percent in town. Because Salem Village land had become valuable, however, mercantile town leaders did not want to let the village break away completely—like Wenham, Manchester, Marblehead, and Beverly—because of the resultant loss to the town's tax base. This reluctance to let orthodox Salem Village free itself from commercial Salem Town was the economic background for the third crime wave in Massachusetts, the witch accusations that erupted in Salem Village in 1692.[20]

Witchcraft

Throughout European history persons "suspicioned" of witchcraft have typically been women, usually older, outspoken, and without mates or status. They did not conform to the religious and social conventions of the time and were presumed to have sold their souls to the Devil and done his bidding. Confidence in their own feelings made them lacking in deference, and spiritual individualism contributed heavily to their plight. In the Salem episode, more than five out of six among the accused witches had origins in the Northwest of Britain where Celtic Christianity had given women a large role in church life. These women had been reluctant to give up the Old Religion after the Reformation and later were open to a sectarian alternative to patriarchal orthodoxy that developed in Puritan Southeast England.[21]

Men charged with witchcraft in the Salem outbreak have not received as much attention, and focusing on them can be revealing. Although some were not accused directly but drawn into proceedings after their wives were cried out upon, their numbers still indicate the intensity of the epidemic. Fewer men than women were accused of witchcraft in Salem and this was true in England as well. In the home country, men were known for the white magic that helped people, but were seldom charged with *maleficium,* black magic that harmed others and called for drastic punishment. Wallace Notestein in his pioneer study of witchcraft in England found only five cases of accused male witches—wizards—who were executed during the 160 years after Elizabeth ascended the throne. A more recent work indicates that from 1560 to 1680 in Essex, a county of East Anglia especially prone to witch executions, only 8 percent of those killed were male. England's last mass execution of witches in 1645—during the chaos and schism of the Civil War—resulted in at least sixty-seven deaths, only two of them male. And in New England prior to 1692, only two of twenty-two persons probably executed for witchcraft were men.[22]

To find a higher percentage of male victims one must turn to the Continent—the Alps were thought conducive to witchcraft and the occult because of the altitude—where there was a wide variation in the percentage of men charged with this crime in French Switzerland. In Catholic Basel only 5 percent of the victims were male while in strongly Protestant Pays du Vaud 42 percent of the accused were men. In between was the small Republic of Geneva with 24 percent male victims; the average for the Jura district was 20 percent male.[23] The similarity of Salem to Calvinist Geneva is noteworthy. Of 141 persons formally accused in 1692 in Salem, 37 were men, and of the 20 killed, 6 were men, 26 percent and 30 percent respectively.[24]

But in Salem, why were these men in particular singled out? Their surnames offer a common denominator, for two-thirds of the accused wizards and two-thirds of men killed had surnames linking them with the Northwest (see table 3-3). Yet about two-thirds of Salem settlers who had arrived before or during the Great Migration came from south of the cultural line from Old Boston to Exeter, and at least three in ten from East Anglia, the "Cradle of Puritanism." Thus the Northwest minority, less than a third of the early Salem population, furnished a large majority of witchcraft victims. This pattern follows the trend set earlier and elsewhere in New England. Of five men executed in New England prior to 1692, all five were most likely from the Northwest. Three Quakers, probably from the Northwest, had been executed for their behavior, while John Carrington of Derbyshire was killed for alleged witchcraft in Connecticut.[25]

Table 3-3. Accused Wizards, 1692

Name	Probable Origin
Abbot, Nehemiah, Jr.	(Dorset, 20; Oxfordshire)
Abbot, Nehemiah, Sr.	(Dorset, 20; Oxfordshire)
Alden, Capt. John	Hampshire
Andrew, Daniel	(Cornwall, 43; Devonshire)
Barker, William	(Yorkshire, West Riding, 65, North and East Riding, 50)
Barker, William, Jr.	(Yorkshire, North and East Riding, 65, West Riding, 50)
Barry, William[a]	(Lancashire, 44)
Bishop, Edward	(Dorset, 42; Buckinghamshire)
Bradstreet, Dudley[a]	Lincoln
Bradstreet, John[a]	Lincoln
Burroughs, George	(western Devon, 23; western Somerset)
Buxton, John[a]	(Derby, 43)
Carrier, Andrew	Wales
Carrier, Richard	Wales
Carrier, Thomas	Wales
Cary, Nathaniel[a]	(Somerset, 24)
Corey, Giles	(Cornwall, 9)
Draper, Joseph	(Bedfordshire, 20; Lancashire)
Eames, Robert[a]	(Bedfordshire, 25)
English, Philip[b]	(Northumberland, 22; Durham)
Farrer, Thomas, Sr.	(Yorkshire, West Riding, 22)
Farrington, Edward	Buckinghamshire
Frost, Nicholas	(Derby, 30; western Somerset, 29)
Hardy, Thomas[c]	(Leicester and Rutland, 38)

Table 3-3, continued.

Name	Probable Origin
Hobbs, William	(Buckinghamshire, 45; Wiltshire, 32)
Howard, John	(Norfolk, 35; Lancashire and Nottinghamshire, 32)
Howe, James[a]	(Somerset, 24)
Hutchens, Francis	(western Somerset, 27; western Devon, 17)
Jacobs, George, Sr.	(Norwich)
Jacobs, George, Jr.	(Norwich)
Johnson, Stephen	(Cambridgeshire, 100; Northumberland, 96; Cheshire, 92)
Lee, John	(Nottinghamshire, 50; Northumberland, 48)
Proctor, Benjamin	(Lancashire, 40; Yorkshire, West Riding, 28)
Proctor, John	(Lancashire, 40; Yorkshire, West Riding, 28)
Proctor, William	(Lancashire, 40; Yorkshire, West Riding, 28)
Salter, Henry	(eastern Devon, 28)
Sawdy, John	—
Tookey, Job	—
Toothaker, Roger[d]	—
Wardwell, Samuel	(Northumberland, 33; Staffordshire, 30)
Willard, John	Kent

Sources: Paul Boyer and Stephen Nissenbaum, *Salem Possessed: The Social Origins of Witchcraft* (1974), 376-78; Guppy, *Homes;* Charles E. Banks, *Topographical Dictionary,* ed. E. E. Brownell (1937); Rossell H. Robbins, *Encyclopedia of Witchcraft and Demonology* (1959).

Note: Surname frequency per 10,000 from Guppy, *Homes,* appears in parentheses. Other probable origins are from Banks, *Topographical.* In the cases where the accused wizards came from the Southeast but had high frequency surnames, the Guppy figures have been cited. Thomas Brattle reported that a merchant, Hezekiah Usher, was also suspected but escaped. The Usher surname was peculiar to Northumberland (26/10,000). See George L. Burr, ed., *Narratives of Witchcraft* (1914), 178; Guppy, *Homes,* 318, 564.

a. Rossell H. Robbins discovered these names.
b. Philip English was actually from Jersey, in the Channel Islands, had an anglicized name, and was an Anglican. See David T. Konig, *Law and Society in Puritan Massachusetts: Essex County, 1629-1692* (1979), 70-74.
c. Rossell H. Robbins discovered this name. The locus of the Hardy surname in Leicestershire was probably in the Northwest. See Guppy, *Homes,* 496.
d. Although Toothaker's origins are unknown and the surname does not appear in Guppy, he did marry Martha Carrier, sister of Thomas. Five Carriers, a Welsh family, were charged in 1692, and four of them were executed. See Sara L. Bailey, *Historical Sketch of Andover* (1880), 202-3.

The Puritan movement touched a number of pioneers from the Northwest before they emigrated, and ministers were conspicuous— John Cotton, John Wheelwright, John Davenport, Richard Mather— for emphasizing the Spirit and affections in religious change; prayer, prophecy, and millennialism were particularly important to them. Their chief fear was antinomianism because they were close to it, geographically and temperamentally. As a minister from the Northwest, Ezekiel Rogers, who led the young settlers to new Rowley, had exemplified revivalism in Yorkshire but held his followers in check after arrival in New England for fear of potential antinomianism.[26]

Better remembered than these restrained Rowley pioneers are those who could not contain themselves under evangelical preaching and crossed the line into heresy. The ideas of John Cotton, as interpreted by Anne Hutchinson, did arouse the Lincoln element of Boston, and open antinomianism bloomed briefly until ministers, elders, and magistrates suppressed it. For this evangelical minority in seventeenth-century New England, whether antinomian or, like most, merely leaning that way, the label of Puritan seems less appropriate than Spiritual Puritan, sectarian, New Light, or proto-Methodist.

The majority of newcomers from the Northwest, however, were unawakened and nominal Anglicans with vestiges of their Catholic and Celtic heritage. They came to New England to fish and farm, not to flee the religious oppression at home. They were westerers, not exiles, and their Great Awakening would not come until the eighteenth century. Until then, their nonorthodox beliefs left them prey to charges of heresy, including latent Catholicism and Anglicanism, Quakerism, sectarianism, or, at the extreme, witchcraft. Many were poor and powerless like the places they had come from. Some, however, had acquired land and status, and situations could arise when their religious tendencies might seem a threat to social stability.

Northwest people might have appeared stubborn and opinionated to others, but this could have been a surface compensation for a suggestibility, a feeling that they were at times prompted or driven by mysterious forces—God, the Devil, demons, or their ids—beyond their consciousnesses. Perhaps a few had been brushed by subtle orthodox currents from the Southeast and as a result wanted unconsciously to break with traditional society but were unable to do so without help. Only direct inspiration from God or conspiracy with the Devil was potent enough to make this possible. They believed they were vulnerable to prophecy and possession and knew from experience that the Devil could take their shape without their consent. Later, in the Great Awakening, people from the Northwest would claim that regeneration was irresistible because most of them found they couldn't resist God.

Their lack of deference and discontent, noticeable when mingling in Puritan towns, was related to this. Voices from beyond gave them the urge, the courage, to verbalize opinions and to challenge social superiors, especially when they occupied the ground first. In making rules and settling disputes, they preferred informal consultation with neighbors or arbitration in church to the formal court system, which was perceived as impersonal and exploited by knaves. The unconverted from the Northwest also distrusted courts, choosing to settle conflicts by taking the law into their own hands. Northwest people, uprooted from their traditional beliefs and not assimilated to Ramistic Puritanism, could be spiritually restless and troublesome. The more eccentric among them could be the victims of witchcraft proceedings.

The Accused

Most of these cases followed a predictable pattern. Usually a young woman or girl would claim to be pinched, choked, bitten and visited by specters. Nearly everyone—in England as well as in the colonies—believed in witchcraft at this time and nearly everyone could recognize the symptoms of witchcraft at work. Townspeople pronounced these young women, beset by strange ailments, "bewitched" and sought to know who had afflicted them. Both the accusers and the accused tended to have Northwest origins.[27]

The executed wizards reflected the usual characteristics of the people from the Northwest. John Proctor, the hero of Arthur Miller's *Crucible,* is one example. He was a farmer of herculean frame and rash temperament. Some in close-knit Salem Village regarded him as a newcomer because he had moved there from Ipswich twenty-six years earlier. In Proctor lack of deference was strong. He saw the witchcraft episode as a criminal conspiracy and said so forcefully at the outset. When the young women brought their charges against him he warned, "If let alone, we'd all be devils and witches." Mercy Warren, a servant in his house, made severe accusations. She charged him not only with the usual pinching, biting, and choking, but also with "pressing me on my Stomack tell the blood came out of my mouth."[28] Questioning Mercy's credibility undoubtedly worked against him in the minds of the orthodox.

In the Northwest, record-keeping and legalism were weak partly as a result of the oral heritage. Therefore the government did not press prosecutions, even though belief in witches was stronger there than in the Southeast. Individuals and families were left to deal with alleged witchcraft on their own.[29] Proctor reflected his origins when he refused to believe that the courts could deal with it better than he could. In this case, Proctor prescribed whipping to test the genuineness of Mercy's accusations and spinning to ward off her afflictions. Proctor also offered to drive the Devil out of Samuel Parris's accused West Indian servant to prove that he was an ally of God, not the Devil.[30]

Proctor had been drawn into the proceedings while defending his second wife against charges of witchcraft. She kept a tavern and her maiden name was Bassett. A goodwife Bassett had been executed for witchcraft in Connecticut in 1651 and that name had also been linked with Quakerism. In 1692, two Bassetts were in jail for witchcraft.[31]

The most influential men in Salem Village, John Putnam, Sr., Thomas Putnam, Jr., and Samuel Parris, the village pastor, testified against Proctor. But he persisted in his lack of deference. From the Salem jail he sent letters to five ministers maintaining that the Devil was deluding the judges. Even a favorable petition from the Reverend John Wise and friends who had known Proctor years before in Ipswich could not save him from the wrath of Salem's orthodoxy and he was soon executed.[32]

Giles Corey is the best known of the "dreadfull wizzards" because he refused to plead and was pressed to death over several days. In Massachusetts confession led to leniency, not execution, yet Corey refused to take the easy way out. He had been fascinated by the witch proceedings from the start. He came to suspect his second wife, Martha, and testified against her. Both were charged. She told the court that it was blind to truth and hoped the Lord would "open the eyes of the magistrates and ministers." Giles Corey's specter appeared to Ann Putnam, an accuser, and told her things about his background that most people had forgotten. Sixteen years earlier Corey had been indicted for stomping to death a man who worked for him, a person described as being "close to a natural fool." He was not prosecuted and Cotton Mather said he bought his way out of it. Another specter also accused Corey of killing his first wife and other misdeeds reaching back to the 1640s.[33]

Why did Giles Corey, when charged in 1692, refuse to plead and thereby save his life? Did he believe he was doomed and was merely trying to preserve his estate from confiscation by the Massachusetts government? According to David Konig, Corey "was making a powerfully defiant gesture against the official, legal process of 'Trial by Jury' as it operated in the county. His refusal to make any type of open, public statement was the most blatant challenge to the methods and goals of the court." Of course, Corey might have been trying to save his estate, but this is not necessarily true. Although some estates were confiscated, not all were, and John Proctor made out his will despite his indictment.[34] More likely Corey refused to comply because of his character. He was an irascible old man. Chronically unorthodox, he was almost eighty when finally admitted to the church in 1691. His accusation against his wife, a church member, and the stomping death made him a less sympathetic figure to the court and to modern-day readers than John Proctor.

The alleged ringleader of the witches was George Burroughs, a Harvard graduate. There was a hint of heterodoxy in his religious behavior. He admitted that as a pastor, he seldom performed the Lord's Supper and his eldest child had not been baptized. At the last, he voiced a skepticism about witchcraft that seemed to deny the struggle going on between God and Satan in Salem Village. Cotton Mather reminded the public that despite his role as pastor, Burroughs had not actually been ordained over a flock, in either Salem or Maine.[35]

Marion Starkey in *The Devil in Massachusetts* described Burroughs as a swarthy and sinewy little man with black hair who looked more like a *courier du bois* from Canada than an English parson. "There was something of the exotic, something Celtic about Burroughs, and this perhaps was his undoing."[36] He must have been fluent and charismatic. He rendered the Lord's Prayer perfectly at the gallows ladder and his extraordinary eloquence almost persuaded the crowd to intervene and save his life. The common belief was that witches were so accustomed to reciting the prayer backwards at sabbats to mock God that they would stumble when required to recite it correctly under pressure. If the crowd expected a confession after the Lord's Prayer, it was disappointed.

Burroughs claimed some remarkable talents that seemed witchlike to the townsfolk. Witnesses testified that he could reproduce conversations held in his absence. Thomas Ruck, father of the minister's third wife, claimed Burroughs "could tell his thoughts."[37] Burroughs boasted that he could lift a rifle with one finger in the barrel and a keg of molasses with two fingers in the bung hole. Many witnesses testified to what Cotton Mather called Burroughs's "preternatural strength."

Burroughs's claim of superior strength may have resulted from his wrestling. In Cornwall and western Devon, the probable origins of Burroughs, this was a tradition among young men. Arthur Rowse believes that such West Countrymen were better at this sport than the ancient Greeks, Turks, or Bretons.[38]

When Burroughs had come to Salem Village from Maine as a probationary minister in 1680, he seemed peculiar and secretive, at least to the Putnams. He and his wife lodged with Thomas and Ann Putnam, and fearing their gossip, Burroughs bound his wife not to reveal his confidences. When his wife soon died, the Putnams attributed her death to his ill treatment of her. Young women, testifying in 1692, held him responsible for many deaths, including those of his first two wives and the wife of Deodat Lawson, former village pastor. They also blamed him for deaths of village men who had gone eastward to fight the French and American Indians in Maine while he was preaching there. His stay in Maine did not help because during King William's war, people in Essex County felt vulnerable and believed that those who had been "in close contact with the Indians and had survived" were witches.[39]

The surname Burroughs was not new to Salem or eastern Massachusetts when the minister first came in 1680. John Burroughs, a cooper in Salem, had been a peripheral supporter of Anne Hutchinson in 1637. The court admonished him for his deviant beliefs. Hutchinson's lack of deference and bold assertion of her religious views suggested possession and witchcraft to many people. Two decades later when two Quaker women came to Massachusetts to witness, authorities stripped them, looking for witches' marks.[40] At the height of this Quaker persecution in Boston and Salem, Edward Burroughs, a prominent English Friend from western Devon, persuaded Charles II to order the Puritan oligarchy to desist. It was this Burroughs that Roger Williams referred to in his pamphlet on Quakers, *George Fox Digged out of His Burroughs* (1676).[41] Thus the surname Burroughs by 1680 was already associated with Salem, antinomianism, Quakerism, opposition to the Puritan oligarchy, and witchcraft. To this the Putnams added their account of the new minister whose wife died suddenly. Guilt by association was widely accepted in the seventeenth century and religious dissent, sorcery, and witchcraft were believed to be related and run in families.

Yet in Maine, where settlers were overwhelmingly from the Northwest, Burroughs had a better reputation. His preaching was effective despite the instability of constant skirmishes with the American Indians. When the growing community needed land he owned, he yielded it without asking for its equivalent in cash or trade. This lack of acquisitiveness was in sharp contrast to Samuel Parris, the orthodox Salem Village pastor in 1692 and chief clerical supporter of the young accusers.[42] Burroughs felt less paranoid in Maine than in the factionalism of Salem Village. Like other colonists, ministers preferred to settle among their people, and for most of those with Northwest origins, this meant the eastward frontier, the hinterlands of Plymouth, eastern Connecticut, Long Island, northern New Jersey, and, later, the western frontier. During the time of spiritual declension, village leaders had tried out Burroughs—along with James Bayley and Deodat Lawson—in the hopes of finding an orthodox minister to uphold deference while reducing tensions in their new church.[43] George Burroughs's character, eccentricities, and stay on the frontier worked against him as a pastor and made him a major victim in the witch trials.

Samuel Wardwell of Andover was the last wizard executed and fits the Northwest paradigm well. He was a "cunning man" who told fortunes that usually "came to pass."[44] Believing in his own powers, he confessed to a pact with the Devil at the height of the panic, but was executed for recanting his confession. Sarah, his wife, confessed and was one of the very few who never recanted after the excitement subsided. This suggests that her confession was not simply a desperate expedient to escape execution; she may have believed herself a witch.

Wardwell was illiterate and renowned for his ability to make cattle come to him. One witness claimed that he used his powers to "pull" Martha Sprague off her horse. His reputed talents, so useful in a pastoral society, could have been a challenge to the emerging commercial class that preferred to rely on fences and courts to regulate the animals. Like fortune-telling, a talent with animals would be declining among converts to the printed word.[45] Wardwell was also associated with the Barker clan. He was said to have an unrequited love for one of the young Barker women.

Four members of the Barker family were charged with witchcraft. One of them, William, made his heresy explicit and confirmed the fears of church members by revealing a design to destroy the church of God and set up Satan's kingdom in Salem Village. Because William Barker confessed, he was not executed.[46] Barker testified that George Burroughs presided at a sabbat where takeover of the village was discussed. Although the idea of Satan's kingdom may seem premodern, the Devil's goals, as Barker described them, have not only an antinomian but modern flavor. According to Barker, Satan advocated equality of persons, no day of resurrection or judgment, and no punishment for shame or sin. Contemporary critics might have aptly characterized this program "a faire and easie way" to Hell, but these ideas seemed to anticipate the New England of Ralph Waldo Emerson.

Finally, Wardwell, like Burroughs, had a surname linked with religious dissent from the beginning. Puritan magistrates had taken away the right to bear arms from Wardwell's father in 1637 because he was in the core group of Hutchinsonians. The Wardwell surname was from Northumberland, Staffordshire, and Durham. These Salem Wardwells actually hailed from Alford in Lincoln, the town that produced Anne Hutchinson and many of her core adherents. Later several Wardwells were in trouble with the law for their Quaker leanings. Lydia Wardwell was whipped for walking naked into Newbury meetinghouse to protest formalism and intolerance. With this family history, these talents, and a pact with the Devil—although recanted—Samuel Wardwell suffered the extreme penalty. A half a century later in the Great Awakening a descendant, Nathaniel Wardwell, served as the first lay preacher of a Separate congregation in Boston; for this, he was suspended from his regular church. Thus the religious deviation of the Wardwells continued into the eighteenth century.[47]

Samuel Wardwell's links with early dissent and Quakerism were not that unusual. Most men and women accused of witchcraft had such indirect connections with dissent through blood, marriage, friendship, and geographical propinquity. Thomas Maule, the Quaker merchant, recognized the similarity of the witches' ordeal in 1692 with earlier Quaker sufferings at the hands of Puritan authorities. He was very thankful that suspicion of witchcraft did not fall on him or his family. What evidently offended the orthodox and triggered such accusations was a detectable sympathy for religious heterodoxy and pluralism and Quaker-like behavior—heresy, outspoken women, and sexual libertinism. These were characteristics of the Northwest group of which Quakers were only a fraction. The orthodox were local in their loyalties—to Parris's church and Salem Village—but sectarian sympathizers were not; they lived in Salem, but remained apart from it.[48] While execution of witches may have renewed prejudices and inhibited sectarianism in Salem early in the eighteenth century, heterodox individuals would prosper and multiply elsewhere in New England.

The female four-fifths of the accused have received much more attention, but they resembled their male counterparts in most respects: of Northwest origins, at odds with Puritan mores, lacking deference, seeking autonomy. Among those actually executed, women achieved one kind of autonomy; 89 percent had inherited property in the absence of a male heir, sometimes years before being cried out upon. Over the decades, the Puritan oligarchy had been reluctant to depart from inheritance procedures by leaving property to women when they sought to inherit. Thus witchcraft proceedings in Salem could be seen as a way of curbing religious deviation but also of bringing property back under government and male control.[49]

The Puritan authority had reached a plateau of influence in the 1660s. After that, it was weakened by people moving out from town onto farms, Crown displeasure at smuggling, and religious intolerance. On the other hand, it was strengthened by the new economic order that was supplanting communalism. In areas where Ramistic Puritans remained dominant, Northwest people, including women, continued to meet with some prejudice; their position did not markedly improve until after the Great Awakening in the 1740s.

The Judges

The magistrates in the witchcraft cases provide a significant contrast to the alleged witches and wizards. The majority who actually served on the special court had Southeast origins. They represented the Puritan oligarchy on the defensive against what seemed to them a mysterious upsurge of evil.

When Sir William Phips, the new royal governor, arrived in Massachusetts from England in May 1692, he found the witch accusations mounting rapidly. He immediately convened a court of *oyer and terminer* to investigate this strange phenomenon and turned eastward to confront land disputes with the French and American Indians, a problem more familiar to him. Phips was actually a native of Maine the Crown had chosen to appease Increase Mather, the Puritan emissary worried about the impact the charter of 1691 would have on the colony. Because this new charter specifically gave the local legislature the power to create courts and it had not yet met, historians have questioned the legality of the court Phips convened and the executions it sanctioned. The governor looked hastily to Massachusetts for qualified judges and relied on the advice of William Stoughton, the new lieutenant governor (see table 3-4). Other establishment figures from the colony were already in Salem conducting preliminary hearings. On April 11 the entire Massachusetts Council had traveled to Salem Village, and an uproarious hearing raised witchcraft from a local to a colonial concern.

These distinguished men had experience as magistrates although they lacked formal legal education. Nathaniel Saltonstall, from Yorkshire, resigned on June 10 following the first execution. After his withdrawal, it could be argued that the Northwest minority, about a third of Salem's population, was still equitably represented because it held three of the remaining eight seats on the court—Jonathan Corwin, John Richards, and Samuel Sewall. The two East Anglians were Wait-Still Winthrop, magistrate and major general in the provincial militia, and Bartholomew Gedney, a respected physician and the only member from Salem Town. William Stoughton of Surrey, John Hathorne of Berkshire, and William Sargeant of Northamptonshire rounded out the Southeast contingent and reflected the commercial, political, and religious establishment of coastal Massachusetts and Salem Town. That a majority of judges were from the Southeast and a majority of the accused from the Northwest was a natural development.

It would appear that among the judges, the Northwest minority had more doubts about the trial proceedings than the others, although there

Table 3-4. Judges of the Court of Oyer and Terminer

Southeast	Probable Origin
Gedney, Bartholomew	Norfolk
Hathorne, John	Berkshire
Sargeant, William	Northamptonshire
Stoughton, William	Surrey
Winthrop, Wait-Still	Suffolk

Northwest	Probable Origin
Corwin, Jonathan	Cumberland
Richards, John	(Cornwall, 130)
Saltonstall, Nathaniel	Yorkshire
Sewall, Samuel	Warwick

Source: Edwin Powers, *Crime and Punishment in Early Massachusetts, 1620–1692: A Documentary History* (1966), 476–77.

is no record of their deliberations. Saltonstall left the bench because he did not agree with the majority's methods from the outset; presumably he did not like their reliance on spectral evidence, which was not allowed for other crimes. He was soon suspected of witchcraft and began to drink heavily; after the executions resumed, he appeared drunk at a council meeting.[50]

Major John Richards was a wealthy merchant and parishioner of Cotton Mather. He invited his pastor to the first trial. Instead Mather sent a letter to Richards and later, on behalf of a clerical group, another one to the court on June 15. He warned them "not to lay more stress upon Pure Specter testimony than it will bear. . . . It is very certain that the devils have sometimes represented the shapes of persons not only innocent, but very virtuous."[51] We can infer that Richards respected his minister's opinion in this matter. Samuel Sewall, the diarist, sat on this panel and the one after, but did not write down his thoughts until later. For the rest of his life, however, he lamented his role in this affair and observed an annual day of repentance. He was the only judge to make a public apology for his actions.

In sum, at least two and probably three of the four Northwest judges had reservations about the trials at the time or afterward. None of the majority did or did not choose to reveal them until long afterward. Although the judges from the Northwest, like those from the Southeast, no doubt believed in witchcraft, when faced with a crisis they could apparently accept more readily the theory that the Devil could take the shape of an innocent person.

Prior to 1692, only one presiding magistrate had specifically rejected the theory that the Devil could only impersonate someone who had covenanted with him. Governor Simon Bradstreet of Massachusetts Bay is credited with saving the life of Elizabeth Morse in 1680. The governor was "not satisfied that a Specter doing mischief in her likeness, should be imputed to her person, as a ground of guilt."[52] The magistrates let her off despite a clamor from some deputies for conviction. As a young man, Simon Bradstreet had been conciliatory toward Anne Hutchinson, testifying that the meetings in her home were "lawful." As an old man, he opposed the witch proceedings in 1692.

The accused in the witch crisis were drawn heavily from the Northwest and combined piety with skepticism about legal proceedings and spectral evidence. Of the judges, Sewall, Richards, and Saltonstall shared these attitudes. The majority of the court, on the other hand, followed a repressive course. Although Puritan conformity may have declined a bit during the Restoration, it remained relatively well entrenched in eastern Massachusetts. Whereas clerical leaders were familiar with the intellectual trends of nonconformity in England and merchants were becoming attuned to its worldly fashions, these Salem magistrates were changing more slowly and were still apt to be literal-minded and legalistic in things religious. According to Gordon Allport's typology, they would be orthodox, not devotional, in their Puritanism, and therefore less *au courant* in religious matters than the clergy, less sensitive to the feelings involved, more this-worldly but less tolerant than either devotional ministers or the general public.[53] Puritan magistrates, suddenly and inopportunely challenged, would respond favorably to the biblical injunction "Thou shalt not suffer a witch to live."[54]

William Stoughton, lieutenant governor and chief justice, has been perceived as the prime villain in the Salem affair. Educated for the ministry at Harvard, he had gone to England in 1650, preaching in Sussex. Upon returning, he chose a secular career, like a number of his generation, and became an important officeholder. Stoughton was successful but some tarnish came from his stance as a "moderate," pragmatically cooperating with the hated royal governor, Sir Edmond Andros, who challenged land titles by established settlers and attempted to take away some charter liberties from Massachusetts while imposing a dominion scheme which consolidated the New England colonies and gave power over them to England.[55]

On the conscious level, political motives could have been uppermost with Stoughton in 1692. He needed to reaffirm loyalty to the New England way at the moment when the royal charter of 1691, properly implemented, could give Puritanism a new lease on life. His collaboration with the swashbuckling Andros could be forgotten more quickly if he were the leader in the reassertion of Puritan political authority and deference to Southeasterners. Trying and executing witches offered such an opportunity, and he was used to taking decisive action.

Stoughton was conspicuous for his severity at the trials. When the jury found Rebecca Nurse not guilty, the chief justice sent them back for further deliberation; they finally returned a guilty verdict. In 1693, when the court appointed by the legislature began to eschew spectral evidence and was therefore acquitting the accused, Stoughton left the bench for a while in disgust, claiming witches were getting away, that the opportunity for cleaning them out was being lost.[56] Stoughton was a literate, rational, orthodox individual. He epitomized Puritan South-east England in his support of the Calvinistic concept of consent and covenant. It was therefore consistent for Stoughton to take the position that the Devil could only assume the shape of someone who had covenanted with him. He took this view in the face of contrary advice from Cotton Mather's group and may have persuaded other magistrates to do the same.

There is an interesting precedent for Stoughton's reliance on spectral evidence. In 1669 some Connecticut magistrates had requested an opinion from clerical experts on this issue. The Reverend Gershom Bulkeley responded for the group, and in contrast to Cotton Mather in 1692, declared that "the Devil could not assume the shape of an innocent person in doing mischief to mankind." He offered no scriptural evidence but reasoned that if the Devil could so impersonate, "it would subvert the course of humane Justice, by bringing men to suffer for what he did in their shapes."[57] As pastor of Wethersfield, Bulkeley had pioneered the presbyterian polity. Like Stoughton, he had quit the ministry and later supported Andros. His father, Peter, had been a leading ministerial advocate of preparation for conversion. The Bulkeleys' views reflected those of other Puritans from the Southeast.[58]

At the preliminary examinations conducted in Salem Village, Jonathan Corwin remained silent. In his leading questions, John Hathorne assumed guilt and hoped to evoke new admissions. For example, in questioning Rebecca Nurse, a church member charged with witchcraft because her shape had appeared to her accuser, he reminded her about the case of Tituba. A West Indian servant in the Parris household, Tituba had confessed, saying that she had in fact loved young Betty Parris and wished her no harm. Yet the court found that Tituba's shape, without her knowledge, had caused mischief to Betty Parris. This suggested to the pious Nurse that good behavior would not be an adequate defense if a secret pact could be "proved" through spectral evidence. At her trial Mary Easty asked, "Would you have me accuse myself?" "Yes, if you be guilty," Hathorne answered.[59]

John Hathorne was the surviving son of Salem's most prominent leader, William Hathorne, who had been speaker when the legislative body passed the first Quaker penalties. As a magistrate in Salem he had described Quakers as distempered and blasphemous, ordering the constable to search out their meetings in the township. He heard the case of Deborah Buffum Wilson, a shy housewife who had walked naked in public, like Lydia Wardwell, to protest established religion. Hathorne sentenced her to be whipped and dragged at the tail of a cart. He attempted to sell the two Southwick children into servitude in the West Indies when their Quaker parents couldn't pay fines and were banished, but there were no takers. Hathorne, Batter, and Endecott were all drastic in their suppression but became more temperate with age. Yet John Hathorne seemed to be following in his father's footsteps in resisting dissent as late as 1692, although the battle for "good order" had been lost and the community had become fragmented in many respects.[60]

It might seem that Hathorne and Stoughton were extreme in their examination of these accused witches but it could be argued that they were playing by the book. In England, witchcraft, like murder by poison, was tried according to different rules. Because witnesses to actual acts of witchcraft were virtually impossible to obtain, spectral evidence and extraordinary witnesses were allowed. In these secret crimes, reputation and ancestry of the accused had to be considered, including the extent of their religious conformity.[61]

There may have been skeptical, urbane gentlemen in Boston who would have maneuvered and stalled to save some eccentric men and women from the gallows but they were not appointed to this court. The panel of judges was representative of the Puritan establishment and the views of the majority. People still respected the clergy, but with arrests increasing and the jails filling up, they looked to magistrates for action. Most believed that Satan particularly resented the godliness of New Englanders and his efforts to recruit defectors to undermine society had brought on a crisis.[62]

Under these circumstances, the decisions of Stoughton, Hathorne, and the majority make sense. To admit that the Devil could take any person's shape without consent would be to admit their impotence against witches and weaken their political authority at a time when they were trying to reassert it. To let witches off on the ground that there was too little evidence other than the spectral would also make them appear ineffectual in a crisis. They chose a middle position, for which there was precedent: the Devil could impersonate only those who signed a pact and sold their souls to him. This interpretation led to the heavy reliance on spectral evidence and consequent prosecutions and convictions. Further, the behavior of the court majority in 1692 was consistent with that of earlier magistrates who had punished Roger Williams, Anne Hutchinson, and the Quakers for their heterodoxy. As it turned out, of course, the court decisions were counterproductive; if magistrates expected collective expiation to follow the executions, they were mistaken. Piety was not revived, and the public came to doubt the judges' wisdom in the witch cases, although the voters reelected them at the next election.

New England lagged behind the mother country in the treatment of witches. Although English courts still allowed spectral evidence in the 1690s, the last mass executions for witchcraft in England occurred in 1645, and the final single execution was in Exeter in 1685.[63] The Salem episode seven years later demonstrated that although more tolerant views might have existed among some people in Salem Town as well as Boston, they had not reached these magistrates.

This third crime wave had begun when young women, most with Northwest surnames and servile jobs, had "fits" and saw things. This brought them more attention than they had ever had before. It also got them out of work and reduced the authority their masters held over them for a short time at least.[64] What actually turned their accusations of witchcraft into a crime wave was the attention and credence the pillars of the church and Salem Village gave the accusers' charges.[65] These men, Southeasterners and advocates of religious conformity, had lost ground in commercial competition with less orthodox inhabitants of adjacent Salem Town and showed their frustration at this situation during these legal proceedings, which served to escalate the drama, multiply accusations, precipitate executions, and ultimately give Salem a notorious reputation.

It has been suggested that the orthodox villagers started all this by displacing their envy and behaving in a premodern way, bringing witchcraft charges against harmless marginal inhabitants. The worldly merchants of Salem Town were direct threats to the communalism and autonomy of Salem Village yet because of deference, villagers avoided confrontation with their economic and social betters, displacing their resentment onto more vulnerable folk. There is truth in this, but the accused were not harmless from the perspective of the villagers. They represented the growing sectarianism and posed a serious threat to Puritan order. They portended religious divisiveness and pluralism and were closer at hand than merchants on the peninsula. Orthodox Southeasterners feared "enthusiasm" and believed that these people were reviving the religious chaos of the Interregnum.

Magic and witchcraft coexisted with Christianity throughout the

Western world, but waning Calvinism was prone to persecution and prosecution. Witch fears were prominent not when Calvinism was ascendant or in equilibrium, but later when Ramism had set in. Thus prosecutions were heavy at certain times and places, such as in the Genevan Republic, parts of East Anglia, and Salem Village.[66] In 1692 Salem Village in particular was the locus of witch executions because two elements reinforced each other: commerce and cooling Puritanism.

The magistrates presiding over the witch trials found themselves in a vulnerable position. In 1684 the original charter that gave the Massachusetts Bay Company almost complete autonomy and power had been annulled, and the years following brought considerable political, social, and religious confusion to the area. Puritans found themselves attacked at home by proponents of other religious views, supporters of Andros and his schemes of dominion, and from those disenchanted with Puritan rule. And they were threatened from the outside as well. As long as the French controlled Canada, they feared invasion and the alliance of the French and American Indians. During King William's War this fear of invasion increased, especially among the inhabitants of the Essex County frontier. At least four young accusers were refugees from the frontier warfare and may have displaced their fear of American Indians onto alleged witches. Cotton Mather had already made a connection, for he viewed Quaker and American Indian "assaults" as similar and coming from the same places. Both preyed "upon the Frontiers and Out-Skirts, of the Province." The Quakers labored "to Enchant and Poison the souls of poor people, in the very places, where the Bodies and Estates of the people were then devoured by the Salvages."[67]

Essex County's vulnerability to attack in the war called attention to sectarian tendencies of the Northwest group and reduced tolerance for non-Puritan behavior. Some of the more peculiar were executed for witchcraft, but this created sympathy and did not stay for long their tongues or numbers in New England. On the other hand, the executions opened doors in Boston and Salem for a few worldly merchants and clerical intellectuals skeptical of the witch accusations and ready to ridicule the hasty actions of the judges. Small but influential, this group would also grow. In Salem defenders of Puritanism occupied the village, middle ground between woods and town. In Massachusetts the orthodox were also in the middle, neither sectarian nor enlightened, an intermediate position that would lose much ground in the next century.

The Great Migration of Puritans from Southeast England was an aberration. These family groups were pushed, but prior to 1630, immigrants from the Northwest had predominated, largely pulled by prospects in New England. When immigration resumed after the Interregnum, it was only a trickle, but more came from the Northwest. This was concurrent with a population shift in New England away from nucleated villages toward farms in the countryside. The pastoral style of the Northwest was more suited to the frontier than the Southeast pattern of close-knit settlements. Puritan clergy and magistrates, by this time largely orthodox and legalistic, lamented the erosion of control and discipline this shift of settlers augured, but devotional clerics also recognized a significant challenge to their ideal of a religious community. Newcomers from the Northwest were a minority that had to "peep and mutter" in the repressive atmosphere of Puritan New England that followed the Hutchinson crisis, but were augmented by the evangelical Scots-Irish in the next century. By 1800 these folk had moved far enough along the road from periphery to center to give the new United States a distinctively revivalistic and sectarian character that European visitors found surprising.

As the histories of Rowley and Hingham have indicated, in terms of religion there were almost two New Englands. Emigrants of Southeast origin settled one of them during the Great Migration decade. By the 1690s this settlement had produced a few religious liberals but most were orthodox, and Ramistic Puritans with presbyterian tendencies predominated and occupied the magistrates' benches. Precursors of the Old Lights, they used the legal system to maintain order against religious dissenters and witches, and in New England it was where these people ruled that actual executions for witchcraft occurred.

The other New England included the frontier that was sparsely settled and unorganized but growing by the end of the century. Its settlers, predominantly from the Northwest, were restless and potentially evangelical, retaining more orality than the others. They believed in witches but not in the government's ability to apprehend and punish the right ones. They were more willing to distinguish between helpful white magic and maleficent black witchcraft and to try countermagic in an attempt to avoid the courts. As a result, there were few prosecutions and no executions for witchcraft in their territory.[68]

The Salem witch episode has been viewed as a turning point in the waning of the later Middle Ages and the demise of the Puritan oligarchy, signaling the emergence of "modern" America. But 1692 was only a minor episode in this gradual change, and it was the less prosperous Southeasterners who suffered most in the transition from a communal to a more commercial society. Northwest dissenters were not silenced by the witch trials and retained their individualism and sectarianism, adjusting to the more pluralistic religious order that followed, but they were still seekers, open to "further light" and antimaterialist appeals for "soul liberty." Therefore 1692 should be seen as merely an early skirmish in the intermittent and continual tension between the evangelical-pietistic and the legalistic-rationalistic subcultures on American soil that was preceded by the Antinomian Controversy and persecution of the Quakers and followed by the Great Awakening.

After 1692, popular religion grew and witchcraft was decriminalized; interest in remarkable providences and the invisible world continued. Charles Levermore, the distinguished historian of New England, noted in 1885 that witchcraft had changed in name and form but not much in substance. "Now," he wrote, "seers find their best customers, not among servant girls, but their mistresses; Spiritualism has become aggressive." Mary Baker Eddy called herself a Christian Scientist but was called "the Witch of Concord" because she tried to heal persons from a distance.[69] Although witches are not prosecuted any more, differences between priest and prophet, rationalist and empiricist, did not disappear in the eighteenth century, were evident on both sides of the Atlantic in the nineteenth century, and can still be detected in American religion and politics in the twentieth century.

Notes

1. "From the start English migrants to the New World regarded native peoples as 'Devil-worshippers.'" John P. Demos, *Entertaining Satan: Witchcraft and the Culture of Early New England* (1982), 71.

2. Richard M. Gildrie, *Salem, Massachusetts: A Covenant Community* (1975), 1–101.

3. The Southeast majority in Salem was 67.5 percent of the population; the minority of 13.7 percent was from the Northwest; another 18 percent had Northwest surnames. These estimates are calculated from Charles E. Banks, *Topographical Dictionary*, ed. E. E. Brownell (1937), and Frank Holmes, *Directory of the Ancestral Heads of New England Families, 1620–1700* (1964 ed.).

4. Kai T. Erikson, *The Wayward Puritans: A Study in the Sociology of Deviance* (1966), ix, 67–159. The persistence is calculated from Banks, *Topographical*, and Holmes, *Ancestral Heads*. The conflict between the two religious sub-

cultures brought from England was evident long before the first crime wave. Philip Ratcliffe suffered severely for religious dissent in 1631. He lost his ears and was whipped, fined, and banished for criticizing the new Puritan establishment. He charged that the Salem church had departed from the ways of the Church of England and that Massachusetts Bay was on a course of rebellion. According to William Hubbard, writing in the seventeenth century, Ratcliffe "was accustomed to a loose and dissolute kind of life" and therefore opposed Puritan authority. See Hubbard, *The General History of New England* (1972 ed.), 137. James Truslow Adams labeled him "mentally unbalanced." See *The Founding of New England* (1921), 151. His relevance here is his Northwest surname, prevalent in Yorkshire; his actual origins are unknown. The year before Thomas Morton of Merry Mount had been banished for similar reasons. He was from Axbridge in western Somerset and best known for constructing his maypole and frolicking with young American Indian women. Ratcliffe and Morton represent the feudalism of the Northwest threatened by the Puritan lifestyle. Henry Guppy, *Homes of Family Names in Great Britain* (1890), 540; Banks, *Topographical*, 138. Roger Williams, of Welsh origin, came to New England from London in 1631. Later he became the pastor of Salem, but was charged with unorthodox beliefs. The magistrates banished him from the Massachusetts Bay Colony in 1636 and, with some of his followers, he moved southward to Rhode Island. Williams was a strict congregationalist, skeptical of established churches. He interpreted the Bible figuratively and has been labeled a Seeker because his religious views evolved. He questioned Puritan claims to the lands of American Indians and showed interest in their language and culture.

5. William Stoever, *Faire and Easie Way to Heaven* (1978), 161–83; Emery Battis, *Saints and Sectaries: Anne Hutchinson and the Antinomian Controversy in Massachusetts Bay Colony* (1962), 42–44.

6. Patricia Caldwell, "The Antinomian Language Controversy," *Harvard Theological Review* 69 (1976): 345–67. See also Jesper Rosenmeier, "New England's Perfection: The Image of Adam and the Image of Christ in the Antinomian Crisis, 1634 to 1638," *William and Mary Quarterly* 27 (1970): 435–59.

7. Babette Levy, *Preaching in the First Half Century of New England History* (1945), 141–42.

8. William Stoever has concluded that, in John Cotton's case, the issue was not preparation per se, but more fundamentally "the nature of evidence by which a person might be assured of his union with Christ." For Cotton, only "immediate light" from Christ was sufficient. Cotton's view that a "created thing could not reveal anything conclusive about this bond until the Spirit illumined it" set him apart from most New England clergy at this time. See *Faire and Easie Way*, 56–57. See also George Selement, ed., "John Cotton's Hidden

Antinomianism: His Sermon on Rev. 4:1–2," *New England Historical and Genealogical Register* 129 (1975): 278–94.

9. Battis, *Saints and Sectaries,* 108–9, 114.

10. Ibid., 329–44. Robert Keane of Berkshire, the wealthy merchant later fined for selling above the "just price," was not a Hutchinsonian. Northwest influence in Boston at the top—the "gentry"—was obviously considerable when this crisis occurred and declined when Anne Hutchinson was banished and her followers departed or were disarmed and disenfranchised.

11. Gildrie, *Salem,* 77–83, quotations from 81 and 82.

12. Battis, *Saints and Sectaries,* 106, 304–28; Philip F. Gura, *A Glimpse of Sion's Glory: Puritan Radicalism in New England, 1620–1660* (1984), 146. Thomas Savage believed that the Bridget Oliver charged with witchcraft in Salem in 1680 and a Bridget Bishop executed for a similar charge in 1692 was Mary Oliver's daughter. See Savage, *Genealogical Dictionary of the First Settlers of New England* (1861), 3:311.

13. Arthur J. Worrall, *Quakers in the Colonial Northeast* (1980), 8, 10.

14. In England, Fox and the Quakers faced such charges during the Interregnum. See Keith Thomas, *Religion and the Decline of Magic* (1971), 487.

15. Gildrie, *Salem,* 135–39; Jonathan M. Chu, *Neighbors, Friends, or Madmen: The Puritan Adjustment to Quakerism in Seventeenth Century Massachusetts Bay* (1985), 93–94.

16. Margaret Hope Bacon, *Mothers of Feminism: The Story of Quaker Women in America* (1986), 1–41; Chu, *Neighbors,* 20–21.

17. Of six Quakers who were banished from Salem for their religion in 1659, all were probably from the Northwest. Joshua Buffum likely came from Yorkshire, Nicholas Phelps from Gloucestershire, Samuel Shattuck from western Somerset, and the Southwick family, Cassandra, Josiah, and Lawrence, from Staffordshire. Forty-seven Quakers who were fined before 1667 also came from Northwest England or had surnames common there. See Chu, *Neighbors,* appendix 2, 172–73. The probable origins are from Banks, *Topographical.*

18. Christine Heyrman, *Commerce and Culture: The Maritime Communities of Colonial Massachusetts, 1690–1750* (1984), 114–15, 133.

19. Gildrie, *Salem,* 88–104; Holmes, *Ancestral Heads;* Christine A. Young, *From 'Good Order' to Glorious Revolution: Salem, Massachusetts, 1628–1689* (1978), 50.

20. Paul Boyer and Stephen Nissenbaum, *Salem Possessed: The Social Origins of Witchcraft* (1974), 153–74.

21. Jean Markale, *Women of the Celts* (trans., 1965), 30–40.

22. Wallace Notestein, *A History of Witchcraft in England from 1558 to 1718* (1912), 384–419. Notestein suggested a ratio of six females to one male (114). Essex County was in East Anglia, a region of strong Puritanism. Cambridge

University faculty claimed Satan was involved in witchcraft. See Enid Porter, *The Folklore of East Anglia* (1974), 137–46.

23. E. William Monter, *Witchcraft in France and Switzerland: The Borderlands during the Reformation* (1976), 119.

24. Paul Boyer and Stephen Nissenbaum, eds., *Salem Village Witchcraft: A Documentary Record of the Local Conflict in New England* (1972), 376–78.

25. For information on John Carrington, see Robert Calef, "More Wonders of the Invisible World," in *Narratives of Witchcraft*, ed. George L. Burr (1914), 389–93. Nathaniel Greensmith was executed in 1662 in Connecticut. A "Mr." Stephen Greensmith was fined as a supporter of Anne Hutchinson in 1637. See Battis, *Saints and Sectaries*, 313; Frederick C. Drake, "Witchcraft in the American Colonies, 1647–1662," *American Quarterly* 20 (1968): 700, 707. A Boston jury found Hugh Parsons guilty of witchcraft in 1651. It relied on testimony taken in Springfield, where Parsons lived, and deferred to the General Court to make the ultimate decision. The principal charge was using witchcraft to kill an infant son. When his wife, Mary, confessed to murdering the child, the General Court reversed the jury verdict and Parsons was not executed. Mary was Welsh, had previously been married to a Catholic, and had long been suspected of witchcraft. Hugh Parsons had earlier lost a libel case because of his wife's "unbridled tongue." See Samuel G. Drake, *Annals of Witchcraft in New England* (1869; rpt., 1967), 66–72, 119; and for Mary's actual testimony heard by a credulous magistrate, William Pynchon, see 239–43.

26. Erikson, *Wayward Puritans*, 120–21, 123. Roger Williams of London belongs in this group. His father had come to the English capital from Wales. The Welsh began flocking to London when the Welsh House of Tudor ascended the English throne. New England contributed two famous millennialists to the Fifth Monarchy movement of the 1650s. Thomas Venner of western Devon emigrated to Boston but later returned to London. William Aspinwall of Lancashire, the political leader of the Hutchinsonians, went into exile in Rhode Island and later sailed back to England. He wrote four books between 1653 and 1655, warning people of the imminent return of Jesus as king. See Stoever, *Fair and Easie Way*, 34–57. On the other hand, the five persons that Norman Pettit chose to analyze as leading "preparationists" of the seventeenth century—Thomas Hooker, Thomas Shepherd, Peter Bulkeley, John Norton, Giles Firmin—were born and raised in the English Southeast. See Pettit, *The Heart Prepared: Grace and Conversion in Puritan Spiritual Life* (1966), 88, 102, 115, 177, 184.

27. Chadwick Hansen, *Witchcraft at Salem* (1969), 30–34.

28. Paul Boyer and Stephen Nissenbaum, eds., *The Salem Witchcraft Papers: Verbatim Transcripts* (1977), 2:683, 687.

29. David T. Konig, *Law and Society in Puritan Massachusetts: Essex Coun-*

ty, 1629–1692 (1979), 136–57. Of the 235 cases of definite execution Notestein cited for the years 1560–1682, 19, or 8 percent, occurred in the Northwest. Ten came from the Pendle Forest near Manchester where a subsidized clergy was encouraging a Puritan enclave noted earlier. Lancashire was a flashpoint for Catholic-Protestant conflict, but C. L'Estrange Ewen has noted that the government took no interest in Wales or the Palatinate of Chester, for example. Executions for witchcraft in both places were rare. Thus 92 percent of English executions occurred in the Southeast, with East Anglia most prominent. See Notestein, *Witchcraft*, 384–419; Alan Macfarlane, *Witchcraft in Tudor and Stuart England: A Regional and Comparative Study* (1970), 74–75; Ewen, *Witchcraft and Demonism* (1933), 413.

30. Boyer and Nissenbaum, *Salem Witchcraft Papers*, 2:683–84.

31. John M. Taylor, *The Witchcraft Delusion in Colonial Connecticut, 1647–1697* (1908), 148–49. Seven weeks after John Proctor was indicted, Sarah Bassett of Lynn, Elizabeth's mother, and Mary Bassett DeRich of Salem Village were also charged. The Bassetts were Quakers, a reason for being accused according to Ernest Flagg, in *Genealogical Notes on the Founding of New England* (1926), 212. See also chart 6, "The Anti-Parris Network," Boyer and Nissenbaum, *Salem Possessed,* 184. Bassett was a Northwest surname, most frequent in Cornwall (24/10,000). See Guppy, *Homes,* 454.

32. Hansen, *Witchcraft at Salem,* 132–33.

33. Ibid., 153–55; quotation from Boyer and Nissenbaum, *Salem Witchcraft Papers,* 1:248; Cotton Mather, "The Wonders of the Invisible World" in Burr, *Narratives,* 250. Corey was a surname peculiar to Cornwall and associated with the town of Bodmin. See Guppy, *Homes,* 106, 472.

34. Konig, *Law and Society,* 174. David C. Brown agrees that Corey intended to show contempt for the legal proceedings. He indicates that Corey actually pled "Not Guilty," but then stood "mute," refusing to give the required consent to trial by jury. He also argues that under the witch law rejuvenated by the new charter in June 1692, only personal and not real property had to be forfeited. See Brown, "The Case of Giles Corey," *Essex Institute Historical Collections* 121 (1985): 282–99.

35. Charles W. Upham, *Salem Witchcraft, with an Account of Salem Village and a History of Opinions on Witchcraft and Kindred Subjects* (1867), 2:157–63; Clifford Shipton, *Sibley's Harvard Graduates: Biographical Sketches of Those Who Attended Harvard College,* 17 vols. (1933–75), 2:323–24.

36. Marion L. Starkey, *The Devil in Massachusetts* (1949), 120–21. People tended to believe that the Devil, like his antagonist, God, looked different from themselves. Among dark-skinned peoples, both were frequently described as pale or white. On the other hand, the English usually described the Devil as black, although once they had emigrated some discerned the Devil in features of the French and the American Indians. The English were very color-con-

scious in the seventeenth century, regarding only the Dutch to be as fair as themselves. Thus this description could be stretched to fit many a foreigner. Considering English history, it is also probable that someone from Ireland, Wales, or the Celtic fringe might seem diabolical, not because of complexion, but because of some cultural traits.

37. Hansen, *Witchcraft at Salem*, 75; Upham, *Salem Witchcraft*, 1:255–57.

38. A. L. Rowse, *Tudor Cornwall: Portrait of a Society* (1969), 439. John Wise, pastor of Chebacco and defender of congregationalism, was another New England parson with a Northwest surname and reputation for wrestling and extraordinary strength. See Joseph B. Felt, *The History of Ipswich, Essex, and Hamilton* (1834), 259.

39. James E. Kences, "Some Unexplored Relationships of Essex County Witchcraft to the Indian Wars of 1675 and 1689," *Essex Institute Historical Collections* 120 (1984): 207. In 1680, trustees of the Salem Village church—three Putnams—promised Burroughs a salary of ninety-three pounds, but then pressed him into accepting sixty pounds with the assurance of permanent settlement. In 1683, he left for Maine because he had not received any pay or that assurance. They saw this as a breach of contract, but to Burroughs "they were violating the spirit of their arrangement no matter what its explicit, legal terms were." The Putnams were a "notoriously litigious family." See Konig, *Law and Society*, 105.

40. Battis, *Saints and Sectaries*, 247–48; Rufus M. Jones, *Quakers in the American Colonies* (1929), 28. The name Burrough, the way the minister signed his name, has been found chiefly in Devon and Somerset and with the final *s*, in Gloucester and Nottingham. See Guppy, *Homes*, 464. Holmes places the family seat near Barnstaple in western Devon. See *Ancestral Heads*, xxxviii. Young Burroughs apparently arrived from London with his mother and was raised in Roxbury. Boyer and Nissenbaum believe he came from "a wealthy Suffolk family." See *Salem Possessed*, 54. If so, he was a member of the important contingent of emigrants from East Anglia with Northwest surnames, a group decidedly New Light in the Great Awakening.

41. Perry Miller, *Roger Williams: His Contribution to American Tradition* (1953), 244–46.

42. Shipton, *Harvard Graduates*, 2:326–27. Boyer and Nissenbaum have analyzed Parris's sermons delivered at this critical time. See *Salem Possessed*, 153–78. The surviving sermons—fifty-two in a series—show that Parris drew frequently on William Ames, the covenant theologian. He emphasized preparation and self-examination "as thorough as a business audit." Grace came after extended pursuit, not suddenly like Paul on the road to Damascus. He said little about heaven or hell and, like many pastors, contradicted himself in preaching about the elect. Parris may have been competent but his eight years in the village were punctuated by the witch trials and increased divisions in

the community. See Larry D. Gragg, "Samuel Parris: Portrait of a Clergyman," *Essex Institute Historical Collections* 119 (1983): 209–37. The pastor was born in London in 1653; the Parris or Parrish surname was peculiar to Essex, East Anglia (27/10,000). See Guppy, *Homes*, 531.

43. Critics of the Puritans once dubbed this period of declension the glacial age because it was culturally stagnant, but this was inaccurate. What was lacking during most of that period was not culture, but the full partnership in New England life of the pastoral, prophetic folk. The Bayley form of Bailey was most frequent in Staffordshire and Cheshire. Lawson's surname had good frequency only in the Northwest (Durham, 40/10,000, and Yorkshire, 20/10,000). See Guppy, *Homes*, 514, 451.

44. Boyer and Nissenbaum, *Salem Witchcraft Papers*, 2:786, 787.

45. Jones, *Quakers in the American Colonies*, 372. Konig emphasizes "polarity" between legalists and the residually oral folk using extralegal means. "Litigation and extralegal force were, to a striking degree, mutually exclusive categories of behavior." See *Law and Society*, 154.

46. Bailey, *Andover*, 212; William Barker, Sr., in Boyer and Nissenbaum, *Salem Witchcraft Papers*, 1:65–67.

47. Guppy, *Homes*, 566; Battis, *Saints and Sectaries*, 307; Christopher M. Jedrey, *The World of John Cleaveland: Family Life in Eighteenth-Century New England* (1979), 42.

48. Worrall, *Quakers*, 28–29; Christine Heyrman, "Specters of Subversion, Societies of Friends: Dissent and the Devil in Provincial Essex County, Massachusetts," in *Saints and Revolutionaries: Essays in Early American History*, ed. D. D. Hall, J. M. Murrin, and T. W. Tate (1984), 38–74; Mathew B. Jones, "Thomas Maule, the Salem Quaker," *Essex Institute Historical Collections* 72 (1936): 1–42. The Maules were Scottish.

49. Carol F. Karlsen, *The Devil in the Shape of a Woman: Witchcraft in Colonial New England* (1987), 77–116.

50. Hansen, *Witchcraft at Salem*, 126; Konig, *Law and Society*, 177. *Oyer and terminer* means to hear and determine.

51. Cotton Mather, "Letter to John Richards," and "Return of Several Ministers Consulted," in *What Happened in Salem?* ed. David Levin (1960), 107, 110–11. In August, Mather wrote, "I do still think that when there is no further evidence against a person but only this, that a specter in their shape does afflict a neighbor, that evidence is not enough to convict. . . . The devils have a natural power which makes them capable of exhibiting the shape they please . . . and I have no absolute promise from God that they will not exhibit mine. . . . Nevertheless . . . use is to be made of the spectral impressions upon the sufferers." Cotton Mather believed most Protestant authorities shared his view of spectral evidence. See Kenneth Silverman, ed., *Selected Letters of Cotton Mather* (1971), 41–42. Both sides of this influential minister's family,

Cottons and Mathers, derived from the Northwest, Lancashire and Warwickshire respectively.

In the autumn, Increase, Cotton's father, perfected his thoughts on spectral evidence and this carried weight with Governor Phips, who suspended court proceedings. He was a member of Cotton Mather's Boston congregation and the son of James Phips, who had come from Gloucestershire to Maine in 1651. Increase Mather inferred from the case of the Witch of Endor (Sam. 28:3–20) that the Devil in Samuel's shape, and not Samuel himself, appeared before Saul. Because this shape lied, it could not have been the real Samuel; therefore, the Devil could assume the shape of an innocent person. See Increase Mather, "Cases of Conscience Concerning Evil Spirits Personating Men . . ." in Levin, *Salem,* 117–18. A few months earlier, at her trial for witchcraft, Susannah Martin had courageously used the same biblical defense: "He that appeared in sams shape a glorified saint can appear in any ones shape." Many testified against her, and she was executed. She came from Amesbury to the north, a town later decidedly Old Light in the Great Awakening, yet her surname had its highest frequency in Cornwall (97/10,000). See Boyer and Nissenbaum, *Witchcraft Papers,* 2:551; Guppy, *Homes,* 44, 520.

52. Upham, *Salem Witchcraft,* 1:449–451; quotation from John Hale, "A Modest Inquiry," in Burr, *Narratives,* 412; David D. Hall, ed., *The Arminian Controversy: A Documentary History, 1636–1638* (1968), 317. The Bradstreet family was from Horbling in Lincoln, Anne Hutchinson's county, and showed a strain of religious heterodoxy. See Banks, *Topographical,* 93. In 1652, magistrates acquitted John Bradstreet of Rowley of witchcraft, but convicted him of lying after he told them tales from a "book of magic." See Drake, *Annals,* 74–75. The Reverend Simon Bradstreet of New London made some astrological prognostications. See Richard Godbeer, *Devil's Dominion: Magic and Religion in Early New England* (1992), 134. The Bradstreets were unusually tolerant of those accused of witchcraft.

53. Gordon W. Allport, "The Religious Context of Prejudice," *Journal for the Scientific Study of Religion* 5 (1966): 447–57. In the days of Queen Elizabeth, before Arminianism, jurists had also been credulous in matters of witchcraft. See John L. Teall, "Witchcraft and Calvinism in Elizabethan England," *Journal of the History of Ideas* 23 (1962): 26. Pastor Parris was active in the legal proceedings. He acted as clerk, recorded testimonies, and testified against many of the accused. He took the position that the Devil needed consent to a covenant before using a person's specter. See Larry D. Gragg, *Quest for Security: The Life of Samuel Parris, 1653–1720* (1990), 123–24. No doubt the clergy were generally alarmed and disheartened by the witchcraft proceedings in 1692, but those with Northwest origins—precursors of the Saving Remnant—were notable for speaking out. This list would include Increase Mather, John Wise, Francis Higginson, George Burroughs, and Michael Wigglesworth.

Cotton Mather belongs here too, but in the minds of scholars, his promotion of remarkable providences and arguments for the existence of witches have more than offset his admonitions about spectral evidence, and he was an irrepressible publisher of material about the "invisible world."

54. Exod. 22:18. All New England colonies had the death penalty for conviction of witchcraft. For the statutes, see David D. Hall, *Witch-Hunting in Seventeenth Century New England: A Documentary History* (1990), 315–16.

55. Samuel Eliot Morison, "William Stoughton," *Dictionary of American Biography* (1935), 9:113–15.

56. Starkey, *Devil in Massachusetts*, 229. William Stoughton's father, Israel Stoughton of Dorchester, an assistant in the Bay government, was given the privilege of making one of the two final statements against Anne Hutchinson in 1637. See Hall, *Antinomian Controversy*, 347. William Stoughton was a bachelor. He is still described as "the most virulent and unrepentant of the Salem judges." See N. E. H. Hull, *Female Felons: Women and Serious Crime in Colonial Massachusetts* (1987), 84.

57. Taylor, *The Witchcraft Delusion*, 57–58.

58. Robert G. Pope, *The Half-Way Covenant: Church Membership in Puritan New England* (1969), 105–6. Stoughton worked with Peter Bulkeley in England (1676–79); they were agents of the Massachusetts Bay Company in charter and land negotiations. See John W. Dean, "William Stoughton," *New England Historical and Genealogical Register* (1896): 50, 9–12; Shipton, *Harvard Graduates*, 1:389–402; Pettit, *Heart Prepared*, 118–21.

59. Boyer and Nissenbaum, *Salem Witchcraft Papers*, 2:288.

60. Gildrie, *Salem*, 135; Chu, *Neighbors*, 41–42, 63–64.

61. Heyrman, *Commerce and Culture*, 112–15.

62. Hansen, *Witchcraft*, 205.

63. Boyer and Nissenbaum, *Salem Possessed*, 25–30, 215–16.

64. John Demos has stressed the orality of the accusers and witches in "Underlying Themes in the Witchcraft of Seventeenth Century New England," *American Historical Review* 75 (1970): 1323.

65. Ingersoll operated an inn at the village center. He was the church's first deacon and firmly pro-Parris. His English origin was Bedford in the Southeast. The Putnam family made ninety-four accusations or complaints, Ingersoll, ten, and Parris, six. See Boyer and Nissenbaum, *Salem Possessed*, 4, 96–97n25, 379–80; Banks, *Topographical*, 2.

66. Calvinism contributed substantially to the witchcraft executions in the lowlands of Scotland in the seventeenth century. Scottish theology was strongly Calvinistic and rooted in the Old Testament; the Scots considered themselves God's people bound by sacred covenant. Judges were therefore inclined to view the witch's pact with the Devil as a "particularly horrific inversion" of the covenant. Calvinism also reinforced the idea that misfortune was not always for-

tuitous but could be just punishment for particular sins. See Christine Larner, *Enemies of God: The Witch-Hunt in Scotland* (1981), 170–72.

67. This interpretation makes their accusations and behavior "comprehensible and appropriate." See Kences, "Some Unexplored Relationships," 186–212; quotations from Cotton Mather, *Decennium Luctuosum*, in *Narratives of the Indian Wars, 1675–1699*, ed. Charles H. Lincoln (1913), 277, 278. Looking at the number of accused witches with conventional ethnic differences from the general population reveals only a few names. Most conspicuous was "Goody" Glover, the Irish Catholic who spoke Gaelic, confessed, and was executed in 1688. During the Salem witch trials, Martha Allen Carrier, Scottish and married to a Welshman, was executed. Philip English was born Philip L'Anglois on Jersey. Much more significant and numerous, I have argued, were the Northwest folk who constituted a high percentage of the deviants, both accusers and accused. See Boyer and Nissenbaum, *Salem Possessed*, 131. Compare Godbeer, *Devil's Dominion*, 201–2.

68. During several decades of "indifferentism" Puritan clergy had dutifully increased their warnings against magic and countermagic as un-Christian, but the people were more concerned with results and convenience than sources and continued to use traditional remedies. See Godbeer, *Devil's Dominion*, 82–84.

69. Charles H. Levermore, "Witchcraft in Connecticut," *New Englander Magazine* 4 (1885): 788–817; Stephen Gottschalk, *The Emergence of Christian Science in American Life* (1973), 206. Eddy retreated to her native Concord, New Hampshire, a town near where Satan was said to have his seat in colonial times.

Chapter Four

Reason and Dissent in Britain: Preparing the Way for Evangelism

Salem Village may have been a flash point for the conflict between Northwest and Southeast, but the tension was also apparent in England during the seventeenth century. After 1660 sectarians were active in the Northwest but in the Southeast fearful recollections of the religious excitement and chaos of the Civil War increased rationalism.

At the Restoration, the Church of England encountered no great difficulty in resuming in Southeast England. This populous section had been, and would continue to be, its stronghold. There were many well-endowed small parishes and the system worked well, serving communities without too many pluralists or absentees. Most links between parish and manor house had not been broken. Population was static, rising only moderately after 1740, compared with the burgeoning North. Anglicanism was strongest in Dorset, Wiltshire, Northampton, Rutland, and Suffolk. Evidently an episcopal polity and creeping Arminianism were satisfactory to a large majority, and the church gained through some defections of faint-hearted Dissenters. There was little evidence of evangelism and many would say, given the compactness and stability of rural parishes, little need of any.

When Charles II returned in 1660 from exile in France and the Stuart monarchy was restored, so was the Church of England, and virtually without conditions. Bishops began to resume their old authority and cathedral buildings were refurbished. Puritans had offered communion infrequently but Anglicans sought to revive it as well as other obser-

vances and rubrics. The Church of England clergy was poor but slowly gained respect, sometimes by copying the Puritans, including delivering sermons without notes.

Puritans, however, did not receive such favorable treatment, for the
return of the Church of England brought harsh restrictions on Dissenters. Although the king was politic and moderate, the Royalist Parliament elected in 1661 reacted against the "enthusiasm" of the religious
during the Interregnum by blocking efforts of nonconformists to reduce
their penalties. Under the Act of Uniformity, the Church of England
in 1662 ejected more than two thousand Puritan clergy from their livings, replacing them with clerics loyal to it and the Crown. In 1664 the
Conventicle Act provided fines and imprisonment for attending non-
conformist religious meetings and in 1670 was tightened. In 1665 the
Five Mile Act kept Dissenting ministers that far away from places where
they had pastored. Although these measures were only sporadically
enforced where Puritans remained, such as in the towns of East Anglia, they still amounted to persecution and served to unify Dissent and
keep it lean and sincere.

Persecution of Dissenters continued intermittently in the 1670s but
the popular fear was of Roman Catholics, a suppressed and dwindling
minority. This was because the king's sympathy for Catholicism and
secret alliance with Louis XIV became known. Parliament passed the
Test Act, a law against Catholics that was also used against Dissenters. Worries over "popish plots" continued and reached a peak when
Charles II declared for Rome on his death bed in 1685. His successor,
James II, openly pushed that faith, causing the Glorious Revolution,
the loss of his crown, and his exile.

The Act of Settlement then brought William and Mary from Holland to England as constitutional monarchs in 1689. William of Orange favored religious toleration since it had proved viable in Holland.
William and Mary sought to promote the Church of England as a compromise and umbrella that could cover a variety of people with differ-
ing beliefs about religious nonessentials. Like Elizabeth earlier, they
wanted to use the church in an Erastian way to give continuity and
respectability to their new regime.[1]

The High Church party could not accept the end of divine right
monarchy and were called Jacobites for supporting the exiled James II.
Naturally William of Orange regarded them as subversive because they
refused to accept the altered nature of government and church and

pledge loyalty to him and his wife. These Jacobites wanted an autonomous church and so resisted Crown efforts to make the Church of England primarily a vehicle for renewed English nationalism. Therefore William and Mary purged from church offices Non-Jurors, those who could not in good conscience consent to the changes of the Glorious Revolution. No doubt the church lost many leaders of vital piety as a result and Erastian and latitudinarian influence increased. Because many of the High Church party were from the Northwest, this region's influence in church affairs was reduced at this time.

Latitudinarianism expanded slowly in the favorable climate following the Glorious Revolution and High Church party purge. John Locke, the most famous of the latitudinarians, was, like Hooker, Hales, and Hobbes, also from the West Country and gained influence during this period. Baptized at Wrington, he was raised at Pensford, Somerset. His grandfather had moved west from Dorset and become a clothier. His father, a lawyer and clerk to justices of the peace, ran a strict Puritan household and dominated young John.

The headmaster at Westminster School, however, was a strong-minded royalist and John sloughed some Puritan notions. He gained a scholarship to Christ Church, the most important college at Oxford. Like Hobbes, he rejected the scholastic curriculum and was drawn instead to the lone don interested in science. In fact, it was probably reading Hobbes that led the young man to a more material view of nature. Locke worried about religious enthusiasm and could not accept religious toleration. He was happy at the Restoration of the monarchy in 1660. Locke sounded Hobbesian when he wrote that the "magistrate of every nation, what way so ever created, must necessarily have an absolute and arbitrary power over all the indifferent actions of his people."[2] With Calvinism defeated and the king and Church of England resuming their earlier powers, a mood of quietism set in among the sects. In this atmosphere Locke did come around to religious toleration, the latitudinarian position he would make famous in his *Essay concerning Toleration,* but he was never willing to include Catholics. In London he mingled with other prominent latitudinarians and joined their church, the Old Jewry, in 1660.

John Locke was a prudent and secretive man. He did not want to discuss speculative and unpopular religious and political ideas in public. In pursuit of scientific truth, sometimes he did not disclose his sources or all that he had discovered. His approach to religion was distinctly rational. While he seemed to retain Puritan reverence for the Bible as the inspired word of God, he believed it had to be tested by the common sense of the late seventeenth century and be consistent with itself. He sought the fundamentals of faith in the gospels, and when he discovered philosophy, did not seek to make it an emotional substitute for religion. His use of reason and pleas for simplicity laid the basis for modern historical criticism of the Bible.

Locke's ideas on child-rearing and education were a mixture of the strictness of Puritanism and the practicality of Whiggism. He suggested that young infants be "broken," that is, denied their wishes and fed irregularly. As a bachelor physician advising his friends with children, he wanted to avoid "cockering," or coddling; he suggested that children's feet be bathed in cold water year round, and they should receive little or no medicine. He worried about "costiveness" among the young, hoping they would have regular stools although he forbade fruit in their diet. Locke favored education by tutor to keep children from the corruptions of even genteel classmates. Parents were to remain firm and aloof, becoming friends with their children only when they reached the age of rationality. He gave little attention to religious education for young children but recommended the New Testament for ethical instruction. This advice was perhaps appropriate for raising a Whig in the new world of commerce and investment. Locke's suggestions, like the more attractive and practical ones of Benjamin Franklin, fit Max Weber's model: print-oriented, puritanical training combined with rational religion, resulting in the Protestant Ethic that was conducive to individualism and capitalism.

In economics, Locke was an ardent and orthodox mercantilist. Although ailing, he served on the Trade Commission of Charles II in the 1670s. He bought stock in the Royal African Company when it was chartered, getting in on the ground floor of what would become the greatest slave-trading enterprise in the world in the next century. He was also the author, with Lord Ashley-Cooper, of the "Fundamental Constitutions," the blueprint for reorganization of the Carolina Colony. Relying on the success of plantations in Virginia and Maryland, he envisioned for Carolina large, structured estates with a titled nobility. His constitution was not adopted and no nobility materialized. Later Locke, sacrificing his health again, chaired the Board of Trade for William III and resumed the task of making the colonies profitable to the home country.

There is less information on his views of social conditions at home, although a report of the 1670s is indicative. He considered the chief societal problem to be lack of virtue among the lower classes and recommended inculcating good work habits and discouraging vice. Thrifty himself, he wanted to convert the population into an efficient and frugal labor force. In short, Locke aimed to "modernize" England and create the working conditions that Dickens would criticize in the nineteenth century.

Locke's comprehensive religion of morality would aid this development while maintaining law, order, and national unity. Unlike Hobbes, Locke wrote his major work after the Civil War and so did not prescribe a leviathan to restrain selfish individualism. While in theory his rational religion was self-evident and therefore contagious, when combined with social conservatism it was not appealing to many sections and segments of the nation. In pioneering a new kind of reason, Locke underestimated the otherworldly, intuitive, affective side of people's nature. The real transformation of the work force and the public, therefore, had to wait until the Methodist-Evangelical Revival, a movement that could provide popular energy for his natural rights ideas.[3]

When the Whigs replaced the Tories in government in 1714 this rationalist tendency and Locke's influence increased. George I and the Whigs were definitely "low church," reducing the ceremony in the Church of England. From modest beginnings in John Hales's time and nurtured by Locke's writings, latitudinarians came into their own under the House of Hanover. They dominated the prominent dioceses of England. The Lockean attitude was fashionable at the height of the Age of Reason.[4]

Benjamin Hoadley in his heyday epitomized this latitudinarianism. He was successively bishop of Bangor, Hereford, Salisbury, and Winchester. He was born in Kent, and the Hoadley surname was concentrated in the Southeast, with two parishes by that name in Sussex and many Hoadleys inhabiting that county. The bishop was a strong advocate of total conformity to the church. He argued that Dissenters who occasionally conformed so that they could hold office were admitting that conformity was not a sin, thereby undermining their own dissent. The church, after all, did not demand that its members agree to every part of the liturgy. He caused the Bangorian Controversy when he condemned Non-Jurors for their belief in divine right and upheld Whig principles, which called for loyalty only to benevolent leaders. He took reasonable religion a few steps beyond Locke. To Hoadley, the Lord's Supper was not a mystery, but merely commemorative. He was ready by 1715 to accept the Arian belief that Jesus was divine but not co-equal in the Trinity.

In most ways, Hoadley fit the pattern of his predecessors in rational religion. He excelled in using the printed word to challenge orthodox religious ideas and did very little preaching. He stayed in London, not feeling well enough to visit his first two bishoprics. He was a poor orator and when he did preach, his sermons revealed a heavy, involved style. He was not always reasonable and moderate; as chaplain to George I, he was excessive in his praise of the king and his family. The years of Hoadley's maximum influence, 1715 to 1725, coincided with the apex of rationalism and nadir of piety in the established church.[5]

Dissenters in the Southeast

The Dissenters remaining after the Interregnum were a small stratum of English society, an estimated 6 percent of the population. In the populous and commercial cloth towns of the Southeast, however, their percentage was higher. During the Civil War, these orthodox people reacted against the war and the radical sectaries by developing further the rational component of Puritanism. Ramism and Arminianism from the Continent continued to advance quietly there, further separating Southeasterners from Northwesterners. The war accentuated these religious differences as Northwesterners responded to evangelism and sectarianism.

Dissenters greeted the Glorious Revolution with relief and optimism. They believed that the Act of Toleration of 1689 and the shift from divine to constitutional monarchy would give them essential religious and civil liberties denied during the Restoration. They soon found out, however, that this optimism was ill-founded. The government's new policy was partial religious toleration, a shift from persecution to discrimination. Dissenters organized to fight for more freedom and oppose the Test and Corporation Acts that remained on the books and made them second-class citizens. As bourgeoisie they prospered but their religion, turning nonevangelical in the years after the Civil War, continued to lose fervor. Dissenters became preoccupied with their civil disabilities and the education of ministers to perpetuate their denominations rather than concerning themselves with new members. The language of the toleration law gave new power to ministers and trustees and they became high-handed; orthodox clerics tended to ignore the needs of the rank and file. And liberals kept their flocks abreast of rationalist developments in theology without much concern for their missionary obligations.

Relaxed restrictions on printing made heterodox religious ideas and freethinking quite fashionable, and even young men of Dissenting families began to forget "the Old Cause"—Calvinism and opposition to bishops. They were attracted by the episcopal polity and Arminian theology of the established church, especially after the House of Hanover, advocates of low church Anglicanism, came to the throne. The Age of Reason reached full tide several decades after the Glorious Revolution. Dissent in the English Southeast survived persecution but could not sustain itself after the fall of the Stuarts by invoking memories of the Cromwell years or the sufferings of the Restoration. In the early eighteenth-century atmosphere of toleration and prosperity, Dissent—Presbyterian, Baptist, and Independent (Congregationalist)—could not maintain its strength and unity.

One reason was the conflict between Calvinists and Arminians. This division in the ranks of Dissenter clergy was exacerbated by the Salters Hall controversy of 1719. A century after the Synod of Dort, where Arminianism was rejected, Calvinists in England proposed creedal subscription to protect the Dissenter pulpits that had already been established from any new ideas coming from graduates of Dissenter academies that might undermine their position. Opponents, labeled Arminians, argued that subscription would be stultifying and urged tolerance and freedom to disagree. At Salters Hall in London, nonsubscription won in a close clerical vote.

The decision against subscription proved to be a watershed. Controversy sharpened distinctions between Calvinists and Arminians and made unity through compromise difficult for all Dissenters. In reality neither faction won at Salters Hall. The narrow victory of nonsubscribers was soon followed by large declines in membership among Presbyterians and General Baptists, chief protagonists of this position. The losers, mostly Calvinistic Independents and Particular Baptists, preserved creed and polity but sacrificed their piety for hyper-Calvinism and made few converts. Looking back bitterly on the Salters Hall vote, they questioned the sincerity of their opponents who had argued so vehemently in 1719 that subscription infringed on Christian liberty, because so many of these people later conformed to the Church of England, which required subscription to all thirty-nine articles of the Anglican creed.[6]

After the Glorious Revolution, Presbyterians emerged with 550 churches, the largest denomination in Dissent. Their opportunity to become the national church had come and gone during the Civil War so they had metamorphosed into a Dissenting sect. Older members had long hoped for reunion with the established church, but an effort toward this end failed again in the 1690s.[7] Because Presbyterians operated without presbyteries or synods, their churches were almost as autonomous as Independents, although the ordination of their clerics was general rather than over a specific congregation and their trustees had great power, including selection of the minister. Many pastorates were endowed and not dependent on voluntary offerings, so ministers felt free to reflect the latitudinarianism or liberalism of an oligarchy of church leaders and checks on heterodox doctrines were lacking. Ministers were constantly on the defense against unbelief, but were more receptive to new theological ideas than the laity. These academic and rationalist ministers had to compete for hearers in the religious marketplace with the Anglican establishment that offered much the same thing—latitudinarianism—but with more tradition, liturgy, and influence. Further, church membership was casual with no requirement of a vital religious experience to join. These conditions resulted in a decline that set in slowly following the Toleration Act and accelerated after the Salters Hall decision.

Freed from doctrinal constraints by the nonsubscription vote at Salters Hall, Presbyterian ministers in the Southeast continued their drift toward openly Arminian, then Arian positions. The loss of membership was concurrent and hereditary wealth and ministers of good academic standing could only cushion the descent. By 1800 the denomination had virtually disappeared from Southeast England, dissolved by a rationalism that ended in Unitarianism in most instances. From a position of numerical leadership, Presbyterians sank to a mere 15 percent of Old Dissent a century later. Only in the North near the Scottish border, where there were pockets of Calvinists, did the denomination retain most of its historic creed and polity.[8]

Baptists had 250 churches after the Glorious Revolution. They adhered, of course, to baptism and immersion for believers rather than infants, but had no church covenants. Their interpretation of church fellowship was centralizing, giving their polity a presbyterian appearance. Thus the door was opened to rationalist ministers and a decline in popular appeal. The denomination was divided into two major factions over theology; General Baptists were Arminians; Particular Baptists, Calvinists.

General Baptists rejected limited atonement, maintaining that Christ died for everyone, but were in some confusion over the Trinity. In the seventeenth century, they had been much influenced by the Dutch Arminian movement. "Obscure," "unstable," "artless," "anticlerical," and "illiterate" were terms critics used to characterize them. The Salters Hall decision relieved them of doctrinal restraints and by 1750, General Baptists had embraced the Arian position that there was one God in three manifestations. Like Presbyterians, they lost the "virility of their witness" in a drift toward Socinianism and Unitarianism. General Baptists were quite concentrated in a few counties of the Southeast: Kent, Buckinghamshire, Sussex, and the southern parts of Leicester and Lincoln. During the Age of Reason, however, their numbers declined quite rapidly.[9]

The Particular Baptists were orthodox, emphasizing autonomy and freedom of belief. Compared with the General faction, they were clear in their creed, yet considered evangelism and missionary work futile because they would happen in God's own time. They did not urge people to believe, repent, or pray because that would be preaching the law, a gospel of works, not faith. Because the divine principle had to enter the soul before genuine belief and virtuous action were possible, members' attention turned away from worship and church activity toward an inward search for evidence of conversion. The result was spiritual pride and tribalism. Particular Baptists were also clustered in the Southeast: Wiltshire, Berkshire, and along the cultural divide in the eastern parts of Devon and Somerset. During the Enlightenment, the Particular Baptists, with Calvinism and congregationalism, held their ground better but remained static.[10]

When the Act of Toleration became law in 1689, the Independents had some three hundred churches. Their congregational polity had been tested and invigorated by persecution during the Restoration and they preferred toleration to union with the Anglican establishment. Although they believed in divine sovereignty, they did not attempt to force this belief upon others. These churches required that the whole flock hear accounts of conversion experience, and covenants made them more resistant to Arianism and deism than the Presbyterians, although they did feel some rationalist pressure. Independents were the direct heirs of East Anglian Puritans of the 1620s. They were stereotypically middle class, characterized by strictness, legalism, and Whiggism. Their ministers showed professional tendencies, assuming some of the original powers given to the congregation, which undermined its polity in the eighteenth century. Yet enough congregationalism remained to keep controversy confined to the local level.

The congregational polity did lend itself to a few evangelical sparks in the midst of religious apathy in the Southeast. Richard Davis, "a fiery thirty-one year old Welshman with a good voice and a thundering way of preaching," became minister of an Independent church at Rothwell, Northamptonshire, in 1690. At his ordination, Davis had church officers, instead of neighboring Independent colleagues, take part. This strict congregational practice offended some clerics. He antagonized more by embarking on a vigorous evangelical campaign, taking the gospel into eleven counties and founding seven churches. He encouraged lay exhorters and created excitement. Thus he kindled some embers of the strong evangelism of the 1640s and 1650s and was accused of antinomianism. Dissenter opinion of Davis was divided, with most clerical leaders resisting his evangelism. He did prove that an evangelist could draw attention and support in the Southeast, but would have to do it in the face of large-scale resistance from ministers and wealthy landowners. Richard Davis was not only an echo of the Interregnum but a herald of the Methodist-Evangelical Revival.[11]

In 1760 the Independents were still concentrated in the Southeast. In the smaller towns of East Anglia, their chapels were often the only alternative to the Church of England. They were also numerous in the high-quality cloth towns of Wiltshire, eastern Devon, and Somerset. Membership in Independent churches rose slightly during this period but did not keep pace with population growth.

The general decline of otherworldliness in the Southeast accelerated during the Enlightenment. Organized religion became the concern of men of affairs who supported it as a force for morality, as the traditional social cement in the community. Women, restricted in their means of expression, provided the preponderance of hearers and active members in the churches. Only in a few enclaves—the wealds, fens, and among emigrants to London and Norwich from the Northwest—did the evangelical spirit survive in the Southeast in the first half of the eighteenth century.

Denominational historians describe this period euphemistically as one of consolidation. Others are blunt, using the terms "decline," "decay," and "worldliness," linking these with political corruption, the "robinocracy" of the Walpole era.[12] The Age of Reason had brought some basic Christian beliefs into question and changed the equilibrium between the Church of England and Dissenters, but it did not sustain or rejuvenate the churches. Where rationalism appeared early—East Anglia and the West Country cloth districts—it continued to evolve, and the gulf between the beliefs of ministers and laity widened. Religious belief was becoming an individual and private matter. Among Dissenters, neither subscription nor nonsubscription could arrest this trend. Pastors ignored or neglected the doctrine of justification by faith alone and the decline in evangelical piety became palpable, pervasive, and seemingly irreversible.

The Northwest

There was continuity between the Civil War and the Methodist-Evangelical Revival in the Northwest. Activities of sects during the Interregnum, particularly the Quakers of the first generation, prefigured the revivalism of the next century. During the Commonwealth, Roundheads held religious meetings in their homes, which echoed the separatist conventicles of Elizabeth's time and were forerunners of the religious societies of Hornbeck, Wesley, and Whitefield. Many groups had surfaced with the defeat of the Stuart monarchy: Seekers (or Waiters), Ranters, Dippers, Grindletonians, Muggletonians, Manifestarians, and Quakers. After Charles I was executed and Oliver Cromwell died, Fifth Monarchy sectarians predicted that Jesus would be the next ruler. This was a time of religious discussion, experimentation, and prophecy; separatism was rampant.

In the Restoration that followed, the Quakers proved to be the hardiest of these separatists. George Fox, founder of the movement, was born at Fenny Drayton in western Leicestershire in 1624. His father was a churchwarden and his mother came from a respectable family. A pious youth, the young apprentice shoemaker and shepherd wandered about in the North for four years during the Civil War seeking religious conviction but kept in touch with his parents. Fox discovered that the power of God was within and that he could feel it in his own heart. Christianity was alive and could be verified from within; it was much more than faith in the report that Christ had died in Jerusalem a long time ago. This Inner Light gave him the confidence to proclaim "the Truth" and challenge clergy as well as laity in religious disputation. The young visionary dismissed as "notions" any ideas not confirmed by inner experience. He was ready to reject the national religious forms of the time with their bishops, priests, tithes, and formal worship because he believed that God dwelt in people, not churches. Fox was an iconoclast with a piercing gaze who critics called blasphemous, bewitching, and mad. He answered the charge that he claimed to be Christ by declaring that everyone could find Christ within. In 1647 he began traveling to publish the Truth and proclaim the Day of the Lord.

When Fox again traveled North from Fenny Drayton and crossed the Humber River, he found many people ripe for his message. Because the fields were "white for the harvest," he and his first converts, "the Publishers of the Truth," were able to convince many groups as well as individuals in a short time. In this environment, Quakers were able to draw converts from several social classes. Even some younger sons of the lesser gentry felt the Inner Light. Young women were conspicuous when they witnessed in public or traveled unescorted. Itinerating was for the young and unattached but more mature converts and sympathizers offered hospitality to these young travelers.

The Quakers drew their support in the North from sectarians generally, but especially from Spiritual Puritans (or Seekers) who had been gathering in small groups and waiting quietly for Light from the Lord. The charisma of Fox convinced many of them that he was a prophet, was in the Light, and spoke the truth. He taught them to explore the indwelling power of God. Fox made his headquarters at Swarthmore Hall in northern Lancashire, home of Judge Thomas Fell and his wife, Margaret. She proved to be an inspiration to Quakers in the field. When she was widowed, Fox married her.[13]

The Quaker Galilee was in the North, chiefly Cheshire, Yorkshire, Lancashire, Cumberland, and Westmorland, some of the highest ground in England. Quakerism found special favor with small farmers or shepherds descended from Vikings. The Norse custom was individual land ownership, so they felt alienated from the Norman-French governing class, its political institutions, and lingering Catholicism. Fox's Quaker ideas and simplicity reinforced evangelical Protestantism in this region's pastoral people.[14]

Fox was most successful in places where Spiritual Puritans had been aroused as the Civil War began. Geoffrey Nuttall has found that the doctrine of the Holy Spirit was present among mainline Puritans, who were wary of reason alone, but was primary among the radicals, who emphasized the personal God and contemporary indwelling of Spirit. This Spirit was not the same as "reason" or "conscience" and was superior to them. Defending themselves against the charge of irrationality, the radicals argued that reason had its intuitive as well as discursive aspect. Having the "gift" to communicate the Spirit was more important than formal education or sacraments.

Fox, in developing the ideas that became Quakerism, had to go only a short distance beyond the positions of these Spiritual Puritans. He saw the same Spirit in latter-day saints as in the apostles. He didn't claim that his direct inspiration revealed anything that superseded New Testament teaching, but he did believe that the Inner Light gave him "dominion" over sin and the ability to detect evil. Fox diverged from Calvinism by declaring that every person was enlightened by the divine light of Christ, the converted completely and the unconverted, incompletely. Nuttall welcomed Fox's interpretations of Calvinistic Puritanism, especially the rejection of humanity's degeneration from a golden age, an idea he labeled a pagan vestige. He saw the Quakers as performing a "real service" by going beyond Spiritual Puritanism in emphasizing the doctrine of the Holy Spirit because the Puritans, in reacting against Catholicism, had neglected the aesthetic element in the human constitution.

In sifting the ideas of Spiritual Puritans for precursors of the Quakers, Nuttall cited a dozen surnames of followers, all from the Northwest. He believed that Morgan Lloyd of Monmouthshire was the most consciously and consistently mystical. Lloyd stressed prayer and did not memorize sermons, relying on the Lord to inspire him. The critics mocked his congregation, calling them "New Lights." Other precursors mentioned were Saltmarsh, Dell, Erbury, Rous, Cradock, Burrough, Lawson, and Baxter. Nuttall noted that the "Celtic element" in Spiritual Puritanism was very high and marveled that Lloyd had not joined the Quakers. Richard Baxter, raised in the Welsh marshes, shared many Quaker tendencies yet charged that group with spiritual pride. Baxter saw in the Quakers links with the Jesuits because Jesuits considered the Inner Light infallible, deemphasized scripture, and refused to take the oath rejecting papal authority.[15]

The Society of Friends, as the Quakers called themselves, conducted missionary efforts in the Southeast during the Restoration, and

Quakerism spread through the trading classes in towns, becoming more and more identified with a few strata of the population. Quakers turned inward, using less evangelism and seeking instead the small, still voice, retreating from a movement with universal claims to a sect. Quietism brought not only respectability and conservatism but sometimes a touch of deism. The followers of George Fox were still a peculiar people. Despite their inroads, in the English Southeast there continued to be many more Puritans than Quakers, with the greatest disparity in East Anglia. Metropolitan London, however, remained a melting pot for religious belief as it had been earlier in the century.[16]

The Quakers were the most successful sectarian survivors of the Civil War era. Yet in 1660, when the Quaker Seventy in the North went south to carry the Truth to the whole country, neither the time nor the place, the Southeast, was anywhere near as responsive as Westmorland had been in the 1650s.[17] The Quaker movement was beginning to turn into a birthright sect. Fox was prophetic, however, in proposing some moral reforms that would concern Methodists and Evangelicals as well as Quakers in the next century. Evangelism lived on after 1660 in the North, but was carried less by Quakers than others as the decades passed.

Making Way for the Methodist-Evangelical Revival

The surge of religiosity that emerged with George Whitefield and John Wesley in the 1730s had several sources. The most obvious was High Church piety. Members of the High Church party developed much frustration with the Glorious Revolution, the House of Hanover, and Walpole's Whiggism. Ritualism and religious societies were not enough to sustain them as worldly England challenged Church of England autonomy and ridiculed supernaturalism. They were ready to react against Protestant rationalism, Lockean assent, and the cult of mere morality. Other sources were the leftover Spiritual Puritans, Seekers, and sectarians who had not internalized the separate peace of quietism and still felt the Holy Spirit.

The application of eighteenth-century reason to scriptures, the beginning of biblical criticism, caused widespread uncertainty and a recoil toward "reasons of the heart." Internal evidence of belief—the Holy Spirit or the New or Inner Light—was popular because it was not confined to an elite and could be shared by males and females, rich and poor.[18] While impetus for this evangelism came from the geographical and social periphery of Britain, the formal beginning of the revival came from the Southeast, from Oxford University where some students from the Northwest, feeling their roots, rejected the indifference of their classmates.

Oxford undergraduates and teachers alike were lethargic and lax in the early eighteenth century. Studying and teaching were perfunctory since sons of gentry were secure enough in their positions not to be too ambitious or intellectual. Gambling and promiscuity at the university corresponded with a low point in the cycle of public morality in England. The majority of students were latitudinarian or indifferent to religion, reflecting the attitude of the upper class in Southeast England. A Northwest minority, concentrated in several colleges, felt the tug of the Old Religion more than others, but they too were adrift and spiritually unawakened.

The faculty at Oxford, however, was much less secular than the undergraduates. The dons were High Church members who defended the clerical prerogatives of the church and attacked the Arianism and deism abroad in the land. They looked back to Richard Hooker and other Caroline theologians who had given Anglicanism a respectable place in the middle ground between the Catholics and the low church and the latitudinarians and the nonconformists. The Whig government believed that faculty loyalty to the House of Hanover was weak, that there were some actual Jacobites among the dons, and intervention at the university might be justified. Because of these suspicions, not unfounded, Oxford received less than its share of Crown patronage.

Charles Wesley started the Holy Club at Oxford in 1728 and his brother, John, became its leader. The Wesleys took their ideas from the religious societies of Restoration England and the *collegia pietatis* of Germany. Members were drawn from the Northwest and were closer religiously to High Church faculty than to other undergraduates. Members sought purity through close association and good behavior, eating together five nights a week and singing hymns. They took weekly communion and went beyond scriptures to observe neglected canons and decretals. They fasted on Wednesdays and Fridays and on Saturdays prepared for the sabbath. They aimed to study diligently and live in a holy manner. These strict practices earned them several opprobrious nicknames—"bible moths," "bible bigots," and "methodists." The last one stuck; it was not a new name, having been applied to some French

Calvinists and English sectarians in the previous century. To some this ascetism and living by rule suggested Catholicism, and this label dogged the Methodist movement long after the club had disappeared.

The Holy Club was also committed to good works. This meant reading to and catechizing the illiterate, caring for the sick, and visiting prisoners in the Castle and Bocardo, the "gaols" of Oxford. Later when an opportunity arose to be missionaries in the new colony of Georgia, the Wesleys sailed so that they could preserve their own holiness as well as convert the American Indians.

Contemporary critics were quick to charge the club with superstition, enthusiasm, and madness. One claimed that members were neglecting or afflicting their bodies in the belief that religion was designed to contradict nature. He also suggested that enthusiasm encouraged restlessness, itineracy, and exotic travel. John Wesley denied charges of excessive fasting, but much of the criticism was true. Of course some club members gave the impression that only they had true faith and would be saved, and this implied slight on the religion of others made enemies.[19]

The Holy Club would turn out to be the most important cadre of the British Saving Remnant in the eighteenth century (see table 4-1). Most came from the periphery of Britain, while no one from East Anglia or the London vicinity joined. High Church and pietistic tendencies predominated, and several members later adopted specifically Moravian tenets, as that perspective became better known. But seeds of evangelism, including the Calvinistic version, were also present and would soon surface. The total membership probably did not exceed forty, with less than twenty active at one time. When the Wesleys departed for Georgia, the club reduced its good works in the community and turned further inward. Women had been the chief supporters of the club outreach in the Oxford town area, and they could not sustain the community work without help from the collegians. After six men from Queen's College joined, the locus of the Holy Club moved farther north, closer to the Tweed.

Behavior of course varied in later years, and not all members were as persistent and evangelical as the founding members. For example, Westley Hall, one of the few members from the Southeast, has been called the Judas of the club. At the outset he had made himself useful to John Wesley and others. Yet when Wesley took him home to Epworth, he secretly wooed two of John's sisters at once, marrying Mar-

Table 4-1. The Holy Club

Original Members	Probable Origin
Broughton, Thomas, M.A.	Scotland
Clayton, John, M.A.	Lancashire
Gambold, John, M.A.	Wales
Hall, Westley	Wiltshire
Harvey, James	Northamptonshire
Ingham, Benjamin	West Riding, Yorkshire
Kinchin, Charles, M.A.	Wales
Kirkham, Robert	Gloucester
Morgan, William	Ireland
Wesley, Charles	Lincoln
Wesley, John, M.A.	Lincoln
Whitefield, George	Gloucester
Whitelamb, John	Lincoln

Later Members	Probable Origin
Atkinson, Christopher	Westmorland
Bell, John	Cumberland
Smith, John	Durham
Washington, Henry	Cumberland
Watson, Robert	Cumberland
Wilson, Roger	Northumberland

Sources: John Wesley, *The Journal of John Wesley* (1909; rpt., 1938), 2:284; Luke Tyerman, *The Oxford Methodists* (1873), 1–411.

tha and jilting Keziah. He changed his mind about going to Georgia with the Wesleys and returned to his home in Wiltshire. Then he became a Moravian, broke with the Wesleys, and withdrew his followers from the Church of England. As a Dissenter he was a smooth talker who used his eloquence to convert female disciples. After drifting into deism, he sailed to the West Indies and remained there with his mistress until he inherited a sizable estate at his parents' death. In the personality of Hall, one of the very few club members from the Southeast, Wesleyan religion had to compete with strong self-interest as well as other trends of the region and time and lost out. As a Holy Club member and brother-in-law, Westley Hall was a conspicuous backslider, a major embarrassment to early Methodism.

Although this affair affected the religious activities of the Wesley family, a more important event was John Wesley's conversion. The day was May 24, 1738, at quarter to nine in the evening at a religious society meeting in Aldersgate Street, London. When he went to the meeting, he was still pondering his ineffectuality as a missionary in Georgia and was in a state of expectancy and anxiety. God did not seize him but merely warmed his heart. At the time he was within a month of his thirty-fifth birthday, already three years older than Martin Luther at his conversion. Wesley later indicated that he had passed through some kind of checkpoint in 1725 when he focused on his call to the ministry and the possibility of Christian perfection. Although the Holy Club contributed to his growth, the episode in Aldersgate Street was more important because it was sudden and definite, resulting in the resolution of doubts and a change in lifestyle; a career of preaching, itineracy, and organization soon followed.[20]

In terms of the Methodist-Evangelical Revival, Wesley's friendship with George Whitefield was also significant. When Whitefield was a lowly and lonely servitor at Oxford, the Wesley brothers befriended him, took him into the club, and nudged him in the direction of ritualism, fasting, and good works. But these activities did not alleviate the sufferings of his sick soul and Whitefield had to turn elsewhere for solace. His anxiety grew during the fall of 1734 and ended with a sudden conversion at Oxford seven weeks after Easter; George was five months past his twentieth birthday. Whitefield always remembered the "unspeakable joy." During his lifetime, he had continual swings in mood, according to how well he preached or expounded yet never seemed to lose confidence in this conversion and the belief that he had become a "new creature."[21]

Notes

1. William H. Hutton, *The English Church, from the Accession of Charles I to the Death of Anne (1625–1714)* (1934), 320–48.

2. Maurice Cranston, *John Locke: A Biography* (1957), 1–46, 60. In his analysis of Virginia, David Hackett Fischer has chosen Robert Filmer to exemplify Wessex and this region of Southeast England. Filmer was a strong defender of monarchy and hierarchy, a traditionalist compared with Locke. See *Albion's Seed: Four British Folkways in America* (1989), 216–24. He was, however, from Kent and the Filmer surname was heavily concentrated in that county. See Henry Guppy, *Homes of Family Names in Great Britain* (1890), 485.

3. Cranston, *Locke,* 124–28, 239–45, 119–20, 399–448. Ernest Tuveson has identified Locke as a visualist. While Locke recognized that sensations came in through all the senses, only sight was vivid to him. He saw error or obscurity as arising from failure to observe attentively or from lack of light. His expectation that his ideas, because they were "self-evident," would spread naturally and quickly were not unfounded, but they did depend on a degree of visualism that sacrificed the other senses and did not reckon with cultural barriers in the British population of that time. See Tuveson, "Locke and the Dissolution of the Ego," *Modern Philology* 52 (1955): 159–74, especially 164.

4. G. R. Cragg, *The Church and the Age of Reason* (1964), 61–86, 117–26.

5. Gordon Rupp, *Religion in England, 1688–1791* (1986), 88–101. There were Hoadleys from Kent in central Connecticut in the midseventeenth century, but no clerics of that name during the Great Awakening. See Charles E. Banks, *Topographical Dictionary,* ed. E. E. Brownell (1937), 81; Thomas Savage, *Genealogical Dictionary of the First Settlers of New England* (1860), 2:429.

6. Russell E. Richey, "The Effects of Toleration on Eighteenth Century Dissent," *Journal of Religious History* 8 (1974–75): 350–63; Anthony Armstrong, *The Church of England, the Methodists, and Society, 1700–1850* (1973), 35; William J. Gibson, "Patterns of Nepotism and Kinship in the Eighteenth-Century Church," *Journal of Religious History* 14 (1987): 382–89.

7. Roger Thomas, "The Non-Subscription Controversy amongst Dissenters in 1719: The Salters' Hall Debate," *Journal of Ecclesiastical History* 4 (1953): 162–86, and "The Salters Hall Watershed," in *The English Presbyterians: From Elizabethan Puritanism to Modern Unitarianism,* ed. C. Gordon Bolam, Jeremy Goring, H. L. Short, and Roger Thomas (1968), 151–74; Rupp, *Religion in England,* 108–15.

8. Michael R. Watts, *The Dissenters: From the Reformation to the French Revolution* (1978), 217–19, 260. The Old Dissent refers to those denominations outside the Church of England before 1791. After John Wesley's death that year, English Methodists broke away from the establishment and joined the group, making it the New Dissent.

9. John D. Gay, *The Geography of Religion in England* (1971), 119, 290; James H. Wood, *The Condensed History of the General Baptists of the New Connexion* (1847), 145–73.

10. Watts, *Dissenters,* 267–85, 393.

11. Ibid., 292–93.

12. Robert G. Torbet, *A History of the Baptists* (1950), 91–96; J. M. Cramp, *Baptist History, from the Foundation of the Christian Church to the Close of the Eighteenth Century* (1868 ed.), chap. 7, "The Quiet Period, 1688–1753," 474–504.

13. Hugh Barbour, *The Quakers in Puritan England* (1964), 1–93.

14. Fischer, *Albion's Seed,* 438–48.

15. Geoffrey Nuttall, *The Holy Spirit in Faith and Experience* (1947), 51–52, 148–70. In "From Seeker to Finder: A Study in Seventeenth-Century Spiritualism before the Quakers," *Church History* 18 (1948): 299–315, George A. Johnson emphasizes the contributions to the Quaker movement of four radical spiritualists with university degrees: William Dell, John Saltmarsh, Thomas Collier, and Thomas Erbury (or Erbery). See also Michael J. Galgano, "Out of the Mainstream: Catholic and Quaker Women in the Restoration Northwest," in *The World of William Penn,* ed. Richard S. Dunn and Mary M. Dunn (1986), 117–37.

16. Barbour, *Quakers,* 257.

17. William Braithwaite, *The Beginnings of Quakerism* (2d ed., 1955), 153–209.

18. John D. Walsh, "The Origins of the Evangelical Revival," in *Essays in Modern English Church History,* ed. G. V. Bennett and J. D. Walsh (1966), 132–62.

19. V. H. H. Green, *The Young Mr. Wesley: A Study of John Wesley and Oxford* (1961), 145–201.

20. Ibid., 238–41, 291–92, 271–78.

21. Arnold A. Dallimore, *George Whitefield: The Life and Times of the Great Evangelist of the Eighteenth Century Revival* (1970), 1:179–98.

Chapter Five

Wesley and Whitefield Triumph: The Methodist-Evangelical Revival

George Whitefield has come to be regarded as the greatest orator in British history. The ultimate source of his astonishing power over the multitudes was the timber and sonority of his "magical voice." He could thunder and whisper; his cadence was exceptional. Benjamin Franklin estimated that he could be heard, without shouting, by thirty thousand people at once. David Garrick, the actor, noticed that Whitefield could convulse an audience merely by pronouncing "Mesopotamia"; others remarked that he could get this same effect with the most ordinary words as well. Dr. Samuel Johnson denigrated Whitefield's ability by attributing it to a "peculiarity of manner—he would be followed by a crowd were he to wear a night-cap in the pulpit or preach from a tree."[1]

The Great Awakener had a fair complexion and was not unattractive; he did have talents as a mimic and raconteur. Without notes, he looked steadily at his hearers and was at his best acting out anecdotes, parables, and history. He often began his flights of fancy with "Methinks I see . . ." and favored surprise endings. He reinforced his pictorial language with a mobile face and active fingers. His taste was vulgar but his wit was ready. When a clergyman on Boston Common in New England told him, "I'm sorry to see you here," he replied, "so is the Devil." When he raised emotions to a high pitch, Whitefield was usually a casualty himself, weeping more or less openly as he preached.[2]

When Whitefield began his sermonizing in the 1730s, the mass market for news and goods was just emerging, and he embraced it. He saw people as consumers and believed in advertising and advance publicity. He was more talented than any other young preacher in using new commercial techniques to promote his preaching and printed material, sermons, and hymns. Thus he reinforced his spoken words with printed words written to be spoken or sung. Merchants admired his dedication and organization and often supported his kind of religion. In Whitefield's case, as in the popular evangelists who came later—Charles Grandison Finney, Billy Sunday, Billy Graham—commerce and religion were not antithetical, but went together.[3]

Whitefield's success began in the Northwest. After his conversion, he left Oxford and returned to his native Gloucester, staying nine months with Gabriel Harris, a well-known bookseller and son of the mayor. In his long career of itineracy, Whitefield would take many sojourns in Gloucestershire. He actually founded the first "Methodist" religious society here in 1735, before he and Wesley had become national figures. The next year, the bishop of Gloucester, Martin Benson, ordained him and he preached his first sermon at St. Mary de Crypt Church with his family, officials, and society members looking on. It was soon reported that the neophyte preacher drove fifteen persons mad, but the bishop hoped that they might remain in that condition until the following Sunday. Benson, from Hereford, was a friend of George Berkeley, the idealist philosopher, and had worked hard to revive religious life in this poor western diocese.[4]

Whitefield did not have to overcome complete apathy in Gloucester. An Aberdeen graduate from Scotland, James Forbes, and his protégé, Thomas Cole, had sustained evangelism in a Dissenter church since 1700. In fact, "old Cole," as the unconverted young Whitefield had called him, became even more active a preacher after Whitefield drew such a strong response in 1735. Whereas Dissenter churches in the Southeast retained their complacency before and reluctance during the Methodist-Evangelical Revival, this church in Gloucester kept its religious fervor. Gloucestershire's historic religiosity has been attributed to the many abbies it sustained before the Reformation. Whitefield spent two more months in the county, pastoring at Stonehouse in the Cotswolds because of delays in his ship's departure for Georgia.

When the Awakener returned to Gloucester in 1739, he had become famous and controversial, and a number of flocks in the county regarded him as their spiritual leader. Yet because so many clerics had closed their parish churches to him, he often had to preach in the open air. Church canons permitted preaching out-of-doors in places where there were not adequate church facilities; in his youth, Whitefield stretched this by going into some parishes without permission from settled ministers. He noted that response in Gloucester had become as rewarding as that in London. Of the thirty-six religious societies looking to Whitefield for inspiration in 1743, five were in Gloucestershire. Long after Whitefield had relinquished any leadership role in the revival, these societies took their cues from him. Whitefield's local origins and Calvinistic style explain this continuing allegiance.

Whitefield visited some county towns many times—Rodborough, Hampton, Dursley, Tewksbury, Stroud. At Hampton, a Holy Club member had paved the way for the Awakener's efforts. But it was here also that a mob routed his hearers. He took the instigators to court in Gloucester, charging them with incitement to riot, and won his case. At Cheltenham, Lord Dartmouth had a summer home that was used for evangelical meetings. Dartmouth was the most important peer and officeholder to share the evangelical viewpoint. In the early nineteenth century, Robert Raikes launched England's Sunday School movement in the county. The proverb "As sure as God's in Gloucester" continued to ring true.[5]

Whitefield lodged with his sister in Bristol frequently, so it became an important revival site. It was a port adjacent to Gloucester and England's second largest town. On the outskirts was Kingswood, a tract of land originally used for hunting that had become a coal mining district with little woods remaining. The men, women, and children who worked in the dark pits were described as sad and sullen, lapsing into a dialect of their own. They had no schools and were not welcome in the parish churches of Bristol because they had terrorized the town on occasion. Told that these colliers were as barbarous as American Indians, Whitefield visited them in 1739. Whitefield's outdoor preaching had strong effects, and he long remembered the streaks of tears running down the blackened faces of the miners. Despite their reputation for violence, these people never attacked Whitefield.[6] In districts like this in Britain, Whitefield and other itinerants were addressing audiences that were largely illiterate, so their message of the New Birth—if followed up by conversion and encouragement to learn to read the scriptures—could improve literacy and educability as well as lead to emotional and personality changes.

Whitefield was having great success in Bristol but wanted to move on and continue the work elsewhere. John Wesley was in London working in the religious societies, worrying about his health, and drifting emotionally after his conversion. Whitefield pressed Wesley to take over for him in Bristol and preach in the open air. He was reluctant and had to overcome the inhibitions of his High Church background. The Holy Club and the Georgia experience had reinforced his preference for decency, law and order, and obedience to church rules. He believed, however, that as a fellow at Lincoln College, he had the right to preach anywhere, but was aware of the charges of "irregularity" that Whitefield's preaching outdoors had already caused. Overcoming his natural reserve, Wesley made his debut in a brickyard on April 2, 1739, with good effect. One authority has argued that this day is more relevant for Methodism and British history than the date of Wesley's conversion because Wesley added evangelism to his piety, giving it the power to change the society and landscape.[7] Once Wesley joined Whitefield in Bristol it became the center of Methodism in western England.

Even before Wesley began delivering his messages in the open air, he produced some strong physical symptoms in his hearers. In his journal, he records many more cases of women being overcome than of men. Because he had read Jonathan Edwards's account of the Frontier Revival in western New England just six months earlier, Wesley may have been more tolerant of these occurrences than he otherwise would have been. According to Edwards, these physical responses were the stumbling blocks of Satan to the work of evangelism and hurt the reputation of those laboring in the vineyard. When Samuel, Wesley's older brother, complained that God didn't work this way anymore, John said he was judging converts, not by their cries or groans, but by the whole tenor of their lives. "I don't believe every spirit, but try the spirits, whether they be of God, using tests from Law and Testimony."[8] Nevertheless, critics labeled the strange behavior in Bristol as "enthusiasm" and "madness," likening the responses to those the French prophets had aroused earlier in the century.

Wesley also proved his drawing power with the colliers of Kingswood, as Whitefield had done, and this set a pattern. Buoyed up by his success and alarmed by the lack of religion amongst the miners, Wesley sought them out in Durham, Stafford, Cornwall, and Wales. Men away from home or in dangerous work—colliers, soldiers, sailors—were vulnerable to his message in the eighteenth century. Much of the power of Methodism came from the ability to reach simultaneously hard-working men of the Northwest and women in the religious societies.

In addition to simply preaching, Wesley could offer medical advice to both groups. He was impatient with physicians of the day. They were scarce, expensive, and ineffective, treating body but neglecting mind. Confronted with despair and melancholia, they prescribed bleeding, drugs, or, in the case of the affluent, a change of scene or companions. In contrast, Wesley's approach was holistic, that the mind had much to do with good health, an early version of mind cure and the power of positive thinking. The one thing needful was faith in God and the consequent relief from sin. What Wesley and the Methodists offered could be viewed as mass psychiatry at a very low cost. Methodists treated anxious thousands in the eighteenth and nineteenth centuries.[9]

More important than medical advice was the singing Wesley encouraged at his services. Hymns provided a bridge between a still oral people and an organized middle-class religion centered on the Bible. Before the Methodist revival, congregational singing had reached a low ebb in the Church of England. In most places there was chanting with no musical accompaniment. In some a choir of young boys sang to the flock—"striplings" who mouthed words without much understanding, according to Wesley. He wanted everyone to participate and opposed "dumb singing" as much as the Puritans had opposed "dumb reading" in the previous century.

Wesley himself was always moved by song. His great concern with the details of Methodist singing was therefore genuine and heartfelt. Luther had given singing to the common people of Germany and Wesley admired that tradition; his first hymn book was a collection of German hymns, published in 1737 in South Carolina. His journals show that he sang with companies of people three or four times a day, in a society, at church, or in a lodging house. Occasionally, as in his first visit to Newcastle, he sang to draw a crowd for preaching in the open.

Singing attracted many who were unaware, indifferent, or even suspicious of Methodist religious views. Wesley decreed that hymns be sung standing and only twice, before and after the sermon, so that people would not tire of them but go away wanting more. He disapproved of complexity—fugues or singing different words at the same time—as well as "meaningless repetition." He reasserted the ancient tradition of singing—melody and a strong beat. John wrote many hymns but was overshadowed by brother Charles, who has been credited with some 6,500 titles. The Wesleys were happy that some of their compositions became popular tunes of the day.[10] Women, children, and unlettered working men, having retained more orality than educated men in commercial towns, were disproportionately affected by the power of song. The mnemonic advantages of rhythm and rhyme were apparent to most revivalists, providing an outlet for poetic impulses and introducing and reinforcing simple religious beliefs and attitudes. Thus singing was democratic and educational yet served to bring the rank and file into conformity with the Methodism John Wesley shaped with little input from others.

George Whitefield sang almost as much as Wesley. He burst into hymns on the road. In 1735 after conversion, he wrote, "Go where I would, I could not avoid singing of psalms aloud." He sang hymns instead of popular songs at public houses. He set sacred words to popular airs, arguing that the Devil should not have all the good tunes. In Wales, where Whitefield exceeded Wesley in influence, the hymns were as important as the sermons.[11]

Yet singing merely introduced the unconverted to Methodism. It was reading that was really important for this burgeoning religion. For his followers Wesley prepared spiritual classics, "the Christian Library," at considerable personal expense. He encouraged reading in his schools and urged people to read as well as pray when alone. Early in life he read devotional works. Later he read major critics of the Methodists and decided whether to reply. Some of Wesley's reading came from the colonies: not only Edwards's account of the Frontier Revival in New England but his biography of the saintly David Brainerd and *Christian History*, with its eyewitness accounts of revivals. The image of John Wesley that has come down from the eighteenth century is of a solitary rider, letting the horse find its own way, reading as he traveled the highways, byways, and hedgerows of the British Northwest.

More surprising was Wesley's secular reading: Voltaire, Pascal, Franklin, and, of course, geography and history, especially about the places he visited so often—Ireland, Cornwall, Wales. After his conversion he followed his doctrine of "think and let think," showing a willingness to read, after his evangelical conversion, pagan as well as Catholic and skeptical authors. He persevered with those he found dull and difficult, closing the book only on the most obscure German Pietists. His view of God as omnipresent, as still active in the world, made him open to new scientific findings. Instead of rejecting the Enlightenment, Wesley remained interested in its discoveries. His readings reflect the tendencies of his home county of Lincoln. There, pietism, sectarianism, and witchcraft could go hand in hand with a lifelong interest in knowledge and science.[12]

Whitefield's reading was much more limited. After college, he did not make time, like Wesley, for broad, secular reading. The Awakener was familiar with Francke and Law but what set him apart from Wesley was his emphasis on Henry Scougal and Matthew Henry. Scougal, a seventeenth-century Scot, had graduated from Aberdeen and joined the faculty. He was the first professor in Scotland to teach Francis Bacon's methods, but shielded his students from the amoral Hobbes. While some called his ideas Arminian, both Presbyterians and Anglicans valued his work. His *Life of God in the Soul of Man* (1677) became a religious classic, and after his death at age twenty-eight, he acquired almost a saintly status in the Scottish church.

Mathew Henry was the son of a Welsh minister. After studying law, he began to preach and was privately ordained as a pastor in Chester. Supporters built a large meetinghouse for him. He was a Dissenter, but Anglicans thought well of him. His *Exposition of the Old and New Testaments* (5 vols., 1708–10) was long regarded as the best commentary in English for devotional purposes. Henry conceded it had no critical value, but the volumes were packed with quaint truths and practical suggestions. Whitefield read through the work four times and urged it on others. Oxford had not offered instruction in systematic theology and the Holy Club did not study it, so this was his early and chief source. Inspired by Henry's work, Whitefield would go on to reassert belief in the power of certain doctrines to produce conversion, the New Birth.[13]

The beliefs of Whitefield and Wesley diverged because Wesley's theology did not change with his conversion but his preaching style did. He came from a High Church home and was affected early on by German Pietism; neither tendency was Calvinistic. Wesley found he could believe in free will and still, by preaching the Law as well as love, purge his hearers before feeding them. Wesley and his Methodist preachers could thus accept the Arminianism of the Church of England and yet be searching and effective in the field. On this ground, there would be no need for Methodist societies to secede from the established church. When Wesley was charged with schism or moving his societies toward a "new religion," he responded by being more explicit in his Arminianism.

This disturbed George Whitefield and led to some estrangement between the two. Whitefield's early experience convinced him that his evangelical power came from asserting Calvin's decrees. Whitefield's admonitions had little effect on Wesley, however, and between 1740 and 1760 they disagreed on these fundamentals of theology, although in practice their messages were often quite similar. In his travels and preaching, Whitefield was becoming more explicit in his Calvinism, which caused tension not only between him and Wesley but with other Methodists and Anglicans too. Although the thirty-nine articles of the church were unchanged and Calvinistic, the Arminian emphasis had predominated for four generations.

The two differed over German Pietism as well. Following his unsuccessful sojourn in Georgia, Wesley returned to London and came under the influence of Peter Bohler, who explained Moravianism and took him beyond High Church formalism to experimental religion based on faith alone. After visiting Germany, Wesley looked upon these people favorably because they took their religion and work seriously, even though their writings were often obscure. When he wrote that the great sin of the British people was godlessness, he may actually have been comparing them with these pious Germans.

Following his conversion and some defections of his helpers to the Moravians, Wesley began to find fault with Pietists. He objected not only to their "stillness," or their belief that perfection came only through passive contemplation, but charged them with excesses we still associate with cults: taking members' worldly goods, assigning inappropriate tasks, and generally exploiting their labor. And although Wesley completely controlled his Methodist preachers and societies, he nevertheless complained that the Moravians tyrannized their members. His chief complaint, however, was that they went "beyond what is written" to "sublime nonsense." He charged that the Pietists tended toward antinomianism, relying on their own feelings too much and the Bible and liturgy too little.[14]

Like Wesley, Whitefield encountered Moravians in Georgia and attended their meetings at Fetter Lane in London and elsewhere. He quarreled with them as early as 1740 over predestination because they soundly rejected it. Thirteen years later, when they made many converts among the new Methodists, he felt compelled to criticize them publicly. He believed they slighted scriptures, were irreverent, waxed sentimental, and used sexual terminology inappropriately in referring to Jesus. More importantly, they were yielding to pomp and taking their indebtedness too casually. This was unusually aggressive behavior for Whitefield, and they responded in kind. He was milder toward them afterward and they soon backed away from the tendencies he mentioned. Whitefield had less feeling than Wesley did for this kind of Continental piety and he continued to doubt Wesley's perfectionism, which the Pietists had reinforced.[15]

Religious Societies and the People

In organizing his religious societies, Wesley drew upon the Church of England and borrowed from the Moravians. Anthony Hornbeck's societies, begun in London in 1676, provided the example for the Holy Club. Hornbeck had come from the Pietistic circles of Germany to London during the Restoration, when Anglican religiosity was at a low ebb. Following his example, some forty societies appeared in the metropolitan area and the movement spread. In 1712, Dr. Josiah Woodward printed rules for society organization and conduct. At meetings a cleric expounded on scripture and there was prayer, singing, reading, and support of charitable works. Organizers hoped that members' presence and example at regular services on Sunday would revitalize the Church of England, threatened at first by Catholic sympathies of the monarch and after the Glorious Revolution by the latitudinarianism of the bishops and indifference of the people. How many of these societies were still in existence when Whitefield and Wesley began their work is not known, but presumably there were few.

At the outset, John Wesley followed Woodward's rules and led the same activities. He soon altered the structure to resemble what Queen Elizabeth had banned as "prophesying." Members were encouraged to share emotions, thoughts, fears, and spiritual fluctuations of the week with each other as well as reactions to exhortations of the minister or lay leader. Wesley quickly learned that discussion of speculative religious opinion was to be avoided; it could cause "vain jangling," separations, and decline in piety. Because Wesley discouraged controversy in the societies, Methodists were criticized for narrowness of thought. But society meetings were meant to reinforce godliness and work toward Christian Perfection, rather than provide forums for theological debate. He constantly used his power to purge the membership lists of those who backslid in behavior or grew cold in religion.

Wesley found he had to continually remind everyone that these societies were Anglican auxiliaries not to be likened to the seditious conventicles of the Elizabethan Separatists. He therefore urged regular attendance at church services and no scheduling of Methodist meetings that conflicted with them. Members should go to church whether the minister was effective or in error. He had to make this plain so often because the natural tendency of the awakened was to look to each other for emotional support and look down on unawakened brothers and sisters at church. Opposers never ceased to claim that Wesley was starting a new religion they viewed as competing with, and inclined to separate from, the Anglican communion.[16]

Wealthy Anglicans offered Wesley his greatest challenge. He was impatient yet tried to deal very plainly with them. He noted that it was hard for the gentry to enter the Kingdom and their souls needed saving too, but he didn't want to be the one to do it. From his perspective, a serious person needed much grace just to converse with great people because of their affectation and adherence to convention. He recognized that they felt confused and threatened too and blamed them, with much justification, for pressuring the clergy, mayors, landlords, employers, justices, and church wardens into denying facilities, promoting confrontations, or using the law against the Methodists. As a result, the wealthy were rare among his hearers in the Southeast, daring to hear him only once, a visit they could explain as mere curiosity. They sometimes drove away in their coaches rather than listen to such an "uncouth preacher." Even among the well-to-do who were inclined toward his message, he saw wealth as a considerable barrier to holiness and happiness. He was aware that Methodism tended to bring prosperity to its adherents, but was unsure if they would be strong enough to resist its accompanying temptations.[17]

Despite his Oxford education and scholarly inclinations, Wesley felt liberty of spirit in bringing "the Glad Tidings" to the simple and artless who were free from conflicting religious opinions. He welcomed their curiosity, honesty, and directness. He believed that God had chosen the foolish of this world to confound the wise. The poor were not in that condition merely because they were idle, as Whig theorists would have it. They were poor because they were without God, the one thing needful, and life without religion was dull, brutish, and short, the description Hobbes had offered for the masses. He felt sorry for them but never questioned the economic system.

Animated by cries of "Church and King," these people sometimes formed mobs to prevent dissemination of what they assumed was a new and subversive religion; they were purposeful, aiming to get Methodists to stop addressing large groups and leave the community. They feared social change, a threat to pastimes, and disruptions to family if a member converted to Methodism. A Methodist preacher could be viewed as a sorcerer seeking to convert them all, spreading "spiritual rabies" that would make them mad dogs. Wesley learned in this situation he could face down mobs, deal with their leaders rationally, and usually transform them into lambs of the Lord. The anti-Methodist mob was a transitory phenomenon and faded as Methodism acquired some respectability.[18]

In contrast, Whitefield felt more comfortable with the gentry and nobility. Lady Selina, Countess Huntingdon, became a disciple and gave the Awakener entree to the upper class. He was her chaplain, preaching in her lodgings and chapels. People of this class were willing to attend Whitefield's services if they did not have to go into the open air or into a tent. Some heard Whitefield out of curiosity, but others had spiritual hunger. He may have tried to remain too respectful of their position, but could still reprove their conduct. He used correspondence to reach them and sometimes asked for contributions to needy causes. Whitefield's association with the forceful countess gave some dignity to the evangelical movement, yet he was able to retain his appeal to the populace.[19]

The Influence of Lincoln County

Wesley was a native of Lincoln, a poor place where the Old Religion had lingered and Dissent had arrived late. He visited it many times in his lifetime of itinerancy, working at Epworth, his birthplace, and in the small villages of Lindsey near the Yorkshire border. He seldom went to the county's two large towns, Lincoln and Boston, or southward to the Kesthaven and Holland sections of the county. There is no mention in his journals of Alford, Anne Hutchinson's hometown.

Epworth was a hillock on the Isle of Axeholme, a small isolated town sometimes surrounded by water although the fens had been drained a century before. As a child, John watched his father, the rector, try to reach the wild fen-dwellers of the parish and knew how stubborn such people could be in resisting God's word. Later when he first visited Epworth as an itinerant, the incumbent preached against him and denied him the pulpit of his father's church. This opposition contributed, John thought, to the dull, "senseless" attitude he encountered in the vicinity. But he kept coming back to Epworth and wore them down; later the gentry became cordial. He happily reported a revival there in 1781–83 among young people who worked in the factories.

Among the northern counties, Lincoln had a special reputation for witchcraft. Wesley's father preached against belief in it, yet the Wesley household itself was said to be beleaguered by a ghost or goblin in 1716 and 1717. While young John was away at school, the parsonage was subject to strange visitations. Servants, then Wesley's young sisters, heard noises—groans, knockings, rumblings, clattering, footsteps. The dog, servants, and children were obviously scared. Susannah Wesley at first attributed these happenings to rats, as did her husband when he was told. The children sweated and trembled in their beds but gradually came to accept the existence of the goblin who occasionally gobbled like a turkey-cock. John's sister, Emilia, dubbed him "Old Jeffrey" after someone who had died in the house years before. The rector himself was shoved three times by the ghost and grudgingly tried to communicate with it. Dr. Joseph Priestley, the skeptical scientist, investigated and suggested a trick of servants or neighbors. Members of the parish had earlier pulled tricks on the rector in resentment of his strong Christian message. There still is no full and satisfactory explanation of these events.

While John Wesley claimed the whole world as his parish, his real world was not England, London, or Oxford, but the parish of Epworth, and that world included Old Jeffrey. This was the age of the Enlightenment and so traditional authorities could be accepted only if confirmed by evidence and experience. While John had not lived in the parsonage with Old Jeffrey, he was in correspondence with the family and investigated the story when he came home in 1720. He was convinced by evidence he heard and the experience of his family. Like Cotton Mather in the seventeenth century, he later collected accounts of remarkable providences, preternatural happenings, and cases of witchcraft. He recorded some interesting manifestations in the Northwest, where he spent so much time. In 1776, he continued to feel the pressure of skeptics. He wrote, "I cannot give up the credit of all history, sacred and profane, and at the present time I have not only as strong, but stronger proofs of this from eye and ear witnesses, than I have of murder so that I cannot rationally doubt of one more than the other." In 1784 he published the records of his investigation of Old Jeffrey. About the same time, he rode once more to Epworth, "which I still love beyond most places in the world."[20] Belief in witches was still alive in the Northwest, and despite his reading and travels, Wesley reflected this. He held to this belief because it made sense to him and his region. His childhood at Epworth and Old Jeffrey confirmed the invisible world. His interest in remarkable providences, cases of possession, and haunted houses never left him.

The North

Wesley traveled to the far north of England, visiting Newcastle for the first time in 1742. His success at Kingswood led him to believe that he could be as effective with the more numerous colliers of Durham. He was drawn to the colliers because they lived in isolated villages and many people despaired of them. He thought evangelism could produce dramatic results and he was right. Although he was strict and anticipated backsliding, many groups proved stable and faithful in his meetings.

Newcastle itself was a port of rough sailors as well as colliers. This was a growing town the established church had neglected and was ripe for Methodism. Wesley bought land for a preaching house and appointed trustees. He called the building the "Orphan House" (after Francke's facility in Germany), but it served many functions: a place of worship, school for preachers, and temporary home for Wesley as well as a few orphans. Wesley noted that God worked differently in different places. In the Newcastle area, grace ran in a wider stream and moved everybody a little, but was not as deep as in Bristol and Kingswood. The "very best people" were as profoundly affected as the "sinful" miners. People who cried out were in good health and had no history of "fits." Moved by the Holy Spirit, they dropped down suddenly while listening or thinking, lost strength, and felt pain. But because some could not provide rational accounts of their experiences, he could not accept their testimonies as genuine. Despite this, Newcastle became the center of Methodism in the North as Bristol was in the West.[21]

He also made Wednesbury in the Black Country a regular stop. This was a town of miners notorious for cockfighting and bull-baiting. After his first visit, the local minister turned against him and some gentlemen and justices instigated riots. There was looting and Methodist sympathizers had their houses pulled down. For a while, antinomian teachers spread the radical doctrines of free goods and free love. It was here that a woman led the mob but changed her mind about Wesley, protecting him by knocking down four men. She was subdued and almost killed. Methodists took hold here fairly readily despite the violence. In the nineteenth century, when Methodists lost some of their fire, Primitive Methodists emerged in Staffordshire to preserve the original faith, and this splinter denomination spread through the North where Wesley had pioneered.[22]

The Northwest proved to be a stronghold for Methodism, so when Wesley organized circuits, he recruited his circuit riders almost exclusively from this vast area. Of the thirty-six itinerants Wesley chose, thirty-two preachers were born in the Northwest, one came from London, and three lived in the Southeast.[23] While converts usually develop a missionary impulse, the pastoral terrain and traditions reinforced this, making these Northwesterners more willing than others to leave friends and relatives to respond to Wesley's call. Methodist itinerants led an arduous and lonely life, constantly changing their circuits and receiving less respect and more abuse than Wesley himself.[24] Because they lacked university degrees, they do not qualify as members of the Saving Remnant. But these preachers had many talents and were natural leaders essential to the movement, and Wesley encouraged them to study further when they could find the time.

Evangelicals

Whitefield toured the North when he could, usually on his way to Scotland. He tried to visit and assist the small minority of the established clergy who called themselves Evangelicals to differentiate them from Methodist preachers (see table 5-1). They were university graduates but comprised only 5 percent of the Anglican clergy, and many bishops discriminated against them. Like the Holy Club and the Methodist preachers, virtually all the Evangelicals had roots in the Northwest. While they welcomed Wesley, their natural affinity was with Whitefield.

The influence of the Evangelicals increased in the next generation when some sons of prominent Northwesterners were successful in business while living near London. Called "Saints" at the time, they were later dubbed "the Clapham Sect" because many of them lived or met together in Clapham, a village four miles south of the metropolis (see table 5-2). They lived well and were not ascetic, yet retained their otherworldliness in private. Their heritage of pastoral religion led them to

Table 5-1. Early Evangelical Clergy in the British Isles

Name	Probable Origin	Parish
Bateman, Richard T. (1713–60)	Wales	Llysyfran, London
Berridge, John (1716–93)	Nottinghamshire	Everton
Davies, Howell (1716–70)	Wales	Prengast
Fletcher, John (1729–85)	Switzerland	Madeley
Grimshaw, William (1708–63)	Lancashire	Haworth
Haweis, Thomas (1732–1820)	Cornwall	London
Jones, Griffith (1713–61)	Wales	Llangdowror
Madan, Martin (1726–90)	Hertfordshire (France)	London
Milner, Joseph (1744–97)	Yorkshire	Hull
Romaine, William (1714–95)	Durham	London
Rowland, Daniel (1713–90)	Wales	Llangeitho
Thompson, George (1704–82)	Wales	St. Gennys
Venn, Henry (1725–97)	Surrey (western Devon)	Huddersfield
Walker, Samuel (1714–61)	Exeter	Truro
Williams, William (1717–91)	Wales	Llangwrstsd

Source: Arnold A. Dallimore, *George Whitefield: The Life and Times of the Great Evangelist of the Eighteenth Century Revival* (1970), 2:310–14.

Table 5-2. The Clapham Sect

Name	Probable Origin
Babington, Thomas	northern Leicestershire
Clarkson, Thomas	Yorkshire
Gisborne, Rev. Thomas	Staffordshire
Grant, Charles	Scotland
Macauley, Zachariah	Scotland
Milner, Rev. Isaac	Yorkshire
More, Hannah	Gloucester
Sharp, Granville	Lincoln
Shore, John (Lord Teignmouth)	Scotland
Stephen, James	Scotland
Thornton, Henry	Yorkshire
Venn, Rev. John	western Devon
Wilberforce, William	Yorkshire

Source: Ernest M. Howse, *Saints in Politics: The "Clapham Sect" and the Growth of Freedom* (1951), 10–18.

continue trying to change society by changing individuals without altering economic institutions, although Britain was in the throes of its Industrial Revolution. They knew from experience that the manners and morals of individuals could be changed by exhortation. They differed from early Whigs like John Locke in being much more willing to spend their own funds to achieve their religious and philanthropic goals. They were men of the Northwest reaffirming a personal God and paying back their region and country for worldly success.

The sect was at the same time pious and pragmatic. In Parliament they generally were influential as active church members ready to act with any faction to advance their reform agenda. Evangelical concern for "soul liberty" made them fear the deism, libertinism, mobbism, and aftereffects of the French Revolution. In reaction, they pushed for human rights in the British Empire, challenging the caste system in India and leading the crusade against African slavery in the British West Indies, a struggle they finally won in 1833, providing a major inspiration to abolitionists in the United States.

William Wilberforce quickly emerged as the leader of the Clapham Sect. His convictions and talents made the reform group powerful in Parliament and among the middle class. Through him the religiosity of the Northwest—the Calvinism of George Whitefield, Countess Huntingdon, and the Evangelicals—was brought to a new effectiveness in public life. The Wilberforce roots went deep in the East Riding of Yorkshire. The surname came from Wilberfoss, a village eight miles from York. Some of this family moved to Beverly and Hull. William's grandfather had been mayor of Hull and his father, a wealthy Baltic trader, lived in that borough. This made it possible for William to be elected to the House of Commons from Hull at age twenty-one and from the whole of Yorkshire four years later.

Although little has been reported about religion in his home, a visit to his aunt, Marianne Thornton Wilberforce, may have influenced him. She was an Evangelical and tried to convert him, but his mother thwarted the attempt. This seemed to have had little effect because as a young adult he engaged in the diversions of his time and class: cards, plays, operas, assemblies, horse racing, and repartee. At Cambridge he was an indolent student. He enjoyed politics and formed a friendship with William Pitt, who was his age and a rising political figure.

The great change in Wilberforce's life came late in 1785. He was taking some family members with him on a grand tour on the Continent and, on impulse, invited Isaac Milner to come along. Milner had been an usher at Wilberforce's grammar school in Yorkshire, but had risen rapidly to be a Cambridge don. He was a large affable man with a worldly manner, and Wilberforce did not anticipate that he would be "methodistical" in religion. At Milner's urging, however, they read Philip Doddridge's *The Rise and Progress of Religion in the Soul* (1745) and the New Testament in the original Greek, discussing them while they traveled. Wilberforce became introspective, and when he felt real anguish, consulted Captain John Newton, the slave-trader-turned-preacher, who consoled him. Printed words were important, but it was the spoken words of Milner and Newton that made the difference in Wilberforce's situation.

It is noteworthy that Wilberforce's conversion occurred during the skeptical phase of the Enlightenment and before reaction to the French Revolution diminished its influence. In Britain the deistic pressure on supernatural religion was considerable, yet it did not prevail with Milner or Wilberforce. In fact, Milner at the time was one of the nation's brightest stars in mathematics and science. With only a bachelor's degree he had been elected Fellow of the Royal Society and in 1782 became the first holder of the chair of natural philosophy at Cambridge. In later life he retained his mathematical interest but gave less attention to science and more to religion. Milner made Queen's College a "nursery of Evangelicals" when he was its president in the 1790s. Among the Saving Remnant, science and reason were not in conflict with religion, even at the height of the Enlightenment.

Wilberforce's conversion at age twenty-six did come as a surprise to his carefree friends. The born-again Wilberforce of 1786 retained his charm, but was more controlled and serious. His life had been permanently altered. He was ready to study, to do the reading he had neglected at Cambridge: Montesquieu, Locke, Adam Smith, Blackstone. Eleven years later he married Barbara Ann Spooner, the Evangelical daughter of a Birmingham merchant. Afterward, he led a happy domestic life with many children, much horseplay, but strict sabbaths.

Wilberforce's power in public did not come from his appearance although it may have been more arresting than that of Whitefield. He was a small, frail man with bad eyesight and a poor posture. His talents were chiefly oral. He enjoyed and was good at lively conversation. Although his voice was untutored, he loved to sing and everyone asked him to do so, even before his conversion. In his public speaking he resembled Whitefield, for he was spontaneous and animated; his musical voice carried a great distance. In print, his words did not reveal their power. He was ecumenical and not censorious and this facilitated religious and political alliances for his reform causes. Among people who held on to their orality in an increasingly visual culture, his combination of voice and word was peculiarly effective.[25]

While the Claphamites gained prominence from Wilberforce and other lay leaders, the clergy also contributed to their growing strength. Wilberforce met Thomas Gisborne at Cambridge and they became life-long friends. Gisborne, son of a mayor of Derby, was a high-minded Evangelical who debated theology and wrote books. In his ethical writings he sought an alternative to the moral expediency of William Paley. When Gisborne obtained a living in Staffordshire, his home, Yoxall Lodge, at the edge of Needwood Forest, became a Midlands retreat for Wilberforce and allies planning their campaigns for reform in Parliament.

The Venn family was also influential with Thornton, Wilberforce, and others. As a young man, Henry Venn spent five years (1754–59) as curate at Clapham. The village was well-to-do but Venn, an earnest Evangelical, was grieved by prominent people who obstinately rejected the gospel. When Lord Dartmouth secured a living for him in Yorkshire, he found a much more receptive audience at Huddersfield.

Henry Thornton was a pioneer in Clapham and encouraged like-minded friends to move there; Wilberforce heeded his advice in 1792. He also made the shy John Venn, Henry's son, the rector of the parish. John was an Evangelical but did not emphasize God's conflict with Mammon, and his Calvinism was more moderate than his father's. Theological accommodation and the arrival of more of those from the Northwest together with Venn's popular preaching made the Evangelicals dominant by the turn of the century.

But Clapham was exceptional in the Southeast. The Evangelicals had increased to about 10 percent of the Anglican clergy nationwide; they had to face opposition from the large majority on many issues. As active Anglicans and university graduates, the Claphamites had more standing and patronage than the Methodists or other Dissenters. They were the natural descendants of the religious societies of the Restoration that had attempted to "do good" in the community.

Wilberforce and the other Claphamites wanted to arouse consciences and open pocketbooks of the well-to-do rather than provoke rebellion. He was interested in improving prisons, establishing charity schools, and protecting British agriculture. His specifically religious causes were the Bible Society, the Church of England missionary society, Sunday schools, and the Elland Society, which encouraged pious young men to enter the ministry. He believed in what the Scottish-American Andrew Carnegie would later call the "Gospel of Wealth": people of influence, acting as the stewards of society, should use their wealth to perfect the system while preserving religious and economic individualism. Wilberforce could accept some socialistic ideas if they did not come from those hostile to Christianity as he understood it. As his critics liked to point out, he was more concerned with soul liberty than economic reform. Apparently he gave away so much of his annual income early that he had to live in straightened circumstances late in life.

The Clapham reformers received middle-class support for their many causes and won their biggest victory over the slave interest. Because they came from the parts of Britain that had pioneered exploration and colonization, they had more interest in and knowledge of peoples overseas than did most other Britons. Some Claphamites were "old hands" in the empire, the affairs of India, the West Indies, and Africa and were as much or more concerned about soul liberty abroad as at home.

When the antislavery crusade began in the late eighteenth century, many religious people looked for a scriptural criticism of slavery. Unfortunately, the references were inconclusive and the strictures on slavery, moreover, were only a small cluster among many indictments of social injustice in the world. The Evangelicals brought another perspective to the cause, one that would prove more popular and effective. Instead of relying on scripture, Wilberforce rested his case on liberty, justice, and compassion. He emphasized that the Chosen People had not only been delivered from Egyptian captivity but also redeemed from bondage. Of course, spiritual freedom was uppermost for Evangelicals, but physical release was important also. Granville Sharp and Thomas Scott found this deliverance a command to godly people to show humanity toward slaves precisely because God had showed mercy to the Chosen People in Egypt.

The theology of the Evangelicals was narrowly focused, but it did create great intensity in their work for this reform. And because they had overcome their own bondage of sin, they perceived the bondage of slavery, and its inherent sin, more readily. They believed in Providence and worried that conditions in the West Indies or Africa could bring divine retribution on the British homeland through defeat in a foreign war. Although they had concern for soul liberty they did accept much of the moral philosophy of the day. Unlike less altruistic reformers, they did not use emancipation as a cloak for free trade, but nearly the opposite, using economic arguments and downplaying their religious motivation. Like the Spiritual Puritans and Quakers before them and the Victorians and Progressives who would inherit from them, Claphamites were lobbyists for the Lord but, reflecting the times, were more businesslike in organization and more willing to compromise in politics. These beliefs and tactics made them a formidable force when they entered the political arena in the 1790s.[26]

Scotland

Whitefield had a long and affectionate association with the Scottish people, visiting the country fifteen times over a span of thirty years. The first time, in 1741, he found the northern kingdom, like England, still in a spiritual trough but beginning to stir. The established Presbyterian church was paying lip service to the Westminster Confession of 1648 but the life of the spirit had grown cold. Calvinism had degenerated into fatalism and discipline had weakened. The Moderate party had come to dominate the church, reflecting the Enlightenment and paralleling the latitudinarianism of the Church of England.

Scotland had strong roots in scripture, however. Scots still read the Bible in their homes, and religious societies kept alive the hope for revival. Its first signs came with the reprinting of a Puritan work, *The Marrow of Puritan Divinity*, in 1718, which advocated direct personal preaching to everyone. The Moderates denounced this as universalism, but the small evangelical faction hailed it as true Calvinism. These evangelicals, allied with the religious societies, laid the groundwork for the revival in Scotland.

The Moderate-evangelical conflict led to an open schism and the formation of the Associated Presbytery in Scotland. The leaders of this faction, the Erskine brothers, pioneered open air preaching and were the first to invite Whitefield to their country. They hoped to make this already famous preacher a partisan of their schism and new presbytery. But Whitefield was characteristically ecumenical and refused to take sides in what he thought was primarily an argument over the form of church government. Instead of siding with the Erskines or others who had invited him, he said he came to Scotland as an occasional preacher to appeal to "anyone who would hear me."

The Awakener spent about three months in Scotland the first time. He was surprised by rustling in the pews after he announced his text; hearers were turning the pages of their Bibles. Using Edinburgh as his base, he visited Perth, Dundee, Glasgow, and Aberdeen. He planted seeds on the first visit, returning later to reap the "harvest." Seeds in the villages of Cambuslang and Kilsyth sprouted spectacularly in February 1742, when the orthodox local pastors, William McCulloch and James Robe, began to preach the New Birth. Their flocks responded several months later. Hundreds of hearers, about 20 percent, were affected and swooned, including stout men. Emphasis on love as well as the terrors of the law got results. When Whitefield arrived in June, he claimed these reactions were greater than any he had seen elsewhere in Britain or the colonies. At Cambuslang there were over three thousand communicants and it took from dawn to dusk to administer the sacrament, despite the fact that ministers worked hard to separate the wheat from the chaff, issuing tokens only to those whose faith appeared to be sincere and strong. Later New Lights would argue that it was the Holy Spirit responding to sacred doctrine, not the talents of McCulloch and Robe, that brought this about. It could also be viewed as a true revival because the preachers recalled hearers to the Reformation, when Scotland was second only to Geneva in its support of the Calvinist system. New Lights in New England drew inspiration from these events. The Reverend James Hamilton provided a detailed account to the *Christian History* in Massachusetts.[27]

Wesley did not travel to Scotland until 1751. He noted that his Scottish auditors listened like statues. Whitefield thought that it was because Wesley's Arminianism was too well known in Scotland by this time. Whereas people in the North of England were relatively creedless, the Scots were well versed in Calvinism and therefore found Whitefield's evangelism more to their liking. Despite this, Wesley revisited Scotland, prescribing more field preaching to overcome this resistance and insisting that he would treat the Scots no differently than the English. There was an obstacle to setting up Methodist circuits because the Scots were already well organized religiously and opposed itinerancy. Moreover, Wesley converts in Scotland never regarded themselves as members of the Church of England because the Anglican clergy refused them the sacraments. Wesley finally ordained his own ministers there, following the precedent in the colonies. Perhaps because of this separation, the Wesleyans constituted only a small supplementary force of evangelism. In 1826, Adam Clarke concluded that Wesleyanism made real headway only in the two large towns of Glasgow and Edinburgh.[28]

Wales

In Wales early in the eighteenth century, Calvinism was still evident among both Church of England people and Dissenters. The Puritanism and Dissent of England had by-passed many parts of the principality in the seventeeth century, but both were arriving in the 1730s. This was frontier territory, religiously speaking, when Griffith Jones and Daniel Rowland pioneered itinerant evangelism. Howell Harris, Whitefield, and others were able to build on this base several decades later.

Whitefield's connections with Wales were many. He belonged to Pembroke College at Oxford and after joining the Holy Club, gained a patron, Sir John Phillip of Picton Castle, who provided him with twenty pounds. Phillip had been praying for a religious revival in Wales for a long time. He died in 1737, however, before the Methodist Revival was underway. Whitefield heard about the earlier work of Howell Harris and wrote him in 1738. He learned that Harris, a Welshman, had been converted just a few weeks after himself and had been preaching outdoors for three years. After his conversion, Harris had gone to Oxford but found the university too complacent and immoral for an evangelical Christian. Returning home, he started preaching in the open as an unordained itinerant. Whitefield and Harris found they had much in common when they met in 1739 and became friends. Indeed, when the Awakener decided he needed a wife, Harris encouraged him to court Elizabeth James, a Welsh widow in her thirties, and Whitefield married her in 1741. She owned a house at Trevecca on the west coast of Wales. Harris later organized a religious "family" there.

On his first visit, Whitefield noted that the Welsh people were ripe for his efforts. Whitefield described them as "sweetly disposed to the Gospel." "People make nothing of coming twenty miles to hear a sermon, and great numbers there are who have not only been hearers, but doers also of the Word." Whitefield found his power was in the spoken word, not the printed; hymns and spontaneous prayers were far more popular in Wales than prose or written sermons. Harris and Whitefield agreed on a Calvinistic emphasis in their preaching so some thirty societies looked to them rather than Wesley for guidance, and

Whitefield became moderator of the Welsh Calvinistic Methodists in 1743. He did have some organizational ability, but not the talent of John Wesley in such matters.[29]

Wesley visited Wales more often than Whitefield, making fifty-three trips between 1739 and 1790, the last within a year of his death in 1791. He first went to Wales not to launch a movement but to unite forces with Howell Harris. He went where Harris suggested and expounded to small groups—open and closed, Anglican and Dissenter—that had already been stirred by evangelism. Harris had preached in his native tongue since 1735, and Wales was tilting toward his brand of evangelism, but Wesley nevertheless found some people friendly to his message. Marmaduke Gwynne, a large landowner, befriended Wesley early and later his daughter married John's brother Charles.

Wesley knew beforehand about the lack of organized religion in Wales, but was surprised that one place resisted his long-term efforts: the anglicized county of Pembroke. In contrast to the rest of Wales, Puritanism had been quite evident in the anglicized county of Pembroke in the seventeenth century. But Wesley found the people cold and careless, coming to church dancing and laughing as if to a playhouse. Despite many visits and much exhortation, Pembroke's Methodist societies and preaching places languished. And Howell Davies, the Evangelical "Apostle of Pembroke," attacked Wesley's helpers for their Arminianism, gathering in what serious, susceptible folk there were in the county. This Puritan enclave, like Southeast England, was not very responsive to Methodism in the eighteenth century.

From the beginning, Wesley's efforts in Wales suffered from his failure to study the Welsh language or employ native speakers as helpers. While many people could understand English without speaking it themselves, in some places local leaders had to repeat Wesley's words to everyone. Wesley was further criticized for arriving late with his Arminian theology, perceived as an English import, and with inferior organization compared with what Harris and other Calvinistic itinerants had already arranged. Sometimes Wesley's aides were criticized for presenting the unfamiliar Arminian view to small groups and confusing them.

When the gulf developed between Whitefield and the Wesleyans over theology, Wesley visited Wales less often. He made only two specific visits there between 1750 and 1762, but as the conflict subsided, Wesleyanism in Wales revived. Between 1762 and 1790, eighty preachers spent a year each on circuits in the principality. When Wesley died in 1791, Wesleyans had six hundred members, three circuits, and seven itinerants preaching from Monmouthshire to Flintshire. Afterward Thomas Coke of Brecon encouraged more Welsh-speaking preachers, and Methodists grew along with industry in the nineteenth century, especially in northeast Wales.[30] Thus Harris, Whitefield, and Calvinistic Methodists were first on the scene and preferred by the majority, but Wesley and the Arminians did close some ground on them later. Together they made Methodism overwhelming and permanent in Wales.

Cornwall and the Far West

The people of Cornwall had a reputation for lawlessness and violence because of their brutality toward persons shipwrecked on the coastline and their smugglers who robbed the king of custom duties. But the Wesley brothers felt challenged by this Cornish ferocity and the weakness of the Church of England there. After successes with colliers at Kingswood, Newcastle, and Stafford, the brothers were confident that they could also convert the tinners of Cornwall. John and Charles went to Cornwall in 1743 and set up a circuit in 1746. While English had been spoken for a long time, there was little history of Puritanism or Dissent. The people gaped at them, but convictions came hard at first.

Mobs were active at the start. John Wesley was almost killed by a crowd at Falmouth in 1745, but showed poise and courage in facing them down. That was the year of an uprising in the North, and rumors circulated that the Wesleys were agents of the Stuart Pretender, Charles Edward, and the Jacobites. Where Catholicism lingered, in Cornwall and elsewhere, this charge appeared plausible because the Wesleys' parents had held High Church views, had Jacobite sympathies, and had educated their children at Oxford. John answered this talk by professing his loyalty to the House of Hanover.

After the first decade, mobs subsided and the Methodist work took hold. Much opposition came from the clergy, some of whom held government positions. Local officials impressed into the army several Methodist itinerants to keep them from preaching. Yet the Wesleys remained undaunted. Once when a minister read the Riot Act while John Wesley was preaching, he moved over three hundred yards and finished his discourse. He did complain that even members of his societies—supposedly awakened—were trafficking in "uncustomed goods." Wesley also noted that his preachers in the county were sometimes "unfaithful," lured by Whitefield's Calvinism and Evangelicals like Davies in the Church of England, though Whitefield seldom visited the country.

Within twenty years, the Evangelicals and the Wesleyans had become the most vital force and agent of change in Cornwall. Wesley made Cornwall a special target, but was troubled by a revivalism that was too emotional, pervasive, and disruptive. He had always cautioned against enthusiasm, yet Methodism in Cornwall did lead supporters as well as opponents to mob action. The excessive revivalism of Cornwall, especially in the west, has been attributed to clerical neglect, the heritage of the Celtic church, the physical isolation of the peninsula, and the autonomy of the miners and fishermen. In the nineteenth century, evangelism was stronger here than anywhere else in the realm, and Methodists by themselves constituted a large majority of churchgoers on the day of religious census in 1851. Evangelical religiosity was a badge of identity and regionalism, helping the Cornish preserve their subculture in a rapidly changing world.[31]

In the remainder of the Far West—western Devon and western Somerset—Whitefield's efforts were more important. He got an unexpected opportunity to work beyond Gloucester and Bristol in 1744. Waiting for a wartime convoy across the Atlantic, he spent six weeks of powerful evangelism in the Plymouth district and he preached twice a day, counseled the awakened, and founded two religious societies. He was particularly popular at Dock, two miles from Plymouth Town. In the evenings he and his followers came to Dock, singing and praising God. His most important convert in Plymouth was Henry Tanner, who had come to mock but joined the group. Tanner later became a minister of a "tabernacle" at Exeter in 1769. In Exeter, Whitefield converted Andrew Kinsman, who moved to Plymouth and later put Whitefield up on subsequent visits. The effects of Whitefield were also notable at Biddeford, Taunton, Kingsbridge, and Wellington.[32]

Ireland

John Wesley had always been attracted to the people and the beauty of Ireland. On each of his forty-two trips there, virtually every Protestant turned out to hear him. The presence of British officers in uniform awed the Catholics, however, who remained at the edge of the crowd. He realized that preaching in the open was especially important in Ireland because the priests had forbidden their people from entering Protestant places of worship. Wesley wanted priests to let their parishioners worship as they pleased.

Methodists were the victims of many violent episodes in Ireland in the early days. Mobs got away with more harassment than elsewhere because most Irish jurists were Catholics. Wesley believed that the Irish had a long history of tribalism, that they had changed little since the Reformation and that they were still ready to cut Protestant throats. He found that the Irish needed "stronger discipline than any other nation, being so soft and delicate that the least slackness utterly destroys them."

Whitefield made only three visits to Ireland. The first was inadvertent and brief; in 1738 his ship, returning from Georgia, was carried off course and struck the west coast. The bishop invited him to preach in the Limerick cathedral, and the Anglican clergy in Dublin treated him well. When he came back in 1751, it was as a promoter of societies Wesley had started in the 1740s. Whitefield got good responses in Dublin and stronger ones in Protestant northern Ireland. On his third visit in 1757, some men blocked his line of exit after preaching in Dublin and he was wounded in the head. Methodist converts, after hearing Whitefield, wanted to break with Wesley, but the Awakener discouraged this, trying to preach what he and Wesley had in common to avoid divisiveness. Wesley was to lament Methodist results here, and he and Whitefield were tempted to think of Ireland as the darkest corner of the British Isles.[33]

London

In London the chief scene of Whitefield's work was Moorfields, a large open area where crowds gathered to play games and watch spectacles. He preached there and built a shed to shelter his hearers from the weather. He dubbed it the "tabernacle" and later rebuilt it, making it sturdy and more permanent. Sometimes the crowds outside were hostile and violent, using fists and staves to break down the doors. The enlarged tabernacle became the headquarters of all the religious societies associated with Whitefield. He and like-minded protégés preached continually there. He also preached often at Long Acres Chapel along Tottenham Court Road and criticized the theaters nearby. The actors retaliated by ridiculing him as "Dr. Squintum" because of his crossed eye. Whitefield divided his time, especially in winter, between the tabernacle and the chapel, preaching and expounding several times a week.[34] Although it is hard to determine who attended Whitefield's sermons in London, he presumably attracted those who were evangelically inclined and preferred his Calvinistic emphasis to that of the Arminian Wesley.

John Wesley shifted his operation back to London from Bristol in 1739, where Whitefield continued to encourage him to preach in the open. At the Awakener's invitation, Wesley offered the Word to 14,000 people at Blackheath. His chief work was in the societies and Wesley's message sometimes produced strong physical symptoms, not only tears and cries, but dropping down.

Wesley soon became concerned about the inroads of Pietism at the Fetter Lane society. Philip Molther, a leader in that society, had imported his extreme perfectionism from Germany. Although he had worshipped with Count Zinzendorf, he denied that there could be degrees of faith and believed those with faith would find perfection in the annihilation of the will and passive contemplation of God. The result of this influence of stillness in the little society was that many members who had been joyful in the faith became doubtful and withdrawn, unwilling to participate in communion, and content to do nothing but lie at Christ's feet. Some did not attend church, search scriptures, or even engage in private prayer. Wesley was impatient with this and "vain janglings," idle reasonings, and other divisions in the society and gained no satisfaction from Molther. Wesley was much more inclined toward perfectionism than Whitefield, but could not accept Molther's doctrines and their results at Fetter Lane.[35]

Aware that stillness had already claimed a majority in the society and believing that God's ordinations must be performed, Wesley led a separation of nineteen persons. He soon formed a new society in Moorfields near Whitefield's tabernacle. Wesley purchased and renovated what came to be known as the Foundry. It could seat fifteen hundred on plain benches, and there were classrooms and living quarters attached. His new society began with twenty-five brothers and forty-seven sisters. These figures are a reminder that Wesley in his early society work attracted more females than males, in contrast to the New Light pastors in New England. Three years later, Wesley counted 1,100 in his societies in the London vicinity. For the rest of his life, while wintering in London, he checked the society lists, removing those of doubtful character that could hinder the holy enterprise. Later Wesley would bring to the Foundry several of his best preachers. Although denied access to the city's churches for a long time, Wesley's perseverance, longevity, and growing respectability caused them finally to open up to him in the 1780s.[36]

Thus the evangelically inclined in London could choose between Whitefield and Wesley. Whitefield's mannerisms were easier to imitate. Wesley was better at using his presence to silence and even convert workers who had been drawn to hear him by their curiosity and vulnerability. Whitefield and Wesley had somewhat different constituencies, but their effects were often similar. Wesley did suffer from defections to the Moravians. In the beginning the metropolis seemed more important to Wesley than Whitefield but was less so after he had traveled widely, organized well, and the population shift to the North was under way.

The Southeast

The Southeast did not lend itself readily to evangelism, Methodist or Evangelical. In the West Country, in the land of Hooker, Hales, Hobbes, and Locke, where Arminian rationalism had surfaced in the seventeenth century, Wesley made little progress even after his movement had gained some status and his journal reflects his dissatisfaction. Wincanton was the dullest place in Somerset. In Dorset, at Shaftesbury the flock was numerous but "wonderfully unconcerned." Mobbism had declined at Devizes but Methodist preachers worked Trowbridge and Reading for many years to no avail. In Hampshire at Winchester, Wesley found a "careless, self-conceited people," but at Portsmouth they "were more noble than most in the south of England." At Rye in Sussex, smuggling among members hurt the Methodist cause.

Conditions were similar in East Anglia. Yarmouth on the Norfolk coast was particularly discouraging to Wesley: "I know there is nothing too hard for God, else I should go thither no more." The religious societies were shattered by disputes of all kinds. The tradition of Dissent was also present in these counties, so Wesley reminded his people to attend church services. At Lynn people were affable but "the prospect of doing good has almost vanished." Beccles had few converts although fifty people came into the meetinghouse just to see and hear. Norwich, the large town with a history of antinomianism and separatism, was very unstable for Methodism. Despite extraordinary efforts, membership fluctuated widely there, much to the annoyance of Wesley.

The rest of the Southeast was generally unresponsive. George Shadford, a Methodist preacher, recalled that Kent seemed to be a profane place when he was stationed there. There was revelry in the pubs during Sunday services. Preaching to a half-filled house in Canterbury, Wesley acknowledged that people reproved too often for "coldness" could become discouraged. In Surrey, near London, people were curious but unmoved by his message. None were "cut to the heart." Wesley concluded that the Methodists were "ploughing upon the sand" in this part of Britain.[37]

There were some exceptions. At Shoreham in Kent, the vicar, Vincent Perronet, a pious Swiss, befriended Wesley early and let the Methodists use his facilities. His support, his long tenure, and the hard work of his daughter resulted in a small enclave of Methodist sympathy. And on the Isle of Wight, where organized religion had been weak, Methodists gained much ground.[38]

Whitefield spent even less time in the Southeast than Wesley, perhaps 2 percent of his days between his conversion in 1735 and his death thirty-five years later. When Whitefield did make a visit, he reported good crowds. After the first years of his itineracy, the Awakener no longer felt the need to invade parishes without the permission of local pastors. With fame he had many invitations and could choose where to go. These requests often came from Evangelical clergy within the established church. Sometimes Evangelical ministers—the small, resented minority—could not obtain even moderately important parishes in the Southeast and had to accept obscure livings or lectureships. Olney in Buckingham became a stop for Whitefield because Moses Browne, and later John Newton, Evangelical clerics, were there. He went to Northampton to see Philip Doddridge, a church leader trying to be ecumenical and maintain good relations with both Evangelicals and opponents. Whitefield's visits to Bath and Brighton were at the behest of Countess Huntingdon. She had built chapels on her property to bring the New Birth to the gentry and peerage. At Everton in Bedfordshire, John Berridge, the Evangelical from Nottingham, generated some revivalism and physical symptoms; both Whitefield and Wesley made several trips to this outpost.[39]

Yet the Southeast was simply not very responsive to evangelism of any kind, and when there were outbursts of revivalism, they were hard to sustain. Even in the nineteenth century, when Methodism had become a separate denomination and its members were consolidating their position nationally, much of the south coast—Dorset, Sussex, Hampshire, and Northamptonshire—remained a "Methodist Desert."[40] A generation after he began his work, Wesley's organization was still weak in the Southeast and heavily concentrated in the Northwest. Yorkshire and its vicinity was home to more than one-third of all Methodists (see table 5-3).

Of course, Wesleyan Methodists did not constitute the whole evangelical population. To estimate that, the Evangelical wing of the Anglicans, the Calvinistic Methodists, and some other Dissenters—Independents, Baptists, and sectarians—would have to be added. It is safe to say that adding them would only reinforce the sectional division of evangelism running through Britain. In the Southeast, outside of London, where the Church of England parish system was long standing, the movement had made little headway. Where Dissent had been

Table 5-3. Wesleyan Methodist Membership, 1767

Northwest		Southeast	
Yorkshire	7,226	Wiltshire	840
Cornwall	2,160	East Anglia	438
Lancashire	1,875	Bedfordshire	208
Newcastle	1,837	eastern Devon	206
Lincoln	1,462	Sussex	176
Bristol	1,064	Kent	147
Staffordshire	906	Oxfordshire	142
Derbyshire	741	London	2,250
Cheshire	525		
Wales	232		
western Devon	207		
Scotland	468		
Ireland	2,801		
Total	21,504		4,307

Source: Luke Tyerman, *The Life and Times of John Wesley* (1870), 2:608.

Note: The disparity between Northwest and Southeast was even greater than this table reveals because as chap. 1 has indicated, London was an *entrepôt* and a large fraction of its population had Northwest origins.

strong—East Anglia—Methodism was weak, with less than 2 percent of the total number of converts for Great Britain.

The face of England was changing rapidly after 1740; the transition from commerce to industry in the North meant population growth and strengthened evangelism at the expense of its opponents. The revivalists overcame early and violent opposition there, gaining acceptance and gradual respectability. Their opponents, the conservative rationalists pursuing their own interests and not disposed to itineracy, popular preaching, and missionary work, were thus less able to adjust to the population shifts industrialism was bringing. In Britain, Whitefield and Wesley complemented each other and shared religious success. If Wesley's Methodism made its converts more submissive and efficient for an industrializing society, Whitefield's evangelical Calvinism made his followers more anti-authoritarian, more open to soul liberty, individualism, natural rights, and republicanism.

Britain and the Colonies

Whitefield's early tours through the tidewater plantation country of the colonies seemed like an extension of those in Southeast England and were disappointing. Hearers were reticent and subdued for the most part, inhibited by the Anglican establishment and the presence of slavery. The Church of England, established early in Virginia, had a Puritan flavor early in the seventeenth century but took on a latitudinarian cast after 1700, as it did in the Carolinas. Therefore Alexander Garden, the Bishop of London's commissary in South Carolina, had the support of most clergy and gentry in resisting Whitefield when he came the first time in 1740. Garden was determined to maintain order and publicly questioned the Awakener's right to itinerate. Of course Whitefield claimed he was merely traveling to raise funds for the orphanage he had founded in Georgia.

Slaves were being brought to work on the plantations in good numbers, and planters wanted to emulate English gentlemen by retaining control over them. The planters in the tidewater, a white minority, worried that religious enthusiasm could lead to disorder and black insurrection. They feared the orality, spontaneity, and leveling implications of Whitefield's message. The slaves did respond to Whitefield, confirming such fears. When Whitefield set up a school for black children, planters countered with one of their own and were not persuaded by arguments that black converts to Christianity made better slaves. When English Methodists later visited the British West Indies, most of the converts were black.[41]

If Whitefield had gone to the piedmont backcountry of the South in his later visits, he would have received a much warmer welcome. When his converts, Shubal Stearns and Daniel Marshall, moved from New England to Sandy Creek on the Carolina frontier in 1755, they got an overwhelming response, especially from the Scots-Irish.

In the Middle Colonies Whitefield naturally got his best results from the Calvinists or those fallen away from that tradition but not yet in the camp of the Arminians or Pietists. Theodore Freylinghuysen, William Tennent, and Princeton graduates had already stirred many Calvinists, and Whitefield's activities divided Calvinist clerics there. The Presbyterians split formally in 1741, very early in the Great Awakening, into New Sides (New Lights) and Old Sides (Old Lights). After feelings had cooled somewhat, the New Sides reunited with the Old Sides in 1758. In the intervening years, the evangelicals gained fifty ministers, and the antirevivalists lost five. The disparity in the number and size of flocks was even greater. The former simply outreproduced opponents. Among Presbyterians, Old Siders were mostly those educated at Scottish universities, especially Edinburgh, and influenced by the Enlightenment.[42]

John Wesley never came back to the colonies after his conversion in 1738. What Wesley stood for—Arminian evangelism within the church's episcopal hierarchy, some sympathy for German Pietism and perfectionism, passive obedience to the authority of the House of Hanover and George III, an emphasis on the working class—did not fit the frontier and the Northwest folk there as well as what Whitefield had to offer. Without the presence of Wesley, Whitefield set the religious tone in the colonies, even for several decades after his death in 1770. While he could reach both workers and gentry in Britain, he was more willing than Wesley to spend time on the middle class, and the colonies were middle class from the start.

Whitefield drew his biblical inspirations primarily from Scougal and Henry, a Scot and a Welshman, neither of them Anglicans. The pastoral places on the periphery of Britain were where Whitefield cultivated his evangelical Calvinism inside church establishments and among Dissenters. In New England and among people with Northwest origins Whitefield found conditions similar in geography and religion to

Gloucester and upland Scotland and at an optimum for his message of the New Birth.

Notes

1. Stuart C. Henry, *George Whitefield: Wayfaring Witness* (1957), 156.
2. Cedric B. Cowing, *The Great Awakening* (1971), 59.
3. Frank Lambert, "'Pedlar in Divinity': George Whitefield and the Great Awakening, 1737–1745," *Journal of American History* 77 (1990): 812–37.
4. Arnold A. Dallimore, *George Whitefield: The Life and Times of the Great Evangelist of the Eighteenth Century Revival* (1970), 1:96–97, 109, 284, 389.
5. Geoffrey F. Nuttall, "George Whitefield's 'Curate': Gloucester Dissent and the Revival," *Journal of Ecclesiastical History* 27 (1976): 369–86.
6. Dallimore, *Whitefield*, 1:250, 255–57, 263–64, 2:38–40, 76, 295.
7. John Wesley, *The Journal of John Wesley* (1909; rpt., 1938), 2:112–19, 167–92, 201, 220. In 1903 Élie Halévy suggested that Wesley's Methodism, begun in 1739, transformed a rural proletariat into a docile and efficient work force, averting a revolution against emerging industrial capitalism. His thesis was that evangelical religion diverted the working class from aggressiveness in the economic world. This "Halévy thesis" is plausible and it has been obv ously attractive to British scholars, especially Marxists. Gertrude Himmelfarb has said that it remains a "historical working hypothesis." See Gerald W. Olsen, ed., *Religion and Revolution in Early-Industrial England: The Halévy Thesis and Its Critics* (1990), vii–xi.
8. Wesley, *Journal*, 4:156, 196, 313, 509.
9. William Sargent, *The Battle for the Mind: The Mechanics of Indoctrination, Brain-Washing, and Thought Control* (1957), 73–104.
10. Wesley, *Journal*, 2:79–81, 5:47, 281, 290; Anthony Armstrong, *The Church of England, the Methodists, and Society, 1700–1850* (1973), 76–80; Protestants had been adapting hymns to folksongs ("counterfeiting") since the Reformation, when Luther sanctioned it. See Peter Burke, *Popular Culture in Early Modern Europe* (1978), 226–27.
11. George Whitefield, *A Continuation of the Rev. George Whitefield's Journal* (1741; rpt., 1960), 58; Dallimore, *Whitefield*, 1:25, 184–85, 357; Henry, *Whitefield*, 37, 43, 161.
12. Wesley, *Journal*, 3:320, 4:45, 51, 53–54, 190, 357, 5:13, 81. Wesley was suspicious of Cartesian philosophy and the Continental Enlightenment generally and therefore reflected its influence only indirectly. But he drew on Locke and was an empiricist whose scientific insights were ahead of his time according to Richard Brantley, who places Wesley close to the central tendency of the Anglo-American Enlightenment. See Brantley, *Locke, Wesley, and the Method of English Romanticism* (1983), 17–19, 76–83.

13. Dallimore, *Whitefield,* 1:72–73, 82, 224.

14. Wesley, *Journal,* 2:112–19, 4:177, 222, 359, 5:58, 70.

15. Dallimore, *Whitefield,* 1:172–73, 2:325–32, 466–67.

16. See, e.g., Wesley, *Journal,* 4:177, 222, 259, 276.

17. Ibid., 3:455–56, 5:82.

18. Wesley, *Journal,* 2:315, 327–30, 336–37, 472, 490–500, 3:258–61, 265–66, 499, 501–7, 511; John Walsh, "Methodism and the Mob in the Eighteenth Century," in *Popular Belief and Practice,* ed. G. J. Cuming and Derek Baker (1972), 213–27.

19. Dallimore, *Whitefield,* 2:261–81.

20. Wesley, *Journal,* 1:273, 501, 4:358, 422; C. E. Vulliamy, *John Wesley* (1954 ed.), 245, 259. Wesley, *Journal,* 6:109, 520. See 2:299, 3:351, 4:23, 5:265–75, 374–75 for some interesting cases. See also Robert Southey, *The Life of Wesley: The Rise and Progress of Methodism* (1889), 14–18, and Marjorie Bowen, *Wrestling with Jacob: A Study of the Life of John Wesley* (1938), 40–46. In the seventeenth century, Joseph Glanvill, a member of the Royal Society, was influential in supporting the belief in witches. He was born in Plymouth and therefore, like the Mathers and the Wesleys, had Northwest roots. He opposed scholasticism and Hobbism, but admired the Cambridge Platonists. Wesley read his work a century later, seeking empirical evidence to shore up his belief in witchcraft but had to concede that Glanvill's descriptions of "astral spirits" were "stark nonsense." Wesley, *Journal,* 5:311.

21. Wesley, *Journal,* 3:13, 54–55, 59–60, 66–71, 210–14.

22. Ibid., 3:62, 74, 98–99, 225, 237.

23. John D. Gay, *The Geography of Religion in England* (1971), 150–52, 305.

24. Frank Baker, *John Wesley and the Church of England* (1970), 79–84; Thomas Jackson, *The Lives of Early Methodist Preachers* (1871 ed.).

25. This account is drawn from Ford K. Brown, *Fathers of the Victorians: The Age of Wilberforce* (1961); Ernest M. Howse, *Saints in Politics: The "Clapham Sect" and the Growth of Freedom* (1951); and Reginald Coupland, *Wilberforce: A Narrative* (1923), 2–144. See also Robert J. Hind, "William Wilberforce and the Perceptions of the British People," *Bulletin of the Institute of Historical Research* (1987), 321–35. Doreen M. Rosman, in *Evangelicals and Culture* (1984), finds that the Claphamites shared the general upper-class culture to a surprising degree.

26. Roger Anstey, *The Atlantic Slave Trade and British Abolition, 1760–1810* (1975), 184–99, and "Religion and British Slave Emancipation," in *The Abolition of the Atlantic Slave Trade,* ed. David Eltis and James Walvin (1981), 37–61.

27. Dallimore, *Whitefield,* 2:77, 83–88, 121–37, 251–53.

28. Wesley, *Journal,* 3:522, 5:15, 72, 171, 225, 457.

29. Dallimore, *Whitefield,* 1:283, 357, 402, 157–58.

30. Wesley, *Journal*, 2:292–96, 341, 505, 532; 3:29, 76, 133, 195.

31. Ibid., 3:86, 194, 305, 5:147, 7:528; David Luker, "Revivalism in Theory and Practice: The Case of Cornish Methodism," *Journal of Ecclesiastical History* 37 (1986): 603–19.

32. Dallimore, *Whitefield*, 173–76.

33. Wesley, *Journal*, 3:311–15, 337–53, 395–417, 463–86, 4:38–45, 155–83, 257–81, 374–402, 493–521.

34. Dallimore, *Whitefield*, 2:49, 149–59.

35. Wesley, *Journal*, 2:108–11, 222–23, 312–16, 326, 343–45, 363–70, 395–99.

36. Vulliamy, *Wesley*, 334–36.

37. Wesley, *Journal*, 5:294, 347, 355, 392, 393, 394, 395, 431, 437, 438, 441, 487, 495.

38. Wesley, *Journal*, 3:145, 265, 319, 448, 453, 4:89, 480; and on the Isle of Wight, 1:121, 420, 4:74, 83, 286.

39. John Gillies, ed., *The Memoirs of George Whitefield* (1838), 68, 96–97, 130, 135–36, 143, 166, 171, 179, 183–84, 187, 196–97. William Cowper, poet and Evangelical, also lived in the village, giving Olney some visibility as an Evangelical outpost. Dallimore, *Whitefield*, 2:317.

40. Gay, *Geography of Religion*, 156–57.

41. S. Charles Bolton, *Southern Anglicanism: The Church of England in Colonial South Carolina* (1982), 50–56; *Dallimore*, Whitefield, 1:511–23; Henry, *Whitefield*, 138–41.

42. Lester J. Trinterud, *The Forming of an American Tradition: A Re-Examination of Colonial Presbyterianism* (1949), 144–65. For the statistics, see p. 151. More recent figures show New Side (New Light) ministers increasing their numbers from twenty-eight of fifty-four during the Great Awakening to seventy-two of ninety-two in 1758. Among New England clerics serving Presbyterian churches in the Middle Colonies, New Light numbers rose from eleven to twenty-four, while Old Lights shrank from four to three during this period. Marilyn J. Westerkamp, *The Triumph of the Laity: Scots-Irish Piety and the Great Awakening, 1625–1760* (1988), 204–5.

Chapter Six

Spreading Evangelism:
The New Light Regions of
Massachusetts and New Hampshire

In his tours of America, George Whitefield preferred New England to the Middle Colonies or the tidewater South because people there seemed more godly and more responsive to him. Before his arrival in 1740, some ministers had prepared the way for him, inspiring and witnessing minirevivals in various localities. The term "Great Awakening" came into use in the nineteenth century to describe the powerful religious revival that reached its height during the 1740s but was actually the culmination of a long cycle of evangelism, with responses stronger and closer together than before.[1]

Whitefield's evangelical message drew some reaction everywhere he went, but was especially strong in those places that geographically and religiously resembled the Northwest of Britain, where revivalism and itinerancy were already beginning to take hold. A large majority of settlers in northern New England had Northwest origins; their backgrounds, as well as the terrain, made these people ripe for the New Light. And there was little High Church Anglican sympathy or German Pietism there compared with the North of England. The Arminian evangelism of John Wesley did not arrive in New England until the decade preceding the Revolution and would not attract a sizable following until the beginning of the nineteenth century. Therefore Whitefield's Calvinistic emphasis was not diluted and he received favorable religious responses in many places that were comparable to those in Scotland and Gloucester. Whitefield and the revival were able to arouse people and ministers of Northwest origins. The prestige and support of these clerics—the Saving Remnant—sustained Whitefield's efforts, turned convictions into conversions, and brought many religious and social changes.

Although the American Indian place names are perhaps better known—Kennebec, Kennebunk, Passamaquoddy, Penobscot, Saco, Sagadahoc—many place names derive from the British Northwest: Arundel, Belfast, Biddeford, Brunswick, Chester, Cumberland, Durham, Falmouth, Harpswell, Kittery, Limerick, Londonderry, Nottingham, Scarsborough and York.[2]

Emigrants from the British Northwest pioneered northern New England, dominating it in the colonial period. In the settled lands north of Exeter, New Hampshire, over three-quarters of the population had come over from the Northwest.[3]

James I made large proprietary land grants in northeastern New England to Sir Fernando Gorges and Captain John Mason, loyal West Country supporters of the Stuart monarchy and the Church of England against the rising tide of Puritanism and Parliament in Southeast England. Their plans for this stretch of the North American coast—site of the legendary city of Norumbega—were accordingly feudal and premodern, in keeping with the lifestyle of the few fishermen already there and retainers Gorges and Mason planned to send over. While they were never able to implement their plans and battles over land titles lasted for many decades, the region would reflect this early history.

Before the Pilgrims landed at Plymouth Rock, there were small fishing and trading stations on craggy islands and at salt marsh harbors of the northeastern coast. Adventurous men from the West Country and the Midlands supplemented fishing with trade and led a precapitalistic existence, eating, drinking, and lamenting the lack of women. To fishing and trading the men added, by 1630, exploitation of the forest, but warfare with the local American Indians kept the area a frontier for more than a century. The inhabitants were unruly and only nominally religious. They might occasionally listen to an itinerating Anglican priest, but the two that tried to stay, Richard Gibson of Worcestershire and Robert Jordan of Yorkshire, were not well treated. The settlements were twenty years old before the political and religious influence of the Massachusetts Bay Colony encroached on this sea and forest land.

After 1700, newcomers from the western Midlands augmented the migrants from Cornwall, Gloucester, western Devon, and Somerset and the Scots-Irish began to arrive from Ulster.[4] People from the periphery of the homeland settled on the periphery of New England. These pioneers came from the parts of England where farming was not intensive and settling in the eastern country did not change this. It would take the eighteenth century and evangelical religion to move the pastoral folk toward Yankee yeomanry.

To this early "Merry England" atmosphere some Northwest sectarianism was added. After the Anne Hutchinson controversy of 1636–38, her brother-in-law, John Wheelwright, was banished and led his antinomian sympathizers north to Exeter, which he thought was beyond Massachusetts Bay jurisdiction. When the colony extended its control, Wheelwright and some others moved again, settling on the Maine coast at Wells. Also, Hanserd Knollys came from Lincoln to Boston, but moved north to Dover when suspected of antinomianism. There he set up an independent church, the second in New Hampshire. His fervor brought him a pious following. But several years later an orthodox minister and Massachusetts authorities challenged his little congregational republic. Knollys returned to England, attracted by the prospects of religious freedom in the Civil War. He gained fame in London as a preacher and founder of the Particular (Calvinistic) Baptists. The church in Dover survived, but most of Knollys's followers sought religious freedom on Long Island and, later, New Jersey.[5] Thus a sectarian tendency was planted at Exeter, Wells, and Dover by 1640, and would develop later.

The influence of the Bay Colony grew in the 1640s and the Maine District came formally under its jurisdiction in 1652. Church attendance and tax support for the minister became mandatory, but church membership as a prerequisite for voting, so important at Massachusetts Bay, was never instituted in Maine. Preaching was intermittent along the coast and only one church, York, was organized in the seventeenth century. The lone Bay Colony minister invited to the pastor's ordination in 1673 was Samuel Phillips of Rowley, an early indication of Rowley-Maine affinity. Two other churches were formed before the end of Queen Anne's War in 1713: Wells in 1701 and South Berwick in 1702.[6]

Although the seventeenth was the century for witchcraft in the colonies, northern New England apparently had only a couple of court cases and the results were acquittals. This was true despite frontier conditions and proximity to American Indians, believed to be minions of the Devil. In 1656, Jane Walford of Dover was accused but acquitted on a promise of good behavior. The most well-known episode was described as "lithobolia," rock throwing in the middle of the night. Rocks coming to and fro through John Walton's parlor convinced him that his neighbor, the widow Hannah Jones, had put a hex on his property after he had refused to sell it to her. No one was seriously hurt and despite the testimony of the Waltons and the fact that Hannah Jones was the daughter of Jane Walford, the council in Portsmouth did not pursue the accusation. People in this region had suspicions about the behavior of their neighbors, but did not press them very hard in court.[7]

Maine

Before the Great Awakening, the religious atmosphere of Maine—indifference of many, dormant Anglicanism of some, and antinomianism of few—was disturbed only once. Ammi Ruhamah Cutter was dismissed from his pulpit in North Yarmouth for Arminianism. Despite the shortage of clerics in the region in 1735, the people would not tolerate overt Arminianism and finally dismissed him after repeated warnings. Cutter had been offered a comfortable post in Massachusetts, but chose instead the Maine frontier where his family owned property.

In many ways Cutter did not fit the profile of the typical Arminian. Clifford Shipton noted that Cutter belonged to a piety society at Harvard College and through seven years of residence his conduct was "flawless." Shipton learned early in his biographical research that good conduct as an undergraduate was a reliable predictor of later piety and New Light tendency. Before the Great Awakening, ministers leaning toward Arminianism did not usually make this explicit but were so labeled for neglecting to preach the five doctrinal points of Calvinism and implying free will. Cutter, however, flaunted his free will views; he was an imposing man with piercing eyes and a lively delivery. He appeared to be liberal in theology, yet evangelical in preaching style. He liked Maine and stayed on in North Yarmouth after his dismissal, serving as doctor, surgeon, and town representative.

The first Cutters had emigrated from Newcastle-on-Tyne, Northumberland, to Massachusetts in the 1630s.[8] It is interesting to note that Barbary Cutter, one of Ammi Cutter's ancestors, made a confession, or public relation, that has survived. She gave an account of her conversion experience to the pastor and church in Cambridge, Massachusetts, a town of settlers from the English Southeast. The pastor, Thomas Shepard, managed to record fifty-one conversion experiences. Barbary's was longer than most and differed from the others because she identified "the moment of vocation as a . . . distinct instant" and said explicitly that God "overpowered my heart at that time."[9]

Examples of typical Old Light clerics were few on this frontier and surfaced late. One was Solomon Lombard, who was born on Cape Cod and preached part-time while serving as justice of the peace. When he inherited a proprietor's share of land in Maine, he moved up to Gorham and was ordained in 1750. He was "notoriously unpopular" because of dull sermons, autocratic opposition to revivals, and stinginess toward clerical colleagues. Only a quarter of his flock supported him, and after several failures at compromise, he was finally dismissed in 1764. The Gorham church replaced him with a New Light graduate of Princeton. Solomon's ancestor, Thomas, had arrived in Dorchester in 1630 from Kent in Southeast England. Lombard, not Cutter, exemplified the Old Light ministers who appeared often in Shipton's biographies of clerics, but were rare, even after 1750, in the Maine District.[10]

The Great Awakening in Maine began when George Whitefield reached York late in 1740. He had come to see Samuel Moody, who had endured almost half a century of raids by American Indians and desolation to tend his flock. Moody had a reputation for otherworldliness and had been a missionary to Rhode Island. Many Puritans regarded with favor such efforts among the religiously heterodox inhabitants of that small colony. Moody's belief in the immediate presence of God and faith that the Almighty would provide usually worked out; the town did provide and he achieved unity there. By preaching extemporaneously, not neglecting Hell, and condemning vanity and evil in the community, he strengthened his position as religious leader. In his piety he anticipated Whitefield, but he was also a scholar who agreed with John Wise's arguments for congregationalism. In his journal for 1740, Whitefield described "Father Moody" as "worthy, plain, powerful" but slowed by age. Mindful of the religiosity Moody had cultivated, the Awakener preached consolation to the flock, not terrors of the law of God.[11]

Whitefield's preaching affected other ministers of the region as well. During the Great Awakening, the pastor at South Berwick was Jeremiah Wise, the oldest son of the famous defender of congregationalism, John Wise of Chebacco parish. Young Wise had served as chaplain at Saco before ordination in 1707. "The martial fire in his constitution" was tempered by "courage and resolution." He approved of New Light tactics and the revival but worked to prevent what he called antinomian "errors."[12] The results were similar at Wells. The minister, Samuel Jefferds, had married John Wheelwright's granddaughter. He was the son of a Scot who had come to New England late in the seventeenth century. Jefferds was an evangelical seeking souls and felt sectarian competition from Quakers and Scots-Irish. There were several revivals in Wells in the 1730s and one in 1756. Jefferds welcomed Whitefield and the revival but drew the line at accepting the itinerant Daniel Rogers.[13] Ardor for the New Light in the Wells church was strong in 1742 compared with the previous seven years, and the male percentage of converts increased (see table 6-1).

Daniel Rogers was another prominent New Light in this region. He had been affected by the visions of his French instructor at Harvard. The grandson of President John Rogers of Harvard, he was rule-abiding, graduating fourth in his class of forty-nine. Harvard retained him as tutor and he was called to Boston's North Church. Instead, he rode off with Whitefield, leaving students and the church behind. He itinerated in northern New England but also invaded parishes in Essex County early in the revival. Some New Light ministers ordained him as an evangelist in 1742 although Congregationalists taught that ordination was valid only over a specific church, not at large. Old Lights decried Rogers on this ground among others. He prayed at Whitefield's funeral in 1770, indicating that he had retained his evangelical sentiments even late in his life.[14]

Thomas Smith of Falmouth was perhaps the most prominent minister in Maine. Entering Harvard at fourteen, he graduated fourth in his class. He relied on the generosity of the town and church to provide him with a comfortable parsonage and he became a large landowner. In the pulpit his elocution and pathos were effective, but his vigorous Calvinism moderated after the revival. "Bishop Smith," as he was affectionately called, had to compete with itinerant Scots-Irish Presbyterians and contended, probably rightly, that their ministers tried to win adherents by exaggerating denominational differences. Lifelong service as a physician may have increased his acceptability to some less warmed by the New Light than he.

Smith had a good sense of humor and was not constrained by clerical mores, yet had a tendency to despondency and could be volatile.

Table 6-1. Church Admissions in Maine

| | 1735-41 | | | | | 1742 | | | |
	Male	Female	Total	Average per Year	Percent Male	Male	Female	Total	Percent Male	Percent Male Change
South Berwick	28	38	66	9.4	42.4	30	28	58	51.7	+09.3
Wells	22	34	56	8.0	39.3	27	20	47	57.4	+18.1
Scarsborough	6	20	26	3.7	23.1	17	19	36	47.2	+24.1
Biddeford						16	18	34	47.1	

Sources: "Records of the First Church of Wells, Maine," New England Historical and Genealogical Register 76 (1922): 192-95; "Records of the First Church of Berwick, Maine," New England Historical and Genealogical Register 82 (1928): 71-98, 204-18, 312-33; "Records of the First Congregational Church in Scarsborough, Maine," Maine Genealogical Register 1 (1883): 51-54, 4 (1887): 256-57.

Note: At Biddeford, Morrill replaced Willard and admitted sixteen males and eighteen females in the years 1742-44. See "Records of the First Church of Christ of Biddeford," Maine Historical and Genealogical Recorder 5 (1888): 204.

He invited Whitefield into his pulpit in 1745, reassuring people about the visit although he and other ministers in Maine were uneasy about religious excesses that might occur. Some merchants opposed Whitefield's appearance either because they feared disorder or disagreed with him religiously or both. But when most of them were out of town, Smith set the date for Whitefield's sermon. When the Awakener came, his words set Smith's emotions "ablaze" despite his "resolution to be calm and moderate lest people think it was wildness and affectation to ape Mr. Whitefield."[15]

Although Whitefield had become persona non grata in some places by 1745 because of New Light–Old Light divisions after the revival, his reputation and that of other New Lights were strengthened during King George's War. When New Englanders decided to make a concerted attack on Louisbourg, the French fort on Cape Breton Island, the pious commander, William Pepperrell, consulted his personal hero and houseguest, George Whitefield. After some hesitation, the Awakener gave his blessing to the expedition and provided a motto, *Nil desperandum Christo duce* (If Christ be captain, no fear of defeat). This endorsement spurred recruitment in Maine, and when a besieged French garrison surrendered Louisbourg to the spirited but inexperienced Yankee forces, Whitefield and the New Lights gained esteem. "Father Moody" of York, at sixty-nine, went along as senior chaplain. He exemplified the New Light combination of humility and violence, using his hatchet to destroy idolatrous images in the Catholic church. Not surprisingly, New Lights interpreted this victory as Jehovah's approval for renewing the Protestant crusade for North America.[16]

New Hampshire

In northern New Hampshire, the New Light was also predominant. Whitefield's audience was small and restrained on his first visit to Portsmouth, but the South Church soon responded favorably and Pastor William Shurtleff welcomed Whitefield on several occasions. Shurtleff, a descendant of William Shercliffe of Yorkshire's West Riding, was a native of Plymouth who had come north to New Hampshire in 1712. He emphasized original sin and criticized others for neglecting it, so the Great Awakening was an answer to his preaching as well as his prayers.

The people of Portsmouth responded favorably to the revival message: "Some members of the church were awakened and converted; but the greater part of the converts were persons who had very little of the form of religion before. Many of them, upon their first being brought under conviction, manifested a deep sense of their original sin as well as their actual sins, complained sadly of the wickedness of their hearts, and bewailed their sin in rejecting and making light of the Savior." The pastor cited the good effects following Whitefield's visits: a rise in family worship and sabbath observance, a decline in swearing, and charity that replaced a selfish, worldly spirit. Some had fallen off from good beginnings and others failed to progress beyond conviction, "but there is a considerable number who are exhibiting all the evidences that can be expected of real conversion to God." That Portsmouth had been revitalized would be conceded "by every unprejudiced observer."[17]

Increased church admissions and the higher percentage of male converts confirm Shurtleff's report. Afterwards, he addressed a letter to his colleagues defending Whitefield and the Great Awakening. He explained this as an "Exercise of brotherly Love" and endeavored "to preserve that Gentleness and Meekness that so peculiarly becomes our high and Heavenly profession," but criticized the clergy for "being too dull and sluggish, careless and negligent" before the revival. While acknowledging some irregularities, he was still claiming in 1745 that "a great many in one Place and another . . . are exhibiting all the Evidence that can be expected of an effectual and thorough Change."[18]

The Shurtleff influence continued after the Revolution when James Shurtleff came north from Plymouth to northern New England. According to Alan Taylor, he was the principal ideologue of the "Liberty Men" in their violent struggle with the "Great Proprietors" of central Maine. He invoked John Locke, claiming that the labor of settling families gave them "a natural and divinely ordained right to the free wilderness land."[19] James Shurtleff was an elder in Litchfield of the Calvinistic Baptist church, the denomination that had become the leader on this frontier.

Evangelical religion, revolutionary rhetoric, and frontier conditions combined to intensify conflict between agrarian "squatters" and Great Proprietors over land. Religious conversion turned anxious sinners into aggressive and political saints. In the early years of the American republic, the connection between religion and political culture was more obvious than during the First Great Awakening.

The responses of churchgoers in northern New Hampshire were similar to those in Maine, but more mixed (see table 6-2). A 1735 revival

Table 6-2. Church Admissions in Northwestern New Hampshire

	1735-41					1742				
	Male	Female	Total	Average per Year	Percent Male	Male	Female	Total	Percent Male	Percent Male Change
Kingston	47	39	86	21.5	54.0	58	68	126	46.0	-08.8
Portsmouth, 2d	7	25	32	4.6	21.9	27	36	63	42.9	+21.0
Newington	9	13	22	3.1	40.9	15	20	35	42.9	+02.0
Greenland	22	38	60	8.6	36.7	14	16	30	46.7	+10.0
Gosport	3	18	21	3.0	14.3	3	8	11	27.3	+13.0

Sources: "Early Ministerial Records of Greenland, New Hampshire," New England Historical and Genealogical Register 28 (1874): 251-56; Kingston Church Records, New Hampshire Historical Society, Concord, 139-45; "Records of the South Church, Portsmouth, New Hampshire," New England Historical and Genealogical Register 81 (1927): 419-37; "Records of the First Church of Newington, New Hampshire," New England Historical and Genealogical Register 22 (1868): 447-51; Clifford Shipton, Sibley's Harvard Graduates: Biographical Sketches of Those Who Attended Harvard College, 17 vols. (1933-75), 5:180; "Church Memberships, Marriages, and Baptisms on the Isles of Shoals in the Eighteenth Century," New England Historical and Genealogical Register 66 (1912): 141-43.

Note: Gosport was a fishing village on Appledore (Star) Island, one of the Isles of Shoals.

in Greenland had already gathered many in, so the numbers in 1742 were only moderately higher than those for the previous seven years. Members of the farming and lumbering community of Kingston, just north of the East Anglian town of Hampton, organized their church in 1725. A decade later this community was the center of an epidemic of "throat distemper" that killed the minister and his family. Joseph Seccombe was the unanimous choice to succeed him. Grandson of a Casco Bay pioneer, Seccombe had been ordained as a missionary in Maine. He resisted a basic Puritan tenet by defending sport and pleasure and his evangelism developed as he competed with the Jesuits for souls; as a result the church membership at Kingston surged. After supporting the revival early, he became more cautious but "abstained from joining the opposition to Whitefield." Nevertheless, his church admissions for 1742 climbed.[20]

The New Lights in northern New England were usually fervent but rarely excessive in behavior. An exception was Nicholas Gilman, Jr., ordained at Durham in 1742. After hearing Whitefield he became excited and triggered enthusiasm in his flock by reading a sermon by Jonathan Edwards. His sermons and prayers produced trances and visions in the beginning, and outsiders reported turning lips, awry mouths, strained eyeballs, and falling. New Light parsons visiting Durham were dismayed by the moans, groans, and cries of "glory, glory." Gilman's two sons had died young, from "throat distemper" and sublimation of grief has been offered as an explanation of his "fanaticism." He kept Durham Church in an excited state until his early death from consumption in 1748.[21]

Exeter lay right on the cultural dividing line next to Southeast territory. Its minister, John Odlin, was descended from another John Odlin, who had been disenfranchised in 1637 as a Hutchinson sympathizer, and was not a typical orthodox minister himself. When he denied Whitefield the pulpit, many in the congregation were "aggrieved" enough to break away from the church. Among those remaining on Exeter's church rolls, Odlin kept a precarious two-thirds majority, but then pushed the New Light minority too far by choosing his son, Woodbridge, also an Old Light, as his colleague. The New Lights drew off to listen to itinerating Daniel Rogers and invited him to settle. The Odlins vehemently and in vain protested Rogers's settlement and the irregularity of the new church, but the schismatics prospered, attracting a share of the town's prominent families. At the founding of the evangelical church, there were thirty male and eleven female members; twenty-two men and thirty-nine women later joined. Exeter was divided in the revival, but before midcentury and despite the Odlins, the New Light had come to prevail.[22]

Unlike the Odlins, the Old Light minority was inconspicuous and had little impact elsewhere on this frontier. Jonathan Cushing of Dover was prudently neutral. Stephen Emery departed Nottingham during a raid by American Indians and accepted a call to Chatham on Cape Cod, where his wife owned property. Proprietors from Massachusetts sent Phineas Stevens and Jacob Bacon north as ministers to the frontier. Stevens died in obscurity at Boscawen; Bacon left his post at Keene for the safer and more congenial atmosphere of Plymouth's schismatic Old Light church. Henry Rust survived in Stratham but had to endure the competition of Dudley Leavitt, a hometown evangelical ordained over a Separate church.[23]

At Londonderry, the Scots-Irish went to the trouble of importing William Davidson from Scotland. He was a graduate of Edinburgh, seat of the Scottish Enlightenment, and an Old Light. The people of Derry in the western part of this popular parish, however, supported David McGregore, who was the son of the first pastor and had been informally educated in the colony. He was an animated preacher who reported a thirst for doctrinal knowledge, greater insight, and no visions or antinomian errors during the revival. The congregation separated, and McGregore's flock grew rapidly while Davidson's remained static.[24]

Timothy Walker was the rare instance of an Old Light not only surviving but prospering a bit in New Light territory. In 1730 the proprietors of Penacook (Concord), some forty miles beyond the nearest settlement, called him to preach. He kept his sermons to thirty minutes, stressed duty over dogma, and adopted the Half-Way Covenant. Although approving of the ideas of Charles Chauncy, the Old Light leader, he rejected the Arminian label, describing himself as a moderate Calvinist. He sought to avoid controversy but put caution aside long enough in early 1743 to defend reason and warn his people of the danger to their souls of listening to itinerant evangelists. Walker managed to outlast itinerants, but the New Light was strong in the area.[25]

For those disturbed by the irregularities of the revival, the Church of England offered a sanctuary in New Hampshire. In the Piscataqua area where Gorges and Mason had tried to plant Anglicanism a century earlier, a new Anglican church was finally founded. Queen's Chapel opened in Portsmouth in 1734; it soon had sixty of the town's seven hundred families attending. Chief promoters of this renewal of the Church of England were the Wentworths. They had come with Wheelwright in Exeter in 1636, taking refuge beyond Massachusetts jurisdiction, or so they thought. Wentworth's political ambitions and continuing resentment toward Bay Colony politics and culture led him to disengage himself politically and religiously from that colony.[26]

Because of the rising status of the Wentworth family in New Hampshire, Queen's Chapel would provide political opportunity as well as religious sanctuary from the revival. But the spiritual leader church members accepted leaned toward the metaphysical, not the rationalist or latitudinarian side. Arthur Browne, an Anglican missionary, was the first rector. Browne felt the call to convert American Indians while he studied at Trinity College in Dublin. He arrived in New England in 1729, probably at the behest of George Berkeley, the idealist philosopher and dean of Derry who had come from Ireland to Rhode Island for a visit. Browne seemed quite favorable to the revival at first. He developed some doubts, however, when he saw it close up at a meetinghouse in Portsmouth. He wrote, "I have added numbers but the fruits must convince us. Some in my parish are wavering. I don't approve of every thing I've seen."[27] Browne represented a metaphysical and aesthetic Anglicanism that was an alternative to the New Light for a very few who were uncomfortable with the worldliness of rational Anglicanism. Most of his hearers in Portsmouth could be described as liturgical, however, following the sociopolitical course of the Wentworths in differentiating New Hampshire, a royal colony since 1679, from the Massachusetts jurisdiction that circumscribed it.

Although Queen's Chapel was a minor enclave of the Church of England, in other New Light areas this Anglicanism had some appeal, especially in the midst of sectarian controversy. The religion was traditional, the missionaries subsidized, and the legalism minimal. During revivals, however, the few metaphysical Anglicans could feel the evangelical undertow and, despite their tradition and respectability, might still be vulnerable if exposed to the revival fervor.[28]

The clergy of this region were warm supporters of the revival; Browne and the neutrals and Old Light opposers were few. In July 1743, after revival excitement had subsided and critics had multiplied, the clerical New Lights of New England signed a testimonial on behalf of George Whitefield (see table 6-3). This gesture of support was a reaction to an

Table 6-3. Ministers in Northern New England, 1741–44

Church	Minister	Rank[a]	Religion of Minister
Maine District			
Arundel			
(Kennebunkport)	John Hovey	36/49	New Light[c]
Biddeford			
(Winter Harbor)	Samuel Willard	*7/43*	New Light
	Moses Morrill[b]	29/40	New Light[c]
Falmouth, 1st			
(Portland)	Thomas Smith[b]	*4/21*	New Light[c]
Falmouth, 2d	Benjamin Allen[b]	3/3	New Light[c]
Kittery, 1st			
(South Berwick)	Jeremiah Wise[b]	*6/15*	New Light[c]
Kittery, 2d	John Newmarch	16/23	Neutral[d]
Kittery, 3d (Eliot)	John Rogers[b]	*2/12*	New Light[c]
North Yarmouth	Nicholas Loring[b]	18/29	New Light[c]
Scarsborough	William Tompson[b]	19/23	New Light[c]
Wells	Samuel Jefferds[b]	31/32	New Light[c]
Windham	John Wight	37/37	New Light
York, 1st	Samuel Moody	8/14	New Light[c]
York, 2d	Samuel Chandler[b]	30/40	New Light[c]
Southeastern New Hampshire			
Amherst	Daniel Wilkins[b]	29/29	New Light
Boscawen	Phineas Stevens	28/34	Old Light
Chester	Ebenezer Flagg	42/49	New Light
Derry	David McGregore[b]		Presbyterian/ New Light[c]
Dover	Jonathan Cushing	12/20	Neutral
Durham	Nicholas Gilman[b]	*14/40*	New Light
Exeter, 1st	John Odlin[b]	9/14	Old Light
Exeter, 2d	Daniel Rogers[b]	*4/49*	New Light
Gosport	John Tucke[b]	*17/43*	New Light[c]
Greenland	William Allen[b]	9/14	New Light
Hollis	Daniel Emerson[b]	22/32	New Light
Keene	Jacob Bacon	20/37	Old Light
Kingston	Joseph Seccombe[b]	37/37	New Light
Litchfield	Joshua Tufts	*9/31*	Regular Light
New Castle	John Blunt[b]	32/37	New Light[c]
Newington	Joseph Adams	10/14	New Light[c]
Newmarket	John Moody	*15/37*	Old Light
Nottingham	Stephen Emery	*9/33*	Old Light
Penacook (Concord)	Timothy Walker[b]	29/49	Old Light

Table 6-3, continued.

Church	Minister	Rank[a]	Religion of Minister
Portsmouth, 1st	Jabez Fitch	8/8	New Light
Portsmouth, 2d	William Shurtleff[b]	10/19	New Light
Portsmouth (Queen's Chapel)	Arthur Browne[b]		Anglican
Rochester	Amos Main	26/28	New Light[c]
Somersworth	James Pike	*24/49*	New Light[c]
Stratham	Henry Rust	19/19	Old Light
Stratham (Separate)	Dudley Leavitt	*13/32*	New Light
Suncook (Pembroke)	Aaron Whittemore	20/34	Neutral
Swanzy	Timothy Harrington	25/40	Old Light

Sources: Names, churches, ranks, and religious preferences compiled from Shipton, *Harvard Graduates;* probable origins come from Henry Guppy, *Homes of Family Names in Great Britain* (1890); names of signers compiled from Joseph Tracy, *The Great Awakening: A History of the Revival of Religion in the Time of Edwards and Whitefield* (1842), 299-301.

Note: Charles E. Clark calls John Newmarch of Maine a moderate New Light. See *The Eastern Frontier: The Settlement of Northern New England, 1610-1763* (1970), 288. Elizabeth C. Nordbeck sees him as a "closet Old Light." See "Almost Awakened: The Great Revival in New Hampshire and Maine, 1727-1748," *Historical New Hampshire* 35 (1980): 41. Newmarch was not a Northwest surname, and his successor at Kittery was an Old Light.

a. Numbers in italic indicate those who graduated in the upper half of their classes. Clifford Shipton explained that the faculty ranked freshmen according to the social standing of their fathers, but sometimes modified them to account for deportment and scholarship as well as dropouts. See *Harvard Graduates.* Benjamin Allen of Falmouth, the lone Yale graduate, was a native of the Massachusetts Bay Colony who came north from Bridgewater to his Maine pulpit in 1734. See Franklin B. Dexter, *Biographical Sketches of the Graduates of Yale College* (1885-1919), 1:74.
b. Probable origins or high surname frequency in the Northwest.
c. Signed Whitefield testimonial in 1743.
d. There were two kinds of neutrals, those for whom information is lacking, and those who have been so classified because they did or said things that were contradictory and offsetting. David Harlan has called this latter kind of neutral a "Regular Light." Tufts of Litchfield fits this category because he subscribed to Chauncy's attack on the Great Awakening, but later signed the testimonial of 1743 without reservations. See *The Clergy and the Great Awakening in New England* (1980), 4, 5.

earlier and smaller conclave in Boston where Charles Chauncy and his Old Lights had taken advantage of the absence of many New Lights to push through a statement quite critical of the revival. While acknowledging some excesses, the signers praised Whitefield and affirmed the Great Awakening as a remarkable work of God. These ministers, overwhelmingly of Northwest origins, made their New Light views known because of their own convictions and experimental preaching and were in accord with the large majority of hearers. It is reasonable to assume, in the virtual absence of dissent, that the congregations and the ratepayers who paid the ministers found their evangelical opinions acceptable.

The New Light clergy of northern New England were spiritual and community leaders before the Great Awakening and had a good public image. They combined piety with practicality and their competence in secular affairs was appreciated. After the revival, ministers remained in harmony with their people. They were Harvard graduates—except Benjamin Allen of Yale and McGregore—but they did not feel unduly challenged by a restive laity and were willing to share some power with ruling elders. In this region there was continuity in religion; the Great Awakening stirred people, primarily of Northwest descent, predisposed to the New Light.[29] Eastern New Hampshire along the coast and the Massachusetts border was Old Light country (see map 2). East Anglian settlers pioneered the Hampton area in 1638, and the religious ethos of eastern Massachusetts extended across the boundary, not officially drawn until 1741.[30]

The spirit of the pioneers from the British Northwest remained relatively unchallenged in northern New England for over a century, from the days of James I to the Great Awakening. Continual conflicts with the American Indians and the resultant instability prolonged the frontier atmosphere and kept the region thinly populated beyond midcentury. Protracted disputes over land among the proprietors and heirs, combined with cultural resistance, retarded accommodation to the ways of Massachusetts. In the eighteenth century, Scots-Irish newcomers reinforced the heritage of pioneers and there was also a renewed influx from western Devon and Somerset. Although Massachusetts had extended its claim to the eastern country early and proprietors were active in the development of these lands, the compact town model failed to take hold among pastoral people in the woods. This "Puritan imperialism" was not very effective in religion either.[31] When the Great Awakening came, northern New England was ready for "the Good News."

The impact of the revival in northern New England was overwhelming and met with very little opposition. Available church statistics show an upsurge of converts in 1742 and an accompanying improvement in the percentage of male converts. A large majority of the ministers pro-

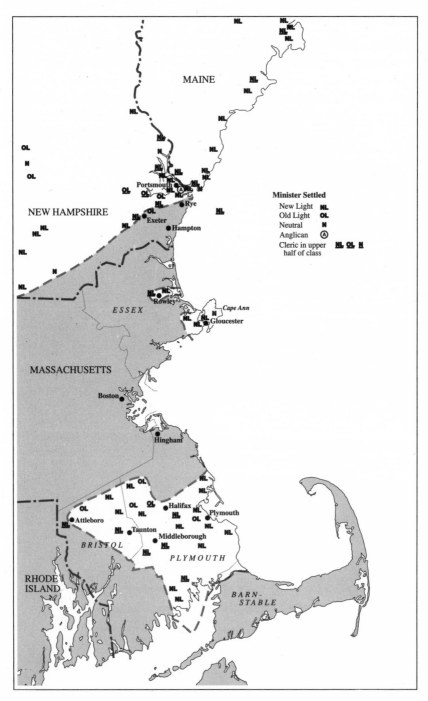

Map 2. Churches in the New Light Regions of Massachusetts and New Hampshire

moted the revival, and some offered accounts of its good effects. Nineteen pastors signed the testimonial of 1743 for Whitefield without reservations; none signed the opposers' statements of 1744 and 1745.[32] This part of New England provided the earliest seedbed for the New Light—sojourners from the Northwest were on the coastal islands before 1620—and in the eighteenth century extended very warm support for the Great Awakening. It was 1750 before Old Lights began to influence the religious culture that had taken root.

Despite their strength in the established churches of this region, some New Lights still wanted to separate; the eventual result was forty permanent Baptist churches. Converts wanted to sustain the New Light and the way to do it, some concluded, was to separate from the unawakened and uninspired. The Separates who persisted in the quest for purity and autonomy went on to abandon baptism in infancy in favor of baptism following conversion, taking the plunge to symbolize resurrection and rebirth. In Maine the Baptists founded most of their churches after conflicts with the American Indians subsided; in New Hampshire they had fewer skirmishes and established their churches sooner. Emigrants from Plymouth and eastern Connecticut, hotbeds of the New Light, stand out as creators of religious excitement and new flocks on this frontier.

During and after the American Revolution, New Lights spread evangelism to maritime Canada. The charismatic leader north of the border was Henry Alline, who had emigrated from New England to Nova Scotia in 1760. His conversion led to what has been called the New Light Revival of 1778–82. Alline rejected predestination in favor of free will. He was eclectic, combining a Whitefieldian style with Arminianism, the New Birth, the Second Coming, and gathered churches. Jonathan Scott, a minister from Middleborough in Plymouth, opposed some of Alline's views, and William Black, a Methodist itinerant, competed with him for hearers. The New Light Revival gave transplanted Yankees a new religious identity, a substitute for American nationalism.[33]

At the same time a revival occurred south of the border in the hill country of Maine, Vermont, New Hampshire, and the Berkshires of western Massachusetts. This "New Light Stir" affected Quakers, then Congregationalists, Separates, and Baptists and peaked in 1780. Baptists experienced the greatest rise in membership. Isaac Backus, the Baptist leader and historian, calculated that the denomination rose from fifty-three churches in 1777 to eighty-nine in 1782, an increase of 68 percent. Benjamin Randall of New Hampshire heard George White-field in 1770 and converted after hearing of the Awakener's death a few weeks later. He joined the Congregational church in his hometown, New Castle. It was Old Light and he soon departed, emerging during the Revolution as a Baptist itinerant with free will views and founding the Free Will Baptist Church, which was active in the Stir on the north-eastern frontier.[34]

Frontier conditions and uncertainties of the Revolutionary War con-tributed to the growing religious volatility and radicalism. Revivalism and sectarianism were continual and would increase with the Second Great Awakening. Northern New England, in parallel with its parent, the British Northwest, was ready for the religious and romantic resur-gence that occurred in Anglo-America in the 1790s. This region had yet to reach its apogee in mysticism and romanticism. Still to come were the prophets—Joseph Smith, Ellen White, Mary Baker Eddy—and the poets—John Greenleaf Whittier, Edward Arlington Robinson, and Robert Frost.

Cape Ann

In eastern Massachusetts, Gloucester was second only to Rowley as an enclave of Northwest folk and, consequently, the New Light. Cape Ann, like the Maine coast, had provided sites for wintering fishermen long before the Great Migration to New England. About two-thirds of Gloucester's pioneers came from beyond the Southeast zone, especial-ly western Devon, Gloucester, and Wales, or had surnames with a high frequency in the Northwest.[35]

Gloucester, not far from Salem, was touched by witchcraft accusations. Pastor John Emerson sent "A Faithful Account of Many Wonderful and Surprising Things Which Happened in the Town of Gloucester in 1692" to Cotton Mather. In it Emerson described strange-looking men "skulk-ing" in the swamps and cornfields who could not be apprehended. He decided that these were specters, that "Gloucester was not alarumed by real French and Indians, but that the devil and his agents were the cause of all the molestation which at this time befell the town." Mather pub-lished the account in 1702, noting that "gentlemen in the neighborhood" still believed that this was an instance of "strange descent from the invis-ible world." Yet Emerson had publicly endorsed Increase Mather's warn-ing against spectral evidence that finally ended the Salem witch panic.

In this way he reflects the typical Northwest view of witchcraft, i.e., strong belief in the invisible world but wariness of pact theory and spectral evidence in court.[36]

Early in the eighteenth century, John White, Emerson's successor in Gloucester, began to worry about the effects of the erosion of Calvinistic evangelism on the spiritual life of the town. He published *The Danger of Arminianism* in 1734, the same year Jonathan Edwards issued his more famous philippic against that "heresy." In *Christian History,* White noted two seasons of "freshening" in Gloucester before the revival: after the Great Earthquake of 1727 when converts were mostly "ignorant and wicked" and following his reading of Edwards's description of the Frontier Revival in Northampton to his flock.

The Great Awakening began in Gloucester at Moses Parsons's school in January 1742. Parsons taught school and singing, and his pupils, largely affluent, suddenly had a great appetite for the Word. They put aside diversions, even though "lawful and innocent," in favor of the hymns of Isaac Watts. The revival spread in many directions but was conspicuous among young people and black servants. There were outcries and—in the beginning—visions, but White said he worked to suppress them. "Scores who had closed with Christ but fallen away, had been anointed with fresh oil." Hearts were "enlarged, quickened," and enabled "to run the ways of God." He recalled that at his ordination in 1703, the church had 21 male and 47 female members but in 1743, at the close of the revival, the figures had risen to 160 men and 180 women, a significant shift toward greater male membership as well as good growth, considering that three parishes had been set off from the main church in the forty-year interval.

At Gloucester's Third Church (Annisquam), Benjamin Bradstreet reported "a considerable reformation in my little parish. . . . We have no divisions or separations . . . and we are without dreams, visions and trances. People have a greater desire than ever to hear the word." Noting that his weekly lectures were better attended than before, he commented that the revival was "a blessed work of God and I hope it continues."

Of the four ministers in Gloucester, three were New Lights who graduated in the upper half of their classes at Harvard: White, Bradstreet, and John Rogers. The other, Richard Jacques, although described as neutral, allowed Whitefield to preach from his pulpit in 1745 when the Awakener was encountering much opposition on his second tour of New England. Whitefield preached for all of Gloucester's pastors at that time, noting that they "were exceedingly kind" and "the congregations large." Parsons, the New Light schoolmaster, Gloucester-bred and Harvard-trained, augmented efforts of the town's clergy. After the Awakening, he was ordained at Byfield and was a pallbearer at Whitefield's funeral in 1770.[37]

This community had a history of pietistic sensibility so the revival was not very unsettling. As in Rowley, the New Lights, by and large, were prominent members of the community and were able to express their religious beliefs without challenge from Old Lights. Support for the revival came from all parts of town, not just the economically successful families in the two parishes where commercial fishing was expanding. And because black servants in harbor households were so strongly affected, the revival did bring the extremes of social order together to worship. By reasserting their traditional piety, the New Lights in Gloucester were able to react against the worldliness of Boston and Salem while maintaining their optimism.[38] The English saying "As sure as God's in Gloucester" also applied to its counterpart in New England.

Adjacent to Gloucester on the north and also susceptible to the New Light was Chebacco (Essex) parish in Ipswich township. Settlers from East Anglia with Northwest surnames moved into this district in the 1670s and 1680s, but it remained wooded and pastoral well into the next century and the people raised cattle and sheep. This was the parish of John Wise, champion of congregationalism against the presbyterian tendencies of his time. When the Great Awakening came to this town, there was an evangelical consensus among the leading families, who called John Cleaveland to their church. He was from the Quinebaug country of eastern Connecticut and descended from Moses Cleaveland, who arrived in New England in 1635 from Ipswich in East Anglia. Like many pioneer families here, Cleaveland had a northern surname; a district in the North Riding was known as Cleaveland.

Young Cleaveland had been expelled from Yale College for attending a Separate church service with his parents. As a New Light preacher he was very effective, using only incomplete notes, and in his later years stayed with Calvinism. He was not afraid to challenge publicly those ministers who were drifting into Arminian and Arian tendencies and had a revival in his church in 1763–64. Even in his later years, he proved steady in his evangelical faith, so Chebacco parish should be added to the New Light enclave of Cape Ann.[39]

New Light Plymouth

The Separatists of Elizabeth's reign, those who sought soul liberty outside the Church of England and fled to Holland, were the antecedents of New Plymouth. When the English turned back the Spanish Armada and the queen no longer needed support from religious malcontents, she attacked nonseparating Puritans and Separatists. This persecution brought an evangelical reaction and increased Separatism. True believers went into exile in Holland, where there was religious toleration, and continued to flee under the reign of James I.

In the United States interest in Separatism has focused on Scrooby in Nottingham near the Yorkshire border, because two renowned Plymouth leaders, William Bradford and William Brewster, came from that vicinity. Separatists from the Scrooby area soon gained fellowship with other religious refugees from England. Richard Clifton and then John Robinson, an ex-minister of the Church of England, were their leaders. They settled in the university town of Leyden and perfected their congregationalism. After a decade of Dutch toleration and hard work at new callings, the religious emotions of Robinson's flock ebbed.

But in contrast to English Protestants quarreling and improvising elsewhere in the Low Countries, Robinson's group at Leyden was unified and held beliefs and practices that would furnish the seeds of evangelism in America. Specifically, the Leyden church retained prophecy. On a sabbath afternoon, under the guidance of elders, members in good standing, including women, could exercise their "gifts" and share pious thoughts with the congregation. Robinson also taught that God had not spoken his final words in the Bible, but remained an interested observer of people and from time to time would provide "further light." "Prophesying" could produce further light, and retaining it during the religious lull in Leyden made an upward swing in sectarian piety more likely under the right circumstances.[40]

Like those on the northern New England coast that had preceded them, Separatists were primarily pulled rather than pushed to the colonies. They were free from religious persecution in Holland although they could not proselytize among the Dutch. As emigrants from England they were making it economically through long hours of labor, but received less wages than the Dutch doing similar work. The prospect of renewed civil war when the truce between Dutch and Spanish forces ended in 1619 offered some incentive to leave, but the opportunity to preserve their cultural identity under the English flag but not in profane, corrupt England itself proved more important. These emigrants were more pious than other members of the Leyden church and wanted to preserve their particular form of piety and polity away from the cosmopolitanism and toleration of Holland that opened the door to secularization. They sought to maintain their faith by returning to the pastoral life, by migrating to English land in the colonies.

When they sailed to New England in 1620, however, they lacked a typical element of evangelical faith. Robinson's church had not required testimony of saving grace for membership but only assent to creed and discipline. Edmund Morgan has concluded that while it is possible that the Pilgrims wished to change this requirement, it is unlikely since no evidence of it survives. He believes that Pilgrims acquired this practice from Puritans in the Massachusetts Bay Colony and not directly from Robinson's church in Leyden. The public confession, the narrative of conversion experience, was instituted after the settling of Massachusetts Bay, long after the Separatists had fled to Holland and the Pilgrims had come to the colonies.[41] John Cotton and John Davenport were the chief architects of this higher standard of membership in New England.

The Southeast clerics who first arrived in New Plymouth were impatient with Pilgrim reliance on voluntary offerings to support a minister. Therefore they did not stay long, although the colony needed religious leadership. Charles Chauncy of Hertfordshire stayed at Plymouth Town only three years before moving to Scituate. He was about to return to England in 1654 but then accepted the presidency of Harvard College. John Norton, also from Hertfordshire, disliked Plymouth mores and found a better opportunity at Ipswich in the Bay Colony. William Hooke of Hampshire spent three years at Taunton. He left for New Haven in 1641, returning to England in 1656.[42]

John Lyford was the most notorious minister in Plymouth. He had come over in 1634 from Wiltshire at the behest of the secular joint stock company financing settlement. He was obsequious and after confession of "disorderly walking," was admitted to the church. Elder William Brewster allowed Lyford to alternate preaching with himself, but Lyford was apparently a conspirator against the Pilgrim way and Plymouth government. Although he had not actually taken holy orders, he was discovered to be engaging in Anglican ceremonies and sending slanderous letters to England. He was forced to leave the colony and died in Virginia a few years later.[43]

Ministers from the Northwest, like the majority of settlers, were peripatetic but less apt to move away from Plymouth. Edmund Winslow invited the Reverend Richard Blinman and his followers to come from Wales to Marshfield; they stayed only briefly before moving on to Cape Ann and eastern Connecticut. James Keith, an Aberdeen graduate from Scotland, was successful as the pastor at Bridgewater from 1662 until his death in 1719. The "father of Taunton" was Richard Williams of Wales. He was town deputy and deacon, attending church even after he was deaf and blind. Nicholas Street of Bridgewater, Somerset, rendered effective service at Taunton until 1659, when he succeeded Hooke at New Haven. Ralph Smith served for six years at Plymouth and Roger Williams came down from Massachusetts Bay to assist him for three years. John Rayner spent a longer time in this pulpit before moving to Dover, New Hampshire, in 1654.[44]

Finding a minister for the original church at Plymouth was a problem from the outset. Pastor Robinson had stayed in Holland with the majority of his Leyden flock; this left elder William Brewster as the Pilgrims' religious leader, but he was without ordination and could not administer the sacraments. The Pilgrims were still hoping for the emigration of Robinson when they learned of his death in 1625. Then came the years of Smith and Rayner, but it was John Cotton, Jr., son of the Boston cleric, who finally gave the Plymouth church order and continuity at the end of the 1660s. He implemented the requirement of a personal narrative of saving grace for communion, following the standard developed principally by his father and widely imposed by churches in the Bay Colony a generation earlier. He preached without a script, catechized children, instructed the American Indians, and started monthly religious conferences. His "days of humilation" were successful and prepared the way for later "harvests" here.

In the first decade of the Plymouth Plantation, the small population was quite mixed in motive, region, and religion. It was not the group of single male adventurers as in northern New England, but it was not the ardent company that Ezekiel Rogers gathered into the Rowley church either. Plymouth fell somewhere in between. The protagonists on the *Mayflower* and in the history books were the Pilgrim families from Holland who sought to preserve their religious perspective. Also on board, however, were single young men the promoters had recruited in London to work the plantation. Although these men died in disproportionate numbers during epidemic sicknesses in the first few months, the survivors held and expressed varying attitudes toward the Pilgrim group. Lastly, there were those men who joined the colony later who had been sent by the company but were free of most plantation work obligations and indifferent to Pilgrim religion.

It could be argued that John Robinson had prepared his followers in Leyden for such a situation. They had learned to accept into their midst persons of varying theology and polity. Robinson taught them the need for a tolerant attitude, a good lesson for a small religious and ethnic minority in Holland. But it was largely because of this tolerant atmosphere that the Pilgrims sailed to North America; they still wanted to preserve their religious and social values. Their evangelical tendency had diminished in Holland and was not stirred that much by crossing the Atlantic. Pilgrims in this mixed multitude were content to farm and fish. They did draw a line at church membership, of course, between Saints and Strangers, and only the former could vote, but public relation was not required until the 1660s. They were congregationalists in the downward cycle of piety and therefore not as strict as the religiously aroused. Their millennial hopes and their evangelical mood fell short of the pioneers at Rowley, New Haven, and some groups at Massachusetts Bay.[45]

Plymouth inhabitants continued to sort themselves out for three decades. Some disgruntled men "on their own particular" went out on Cape Cod, others departed for Massachusetts. After boom days of selling cattle and grain to newcomers at Massachusetts Bay, and depression when this immigration stopped, Plymouth folk spread out. They had some success with fur and cattle, much less with fish, and began to concentrate on grain—wheat, barley, and oats in addition to maize. With sandy soil and little knowledge of scientific farming, their crop yields were quite low even by traditional English standards.[46] Eventually Plymouth Town, although a governmental and ecclesiastical unit, became a collection of neighborhoods, further separating the Pilgrims from their neighbors. Of those who chose to stay in the town vicinity, some 36 percent were from the Northwest and another 19 percent, many from London, had Northwest surnames. Although Plymouth has been described as a quiet backwater, a place economically and culturally stagnant compared with the Bay Colony, the period from 1650 to 1700 should be seen as an incubator of pastoral and sectarian evangelism.[47]

Plymouth Church took an important step toward revivalism when it settled Nathaniel Leonard in 1724. The Leonards had emigrated from Wales and were known for their iron works; some of them had gained status. Young Nathaniel had been a good and pious student at Harvard. In the pulpit, he had brought the congregation to accept the Half-Way Covenant at last. Then the revival changed everything.[48]

When the Great Awakening reached Plymouth Town in the winter of 1742, Leonard and his people were swept off their feet. The flock had been lackadaisical and the cleric himself slowed by "bodily indisposition and heaviness of spirit" and worried about rising intemperance. According to Leonard, who would be inclined to exaggerate pre-revival conditions, the town had been drifting into a degenerate state, with impiety and profaneness widespread. When Whitefield couldn't visit, Gilbert Tennent came from the Middle Colonies instead, preaching original sin and people's inability to respond to God's Word without conversion. His sermons received "general acceptance" and "many men, women and children" were perceptibly altered. Andrew Croswell, the fiery New Light, visited in February 1742 and the gospel came "not only in word but in power." Hundreds cried out in public. A variety of persons turned to Bible study and the old Separatist practice of prophecy reappeared. Only a few of the awakened later fell away and returned to old vices. Most converts joined churches and demonstrated the Christian virtues of sobriety and humility, although only God could know the true state of their hearts, Leonard added cautiously.[48]

The resulting shift toward a larger male congregation was dramatic, with the number of male converts rising from 20 percent of the total number in the preceding seven years to 44 percent in 1742. Leonard even accepted blacks into full communion. Leonard was assisted by a congenial neighbor, the New Light Jonathan Ellis, minister of the Second Church formed in 1739 by the Manomet Ponds part of the town. In fact, Ellis threw himself so fully into the revival fervor that some people went to church elsewhere.[50] The convicting spirit waned in 1744, but outsiders were impressed by the reformation in Plymouth Town. Whitefield described Leonard as a "humble, judicious, Minister of Christ," a downright Nathaniel who had undergone a surprising alteration in principles and conduct. He noted that "the outpouring of the spirit was not small" and he preached six times to "larger and larger auditories."[51]

In Plymouth Town, unlike Rowley or Gloucester, there was no religious consensus, however, even during the revival. Leonard, Ellis, and the awakened majority offended some church members enough to cause them to withdraw and form the Third Church. These separatists thought they would prefer an Old Light minister to Leonard's evangelism and called Thomas Frink. He took the opportunity to escape his unhappy parishioners on the Massachusetts frontier and move to Plymouth, presumably a more receptive congregation. Chauncy, the Old Light leader from Boston, delivered the installing sermon. But Frink and the new Third Church were both disappointed at the outcome. The new pastor lacked emotion in his sermons and interest in theology so instead offered long-winded historical discourses. He was contentious and too concerned about compensation.

The congregation was bored and then annoyed; Frink was dismissed after four years for lack of support. Yet the new church held to its non-evangelical course, despite the conciliatory attitude of Leonard toward the schismatics. Third Church continued its decline in membership, finally rejoining the First Church after the Revolution. This separation at Plymouth was, of course, a reversal of the usual pattern of dissident evangelicals breaking off from Old Light churches. This was the very rare case of an Old Light minority in New Light territory withdrawing and trying to fend for itself.[52]

When Leonard retired, First Church searched hard for an evangelical but respectable successor and found Chandler Robbins, a 1756 graduate of Yale. His father was Philemon Robbins, pastor at Branford, Connecticut, and his great-grandfather, a minister in Scotland. He studied theology with Joseph Bellamy, Jonathan Edwards's disciple, and was ordained in 1760, one of the first "Edwardseans" to gain a pulpit. Excellent in conversation, he was more talented in sermons and speaking and praying; he was lively as well as evangelical. Robbins was a scholar and spoke fluent French but avoided polemics, remaining practical in his discourses. During the Revolution, he was an ardent patriot and chaplain. His effort to repeal the Half-Way Covenant failed, but he inspired an important revival in 1791, anticipating the Second Great Awakening by several years. By 1795 the church had 2,500 hearers, the largest in the state, and this was the time of the French Revolution and fashionable deism.

Following Robbins's death, Plymouth's New Light persisted even after an avowed Unitarian from Harvard was ordained as his successor. Forty-two of the eighty-five members withdrew to form the Third Church again, this time on evangelical principles. When Adoniram Judson came as minister in 1802, he found only 154 persons at the Third Church and remained fifteen years until he went over to the Baptists. His son and namesake gained fame as America's missionary to Burma.[53]

The religious leaders of Plymouth from Robinson and Brewster to Judson were of Northwest ancestry while the pattern of settlement and religion remained congregational and cyclically evangelical. Thus Plymouth Town, although larger and more diverse than Rowley, managed to maintain its New Light into the missionary decades of the nineteenth century.

The hinterlands behind Plymouth Town were settled very largely by those from coastal towns and only slightly by emigrants from England after 1660. Pioneers of Northwest affiliation were in the majority here; Scotland and Wales were well represented. East Anglians were scarce, seeming to prefer the Bay Colony, Cape Cod, or the coastline.[54] This part of the Old Colony—Plymouth County and northern Bristol County—was more pious and less decadent than Plymouth Town and a bastion of evangelism in the eighteenth century (see table 6-4). Ministers from the interior, contributing to *Christian History*, did not claim real impiety or profaneness prior to the revival, but saw their people as dutiful, secure, and indifferent. God had opened the eyes of some who had built on the sandy foundation of their own righteousness, John Cotton of Halifax observed, and a few converts from Arminianism were driven by conviction and temperament to the opposite extreme of antinomianism. He reported that "the vocal opposers were Arminians, loose livers, or both and remained aloof from the revival although they circulated gross misrepresentations about it; they were utterly unwilling to examine the evidence of experimental religion," even in their own neighborhoods.[55]

Pastors reported no cases of visions and very little censoriousness; they claimed to have minimized crying out and falling down. Thirst for the Word was universal, and most persevered in holiness. Itinerants and lay exhorters did not cause much conflict because clergy welcomed assistance from anyone who could further God's work. Whitefield, Tennent, Croswell, and Wheelock, among others, were well received. Pastors exchanged pulpits to keep the interest of the congregations and further promote the revival.[56]

Taunton was the central church of the interior and the source of early revivalism. The pastor worked with youth and American Indians and also offered medical advice. Then in the course of renewing the covenant, some three hundred signers reacted strongly, shedding many tears of affection and giving Taunton a revival in 1705.[57] Later Thomas Clap served for a decade in Taunton before being dismissed. He seemed competent but was preoccupied with salary and science. The people

Table 6-4. Church Admissions in Plymouth's New Light Region

	1735-41					1742				
	Male	Female	Total	Average per Year	Percent Male	Male	Female	Total	Percent Male	Percent Male Change
Middleborough	14	24	38	7.6	36.8	86	78	164	52.4	+15.6
Plymouth, 1st	19	75	94	13.4	20.2	34	45	79	43.0	+22.8
Halifax	23	32	55	7.9	41.8	28	30	58	48.3	+6.5

Sources: *Plymouth Church Records*, 2:521-28; "Records of the First Church of Halifax," *Mayflower Descendant* 26 (1924): 176-84, 24, 117.

Note: Two-thirds of those admitted in Middleborough between 1740 and 1744 had Northwest origins. Of these 217 converts, 5 were African Americans, 3 were American Indians, but only 4 or 5 had East Anglian origins. Calculated from Thomas A. Weston, *The History of the Town of Middleborough, Massachusetts* (1906), 656-64, using Charles E. Banks, *Topographical Dictionary*, ed. E. E. Brownell (1937), and Frank Holmes, *Directory of Ancestral Heads of New England Families, 1620-1700* (1964 ed.).

resented his pecuniary demands because, by their standards, he was a person of considerable means. He was dismissed because even in this period of religious dormancy, the evangelical people of Taunton did not feel comfortable with its liberal pastor and his "clean, happy sermons." Clap returned to his home in Scituate, an Old Light community on the coast, where he later went into politics and the law.

Gilbert Tennent inaugurated the Great Awakening in Taunton with a visit in March 1741. Josiah Crocker, who was serving there on probation after Clap's dismissal, detected Arminian formality among the people and invited Daniel Rogers, who was itinerating in nearby Raynham, to come over and continue Tennent's emphasis on the sovereignty of God and original sin. Then Crocker preached in Middleborough with great effect and some people from there brought religious urgency back to Taunton. Eleazar Wheelock of Connecticut was the next visitor. He was a close, experiential preacher skilled at exploring hypocrisy and self-deception. He called for those under conviction to come forward and occupy front seats, anticipating the "anxious benches" of Charles Grandison Finney and the revivalists of the nineteenth century.

Amidst these religious stirrings, Crocker was ordained in May 1742. In November 1744 he could still describe the results as a "wonderful reformation." Few failed to evince "the reality of their conversion by preserving holiness in life," and they demonstrated a good understanding of scriptures. Crocker used his knowledge of revivals in Plymouth, Middleborough, Bridgewater, Raynham, Berkley, Norton, and Attleborough to continue the work with his flock. Many came into his church, some joined nearby churches, and some Taunton communicants were "refreshed." Crocker was a man of "considerable power," but liable to "strong excitement" often inspired by his audience. He managed another weaker revival in 1759, but was dismissed in 1765 for intemperance. Despite his disgrace, he chose to stay in Taunton and preach on occasion.[58]

Following Crocker's dismissal a strong beacon of New Light continued to come from Taunton. During the Revolution, the church and town settled Ephraim Judson of eastern Connecticut, formerly of the Second Church in Norwich. Ephraim was a descendant of William Judson, who arrived in New England from Yorkshire in 1634, the brother of Adoniram Judson of Plymouth, and the uncle of the famous missionary. He was a native of Woodbury, Connecticut, and a Yale graduate. Pastor Judson has been described as a positive person with logical acuteness. He could be stern, but was mild, courteous, and hospitable. On occasion he was exceedingly engaging in the pulpit, becoming more animated as he proceeded and arousing "deep interest." He was a typical New Light in behavior and belief.

During his probationary period he had been carefully examined on doctrines of grace and experimental religion. He was reassured by conversations and questions as well as the church's articles of faith that he and the flock were in agreement on these "interesting doctrines." Ephraim Judson believed he was in complete rapport with his church members and later said he never had any reason to believe they differed with him on doctrine. In 1790, however, a council of churches recommended that Judson be relieved of his pastorate. The council was generous in its praise of his character and discipline and found that he was indeed in accord with his flock. The council explained, however, that the recommendation had come about because of the "opposition of a few in the Society to some of the distinguishing doctrines of the Gospel, contained in the Westminster Confession of Faith." In other words, a few influential nonchurchgoing ratepayers had become insistent in their Old Light beliefs and brought pressure on the church to get rid of this Calvinistic evangelical. Judson resigned and was installed at Sheffield on the Massachusetts frontier.[59]

After Judson's dismissal, Taunton's church split more formally. Four church members joined with the Taunton Society, made up of those who paid the minister's salary, in calling a recent Harvard graduate to preach. He was dismissed in 1799 and later moved from universalism to "infidelity" in New York City. The rest of the church members withdrew to the western part of town and Judson preached for them a while before moving on to the frontier. The Westville Congregational Church, as these remaining evangelicals called their place of worship, was the site of the first Sunday school in Bristol County in 1816 and participated fully in the revivals of 1815, 1825, 1830–31, and 1838–39. Alvan Cobb, pastor from 1815 to 1861, was Scottish and fit the New Light pattern; he prepared many young converts for careers in the ministry.[60] Taunton did not abandon its evangelical tradition in the 1790s; an overwhelming majority of church members supported Judson's evangelical Calvinism and later took part in the Second Great Awakening. Response to the Great Awakening was obviously good in this part of the Old Colony. Three quarters of the ministers and virtually all the clerics born here proved to be New Lights (see tables 6-5 and 6-6).

Table 6-5. The Revival in Plymouth's New Light District

	Founded	Religion	Admissions, 1741-45	Average per Year
Coastal				
Plymouth, 1st	1620	New Light	116	23.2
Duxbury	1637	New Light	53	10.6
Marshfield	1632	New Light	25	6.0
Kingston	1717	New Light	19	3.8
Inland				
Attleborough	1712	New Light	189	37.8
Middleborough, 1st	1694	New Light	174	34.8
Halifax	1734	New Light	87	17.4
Rochester, 1st	1703	New Light	83	16.6
Bridgewater, 2d	1723	New Light	71	14.2
Bridgewater, 4th	1740	New Light	71	14.2
Abington	1712	Old Light	70	14.0
Raynham	1731	New Light	66	13.2
Norton	1712	Old Light	62	12.4
Berkley	1737	New Light	60	12.0
Rochester, 2d	1737	New Light	48	9.6

Source: John Michael Bumsted, "The Pilgrims' Progress: The Ecclesiastical History of the Old Colony, 1620-1775" (Ph.D. diss., Brown University, 1965), 438.

Note: The combined average number of admissions per year was 16.0.

Table 6-6. Ministers in Plymouth's New Light District, 1741–44

Church	Minister	Rank[a]	Religion of Minister
Abington	Samuel Brown[b]	9/10	Old Light[d]
Attleborough	Habijah Weld	*18/42*	New Light[c]
Berkley	Samuel Tobey[b]	25/39	New Light[c]
Bridgewater	John Shaw[b]	22/28	New Light[c]
Bridgewater, East	John Angier	*2/21*	Old Light[d]
Bridgewater, West	Daniel Perkins[b]	15/17	Regular Light[d]
Brockton	John Porter	29/31	New Light[c]
Carver	Othniel Campbell[b]	37/49	New Light[c]
Duxbury	Samuel Veazie	28/31	New Light[c]
Easton	Solomon Prentice	31/37	New Light[c]
Halifax	John Cotton[b]	*7/33*	New Light[c]

Table 6-6, continued.

Church	Minister	Rank[a]	Religion of Minister
Kingston	Thaddeus Maccarty[b]	20/32	New Light[c]
Lakeville	Benjamin Ruggles	*1/14*	New Light[c]
Marshfield	Samuel Hill	38/40	New Light[c]
Marshfield, North	Atherton Wales[b]	27/34	New Light
Middleborough	Peter Thacher	*3/7*	New Light[c]
Norton	Joseph Avery	6/7	Old Light[d]
Plymouth, 1st	Nathaniel Leonard[b]	22/27	New Light[c]
Plymouth, 2d (Manomet)	Jonathan Ellis[b]	31/38	New Light[c]
Plymouth, 3d	Thomas Frink	29/38	Old Light
Plympton	Jonathan Parker	21/34	New Light[c]
Raynham	John Wales[b]	48/49	New Light[c]
Rochester, 1st	Timothy Ruggles	10/19	Neutral
Rochester, 2d	Ivory Hovey	35/40	New Light[c]
Taunton	Josiah Crocker[b]	*11/37*	New Light[c]
Wareham	Roland Thacher	*12/39*	New Light

Sources: Names, churches, and religious preferences compiled from Shipton, *Harvard Graduates,* and Dexter, *Yale Graduates;* probable origins come from Guppy, *Homes;* ranks compiled from Dexter, *Yale Graduates,* and Shipton, *Harvard Graduates;* distinctions between neutrals come from Harlan, *Clergy,* 4, 5; names of signers compiled from Tracy, *Great Awakening,* 299-301.

a. Numbers in italic indicate those who graduated in the upper half of their classes.
b. Probable origins or high surname frequency in the Northwest.
c. Signed Whitefield testimonial.
d. Signed anti-Whitefield statement.

Frink of Plymouth's Third Church is an obvious exception, as is Joseph Avery of Norton. When the revival started in 1741, Avery and his parishioners welcomed the itinerating Wheelock. By 1745, offended by Whitefield's insinuations against some settled ministers, Avery signed the anti-Whitefield statement. Avery was charged with being too loose in admissions and failing to consult members about changes in church rules; as a result, he was dismissed in 1748. Avery's negative views late in the revival may have reduced the number of converts in Norton. Samuel Brown, first minister of Abington, seems to have been a genuine Old Light on the edge of New Light country. He leaned toward Arminianism, emphasizing moral living and not conversion. In 1745, he signed the anti-Whitefield statement, and John Cotton fostered a

New Light separation, albeit a temporary one. Brown died of a fever in 1749 before Abington could accept his resignation. Daniel Perkins of West Bridgewater had been pro-revival but changed his mind by 1745. John Angier of East Bridgewater was probably the most outspoken Old Light, but was bucolic and practical. Significantly, he was a native of Watertown and a great-grandson of William Ames, the East Anglian theologian of the covenant. Angier rode out the Great Awakening in Bridgewater, but New Lights forced him out of the Plymouth association of ministers.[61]

Church admissions indicate that the New Light was only moderate along the coast of this region. The revival seemed weak in Kingston and Marshfield. In Duxbury, pastor Samuel Veazie was an open Arminian before suddenly going along with the revival in 1742. Undoubtedly there were people who were indifferent or hostile to the Great Awakening in most communities, even in the interior, but this has not been fully explored. The chief conflict in this region, however, was between moderate and radical New Lights, those who questioned certain features like itineracy and extemporaneous preaching, and those who stuck with Whitefield, Wheelock, Tennent, and Croswell and accepted some excess and divisiveness as part of God's work.

Although its religious character was similar to that of Rowley, northern New England, and Cape Ann, the geography of this part of Plymouth was different. Rowley township was an enclave on the Massachusetts coastline, not a port but a town beyond the frontier stage by 1741. Northern New England was in a protracted frontier stage, much of it subject to raids by American Indians. Gloucester was a fishing port. New Light Plymouth was none of these. Settlers had developed backcountry Plymouth late in the seventeenth century. Of course, less arable land—wooded, hilly, or sandy—more suited to cattle grazing than intensive agriculture did make good seedbeds for evangelical religion in Britain and America. But people from the Northwest did not require an actual frontier to thrive and could adjust to several types of terrain. Therefore, favorable response to evangelism in New England should not be regarded as a phenomenon strictly limited to the frontier. The kind of people settling, as well as the physical environment, set the pattern for religious and social life.

Massachusetts Bay absorbed Plymouth in 1691 and the population in the Old Colony grew from 7,000 to 35,000 in the fifty years that preceded the Great Awakening. But penetration of Bay Colony institutions and mores, begun in the 1640s, was slow and would never be complete. In Plymouth, as in northern New England, people remained empiricists who wore the garments of eastern Massachusetts lightly. They could be aroused by "the one thing needful," and when they got it, would naturally incline to the beauty of union and the purity of strict congregationalism. This caused sentiment for repeal of the Half-Way Covenant, which had been adopted belatedly during the years of relative religious indifference, and failing this, some separation efforts. The Great Awakening here was a resurgence of the original Separatist spirit, a peak in the cyclical piety of settlers from the Northwest. Afterwards some Separates and Separate Baptists found the Old Colony pastoral interior, with its lack of nucleated villages and territorial parishes, inviting in meeting new religious needs. The sprouting of small Separate flocks in the interstices of the Plymouth landscape did not create much acrimony because they were filling a vacuum, not drawing off worshippers from existing congregations.[62]

Of course the revival altered considerably church membership. Most churches had gains, but these tended to be larger where the minister as well as the congregation responded to the New Light. The average age of converts dropped from the thirties to the twenties. Blacks were deeply affected; in Taunton virtually all of them were at least "wounded." Moreover, at the height of the Great Awakening, males and females were admitted to churches in almost equal numbers. This is what impressed Peter Thacher, pastor of Middleborough, most: "That whereas in the ordinary Excitations of Grace before this Time, there were more females added than Males, as I suppose has been usual in other churches; but in this extraordinary season, the Grace of God had surprisingly seized and subdued the hardiest men, and more Males have been added here than of the tenderer sex." He reported 185 males and 158 females as church members after the revival in Middleborough.[63] Although religious feeling in general had declined in Plymouth and elsewhere after 1700, among men the decline was greater. By the early eighteenth century, preaching in many churches had become instructional rather than exhortatory. The Calvinistic evangelism of the Great Awakening revitalized male laity and restored a measure of the original Pilgrim congregationalism that had been so welcome in this area.[64]

The Great Awakening also heightened the long-term affinity of Plymouth with other major areas of Northwest influence: New Haven, eastern Connecticut, and northern New England. Croswell, Wheelock, and two Yale College students from Bridgewater brought some of

Connecticut's intense New Light back to Plymouth very effectively. A few years later, Isaac Backus, the emerging leader of the evangelical Calvinistic Baptists, moved from eastern Connecticut to Titicut in Middleborough to set up a Separate church that led to eight permanent Baptist churches in the area.

From the beginning, Pilgrims from Plymouth moved up to the Maine coast, building posts on the Kennebec and Penobscot rivers for fur trading with the American Indians. Plymouth continued to provide a trickle of emigrants to northern New England that increased during the Great Awakening, and after the French and Indian War, it became a stream, with some going on to Canada. The New Light Revival and New Light Stir during the revolutionary years were, in part, the results of this migration. Thus the Old Colony contributed substantially to the reinforcement and expansion of New Light culture to the north and west, while reviving its own religiosity.[65]

After the Revolution, the Old Colony remained receptive to Calvinistic evangelism. The theological heirs of Jonathan Edwards, called the New Divinity or Consistent Calvinists for modifying and refining the teachings of Edwards, while daring to make explicit and justify their implications, found favor here. Their Calvinistic harshness was offset, however, by Edwards' optimistic "new departure" or postmillennialism that accepted the idea of worldly improvement in the thousand years before Christ's return. Samuel Hopkins and Joseph Bellamy were the leaders of this movement, primarily identified with Yale graduates. While their arguments in "paper wars" with opponents were abstract and abstruse, they could preach in the Plain Style and hold their hearers. In the Old Colony, Robbins and the Judson brothers were prominent. At a time when clerics elsewhere had lost some status, were restless, and were quarreling with their people, the seven New Divinity ministers in Plymouth together gave 244 years of service, averaging 35 years per pulpit. This suggests that church members were satisfied with their pastors, whose views provided direct links between the Great Awakening and the Second Great Awakening.

Evangelical Calvinism continued to prosper in New Light Plymouth as towns grew after 1790 and the Industrial Revolution in New England approached.[66] If sedate Arminian and Unitarian Christianity was spreading in eastern Massachusetts and elsewhere in New England, it was offset by population growth and high birthrates in Plymouth and other New Light regions.

Most people are aware of the contributions the Pilgrims made to

American history by holding their first thanksgiving feast with the American Indians, and some know that they extended their congregational church polity to civil government as signalled in the Mayflower Compact. A large fraction of Pilgrims also imported seeds of prophecy and evangelism, but this would not be obvious until the next century. These folk, although absorbed politically by Massachusetts in 1691, retained much of their character.

The New Light Legacy

In the regions of Massachusetts and New Hampshire where a majority of settlers in the seventeenth century had come from the Northwest or had Northwest surnames, a majority of churches were New Light in the eighteenth century (see table 6-7). Extant church records indicate a large influx of members during 1741 and 1742, the peak revival years. A sevenfold gain in converts was accompanied by a significant rise in the number of male members. Large shifts occurred in some older towns—Plymouth, Portsmouth, and Rowley. Perhaps males had been drifting away more in these older towns than elsewhere in New Light territory and were brought back to their faith by the strong preaching of Leonard, Shurtleff, and Jewett.

Ministers born in these parts were overwhelmingly evangelical. Moreover, because the New Light was the norm, even among "ancient" families, they were more effective and did not seem as eccentric as some New Light pastors settled in Old Light territory. For the relatively few

Table 6-7. Religion of the Pastors in New Light Massachusetts and New Hampshire, 1741–44

	Number	Percent
New Light	55	74.3
Old Light	12	16.2
Neutral	7	9.5

Sources: Tables 6-3 and 6-6 plus ministers from the enclaves of Gloucester—White, Rogers, Bradstreet, and Jacques—and Rowley—Jewett and Ellis. Religious preferences compiled from Shipton, *Harvard Graduates,* and Dexter, *Yale Graduates.*

Old Lights, the opposite was more nearly true. They were out of step and their outposts suffered from controversy, lack of continuity, and the ostracism of New Light neighbors. They tried, in most cases, to dissemble their rationalist views.

A significant number, 37 percent, of ministers supporting Whitefield and the Great Awakening were from respectable families and graduated in the upper half of their college classes, which was based primarily on the social standing of their fathers (see table 6-8). This list includes Nicholas Gilman, Dudley Leavitt, Thomas Smith, Jeremiah Wise, James Pike, Joshua Tufts, Daniel Rogers, and John Rogers from northern New England as well as Samuel Wigglesworth, John White, and John Rogers from Cape Ann and David Jewett and Jedidiah Jewett of Rowley. Ministers of good social rank were also prominent in the revival at Plymouth. Virtually all were Harvard graduates, but if they missed collegiate Cambridge and metropolitan Boston in some ways, they had as compensation the potential of strong response to their ministerial efforts, working near home and among people they understood. This combination of respectability, good education, and connection with important families turned this group of ministers into the Saving Remnant ready to use cyclical opportunities to expand piety and evangelism in New England.

In contrast, other ministers in these parts had proportionately fewer representatives of good social standing. Presumably higher ranking Old Lights were usually able to obtain more compatible posts in eastern Massachusetts, the heart of Old Light territory.

The religious evolution of Massachusetts and New Hampshire has been explored to confirm the geographic pattern. Most early emigrants from the Northwest had not been aroused by Spiritual Puritanism before they arrived. The Rogers company at Rowley and a few families

Table 6-8. Class Rank of Ministers in New Light Massachusetts and New Hampshire

Rank at Graduation	New Light	Old Light/Neutral
Upper half of class	20 (37.0%)	4 (21.1%)
Lower half of class	34 (63.0%)	15 (78.9%)

Sources: Tables 6-3 and 6-6. Ranks for ministers in Gloucester and Rowley enclaves from Shipton, *Harvard Graduates.*

in the Pilgrim party were exceptions, although the latter seemed quietistic after years in Holland. There was a sorting out in this territory, with some Southeast people moving out, some Northwest people moving in, and the evangelical tendency of the pastoral population relatively dormant in the seventeenth century. In the meantime, before the Awakening there were lingering signs of "Merry England" in northern New England and some apathy in Plymouth.

Once the New Light swept over these areas, however, they would not be so quiet again. Between the First Great Awakening and the Second, there were strong links in ancestry and geography as well as mood and method. Although rationalist religion appeared in northern New England and the Old Colony after 1750, what should be stressed is the continuity and the persistence of cyclical New Light and otherworldliness during the years of the American and French revolutions. After the New Light Stir, these parts of New England were prepared to follow their heritage and embrace the more general romantic and religious resurgence that occurred in the 1790s in Great Britain and the United States.

Notes

1. Cedric B. Cowing, "Sex and Preaching in the Great Awakening," *American Quarterly* 20 (1968): 642; Jon Butler, "Enthusiasm Described and Decried: The Great Awakening as Interpretative Fiction," *Journal of American History* 69 (1982): 305–7.

2. Ava H. Chadbourne, *Maine Place Names and the Peopling of Its Towns* (1955), 10–66, 124–25.

3. In the seventeenth century, 127 of 175 males settling were from the Northwest. See Charles E. Banks, *The History of York, Maine* (1931), 68–74; Banks, *Topographical Dictionary*, ed. E. E. Brownell (1937); and Frank Holmes, *Directory of Ancestral Heads of New England Families, 1620–1700* (1964 ed.). Ethel S. Bolton provides names and origins for another 300 people, 95 percent of whom were from the Northwest, mostly Scots-Irish for the first four decades of the eighteenth century. Thus by 1740, of 475 settlers listed for this region, over 400 had probable Northwest origins. See Bolton, *Immigrants to New England, 1700–1775* (1931; rpt., 1966). In New England as a whole by this time, perhaps close to half the immigrants had probable Northwest origins. Western Massachusetts is discussed with Old Light Connecticut in chap. 9.

4. Douglas R. McManis, *Colonial New England: A Historical Geography*

(1975), 7–9; Charles E. Clark, *The Eastern Frontier: The Settlement of Northern New England, 1610–1763* (1970), 13–35, 37–39, 44–50.

5. J. Newton Brown, "Hanserd Knollys," in William B. Sprague, *Annals of the American Pulpit* (1865), 6:1–7.

6. Calvin M. Clark, *The History of the Congregational Churches in Maine* (1935), 2:35–70.

7. What happened on the Walton farm that night has been called the work of a poltergeist. The Waltons, a prosperous Quaker family, were the victims of this lithobolia in 1682. There are two accounts in George L. Burr, ed., *Narratives of Witchcraft* (1914), 34–36 and 58–77. The first, by the Reverend Joshua Moody of Portsmouth, was included in Cotton Mather's *Remarkable Providences*. Richard Chamberlain, secretary of the colony, wrote the second, longer one.

8. Clifford Shipton, *Sibley's Harvard Graduates: Biographical Sketches of Those Who Attended Harvard College,* 17 vols. (1933–75), 7:502–9, 200–206; Banks, *Topographical,* 130, 131.

9. George Selement and Bruce Woolley, eds., "Thomas Shepard's Confessions," *Colonial Society of Massachusetts Publications* (1981): 92. As noted in chap. 1, most of these neophytes dwelt "more on preparation than on the life of faith" and "not many people openly exhalted in profound joy or sublime peace." See Charles L. Cohen, *God's Caress: The Psychology of Puritan Religious Experience* (1986), 234, 212.

10. Shipton, *Harvard Graduates,* 7:200–206; *National Cyclopedia of Biography* (1945), 32:334.

11. *George Whitefield's Journals* (1737–1741), ed. William Wale (1905; rpt., 1969), 467–68.

12. Shipton, *Harvard Graduates,* 7:356–58; Banks, *York,* 131–41. The Wise surname had its highest frequencies in the Northwest: Yorkshire (14/10,000), Cornwall (8/10,000). See Henry Guppy, *Homes of Family Names in Great Britain* (1890), 116, 573.

13. Shipton, *Harvard Graduates,* 7:83–85.

14. Ibid., 554–60.

15. *The Journals of the Rev. Thomas Smith and the Rev. Samuel Dean in the First Parish of Portland* (1849 ed.), 115–19, quotation from 119. Smith had a younger brother, John, a Harvard graduate and wealthy dry goods merchant in Boston. He was a close friend of Whitefield and a fund-raiser for the school for American Indians that became Dartmouth College. *Whitefield's Journals,* 521–22.

16. *Whitefield's Journals,* 519; Clark, *Eastern Frontier,* 288–92; Alan Heimert, *Religion and the American Mind: From the Great Awakening to the Revolution* (1966), 148–49. New Englanders generally rejoiced in this surprising victory of their soldiers. The Reverend Charles Chauncy, the leader of the Old

Light party and a zealous opponent of Catholicism, followed these events closely. Pepperrell was his brother-in-law. See Edward M. Griffin, *Old Brick: Charles Chauncy of Boston, 1705–1787* (1980), 50–51, 96–99. The Pepperrells were Cornish. William's father came to Maine in 1676 from Tavistock in western Devon and made a fortune in fish, lumber, and real estate. William inherited his businesses in 1734. After the Louisbourg victory, the king made Pepperrell a baronet, the first in the colonies.

17. *Christian History* 1 (1744): 383. Jonathan Edwards suggested that a record be kept of the revival, and several months later on March 5, 1743, Thomas Prince, Jr., brought out a weekly journal, the *Christian History*. It was designed to provide eyewitness accounts and set the Great Awakening in the historical context of the Reformation and Puritanism. Prince had prepared for the ministry, graduating first in his class of twenty-three at Harvard in 1740. He promoted the revival and qualifies for the Saving Remnant, but was never settled in a church; he died in 1748. His father, Thomas, was a New Light pastor in Boston and a historian. See J. M. Bumsted and John E. Van de Wetering, *What Must I Do to Be Saved?: The Great Awakening in Colonial America* (1976), 101; Shipton, *Harvard Graduates*, 4:550–53.

18. William Shurtleff, *A Letter to Those of His Brethren in the Ministry Who Refuse to Admit the Rev. Mr. Whitefield into Their Pulpits* (1745), 3–9.

19. Alan Taylor, *Liberty Men and Great Proprietors: The Revolutionary Settlement on the Maine Frontier, 1760–1820* (1991), 101–2.

20. Shipton, *Harvard Graduates*, 9:87–96, quotation from 95. The Seccombe surname had a significant frequency only in Cornwall. See Guppy, *Homes*, 547. From 1741 to 1745, Kingston's congregation remained, on average, 49.7 percent male despite the drop to 46 percent in 1742.

21. Clark, *Eastern Frontier*, 284–88; Elizabeth C. Nordbeck, "Almost Awakened: The Great Revival in New Hampshire and Maine, 1727–1748," *Historical New Hampshire* 35 (1980): 23–58; Clarence C. Goen, *Revivalism and Separatism: Strict Congregationalists and Separate Baptists* (1962), 103–5, 246. A number of the well-to-do were attracted to Exeter. "The Unpublished Journals of George Whitefield," *Church History* 8 (1938): 312, 338, 341. The Gilman surname had high frequency only in the Northwest: Staffordshire (18/10,000) and Derby (15/10,000). See Guppy, *Homes*, 132, 490.

22. Emery Battis, *Saints and Sectaries: Anne Hutchinson and the Antinomian Controversy in Massachusetts Bay Colony* (1962), 315, 330; the Odling surname was peculiar to Lincoln. See Guppy, *Homes*, 270, 276, 529.

23. Shipton, *Harvard Graduates*, 5:634–35, 8:707–10, 9:18–21, 10:374–79.

24. Robert F. Lawrence, *The New Hampshire Churches, Comprising the Histories of the Congregational and Presbyterian Churches in the State with Notices of Other Denominations* (1856), 41–44; *Christian History* 1 (1744): 193–94.

25. When ordained in 1730, Walker was warned that Penacook was "a place

where Satan years ago had his seat, and had been headquarters of our Indian enemies." During the Awakening, more were added to the flock by covenant than communion. Several decades later, Walker was consulted about two witches in nearby Hopkinton. He advised townspeople that "the most they had to fear from witches was talking about them; that if they would cease talking about them and let them alone they would soon disappear." See John P. Demos, *Entertaining Satan: Witchcraft and the Culture of Early New England* (1982), 388. The proprietors' choice, Walker, the Old Light, was followed by two New Lights who were the settlers' choices: Israel Evans from Princeton and Asa Macfarland, a Dartmouth graduate. The Scots-Irish Macfarland presided over extensive revivals in Concord during the Second Great Awakening. See Lawrence, *New Hampshire Churches*, 365–72.

26. Jere R. Daniell, *Experiment in Republicanism: New Hampshire Politics, 1741–1794* (1970), 4, 10, 16, 18, 63. There was nominal and unorganized Anglicanism here before 1630.

27. "Letter from the Rev. Arthur Browne," *New England Historical and Genealogical Register* 7 (1852): 264–65; the Reverend Charles Burroughs, "Arthur Browne," in Sprague, *Annals* (1859), 5:76–82.

28. For the influence of metaphysical Anglicanism and the case of Samuel Johnson, see chap. 9.

29. Laura B. Ricard, "The Northern New England New Light Clergy and 'Declension' Reconsidered," *Historical New Hampshire* 42 (1987): 125–49; Clark, *Eastern Frontier*, 69–179.

30. For this region see chap. 8.

31. Clark, *Eastern Frontier*, 12, 36–51, 81, 112, 121, 267.

32. Sixty-three pastors publicly signed in opposition to Whitefield at this time, including at least nine "friends of the revival." See Joseph Tracy, *The Great Awakening: A History of the Revival of Religion in the Time of Edwards and Whitefield* (1842), 363. New England as a whole was quite evenly divided between New Lights and Old Lights.

33. Goen, *Revivalism and Separatism*, 244–57.

34. Stephen A. Marini, *Radical Sects of Revolutionary New England* (1982), 40–59, 64–67, 86–88.

35. Banks, *Topographical*; Holmes, *Ancestral Heads*.

36. Cotton Mather, *Magnalia Christi; or, The Ecclesiastical History of New-England* (1820 ed.), 2:538–40; Marshall Swan, "The Bedevilment of Cape Ann, 1692," *Essex Institute Historical Collections* 117 (1981): 153–77. The three Emersons in the pulpit during the Great Awakening—Daniel, John, and Joseph—were decided New Lights. The Emerson surname had a high frequency in Lincoln and Durham. See Guppy, *Homes*, 483.

37. *Christian History* 1 (1743): 41–46, quotation from 187–88; Shipton, *Harvard Graduates*, 4:421–24, 457–60; *Whitefield's Journals*, 546. Jacques's an-

cestor emigrated from Wiltshire but the surname was specific to Yorkshire. See Banks, *Topographical*, 180; Guppy, *Homes*, 414, 508. Jeffrey Parsons, grandfather of Moses, arrived in Gloucester in 1654, emigrating from Ashprington, western Devon. See Banks, *Topographical*, 19.

38. Christine Heyrman, *Commerce and Culture: The Maritime Communities of Colonial Massachusetts, 1690–1750* (1984), 182–208. The New Light had greater impact on slaves in the English colonies than had Christianity before this time. See J. M. Bumsted and John E. Van de Wetering, *What Must I Do to Be Saved?: The Great Awakening in Colonial America* (1976), 133, 135, 136–38.

39. John Wise had used natural law to justify congregationalism, but the case for regarding him as a precursor of the Spirit of '76 as well as the Age of Reason is made succinctly in Cedric B. Cowing, *The Great Awakening* (1971), 18–21. Christopher M. Jedrey, *The World of John Cleaveland: Family and Community in Eighteenth-Century New England* (1979), 17–57.

40. George F. Willison, *Saints and Strangers* (1945), 58–90.

41. Edmund S. Morgan, *Visible Saints: The History of a Puritan Idea* (1963), 27, 57–63; prophesying was revived in the First Plymouth Church during the Great Awakening. See John Michael Bumsted, "The Pilgrims' Progress: The Ecclesiastical History of the Old Colony, 1620–1775" (Ph.D. diss., Brown University, 1965), 390.

42. Willison, *Saints and Strangers*, 343–72.

43. William Bradford, *Of Plymouth Plantation, 1620–1647*, ed. Samuel Eliot Morison (1967 ed.), 146–69. Lyford's name was specific to Berkshire. See Guppy, *Homes*, 518.

44. *New England Historical and Genealogical Register* 7 (1853): 276–77. John A. Goodwin, *The Pilgrim Republic: An Historical View of the Colony of New Plymouth* (1879; rpt., 1970), 534, 525–26, 358, 421. Shipton, *Harvard Graduates*, 1:496–508.

45. Willison, *Saints and Strangers*, 343–72.

46. Darrett B. Rutman, *Husbandmen of Plymouth: Farms and Villages in the Old Colony, 1620–1692* (1967), 1–27, 63–65.

47. Compiled from Banks, *Topographical*, Holmes, *Ancestral Heads*, and Guppy, *Homes*.

48. Shipton, *Harvard Graduates*, 6:324–27.

49. *Christian History* 2 (1744): 315–16.

50. Shipton, *Harvard Graduates*, 10:163–65.

51. *Plymouth Church Records, 1620–1859* (1920), 2:521–28; Whitefield, *Journals*, 536–37. Charles Grandison Finney, the revivalist of the Second Great Awakening, had English origins similar to Whitefield's. His ancestor, Robert Finney, emigrated from Plymouth in western Devon to new Plymouth before 1643. See Banks, *Topographical*, 25; Holmes, *Ancestral Heads*, lxxxiii.

52. Goen, *Revivalism and Separatism,* 113–14.

53. Sprague, *Annals,* 1:573–75, 2:22–23; *Plymouth Church Records,* 2:475–76. His son and namesake gained fame as the missionary to Burma from the United States. Evangelical traits persisted in Adoniram's talented children, but they reacted differently to the religious changes occurring in the Northeast later in the nineteenth century. The missionary's daughter became a Spiritualist in New England, the son, a leader of the Social Gospel among immigrants in New York City. Joan Jacobs Brumberg, *Mission for Life: The Judson Family and American Evangelical Culture* (1984), 145–216.

54. Banks, *Topographical;* Holmes, *Ancestral Heads.*

55. *Christian History* 2 (1744): 257–67; Banks, *Topographical,* 25.

56. Bumsted, "Pilgrims' Progress," 180–86.

57. *Christian History* 2 (1744): 108–11.

58. Shipton, *Harvard Graduates,* 7:494–98, 10:277–82.

59. Samuel Hopkins Emery, *The History of Taunton from Its Settlement to the Present Time* (1893 ed.), 204–10.

60. Ibid., 220–25; Joseph A. Conforti, *Samuel Hopkins and the New Divinity Movement,* (1981), 56, 230; *New England Historical and Genealogical Register* 15 (1861): 280.

61. Shipton, *Harvard Graduates,* 5:334–37, 7:69–75.

62. Bumsted, "Pilgrims' Progress," 220–32, 386; Goen, *Revivalism and Separatism,* 311.

63. *Christian History* 2 (1744): 99. Shipton, *Harvard Graduates,* 6:208–11, 369–70, 10:85–89, 11:231–36.

64. Cowing, "Sex and Preaching," 635, 644.

65. George D. Langdon, *The Pilgrim Colony: A History of New Plymouth, 1620–1691* (1966), 26; Marini, *Radical Sects,* 26, 28.

66. Gloucester, Bridgewater, and Middleborough were among the ten most populous towns in Massachusetts in 1790, and thirty years later they were joined by Taunton and Plymouth. These New Light communities maintained prominence in the state; in this they seem similar to northern England's industrializing towns where Methodism was so strong. See *Return of the Whole Number of Persons within the Several Districts of the United States* (1791), 23–28; *The Census for 1820* (1821), 5–7.

Chapter Seven

Combining Geography with Culture:
The New Light Regions of Connecticut

The pattern of emerging majority with roots in the English Northwest is just as noteworthy in Connecticut as in Massachusetts or New Hampshire, and this evangelism affected a greater percentage of people. While the original towns—Hartford, Wethersfield, Windsor—turned out to be the land of steady habits, the presbyterian Saybrook Platform, and prosecutions for witchcraft, this was not true of evangelical sections that comprised the larger part of the colony. In eastern—and later western—Connecticut, communities generated New Light and eventually triggered over a hundred separations from churches of the Standing Order, the Congregational establishment of Connecticut, proportionately more than in Plymouth or northern New England. Spiritual concern continued in the post-Revolution years. In the 1790s, these places took the lead in missionary work that characterized the first phase of the Second Great Awakening. John Davenport's New Haven, founded separately and the site of Yale College, would become the intellectual capital of the New Light.

New London County

Among the regions of evangelism in New England, New London County in eastern Connecticut resembled in religiosity the burnt-over districts that later appeared in western New York and Yorkshire. The origins and traditions of the settlers explain a large part of this similarity. Over half the settlers, and even more of those going inland, came from the Northwest. This pattern of settlement was set early when pioneers moved on to the coast of Connecticut after the Pequots were driven out in 1637.[1] There was another surge of immigration following King Philip's War in 1676, so that by the end of the century, some towns and churches had been organized. In this process the culture of nearby Plymouth Colony was transplanted, even after communities of Rhode Island were settled in between.[2]

The history of the first town and hive of this region, New London, really began when Richard Blinman, a minister from Gloucester in the Bay Colony, arrived. Before that Thomas Peter had served temporarily after being ejected from a church living in Cornwall for nonconformity. Blinman had been driven out of Wales for the same reason and sojourned in Marshfield and Gloucester, coming to New London in 1650. He brought with him from Cape Ann a group of Northwest settlers who would make a major imprint on eastern Connecticut: William Addis, William Ash, Christopher Avery, James Avery, Hugh Caulkins, John Coit, George Denison, William Denison, William Hough, Thomas Jones, William Kinney, Andrew Lester, William Meades, James Morgan, Robert Park, and Ralph Parker. Others of similar background filled the ranks: Jonathan Brewster, son of William Brewster of Plymouth; Mathew Griswold, who had moved over from Saybrook; Aaron Stark from Scotland; and Thomas Miner, one of the West Countrymen sifted out of Hingham by East Anglians. These men had strong religious convictions that would shape the town. When Blinman moved on in 1659 to Newfoundland and England, he left behind a group that would furnish very many settlers for new communities nearby.[3]

After Blinman departed, the church and town finally called as pastor Gershom Bulkeley, a young scholar of a distinguished family who had married a daughter of Charles Chauncy, the president of Harvard College. His voice was clear enough but weak, he was peaceable, but he expected unqualified obedience to authority. His affinity for presbyterianism caused "uneasiness." Although pastor and church at first tried accommodation, members soon rebelled over departures from "the congregational way." The result was that Bulkeley was not ordained and moved to Wethersfield, where he soon abandoned the pulpit to become a prominent surgeon and chemist.

As the religious fervor of exodus, pilgrimage, and settlement receded among Connecticut's pioneers, the underlying cleavage between evangelical and nonevangelical church members subsided to congregationalist versus presbyterian. The Northwest folk who had been aroused were naturally inclined to prefer a restricted congregationalism over lax admission standards. On the other hand, the well-organized Southeast settlers increased their pressure for presbyterianism during the 1650s and 1660s. Strict and moderate congregationalists drew together in the face of this threat, but some of the latter were willing to adopt the Half-Way Covenant to head off outright presbyterianism. At this time the discussion over adoption of the covenant often obscured the fundamental conflict in belief between pioneers from the Northwest and those from the Southeast. The geographic pattern is blurred, but the early impetus for presbyterianism came from the original towns of Hartford and Wethersfield and spread down the Connecticut River. Opposition to it was most noticeable and vociferous in eastern Connecticut and New Haven, where the Northwest folk were concentrated.

In New London, those from the Northwest did sustain their beliefs through the long tenure of Simon Bradstreet, Bulkeley's successor. But Bradstreet did have some difficulty in the 1670s because James Rogers, the second wealthiest man in Connecticut, defected from his congregation and joined a Baptist church in Newport, Rhode Island. When Rogers tried to organize such a group in New London, Connecticut authorities suppressed it. His son, John, founded the sect that would be known as the Rogerenes. Members combined evangelism with practices of the Quakers and Seven Principle Baptists, holding immersionist beliefs, refusing to pay ministerial taxes, interrupting church services, and working on the sabbath, much in the manner of George Fox before 1660. The sect was punished as much for its tactics and behavior as for its beliefs. But Rogerene activism continued sporadically for a century and kept evangelism alive when the tax-supported Congregationalists were dormant.[4]

The presbyterianism emanating from Hartford was finally prescribed for New London and the rest of the colony in 1708. In that year the legislature adopted the Saybrook Platform and urged the churches of the colony to adopt it also. This plan established ecclesiastical order, called for ministers and churches to form associations, and reduced the autonomy of local congregations that joined. Eastern Connecticut resisted this presbyterian plan, preferring the congregationalism of the Cambridge Platform adopted previously in 1648 instead. Church members were suspicious of centralizing the church polity and the concomitant professionalization of the clergy, and the pious believed that the Saybrook Platform would foster religious security and indifference, diminishing prospects for revival.[5] They wanted more evangelism in religion and more democracy in politics.

In New London, despite the propensity for evangelism, religion seemed to languish. Eliphalet Adams was a good preacher from the outset of his ministry in 1709, but communion was ill-attended and public relation was actually voted out in 1726. Adams, however, continued to work among the American Indians, taking into his home Uncas, "the last of the Mohegans," for Christian tutoring. The neighboring clerics James Hillhouse and his successor, David Jewett, were also maintaining this effort.[6]

There was some sprinkling before "God's mighty deluge" when the Frontier Revival came down the Connecticut River in 1735 from Jonathan Edwards's church in Northampton. When several ministers from eastern Connecticut visited Edwards to see firsthand the reformation going on in his community returned and described the revival to their people, it proved contagious.[7]

Gilbert Tennent's visit to New London in March 1741, however, began the revival in earnest. He was censorious, leaving controversy and conversion in his wake. He gave seven sermons in two days and attracted people from as far away as Groton. Neighboring pastors assisted Adams and offered sermons to children. In May a protracted meeting yielded diverse conversion experiences and turned New London into an important center of revivalism.

Adding to this fervor was Timothy Allen, a radical New Light, who set up a "Shepherd's Tent" for converts in town. This school of prophets was outlawed and did not last long. More trouble came when James Davenport, another radical New Light, arrived and accused Eliphalet Adams of being a "carnal Pharisee." Perhaps he sensed that challenging the spiritual state of a settled minister would produce conversions. Adams was a Bostonian who had assisted at Brattle Street Church, Boston's most liberal flock, and expanded the Half-Way Covenant in New London. On the other hand, he did invite Whitefield and other itinerants into his pulpit during the revival.[8] Because they regarded Adams as at least a moderate New Light, some colleagues were surprised at Davenport's tactic. Later they were embarrassed by his extremism when Davenport staged a bonfire on the common to burn worldly objects, including some theological works deemed not evangelical enough. The crowd had some second thoughts about the project and rescued most of the books from the flames.

After this, a separation occurred that confirmed the spreading pluralism in the region. For several decades Adams's church had been losing ground to Baptists, Rogerenes, and Anglicans. Like most flocks on the eve of the revival, female members outnumbered male members by a margin of two to one (see table 7-1). Of the 115 persons who defected from the New London church, 46 percent were men almost twenty years younger than the other church members. Few were married or paying rates. These New Light "come-outers" could not be identified with any particular neighborhood or occupation and had average wealth. Certain families, however, contributed greatly to this divisiveness. Just three—the Rogerses, Shapleighs, and Caulkinses—accounted for over a third of those separating.[9]

Despite the factionalism in New London, the county remained a

Table 7-1. Church Admissions in Coastal Connecticut, 1740–44

	Average Admissions per Year	Average Percent Male	Percent Male Change	Religion of Minister[a]
Old Lyme	35.6	44.4	+14.7	New Light
Stonington, North	24.1	40.3	+5.4	New Light
Norwich, 2d (Franklin)	23.4	47.0	+13.7	New Light
New London	21.2	30.2	-8.0	Regular Light
Norwich, 1st	19.0	37.9	+4.6	*New Light*
Colchester, 1st	15.2	39.5	+10.9	Old Light
Colchester, 3d (Westchester)	14.8	41.9	+11.9	Old Light
Griswold	12.6	63.5	+29.5	*New Light*
Norwich, 4th (Bozrah)	9.4	46.8	—	New Light
Stonington	8.0	52.5	+3.2	*New Light*
Preston	5.8	34.4	+1.1	Neutral
Average	17.2	43.5	+9.4	

Source: Calculated from church records at Connecticut State Library, Hartford, Conn. Membership numbers include those admitted in full communion only.

Note: The percent male change is calculated from the average percentage of men in the congregations between 1735 and 1739.

a. Affiliations in italic indicate ministers graduating in the upper half of their classes.

stronghold of evangelical activity (see map 3). Old Lyme had the most admissions. Jonathan Parsons, the minister, had explicitly rejected the Saybrook Platform at his ordination in 1731, and people called him "censorious" when he also backed off from what he realized were Arminian principles. Overcoming prejudices acquired from news accounts, Parsons heard Whitefield for himself and was impressed. According to Parsons, when Gilbert Tennent visited Old Lyme, not only sinners but "drowsy saints" were stirred. In the spring of 1741, weeping, sighing, and some more extreme behavior occurred. Several stout

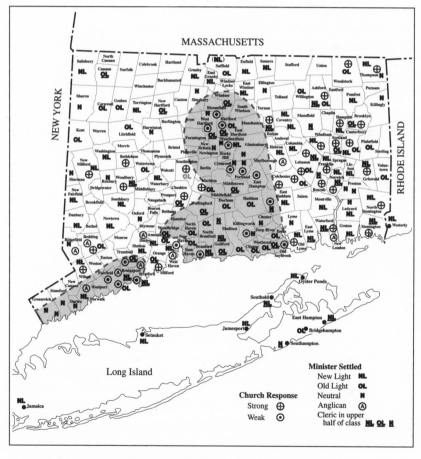

Map 3. New Light and Old Light Regions of Connecticut

men fell as if a cannon were discharged. Convictions went deep, there were many wounded souls, and the truth put some into "fits." Love of God and an increase in religious knowledge became apparent. Persons became humble, kind, patient, educable. While most were young, some converts were middle-aged. Lay exhorters, in imitation of Davenport, attracted some people for a while but there were very few trances or visions among them and 150 persons were added by February 1742. In East Lyme, a smaller community, George Griswold, the pastor, reported that only a minority of the congregation actually cried out. About a hundred whites and thirteen Niantics were converted, and there were no divisions or separations.[10]

In New London, Mather Byles followed Eliphalet Adams as pastor in 1757. His wit and florid style were popular at first, but he became more ritualistic and conservative later as he preached old sermons and neglected his pastoral duties. Byles was particularly exasperated by the tactics of the Rogerenes. Yet the church stuck to its congregational autonomy, still refusing to adopt the Saybrook Platform. In 1768 he suddenly declared himself an Anglican and fled to the company of his liberal friends in Boston. Members of the Byles family were late arrivals in New England, emigrating from Hampshire on the south coast to Boston in 1694. Like his father, Byles was a Tory during the Revolution.[11]

The revolutionary agitation after 1760 reflected the endemic come-outerism of this region. Despite Byles, New London was the first community in Connecticut to protest the Sugar Act as taxation without representation. New Lights captured the colony government in the elections of 1766. Evidently the New Lights were able to convince a majority that "an Arminian and a Favourer of the Stamp Act signify the same man."[12] Many evangelical believers still remained aloof from the political situation, but their religious separatism was spreading into that area.

Norwich

In the county's other port, Norwich, the revival was stronger than in New London. Founded in 1659 at the mouth of the Thames River, Norwich was also an important hive of the region. The town was prosperous, rising from eleventh to first place in taxable property between 1690 and 1742. Its documented history of revivalism began with Benjamin Lord; his ordination in 1717 produced four years of heightened religiosity. Apathy then prevailed until early 1741, when the Great

Awakening took over until the summer of 1743. Lord welcomed the revival and invited Wheelock and Parsons to preach. The age of conversion fell from 33.9 to 25.2 for males and 27.0 to 23.7 for females, and included many single persons.

Norwich had high admissions despite the early separatism in this large township. The percentage of men in the congregation was 37.9 for 1740 and 1744, but higher, 40.2, for 1741–43. The number of converts per year rose more than fivefold from the preceding five years and by 1744 there were twice as many compared to the number in 1717, when Lord was new and earnest.[13]

As the revival receded in Norwich, radical New Lights, with the enthusiasm of converts, criticized Lord's leadership, and the percentage of men in the congregation plunged. They accused him of increasing his fellowship with the Standing Order and thus moving away from the congregational way of the Cambridge Platform, despite the express wish of members. The last straw came in 1745 when he led the church to vote that saving grace was merely desirable and not essential for admission. Although this was simply a reaffirmation of current practice, radicals were very disappointed. They wanted, of course, to make conversion mandatory for communion and criticized Lord for his lax admission standards and dull preaching. They also opposed the prohibition that kept the laity from engaging in prayer and exhortation.

A few weeks later dissenters met at Hugh Caulkins's house and a schism began. The church warned them against "disorderly walking" and some months later suspended thirteen of them for attendance at separate meetings and nonattendance at church (see table 7-2). All thirteen had Northwest ties, and all but Chapman came from Norwich's old families, proprietors who settled the town in the second half of the seventeenth century and therefore had considerable landholdings and political power. Therefore these Separates were not marginal socially, although the younger ones had yet to benefit from their parents' status and land. They were marginal religiously, however, because they were more willing than other New Lights to risk prosecution and double taxation, since they would have to contribute to two ministers' salaries, to found a rival church on the principle of visible sainthood.[14]

Isaac Backus, who would later lead the evangelical Calvinistic Baptists in Plymouth, participated in this separation and viewed his career as the reassertion of precedents set in the Pilgrim era. His ancestor, William, originally from Yorkshire, came from Norwich in East

Table 7-2. The Norwich Separates

Name	Probable Origin
Backus, Elizabeth Tracy	Gloucester
Backus, Isaac	Norwich (Yorkshire)
Backus, James	Norwich (Yorkshire)
Caulkins, Hugh	Wales
Caulkins, Phoebe Abell	Derby
Chapman, Daniel	Yorkshire
Griswold, Joseph	Warwick
Hyde, Jedidiah	Cheshire
Kelley, Lydia Caulkins	Wales
Lathrop, William	Yorkshire
Leffingwell, John	Derby
Leffingwell, Samuel	Derby
Smith, John	(Worcester, 300)

Sources: Francis M. Caulkins, *The History of Norwich, Connecticut* (1874), 321; Charles E. Banks, *Topographical Dictionary*, ed. E. E. Brownell (1937); Henry Guppy, *Homes of Family Names in Great Britain* (1890).

Note: Surname frequency per 10,000 from Guppy, *Homes,* appears in parentheses.

Anglia to Saybrook in 1638. At the time Norwich was the second largest town in England and, as we have seen, had a history of antinomianism, separation, and religious volatility. William was a cutler; he became a proprietor of Norwich in Connecticut and moved there in 1660.[15]

As founders of Norwich in Connecticut, members of the Backus family held many offices and intermarried with Leffingwells, Caulkinses, Griswolds, and Tracys. Isaac had five brothers and five sisters and did not attend college. He attributed much of his religious attitude to his mother, Elizabeth Tracy Backus. At one point Elizabeth went to jail as a Separate, upholding her soul liberty against the Standing Order of churches in Connecticut. The Tracys had come from Gloucester in 1636 and, like the Backuses, were to maintain their missionary zeal well into the nineteenth century. The Backus-Tracy link was a potent Northwest evangelical combination. Azel Backus was Bellamy's successor in Bethlehem and an advocate of the New Divinity. Charles Backus was a leader in the Second Great Awakening. Joseph Tracy wrote inspiring but competent religious history, attaching the label "Great Awakening" to the eighteenth-century revivalism and describing the later missionary enterprise.[16]

These original families, the Tracys and Backuses, as well as the Hydes, dominated the government and the church during this time. Officeholders from the Southeast minority were few—the Fitches and Bushnells had declined service after their second generation of settlement. The desire of some to separate in this situation therefore seems drastic. Scholars have pondered the roots of separatism, which could arise from dissatisfaction over the location or seating in the meetinghouse, the minister's salary, or church discipline and level of piety. Some have suggested that the reluctance to pay ministerial rates, which was often the beginning of separatism, arose from either a return to seventeenth-century religious convictions or newfound eighteenth-century Yankee frugality. Obviously, both are plausible, but it was easier to separate from the established church if dissenters could invoke tradition in rationalizing such an action.

In Norwich and eastern Connecticut, the congregationalism of the Cambridge Platform combined with the evangelism of the Northwest to provide just such a tradition. The original church was organized in Saybrook, and before moving to its Norwich site members ordained its first minister using only deacons and no clergy to make the point that the power of ordination resided in the church as a body. Loyalty to congregational principles had been reaffirmed on several occasions in the intervening years.[17] But it was the emotion of the revival that brought these principles out, that attracted those predisposed toward evangelism, and that revitalized the congregational way.

Thus, the Separates of Norwich, despite their prospects, could still feel in the 1740s the need to be born again. They built a plain meetinghouse on Bean Hill—no spire, bell, or pews, just seats and pulpit—and ordained Jedidiah Hyde in 1747. Following the split, Norwich retained most of its evangelical religiosity and prosperity, growing 700 percent between the Great Awakening and the Revolution. Descendants of the pioneers remained comfortably in control.[18] Evidently the separation affected others in the parish because Benjamin Lord had trouble collecting his salary and three more Separate churches sprouted within the confines of Norwich township. Total evangelical intensity in the original Norwich township was high, and there was no Anglican chapel there as a refuge from the "enthusiasm."[19]

Moving Inland

Moving away from coastal Connecticut, we find that an early indication of readiness for revival came to Windham Church in 1721. Some eighty persons were added to the flock of one hundred in six months. The awakened church was vocal in reaffirming the Cambridge over the Saybrook Platform, the congregational over the presbyterian way. Lebanon, following the Great Awakening, was a leader of evangelism in eastern Connecticut (see table 7-3). In the 1690s, settlers from Norwich, New London, and Plymouth County in the Old Colony, most originally from the Northwest, moved into Lebanon, the first town in Connecticut with a biblical name. They were joined by a group that came over from western Massachusetts in the upper Connecticut River valley, also of Northwest origin, who added to the spirit of the Frontier Revival of 1734–36. By this time, Lebanon was quite prosperous.[20]

Table 7-3. Church Admissions in Windham County, 1740–44

	Average Admissions per Year	Average Percent Male	Percent Male Change	Religion of Minister[a]
Hampton	27.8	42.4	+5.6	New Light
Windham, 3d (Scotland)	27.0	39.2	—	*Old Light*
Brooklyn	24.6	42.3	-6.9	*Old Light*
Ashford	23.4	46.1	+23.1	*New Light*
Windham	23.0	48.7	+5.6	New Light
Thompson	18.4	40.2	+12.9	Neutral
Lebanon Crank (Columbia)	15.0	52.0	+5.6	New Light
Bolton	13.0	47.9	-2.1	*Old Light*
Canterbury	4.6	65.2	—	Old Light
Average	23.0	45.0	+5.4	

Source: Calculated from church records at Connecticut State Library. Membership numbers include those admitted in full communion only.

Note: At Brooklyn and Bolton, the Old Light pastors may have adversely affected the number of admissions and the percentage of male converts. The percent male change is calculated from the average percentage of men in the congregations between 1735 and 1739.

a. Affiliations in italic indicate ministers graduating in the upper half of their classes.

When the Great Awakening arrived, the views of Solomon Williams and Eleazar Wheelock, ministers in Lebanon, assured strong support and made the town into a focal point for the New Light. The town had high admissions, provided many Yale graduates in the 1740s, and also contributed to the ranks of the Edwardseans, pastors who trained young men in the New Divinity and promoted evangelism in the Second Great Awakening.[21] Their concern for evangelism and missions was sustained into the 1830s.

Despite its strength, the revival was as divisive in eastern Connect-icut as it was in many other places. The division here, however, like Plymouth's, was between moderate and radical New Lights. Radicals found some of the regular ministers, although New Light in sympathy, not evangelical enough in the pulpit. Therefore they separated from the established churches, subjecting themselves to prosecution and double taxation. A large fraction of these Separates became Baptists, register-ing under Connecticut's toleration law and gaining exemption from taxes for clergy of the Standing Order.

Separation in Canterbury was particularly divisive. In 1741 James Wadsworth had departed in disgrace after an alleged affair with a wom-an in the flock. Although the people were decidedly New Light and supporters of the Cambridge Platform, without leadership during the Great Awakening they did not add many to the congregation. But in 1744 the Connecticut ecclesiastical establishment increased its pressure for conformity and a faction succumbed, abandoning the Cambridge for the Saybrook scheme. Members of this faction were probably less pious than their opponents, yet few would qualify as Old Lights by the standards of eastern Massachusetts. They were certainly more pragmat-ic, accepting the Half-Way Covenant, requiring no public relation for full communion and the Saybrook Platform they had previously resisted. They were prominent, like the evangelicals, but had greater political interest and involvement. They went on to nominate James Cogswell, a moderate Old Light, for the vacant pulpit. When church members voted, Cogswell lost, sixteen to twenty-three. Rather than accepting Cogswell and the Saybrook Platform, the majority of full members chose to separate. The new pastor was left to begin his ministry with a flock of thirty men and sixty women.

Using itinerants, the new Separate and strict congregational church started with thirty-three men and twenty-four women. Despite criti-cism lodged against it, this church was noted among the Separates for its prosperity and respectability.[22] This gathering of aroused New Lights, although clannish, should not be viewed as exhibiting the same "tribalism" Edmund Morgan has used to characterize New England Puritanism at the end of the seventeenth century. He described those churches as practicing a conservative tribalism. The Puritans turned to their children to perpetuate the faith after several decades of waning religiosity and at a time of legalism and uncertainty about the Puritan establishment under a new royal charter. The Canterbury Separates of 1744, on the other hand, recently aroused and with rekindled interest in the millennium, represented tribalism also but in a different mood, one of expansive anticipation. This may be true of the rest of eastern Connecticut as well. This region produced far more separations and Separate and Separate Baptist churches than the rest of New England. Joseph Fish of Stonington complained in 1767 that he had lost two-thirds of his people to dissenter groups over the years. The basic separatism of the British Northwest finally flowered fully in the wake of the revival.

In addition to separation and accommodation, some people chose to leave the region. For an evangelical after the Great Awakening, the Standing Order or separation were not the only religious choices. Another was emigration to the Wyoming Valley, an attractive option. This part of Pennsylvania was within the western land claim of Connecticut and had good farmland. The end of the French and Indian War in 1760 set off migration. Separatism and millennialism combined with land hunger drained some population from eastern Connecticut to the Wyoming country.[23]

Even in eastern Connecticut there were, of course, pockets of indifference or resistance to the revival. Woodstock was settled from Roxbury in eastern Massachusetts, claimed by the Bay Colony, and called New Roxbury until 1690. Pastor Abel Stiles was an Old Light. Significantly, "the Great Revival of 1740 left relatively little results in Woodstock, but in outlying districts, the spirit was rampant." After Stiles was transferred to Connecticut in 1749, Woodstock finally succumbed to revivalism in 1763.[24] In the Colchester area all three ministers—Ephraim Little, Joseph Lovett, and Thomas Skinner—were Harvard men from Massachusetts and cool to the revival. Little denied his pulpit to the itinerating Benjamin Pomeroy. These churches still gained members but had defections to Separates and Baptists later. In Colchester, people responded to evangelism despite the attitude of their pastors.[25]

Obviously statistics of individual church admissions and the number of separations indicate the strength of evangelism in eastern Connecticut, but a more reliable measure is a roster of ministers. Viewed in conjunction with map 3, this list offers a more complete picture of how evangelism compared with orthodoxy. Table 7-4 shows thirteen Old Lights, ten neutrals, and twenty-seven New Lights, a clear majority. As in New Light Massachusetts and New Hampshire, more New Light pastors in eastern Connecticut had graduated in the upper half of their college classes compared with their Old Light and neutral rivals. Ministers' sons were apt to receive higher placing at Yale than Harvard

Table 7-4. Ministers in Eastern Connecticut, 1741–44

Town	Minister	Rank[a]	Religion of Minister
Ashford	John Hale[b]	*2/14*	New Light
	John Bass	26/40H	Old Light
Bolton	Thomas White	*2/10*	Old Light
Brooklyn	Ephraim Avery	*13/37*H	Old Light
Canterbury	James Cogswell	16/17	Old Light
Colchester, 1st	Ephraim Little[b]	34/49H	Old Light
Colchester, 2d (Salem)	Joseph Lovett	46/49H	Old Light
Colchester, 3d (Westchester)	Thomas Skinner	26/29H	Old Light
Coventry	Joseph Meacham[b]	14/15H	New Light
Coventry, North	Nathaniel Strong[b]	12/17	New Light
Ellington	John McKinstry[b]	(U. Edinburgh)	Neutral
Enfield	Peter Reynolds[b]	13/21H	New Light
Enfield, 2d (Somers)	Samuel Allis	37/40H	New Light
Groton	John Owen[b]	30/42H	New Light
Hamburg	George Beckwith[b]	10/12	Neutral
Hampton	Samuel Moseley[b]	20/28H	New Light
Hebron	Benjamin Pomeroy	11/16	New Light
Killingly, North	John Fiske	10/14H	Neutral
Lebanon	Solomon Williams[b]	*7/27H*	New Light
Lebanon Crank (Columbia)	Eleazar Wheelock[b]	10/16	New Light
Lebanon, 3d	Jacob Eliot	11/21H	Old Light
Ledyard	Andrew Croswell[b]	43/49H	New Light
Lyme, East	George Griswold[b]	*1/5*	New Light
Lyme, Old	Jonathan Parsons[b]	11/17	New Light

Table 7-4, continued.

Town	Minister	Rank[a]	Religion of Minister
Mansfield	Ebenezer Williams[b]	9/13	New Light
Millington	Timothy Symmes[b]	22/39H	New Light
New London	Eliphalet Adams	*4/8H*	Regular Light
New London, 2d (Montville)	David Jewett[b]	*13/31H*	New Light
Norwich, 1st	Benjamin Lord[b]	*4/9*	New Light
Norwich, 2d (Franklin)	Henry Willes[b]	3/3	New Light
Norwich, 3d (Newent, Lisbon)	Daniel Kirkland[b]	6/10	New Light
Norwich, 4th (East, Long. Soc.)	Jabez Wight	35/37H	Regular Light
Norwich, 5th (Bozrah)	Benjamin Throop	*6/14*	Neutral
Plainfield	Joseph Coit[b]	13/14	Old Light
Pomfret	Ebenezer Williams[b]	8/10	New Light
Preston	Salmon Treat[b]	7/8	Neutral
Preston, 2d (Griswold)	Hezekiah Lord[b]	*2/5*	New Light
Stonington, East	Nathaniel Eells	*21/49H*	New Light
Stonington, North	Joseph Fish[b]	29/49H	New Light
Stonington, South	Ebenezer Rossiter	*3/13*	Neutral
Thompson	Marston Cabot	*20/40H*	Regular Light
Tolland	Stephen Steel[b]	9/13	New Light
Union	Ebenezer Wyman	29/37H	Neutral
Voluntown	Samuel Dorrance[b]	(U. Glasglow)	Presbyterian/ Old Light
Willington	David Fuller	12/14	Old Light
Windham	Stephen White	10/19	New Light
Windham, 2d (Scotland)	Ebenezer Devotion	*10/23H*	Old Light
Windsor, East	Timothy Edwards[b]	*7/23H*	New Light
Woodstock	Abel Stiles	13/16	Old Light
Itinerant	Samuel Buell	*7/20*	New Light

Sources: Names, churches, religious preferences, and ranks compiled from Clifford Shipton, *Sibley's Harvard Graduates: Biographical Sketches of Those Who Attended Harvard College,* 17 vols. (1933-75) and Franklin B. Dexter, *Biographical Sketches of the Graduates of Yale College* (1885-1919); probable origins come from Guppy, *Homes;* distinctions between neutrals come from David Harlan, *The Clergy and the Great Awakening in New England* (1980), 4, 5; names of signers compiled from Joseph Tracy, *The Great Awakening: A History of the Revival of Religion in the Time of Edwards and Whitefield* (1842), 299-301.

H = Harvard graduate.

a. Numbers in italic indicate those who graduated in the upper half of their classes.

b. Probable origins or high surname frequency in the Northwest.

because Harvard had more sons of officeholders and they received high-er rankings.[26] Yet Harvard made an evangelical contribution, despite the trio of Old Lights in Colchester; half of its high-ranking graduates were New Lights. Twenty-two of the twenty-seven New Light ministers had probable Northwest origins, compared with three of thirteen for the Old Lights. Thus New Lights and those of Northwest origins, largely the same pastors, had a majority in this region. An evangelical elite, the Saving Remnant, supported and reinforced the tendencies of the people and the results of their work were overwhelming.

It has been customary for scholars to emphasize the decline of religion during the revolutionary era, especially between 1776 and 1790. They point to pastors turning into chaplains, church members dispersing, redcoats occupying church buildings, and millennialists becoming disillusioned at the length and moral ambiguities of the military conflict. It was feared also that the alliance with France and French officers would bring deism to the new republic. New Americans, it has also been said, suffered from spiritual exhaustion during the Revolution, and independence brought constitution-making and economic recession rather than the recovery of organized religion. These descriptions of a religious ebbtide have been written, however, from the perspective of Old Light territory and the Congregational establishments. Douglas Sweet has suggested that historians, lacking evidence from the pews, have relied too much on the recollections of Lyman Beecher, a revivalist who wanted to contrast the dark "before"—the post-Revolution years—with the bright "after" of the Second Great Awakening and promote his mentor, Timothy Dwight, for reviving piety in the 1790s.[27]

In contrast to this notion of religious decline, minirevivals can be found in Connecticut in the 1780s. The Saybrook Platform ended in 1784 and although the Congregational establishment continued until 1818, dissenting churches gained confidence and energy from the Revolution and the discussion of religious liberty that accompanied it. Between 1768 and 1790, The number of Baptist churches in Connecticut grew from twelve to fifty-five. There were serious theological debates in many towns. New Divinity ministers—the Edwardseans—provided evangelical doctrines and long service.[28] While there was declension in parts of New England, in New Light territory "the things of religion" remained as important as nation building.

Then the resurgent Methodist revival in Britain raised the millennial and missionary impulses again. At the beginning of the nineteenth century, one good measure of religious commitment was a decision to go out from New England towns on missions to spread the Word before the Last Days. It is no surprise that the old families of eastern Connecticut—especially those of Northwest origins—played a conspicuous part. Some of the surnames sympathetic to missions were Backus, Bingham, Brewster, Chapman, Edwards, Griswold, Hyde, Jewett, Kinney, Kirkland, Lathrop, Moseley, Nott, Park, Pierson, Storrs, Strong, Thomas, Tracy, Williams, and Winslow. All of these had responded to the First Great Awakening.[29] Even more than northern New England or Plymouth, these Connecticut Yankees stayed with their heritage of evangelism and westering, giving time, money, and lives to the missionary efforts of the young republic.

New Haven Colony

Trade was a major motive for founding the New Haven Colony on Long Island Sound. Some traders from London who accompanied the Reverend John Davenport to Massachusetts wanted a harbor of their own but found the good ones already taken. With the conclusion of the Pequot War in 1637, the Connecticut coastline became an attractive alternative and they resettled at the mouth of the Quinnipiac River. In 1646 a vessel carrying some important traders was lost, however, and never seen again, which resulted in somewhat reduced trading. As a port, New Haven fell short of the traders' expectations.[30]

After this, religious motives for settlement came to the fore. Davenport and his followers—as the name of their town implies—sought peace, prosperity, and isolation to preserve the Christian grace already at work in their hearts. Davenport had come over to found a state "whose design is religion."[31] The explanation for the colony's strong emphasis on grace lies in the background, character, and education of its leaders. The most influential of these men had Northwest origins; surnames from these parts of England included Davenport, Eaton, Gibbard, Gregson, Ling, Nash, Newman, Pierson, Street, Wakeman, and Yale. Fugill and Punderson came from Yorkshire with Ezekiel Rogers but chose to stay in New Haven rather than settle in Rowley. This group was in the majority and East Anglians were quite scarce among the pioneers. The Northwest folk had been touched by Spiritual Puritanism in their education and travels, and their evangelical potential converted into an ardor for grace. The pioneer majority of New

Haven differed, therefore, from their unchurched compatriots in the Maine woods or Strangers in the Plymouth Colony. New Haven's affinity was with Rowley and the awakened people from Yorkshire.[32]

John Davenport left an indelible stamp on the colony he founded. He was the only leader to live within its borders during the entire period of its independent existence from 1638 to 1665. Born and raised in Warwick at Coventry, he married a young woman from that county. He attended Oxford, not Cambridge, and was drawn into the Puritan movement quite late. His stay in Holland caused him to examine the question of church polity and come to favor congregationalism over presbyterianism. As a pastor in Durham and London, the young man showed a special talent for catechizing and preaching to the common people. In the metropolis his church was near the offices of the Virginia and Massachusetts Bay Companies and, caught up in the westering spirit, he joined them. When Archbishop Laud's crusade against nonconformity imperiled his position, he fled to America.

In Boston, during the exciting and divisive time of the Antinomian Controversy, he was the houseguest of his English friend John Cotton. In 1637 Davenport led a party of settlers southwest to New Haven. He hoped to preserve and foster the kind of religiosity there that Cotton, his mentor, had been espousing in the Massachusetts Bay Colony. Cotton, who had lost some status by initially sympathizing with the views of Anne Hutchinson that turned out to be heretical, was urged to join this exodus to the Quinnipiac and implement "Moses His Judicials," the legal code he had compiled for the godly society. Other friends finally persuaded him to stay in Boston, however, so Davenport was left to build the new city on a hill on his own, but he did try to put into use Cotton's code in New Haven.[33]

Without holding public office himself, Davenport was able to dominate New Haven. He relied on his eloquence at public gatherings and worked closely with his childhood friend, Theophilus Eaton, who was governor until 1658. After the banishment and dispersal of Boston's antinomians, New Haven was almost alone in trying to maintain the high level of grace that had been reached briefly in the 1630s. Davenport's quest for purity seemed threatened from all sides during the 1640s and 1650s. In England, Cromwell's victory brought toleration for all sorts of sectarians who had sprung up in the chaos of the Civil War. In New England, recent immigrants were importing some Arminianism and Massachusetts discussed modifying church admission standards.

Even closer to home, Thomas Hooker's colony on the Connecticut River was succeeding although it did not dwell on sudden conversion and tilted toward works over grace. Yet as long as New Haven remained independent, Davenport was able to keep out the "impurities" of the "mixed multitude" and asserted the rule of the elect. Following Cotton, he insisted that converts "speak concerning the gift of grace . . . and the manner of God's dealing with them in working it in their hearts." For thirty years he never wavered in his demand that the experience of grace be described in detail.[34]

The New Haven of Davenport and Eaton was a Bible commonwealth yet it did not prosecute religious deviants. Its laws were a blend of Mosaic and English common law and not as draconian as the theocratic nature of their polity would suggest. The list of capital offenses was short compared with those in England, for example, and Quakers did not often vex the community; one sailor was hustled back to his ship when his Friendly religion became known. The penalty for Quakerism—boring through the tongue and hot irons—was never inflicted.

Six witchcraft cases did arise from neighborhood quarrels in the 1650s. Pastor William Hooke and some prominent families accused Elizabeth Godman, but Eaton and Davenport restrained them from pressing charges. The moderate attitude of New Haven should be contrasted with that of the west coast along the sound. The Fairfield-Stratford area experienced a virtual epidemic of witch charges. Roger Ludlow, the major accuser, had been a deputy governor and held many offices. He was a lawyer who had drafted the Fundamental Orders of 1639, Connecticut's first constitution, and was an honest and blunt legalist. A university graduate from Wiltshire, he had come to the Connecticut coast via Dorchester and Windsor. When he carried his suspicions of witchcraft into the adjacent New Haven jurisdiction, however, Davenport and Eaton rebuffed him. He was fined fifteen pounds for calling a woman a witch and ten more for accusing her of falsehood. Despite his prominence in Fairfield, Ludlow was not trusted in New Haven. Soon after this, he returned to England, later serving Cromwell in his conquest of Ireland.[35] Eaton decided witch cases in New Haven and no witch was ever convicted or stoned there. Although the saints in New Haven had incorporated Mosaic law and restricted participation to the regenerate in the community, they treated Quakers and witches well for the time, especially in comparison with the parts of New England that were strongholds of settlers from the English Southeast.

New Haven was not able to retain its independence for long. With the restoration of monarchy in England, Connecticut moved to strengthen itself by absorbing the smaller New Haven Colony and securing a charter from England. Davenport vehemently resisted this threat to his influence, particularly because it would mean accepting Connecticut's Half-Way Covenant and the consequent dilution of saintly membership in New Haven Colony by persons who lacked grace and could offer only their assent to the creed and discipline of the church. At first he thought of leading his flock of saved to the frontier again—New Jersey—but decided he was too old for another pilgrimage. Instead he entrusted the Reverend Abraham Pierson with the task of establishing still another wilderness Zion, giving him a copy of Cotton's code as a blueprint. Discouraged by Connecticut's annexation of New Haven, Davenport responded to a call from the Boston church where John Cotton had preached. His installation there caused controversy and schism but he died shortly afterward.[36]

Davenport and Eaton had established a kind of theocracy at New Haven that anticipated the communities of the saved that the Great Awakening spawned later. With leaders from the British Northwest who had been touched by Spiritual Puritanism and a high percentage of original settlers from that region, it was natural that New Haven would seek saintliness by emphasizing the covenant of grace and strict congregationalism. John Cotton inspired and John Davenport led this successful effort and New Haven offered an early glimmer of the New Light that would warm New England in the next century.

New Haven responded early and eagerly to the Great Awakening. Ripples from Edwards's Frontier Revival at Northampton reached the Quinnipiac in 1735. During the autumn of 1740, Whitefield preached in the First Church to the adjourned legislature. He reported "sweet melting" and many "Children of God revived under the Word." He also addressed Yale students, starting general concern there, later urging them to be great saints, not polite pastors. Assessing the religious mood, he was characteristically optimistic about the revival, declaring that "Spring is coming on, the Voice of the Turtle is heard in the Land." The next year Gilbert Tennent followed up Whitefield's visit with good results; he noted that "about thirty students came on foot Ten Miles to hear the Word of God."[37] Jonathan Edwards used commencement at his alma mater in New Haven to warn against the excesses of revivalism. The warning was in season because a holy club had surfaced at Yale, and so much religious confusion ensued that the college closed the term early. The demand of the town and the students for New Light preaching continued and was hard to satisfy, especially after the legislature passed a law against itinerants in 1742. Nevertheless, a parade of evangelists—Jedidiah Mills, Joseph Bellamy, Philemon Robbins, John Graham, and Samuel Findlay of New Jersey—had remarkable success in their brief visits.[38]

Acrimony and division appeared in the wake of Whitefield and Tennent, however. When Whitefield's low estimates of grace among the Yale faculty became known, they turned against him and tried to dampen student excitement. And awakened parishioners found the minister of the First Church, Joseph Noyes, if not unsaved, at least too dull and legalistic for their quickened tastes and demanded a separation. The dissidents withdrew and formed the White Haven congregation; it was called the "tolerated church" because members still had to pay rates for Noyes's salary as well as fund their own preaching. It was some time before they were able to free themselves from this burden and form a new society. Over the years these schismatics prospered; by 1759, they outnumbered First Church members 179 to 147. Ten years after that, they called Jonathan Edwards, Jr., who carried the New Light into the revolutionary period.[39]

The revival had special resonance in this town, of course, because of its history of religiosity and because it was the seat of Yale, which attracted young men, such as James Davenport, from Connecticut and western Massachusetts.[40] Davenport commanded attention here because his mother was a native of the town, he was a Yale graduate, and, of course, he was the great-grandson of the founder of New Haven. Before Whitefield set foot in New England, Davenport, pastor of Southold, a town on Long Island that had been affiliated with New Haven Colony, sought to evangelize his neighborhood. Inspired by the Awakener's account of revival success, he heard Whitefield in the Middle Colonies and then accompanied him on tour.

When Whitefield brought the Great Awakening to New England, Davenport was carried away, his emotionalism exceeding that of his mentor. He developed the "holy whine," a singsong preaching style ostensibly good in the open air and wind, but one many found excruciating. He represented the radical fringe of the New Light and, acting on impulses, invaded parishes without permission or warning. As he went through the streets praying, singing, and gesticulating, he was followed by excited women, children, and young men who imitated him. When he found a minister opposed or even lukewarm toward the New Light, he pronounced him unsaved. In New Haven he made this charge against Noyes, calling him a wolf in sheep's clothing, thereby contributing to the separation from the First Church. Wherever Davenport went, he created disorder and was several times admonished and jailed. At New London his enthusiasm reached its apogee with the bonfire. Necklaces, bustles, and wigs did go up in flames. The next year Davenport finally cooled, apologizing at length for his "false spirit" and the "blemishes" he added to the work of God.[41]

Why did Davenport behave in this manner; why did he react so strongly to evangelism? By the standards of the time in Britain or the colonies, he did not fit the stereotype of cultural or rural "deprivation." He was not a product of the actual frontier or the son of an unchurched farmer aroused by an itinerant. His father was the minister of Stamford on the coast. Nor did he lack formal education like Anne Hutchinson and George Fox, the persecuted antinomians of the previous century. On the contrary, Davenport was academically inclined, placing second in his class of twenty-three, and graduating at age sixteen.[42] The explanation for his exaggerated religiosity is to be found in the history of the Davenport family and the cultural milieu of New Haven and Yale College. Young James was of the Saving Remnant that had nurtured the piety of the Northwest and carried predispositions of his famous ancestor—evangelism, experimentalism, perfectionism—into the mid-eighteenth century.

The reports of Whitefield's activities were enough to trigger his feelings. Perhaps his intensity meant that these impulses had been largely suppressed and required the sudden popularity and relative respectability of Whitefield to bring them fully into the open. Although people in New Haven preferred the more moderate New Light of Whitefield to the enthusiasm of Davenport, his behavior and its results demonstrated that the original strain of evangelism that helped found the town was far from exhausted a century later.

Among the larger settlements of New England, New Haven proved to be a particular beacon of the New Light. John Davenport had preserved and cultivated grace carefully in the first settlers and tried to shield them from worldly influence. Although New Haven grew, gaining a college and a somewhat more diversified population, the initial religiosity and preference for grace over works persisted, making the town still open to revivalism when it came along. Evangelical sentiment was not unanimous, but it was remarkably strong, perpetuated in part by the schismatic White Haven Church. New Lights became a political majority in town by the late 1750s.

When the evangelical-romantic mood superseded the Enlightenment in the 1790s, New Haven would lend its name to a modified theology comparable with that orientation. The views of Nathaniel Taylor were dubbed "the New Haven theology" because he was a Yale graduate and its divinity school disseminated his ideas. Of course, Dartmouth, Bowdoin, Middlebury, Amherst, and Williams, new colleges on the north and west periphery of New England, could by this time also provide recruits for evangelical Calvinism and reform.[43]

Western Connecticut

In the early eighteenth century, the upper part of western Connecticut was a natural expansion area for Hartford County proprietors. Ministerial candidates from that county, largely Old Light in disposition, were first on the scene. In the decade before 1741, however, settlers from eastern Connecticut and some religiously restless folk were moving in, and so evangelism grew belatedly and, during the revival, offset the firstcomers (see table 7-5). Western Connecticut was the birthplace of Joseph Bellamy and Samuel Hopkins, founders of the New Divinity, the theology that emerged from Jonathan Edwards's thinking after the revival. When the area filled up and the Second Great Awakening arrived in the 1790s, a dozen New Divinity ministers had been settled and Litchfield was vying with Windham for evangelical leadership of Connecticut.[44]

Milford was one of the earliest settlements on the western coast. The Reverend Peter Prudden of Yorkshire arrived, bringing with him settlers from Hertfordshire. A century later, young members opposed Samuel Whittlesey, Jr., because of his Arminianism, which increased during the Great Awakening. Despite this conflict and the separation in 1743, Milford church statistics show some New Light strength. Eventually in 1747, the Separates chose Job Prudden, great-grandson of the first minister, as pastor, and the Separate church became regular in 1770.[45]

Unlike Milford, Woodbury proved to be a bastion of New Light. At the outset, a religious minority in Stratford was unsatisfied with Israel

Table 7-5. Church Admissions in Western Connecticut, 1740–44

	Average Admissions per Year	Average Percent Male	Percent Male Change	Religion of Minister[a]
Suffield	48.6	47.1	-4.2	New Light, Old Light[b]
Woodbury	22.6	56.6	+19.7	*New Light*
Cheshire	18.6	45.2	-1.4	*Old Light*
Bethlehem	16.2	43.2	—	New Light
Milford	16.2	40.7	+3.3	*Old Light*
New Haven	11.6	39.7	+6.7	*Old Light*
Wilton	10.2	52.8	+2.8	New Light
Southington	9.8	55.1	+15.6	Old Light
New Milford	8.6	49.0	-7.6	New Light
New Canaan	7.8	56.4	+20.3	New Light
Redding	3.2	43.8	-0.6	Old Light
Average	15.8	48.1	+5.5	

Source: Calculated from church records at Connecticut State Library. Membership numbers include those admitted in full communion only.

Note: The percent male change is calculated from the average percentage of men in the congregations between 1735 and 1739. The separation from the First Church in Milford no doubt lowered admissions and the percentage of males.

a. Affiliations in italic indicate ministers graduating in the upper half of their classes.
b. There were two settled ministers at the Suffield church between 1740 and 1744; an Old Light followed a New Light.

Chauncy, the son of the president of Harvard; he was learned, but legalistic. They preferred Zechariah Walker, son of Robert Walker of Lancashire, a Harvard dropout who was an experimental and pungent preacher. When differences with the majority persisted, the dissenters moved from Stratford inland and settled Woodbury in 1670; the new community grew rapidly after King Philip's War. A renewed influx of settlers brought prosperity and a virtual boom between 1737 and 1743.

Anthony Stoddard was the minister of Woodbury from 1702 to 1760. He was the son of Solomon Stoddard, the pastor of Northampton in western Massachusetts, and the Woodbury church evidently practiced his father's "Stoddardism." Until the 1670s, evangelism in the pulpit and presbyterianism in the polity had been largely in conflict, supported by competing groups with the latter gaining membership while fervor

declined. Stoddard found a way to combine these seemingly antagonistic elements into a system that added members and shored up clerical authority at the same time. His first steps were to deliver a strong
evangelical message and invite to the communion table those without
grace but willing to seek it. He justified this by claiming that communion was meant to be a converting ordinance and only God knew who
the truly saved were.

The influx of aroused converts should have led to demands for purity and a higher admission standard, but this did not happen during
Stoddard's lifetime. To check the democratic and anarchical tendency
of aroused converts, Stoddard indoctrinated them with the godliness
of clerical power, the kind of claim used previously but with less success by nonevangelical presbyterians. He also took advantage of his clerical power, personality, and family connections to establish a ministerial association in the upper Connecticut River valley. Thus Stoddard
managed to be evangelical and popular while maintaining discipline and
ministerial prerogatives. This feat earned him the title of "Pope" of the
valley and the esteem of the "River Gods," the merchants of western
Massachusetts, who could appreciate such executive skill. Thereafter
Stoddardism became a viable option, compared to strict congregationalism, in the Connecticut River valley.

In Woodbury, the Stoddardism of Anthony Stoddard meant inviting all baptized persons over age fourteen to communion although they
lacked grace. Of course this was lowering standards, but not everyone
felt worthy enough to take advantage of it. Until 1726, admissions av-
eraged five per year, the average age of church members was 29.2, and
86 percent were married (see table 7-6). Growth was slow but like most
New Light churches, there were minirevivals here in 1714–16 and 1721.
Woodbury was stricken in 1726–27 by a mysterious "Great Sickness"
not shared by neighboring communities. In that year (and the one preceding) the church suddenly gained seventy-five members and the average age dropped to 25.3 with only 47 percent married. The percentage of male converts dipped slightly from 46.0 to 45.3. The effect of
the Great Sickness in Woodbury resembled that of the Great Earthquake of 1727 on the Atlantic coast: new members were added but in
old proportions. Pastors—even New Lights—who "improved" on such
adverse events were not as effective in attracting males as they would
be at the peak of the revival, and this was true of Anthony Stoddard in
Woodbury.

Table 7-6. Church Admissions in Woodbury

	Male	Female	Total	Average per Year	Percent Male
1702–25	52	61	113	4.7	46.0
1726–27	34	41	75	34.5	45.3
1728–38	35	52	87	7.9	40.2
1739	14	19	33	33.0	42.4
1740	11	9	20	20.0	55.0
1741	25	19	44	44.0	57.0
1742	23	18	41	41.0	56.1

Source: James Walsh, "The Great Awakening in the First Congregational Church of Woodbury, Connecticut," *William and Mary Quarterly* 28 (1971): 544.

The long ministry of Stoddard in Woodbury and a history of minirevivals had prepared the way for the Great Awakening. It began unusually early when an eight-year-old girl and two sisters were suddenly converted in 1739. Natives of Woodbury fueled the revival, and the young converts of 1739–42 were sons and daughters of communicants. Children of the unchurched minority, about 15 percent, were not disproportionately aroused. The average age of converts in 1739 was 20.2 but this figure is misleadingly low because no record was kept of communicants "refreshed."

Although the revival in Woodbury began two years early and on the edge of town, it soon conformed to the New Light pattern. The peak years were 1741–42 when converts came primarily from the central, older part of town, and the male percentage of admissions was high. The Great Awakening, compared with the Great Sickness, resulted in more new members and a higher number of men, reaching 57 percent of the total admissions in 1741. Because of the revival, more men joined and at an earlier age than they would have otherwise. Conversions were more sudden and emotion-laden and therefore religious commitment should have been decisive. Thus the already healthy church in Woodbury was invigorated and the piety of its pioneers reaffirmed.[46]

Anthony Stoddard was very successful in Woodbury, but there was always the possibility that Stoddardism would eventually generate a demand for closed communion and cause divisiveness. This demand for purity was one result of the Great Awakening and did eventually bring higher admission standards and repeal of the Half-Way Covenant in much of New Light territory. This left western Connecticut quite evenly divided between New Lights and Old Lights and neutrals (see table 7-7). In origins, fifteen of the twenty-five New Lights appear to have links with the Northwest, compared with only four of the twenty-three others.[47]

Table 7-7. Ministers in Western Connecticut and Long Island, 1741–44

Town	Minister	Rank[a]	Religion of Minister
Bethlehem	Joseph Bellamy[b]	23/24	New Light
Bridgehampton (L.I.)	Ebenezer White	5/8H	Old Light
Canaan	Elisha Webster[b]	*6/15*	Old Light
Cheshire	Samuel Hall	*1/3*	Old Light
Cornwall	Solomon Palmer	14/17	Old Light
Danbury	Ebenezer White	9/16	New Light
Derby	Daniel Humphreys[b]	19/23	New Light
Goshen	Stephen Heaton	14/16	Old Light
Granby	David Rowland[b]	20/24	New Light
Granby, East	Ebenezer Mills	12/15	New Light
Hampton, East (L.I.)	Samuel Buell[c]	*7/20*	New Light
Harwinton	Andrew Bartholomew	12/13	Neutral
Huntington (Ripton)	Jedidiah Mills	6/8	New Light
Jamaica (L.I.)	Walter Wilmot[b]	19/24	New Light
Jamesport (L.I.)	Nathaniel Mather[b]	*1/3*	New Light
Kent	Cyrus Marsh	9/10	Old Light
Litchfield	Timothy Collins	7/13	Old Light
Milford	Samuel Whittlesey, Jr.	*4/17*	Old Light
New Fairfield	Benajah Case	15/16	New Light
New Haven	Joseph Noyes	7/9	Old Light
New Milford	Daniel Boardman[b]	8/9	Old Light
Newton	Elisha Kent	16/17	New Light
	David Judson[b]	*5/15*	New Light
Newton (L.I.)	Simon Horton[b]	*4/13*	New Light
Northbury	Samuel Todd[b]	11/14	New Light
Oyster Pond (L.I.)	Jonathan Barber[b]	15/18	New Light
Poquonnock	Samuel Tudor[b]	7/12	Neutral
Redding	Nathaniel Hunn	11/13	Old Light
Ridgefield	Jonathan Ingersoll	13/19	Neutral
Sharon	Peter Pratt	11/19	Neutral
Setauket (L.I.)	David Youngs	18/20	New Light
Sherman	Thomas Lewis	19/23	Neutral
Simsbury	Timothy Woodbridge	2/3	Neutral
Southbury	John Graham[b]	(U. Glasgow)	New Light

Southampton (L.I.)	Silvanus White	*13/32H*	Neutral
Southington	Jeremiah Curtis	10/17	Old Light
Southold (L.I.)	James Davenport[b]	*2/23*	New Light
Suffield	Ebenezer Devotion	18/19	New Light
	Ebenezer Gay	23/40H	Old Light
Suffield, West	John Graham, Jr.[b]	*6/21*	New Light
Torrington	Nathaniel Roberts[b]	23/23	New Light
Washington (Judea)	Reuben Judd	20/23	Regular Light
Waterbury	Mark Leavenworth[b]	20/24	New Light
West Haven	Timothy Allen[b]	19/19	New Light
	Nathan Birdseye	15/19	Neutral
Westbury (Watertown)	John Trumbull[b]	20/24	Old Light
Wilton	William Gaylord[b]	13/18	New Light
Woodbury	Anthony Stoddard[b]	*2/14*	New Light

Sources: Names, churches, and religious preferences compiled from Shipton, *Harvard Graduates*, and Dexter, *Yale Graduates;* probable origins come from Guppy, *Homes;* ranks compiled from Dexter, *Yale Graduates,* and Shipton, *Harvard Graduates;* distinctions between neutrals come from Harlan, *Clergy,* 4, 5; names of signers compiled from Tracy, *Great Awakening,* 299-301.

Note: At Kent a "mixed multitude," predominantly of Southeast stock, settled in 1738 and called Cyrus Marsh, an Old Light. Later New Lights challenged him and he wanted to resign; he was finally dismissed for "immorality" in 1755. See Charles S. Grant, *Democracy in the Connecticut Frontier Town of Kent* (1972), 160-67.

H = Harvard graduate.

L.I. = Long Island.

a. Numbers in italic indicate those who graduated in the upper half of their classes.
b. Probable origins or high surname frequency in the Northwest.
c. Buell graduated in 1741 and immediately became an itinerant, chiefly in Connecticut. He was much criticized for his youth, ranting, and inexperience and settled on Long Island until 1746.

Connecticut's Legacy

After the Great Awakening, church admissions ebbed for a while because so many of the susceptible had been gathered in, yet evangelical religion continued throughout the eighteenth century. A few pious and scholarly young men in Connecticut found the Saybrook polity unscriptural and Calvinism no longer convincing, but retained their otherworldliness by turning to Anglicanism and episcopacy—not, as in eastern Massachusetts, to Unitarianism. After the turn of the century, many awakened people found the Baptist and the Methodist churches, growing in status and numbers, to provide good alternatives to the Congregational establishments.

Among the laity, some subscribed to Chauncy's *Seasonable Thoughts,* making their Old Light sympathies known. The majority, however, must be classified as neutral in the revival because their views are not sufficiently known. Only a few doctors, lawyers, and businessmen were conspicuous in supporting the revival and qualify for the Saving Remnant.[48] William Adams, son of the New London pastor, engaged in unlicensed preaching and was never settled. Christopher Christophers took part in Davenport's notorious bonfire in New London. Abraham Davenport and Samuel Cooke were leaders in separating from Noyes and the First Church of New Haven. James Pierpont, son of an earlier New Haven minister and Jonathan Edwards's brother-in-law, was a New Light who entertained Whitefield. As a young man, Joseph Hawley rebelled at the New Light and opposed Jonathan Edwards, but in the middle of his legal career, although revivalism had subsided, he embraced Edwardsean views and preached as a layman; he was a strong advocate of separation of church and state in the 1770s.[49] While the New Light was heavily concentrated in the clergy, these men supplemented the cause. They were in as much or more emotional turmoil than their clerical counterparts, pulled back by tradition and forward by "further light." Ready to invoke the Higher Law, they were prototypes of the religious reformers of the early republic. In these religious developments, New Light New England paralleled the British Isles, where Methodism and Evangelism had taken root and was sustained among Northwest people through the second half of the eighteenth century.

In conclusion it may be said that while western Connecticut was merely moving toward revivalism, in eastern Connecticut a combination of geography and culture created a response to the Great Awakening stronger than anywhere else in New England. The churches demonstrate the variations in response and the many flocks that separated after 1746 reinforced the New Light. Certain communities were focal points: the Norwich vicinity, Old Lyme, Lebanon, Windham, New Haven, Suffield, and Woodbury. The Northwest origins of the pastors and their postfrontier distribution reveal the most complete configuration of New Light strength, consistent with the origins and history of these parts of Connecticut. The first families provided links between the religious character of the first settlement and the revival of the 1740s. The Rogerene movement and minirevivals helped to keep religiosity and dissent alive until the Great Awakening. Pioneers from the British Northwest had brought with them their evangelical individualism and their fierce independence, setting the stage for the revivalism and pluralism to come.

Notes

1. A majority of settlers on the Connecticut coast east of Saybrook derived from the Northwest. At New London they made up three-quarters of the population before 1660, but this decreased slightly in the next two decades. This estimate is based on Charles E. Banks, *Topographical Dictionary*, ed. E. E. Brownell (1937); Frank Holmes, *Directory of Ancestral Heads of New England Families, 1620–1700* (1964 ed.); and Henry Guppy, *Homes of Family Names in Great Britain* (1890).

2. Clarence C. Goen, *Revivalism and Separatism: Strict Congregationalists and Separate Baptists* (1962), 186–88.

3. S. Leroy Blake, *The Early History of the First Church of Christ, New London, Connecticut* (1897), 1–30, 91–118.

4. Ibid., 175–90. Like Ezekiel, the founder of Rowley, other people named Rogers also claimed descent from the Protestant martyr, John. Of ministers with this surname in the Great Awakening, five were radical New Lights. Of the three others, one was neutral, another suspected of shakiness on original sin, and the third, a definite Old Light. The last, Daniel Rogers of Littleton, had studied with Ebenezer Gay of Hingham. Leaders of the large Rogers clan that sustained the Rogerene sect in eastern Connecticut did not have liberal educations, but adding them makes the evangelical tilt of religious leaders named Rogers even more pronounced.

5. For a description of the Saybrook Platform and the immediate reaction to it, see Richard L. Bushman, *From Puritan to Yankee: Character and the Social Order in Connecticut, 1690–1765* (1967), 149–56.

6. S. Leroy Blake, *The Later History of the First Church of Christ, New London, Connecticut* (1900), 26–98.

7. Edwin S. Gaustad, *Great Awakening in New England* (1957), 18–20; Howard F. Vos, "The Great Awakening in Connecticut" (Ph.D. diss., Northwestern University, 1967), 37–45.

8. David Harlan, *The Clergy and the Great Awakening in New England* (1980), 59–62.

9. Gaustad, *Great Awakening*, 108; Peter S. Onuf, "New Lights in New London: A Group Portrait of the Separatists," *William and Mary Quarterly* 37 (1980): 625–43; Harry S. Stout and Peter S. Onuf, "James Davenport and the Great Awakening in New London," *Journal of American History* 70 (1983): 556–78. The first Shapleigh in New England, Alexander, a gentleman and merchant, had come to Maine from western Devon before 1650. His son had

Quaker sympathies in the 1660s. See Sybil Noyes, Charles Thornton Libby, and Walter Goodwin Davis, *Genealogical Dictionary of Maine and New Hampshire* (1972 ed.), 623–24.

10. *Christian History* 2 (1744): 115–50.

11. Thomas Savage, *Genealogical Dictionary for the First Settlers of New England* (1860), 1:326; *New England Historical and Genealogical Register* 49 (1915): 101.

12. Alan Heimert, *Religion and the American Mind: From the Great Awakening to the Revolution* (1966), 346.

13. Gerald F. Moran, "The Conditions of Religious Conversion in the First Society of Norwich, Connecticut, 1718–1744," *Journal of Social History* 5 (1972): 331–43. See also John M. Bumsted, "Revivalism and Separatism in New England: The First Society of Norwich, Connecticut as a Case Study," *William and Mary Quarterly* 24 (1967): 588–612.

14. Goen, *Revivalism and Separatism,* 83–85; Frances M. Caulkins, *The History of Norwich, Connecticut* (1874), 318–22.

15. The surname Backus or Backhouse had a high frequency in Cumberland and Westmorland and was also associated with the Darlington district of Durham. See Guppy, *Homes,* 118, 180, 451. The actual origins of the pioneer cutler have been discovered; see Everett F. Bingham, "William Backus of Sheffield, Yorkshire, and Norwich, Connecticut," *New England Historical and Genealogical Register* 142 (1988): 253–54; William G. McLoughlin, *Isaac Backus and the American Pietistic Tradition* (1967), 1–9.

16. Alvah Hovey, *A Memoir of the Life and Times of the Rev. Isaac Backus* (1859), 24–32; Charles R. Kellor, *The Second Great Awakening in Connecticut* (1968 ed.), 50–51.

17. Caulkins, *Norwich,* 149–50.

18. Bruce Daniels, "Large Town Power Structures in Eighteenth Century Connecticut: An Analysis of Political Leadership in Hartford, Norwich, and Fairfield" (Ph.D. diss., University of Connecticut, 1970), 101–47.

19. Goen, *Revivalism and Separatism,* 83–85.

20. Robert C. Anderson, "A Genealogical and Social History of the Early Settlement of Lebanon, Connecticut: A Case Study" (M.A. thesis, University of Massachusetts, 1983), 1–127. Lebanon, still reflecting its fear of presbyterian centralizing, was antifederalist and refused to ratify the federal constitution. Clifford Shipton, *Sibley's Harvard Graduates: Biographical Sketches of Those Who Attended Harvard College,* 17 vols. (1933–75), 13:172.

21. Joseph A. Conforti, *Samuel Hopkins and the New Divinity Movement,* Appendix, 227–32.

22. John W. Jeffries, "The Separation in the Canterbury Congregational Church: Religion, Family, and Politics in a Connecticut Town," *New England Quarterly* 52 (1979): 522–49. First Church did participate in the revival, however, despite Cogswell's conservatism, more men joined the congregation. See

Stephen R. Grossbart, "Seeking the Divine Favor: Conversion and Church Admission in Eastern Connecticut, 1711–1832," *William and Mary Quarterly* 46 (1989): 716. Early in the nineteenth century, William Bradford, mentioned in chap. 2, was pastor of Canterbury Separate Church. He was the brother of the Rowley pastor and also a Princeton graduate. Thus links with the British Northwest, the Pilgrims of Plymouth Colony, and Rowley persisted.

23. See map 3; Goen, *Revivalism and Separatism,* 79, 100, 256, and the map facing 114; Lois Mathews Rosenberry, *The Expansion of New England* (1962 ed.), 118–25; Vos, "Great Awakening," 293–313.

24. Clarence W. Bowen, *The History of Woodstock, Connecticut* (1926), 99; Isaac Backus, *History of the Baptists* (1796 ed.), 2:522–23.

25. Shipton, *Harvard Graduates,* 9:223–26. Four members of the Welsh family of Carrier had been accused of witchcraft in Salem in 1692. Richard Carrier's wife was executed as a witch, and several years later he moved from eastern Massachusetts to eastern Connecticut, from Andover to Colchester, from Old Light to New Light territory. He died in 1735, claiming to be 109 years old and leaving thirty-eight great-grandchildren. Savage, *Genealogical Dictionary,* 1:339.

26. Compiled from Shipton, *Harvard Graduates,* and Franklin B. Dexter, *Biographical Sketches of the Graduates of Yale College* (1885–1919), including only those ordained before 1744. See also Franklin B. Dexter, "On Some Social Distinctions at Harvard and Yale before the Revolution," *American Antiquarian Society* 9 (1894): 34–59. A prominent exception was Benjamin Pomeroy of Hebron, a very active itinerant. Banks has him from the Southeast—Dorset—and Guppy finds the surname specific to that county. Guppy also notes, however, that Pomeroy was an ancient Devonshire name. From the Norman Conquest to the reign of Edward VI, the family owned the manor of Berry Pomeroy and much other property in western Devon. See Banks, *Topographical,* 30; Guppy, *Homes,* 536, 174–75.

27. Douglas H. Sweet, "Church Vitality and the American Revolution: Historiographical Consensus and Thoughts on a New Perspective," *Church History* 45 (1976): 341–57. Statistics from New Hampshire also refute the thesis of religious decline. See George B. Kirsch, "Clerical Dismissals in Colonial and Revolutionary New Hampshire," *Church History* 49 (1980): 173.

28. Conforti, *Hopkins and the New Divinity,* 91–94, 175–90.

29. *Contributions to the Ecclesiastical History of Connecticut* (1865), 154–59. See also "Foreign Missionaries from Norwich, Connecticut," *New England Historical and Genealogical Register* 1 (1847): 46. After 1776, New Light territory was expanding and Old Light territory remained static or was shrinking. The New Light was so pervasive in New Light territory that more and more of the Old Light minority with Southeast English origins living there were accommodating to it.

30. Rollin G. Osterweis, *Three Centuries of New Haven, 1638–1938* (1953), 3–21.

31. Ernest H. Baldwin, *Stories of Old New Haven* (1902), 58.

32. Patricia Trainor O'Malley, "Rowley, Massachusetts, 1639–1730: Dissent, Division, and Delimitation in a Colonial Town" (Ph.D. diss., Boston College, 1975), 14–15.

33. Isabel M. Calder, "John Cotton and the New Haven Colony," *New England Quarterly* 12 (1939): 82–94. Davenport collected "wonder stories." These are said to have inspired the Mathers' later interest in "providences." See Robert Middlekauff, *The Mathers: Three Generations of Puritan Intellectuals* (1976), 143; Richard Godbeer, *Devil's Dominion: Magic and Religion in Early New England* (1992), 57.

34. Norman Pettit, *The Heart Prepared: Grace and Conversion in Puritan Spiritual Life* (1986), 168–73, quotation from 169.

35. George L. Clark, *A History of Connecticut: Its People and Institutions* (1914), 145–54. New Haven policy was "generous" and "restrained." See Arthur J. Worrall, *Quakers in the Colonial Northeast* (1980), 21–24; Charles H. Levermore, "Witches in Connecticut," *New Englander* (1885): 788–817. From his arrival at Massachusetts Bay, Ludlow was "arrogant" and "overbearing." See Frank Thistlewaite, *Dorset Pilgrims: The Story of Westcountry Pilgrims Who Went to New England in the Seventeenth Century* (1989), 100–102, 254.

36. Calder, "John Cotton," 82–94.

37. Gilbert Tennent to George Whitefield, Apr. 25, 1741, in *The Great Awakening at Yale College*, ed. Stephen Nissenbaum (1972), 26–27.

38. Vos, "Great Awakening," 112–19.

39. Whitefield inspired the New Lights and they chose the name of White Haven for their new church. Of those signing a petition against Noyes in 1741, fifty-five were men, fifty-seven were women. See Vos, "Great Awakening," 233–34. The Noyes family came from Wiltshire and played a large role in Newbury; see chap. 8.

40. Nissenbaum, *Great Awakening at Yale*, 254–58.

41. Vos, *Great Awakening*, 76–91.

42. Leonard Bacon, *Thirteen Historical Discourses . . . from the Beginning of the First Church in New Haven* (1839), 75–126; William B. Sprague, *Annals of the American Pulpit* (1865), 3:80–92. Gary Nash finds Davenport's temperament "reminiscent" of religious sectarians in England's Commonwealth era; see *The Urban Crucible: Social Change, Political Consciousness and the Origins of the American Revolution* (1979), 208. Davenport's behavior should not be viewed psychiatrically, but seen in its cultural context as a conspicuous example of "sacred theater," where the actor tells the audience what unconsciously it wants to hear. See Clarke Garrett, *Spirit Possession and Popular Religion: From the Camisards to the Shakers* (1987), 1–9, 119–26.

43. Bushman, *Puritan to Yankee,* 250–66; Ralph H. Gabriel, *Religion and Learning at Yale* (1958), 132–37; Sydney E. Ahlstrom, *A Religious History of the American People* (1972), 1:509–10.

44. Trumbull, *Connecticut,* 2:140–41, 157; Vos, "Great Awakening," 224–40.

45. The pioneer, Reverend Peter Prudden, came from Yorkshire to New England in 1638. See Banks, *Topographical,* 186; Holmes, *Ancestral Heads,* cxvx.

46. James Walsh, "The Great Awakening in the First Congregational Church of Woodbury, Connecticut," *William and Mary Quarterly* 28 (1971): 543–62. In his study of five eastern Connecticut churches (in the Norwich-Windham area), Grossbart confirms Walsh's analysis of Woodbury. He found that a church's admission standard—Stoddardean or "strict"—made no difference during the Great Awakening. The influences of family, church, and community were also more important than socioeconomic factors. He noted as well that age of conversion varied considerably. See "Seeking the Divine Favor," 696–740. The New Light was also strong in the churches that sprang from Woodbury's main church: Southbury, Bethlehem, Judea, Northbury.

47. Ebenezer Devotion nurtured evangelism in Suffield and Whitefield visited the community. After Devotion died in 1741, Jonathan Edwards and Peter Reynolds had great preaching successes there and many converts were gathered in by the time Ebenezer Gay, the Hingham pastor's nephew and a prudent Old Light, arrived. John Pynchon had laid out Southfield (or Suffield) in 1670, but it was not really populated until after King Philip's War. The town ordained its first minister in 1698.

48. Compiled from Shipton, *Harvard Graduates,* and Dexter, *Yale Graduates.* Some prominent New Lights are not on this list, either because they did not graduate in the upper half of their class at Harvard or Yale or because they received their education elsewhere, e.g., Bellamy, Wheelock, Pomeroy, Owen, Whitefield, Tennent. In analyzing Harvard graduates who became ministers, Clifford Shipton noted the prominence of the Old Light and neutral Harvard graduates, compared with those from Yale. Harvard's students were drawn quite heavily from eastern Massachusetts and anti-evangelism was part of the ethos of the college. More recently, Harry S. Stout has gone on to assert that the difference in religiosity between Harvard and Yale was so "striking" as to make them quite literally "different schools of thought" in this respect. While a few Old Light pastors from Harvard may have dampened New Light ardor in eastern Connecticut, this is an exaggeration that is misleading for New England as a whole. Harvard did produce many New Light ministers and a large share of the upper half of the Saving Remnant despite its nonevangelical tradition. While the collegiate atmosphere no doubt affected the students, more important was ancestry and geography, families and communities. See Stout, *The New England Soul: Preaching and Culture in Colonial New England* (1986), 220.

49. These laymen had high class rankings. For Pierpont, see Vos, "Great Awakening," 118. Hawley was from Northampton in western Massachusetts and came down the Connecticut River to attend Yale College, graduating fourth in his class of seventeen. The first Hawley, like the first Cotton, had come from Derby in the Midlands in the 1630s. See E. Francis Brown, *Joseph Hawley: Colonial Radical* (1931), 24–41, 129–32; Holmes, *Ancestral Heads,* cxii.

Chapter Eight

The Old Light Dominates:
Eastern Massachusetts, New Hampshire, and Cape Cod

Refugees from Southeast England arrived in New England chiefly between 1633 and 1640. They were largely bourgeois and pushed out of Britain by the religious persecution of Charles I and Archbishop Laud rather than pulled to the colonies by the prospects of land ownership. At first they spread out into the "howling wilderness," but soon settled in fair-sized towns in eastern Massachusetts, eastern New Hampshire, and on Cape Cod. Because these parts were seedbeds of nonevangelism in New England, there were only a few minirevivals in the decades after 1660. This was concomitant with erosion of evangelical piety in Southeast England that persisted there even after the emergence of Whitefield and Wesley.

Early in the seventeenth century Puritans were still distinguished from their Anglican rivals by their Plain Style of preaching. Puritans emphasized communication, avoided classical references, and used metaphors and similes that could be easily understood. By the time of the English Civil War, however, evangelicals and rationalists were beginning to diverge in interpreting the Plain Style. The evangelicals, not formally dubbed New Lights until the next century, used plain colloquial speech in an effort to create resonance in their hearers, stir their hearts as well as their heads. Their oratory skills made them particularly effective in extemporaneous prayers, sermons, and lectures. Evangelical ministers, even during the formalism that preceded the Great Awakening, regarded the care of their flock as important as the preparation of their sermons. German Pietism inspired a few, and most cultivated contact with the laity. This meant house calls, catechizing, and counseling. In times of religious excitement, it also meant organizing religious societies, giving extra weekly lectures, and exchanging pulpits with other evangelicals or itinerating. With the revival, New Lights significantly extended these efforts, trying to channel the energy released to constructive ends. Some New Light ministers were uncomfortable with a style that required good recall and immediate inspiration, since they had few notes, but those who excelled became the most popular speakers in New England. Records of baptisms and admissions substantiate in most instances the correlation of church vitality with effective sermons and diligent pastoral care.

Rationalist pastors—later Old Lights—on the other hand, because they distrusted untutored emotion, were actually plainer, seeking to convey understanding without unduly stirring affections. Their form of the Plain Style was didactic and predictable and had the legalistic tone that Anne Hutchinson criticized a Boston minister for using. These pastors painstakingly laid out the steps necessary to achieve a godly, moral life, and seemed to be close to preaching the importance of good works. After sectarian chaos in the Civil War, those who had emigrated from the Southeast to New England became accustomed to, and reasonably satisfied with, this approach and respected the learning of their ministers. By the time of the Great Awakening, these men saw themselves as "clergy," professional ministers. Their increasing print orientation made them uncomfortable in touching hearers and dealing with personal problems.

Faced with such a minister, the evangelical minority might challenge the preaching or separate from the congregation. Therefore, some Old Light ministers did suffer divisiveness and loss of authority because of their diffidence and reluctance to reach out to those who were strongly affected by the general revival mood. In reaction to the Great Awakening and New Light preaching, they actually went from sermon notes of six to twelve pages to full sermon manuscripts designed to be delivered verbatim. They emphasized careful sermon preparation to avoid presentation of undigested material and favored gravity over "affected tones," "theatrical gestures," or the "inspired" spontaneity of New Light rivals. They defended their style by invoking traditional texts and Puritan preaching manuals. Old Lights believed that "the speaker did not exist for the sake of the audience, but the audience existed to be edified and enlightened by the minister."[1]

The North Shore

Many arrivals from the Southeast congregated in Watertown, up the Charles River from Boston. From parishes in East Anglia, pioneers brought over to Watertown a preference for oligarchy. They were used to electing "the better sort" and giving them broad power and long tenure. Tudor and Stuart social legislation had facilitated this development in East Anglia and it increased during the depression years of the 1620s. The powers of manorial leet courts had dwindled away, superseded by civil parishes, where churchwardens, overseers of the poor, as well as selectmen of the town exerted their undefined powers in making by-laws and running affairs. This oligarchical tendency continued in the colonies. In the first generation, town meetings were pro forma and inhabitants were content to let leaders make local decisions. Only after 1670 did this begin to change, with the voters slowly reclaiming some of their power. Watertown was agricultural but land was held in closes, not strips, and so individual holders could make their own farming arrangements, free from manorial interference. With its wealth of land, Watertown resembled Hingham in social development. Like that town, it remained relatively passive and unmoved by eighteenth-century evangelism.[2]

Watertown and its church passed through the years of the Great Awakening peacefully, without controversy or division. Seth Storer, who became pastor in 1724, was "pious and blameless" with no hint of Arminianism or liberalism. Despite his Northwest stock and childhood in Maine, what moderate New Light leanings he may have had in the beginning brought very modest results and were soon extinguished by the ethos of Watertown. In 1745 he felt antagonistic enough toward evangelism to cooperate with neighboring ministers in denying Whitefield a pulpit on the Awakener's second visit. Storer died in 1774, esteemed by his people. Eleven natives of Watertown graduated from Harvard between 1690 and 1745; only one of the seven who became ministers was a New Light.[3] Church statistics confirm the mild impact of the revival here. The converts only doubled, and the number of men dropped below 40 percent of the number of newcomers instead of rising (see table 8-1).

Table 8-1. Church Admissions in Watertown

	1735–39	1740–44
Male	13	24
Female	19	40
Total	32	64
Average per year	6.4	12.8
Percent male	40.6	37.5
Percent male change		-3.1

Source: Watertown Records (1906), 4:180–84.

Watertown was part of a line of orthodox settlers that extended from Boston to Rye on the New Hampshire coast, shielding Old Light communities from the New Light to the northwest. Five of the eleven Old Lights along this line in New Hampshire ranked in the upper half of their class, making them part of the Old Light elite (see table 8-2). In a few towns, the Scots-Irish minorities were becoming vocal by this time.

The lone New Light in eastern New Hampshire was Ward Cotton. His father was Rowland Cotton of Sandwich in Plymouth and his mother was a Saltonstall of Yorkshire origin so his heritage was Northwest on both sides. He had taught school and joined the church in Marshfield before coming north to the Hampton pulpit. East Anglians had moved into this district, founding Hampton in 1638 and making it a religious extension of eastern Massachusetts.[4] Despite the East Anglians, Cotton was able to achieve some success there. "Mr. Cotton was of an ardent temperament, and when preaching, sometimes nearly lost control of himself. On such occasions, a signal from one of his deacons . . . instantly restored his self-possession. He seldom confined himself to what he had written, but generally added some *extempore* remarks."[5] He subscribed to Edwards's *Life of Brainerd* but lamented some revival excesses. Whitefield commended him for the plainness of his ways and household. Later in life he was dismissed when his congregation thought a paralytical shock had impaired his moral judgment. After a confession church members welcomed him back and he was so eager to preach that he performed gratis. He died in Plymouth while exchanging pulpits with Chandler Robbins in 1768. Cotton was popular but he was the lone "candlestick" in an Old Light New Hampshire dominated by families from East Anglia and the Southeast.

Table 8-2. Ministers in Eastern New Hampshire, 1741–44

Church	Minister	Rank[a]	Religion of Minister
Hampton	Ward Cotton[b]	*7/28*	New Light
Hampton, North	Nathaniel Gookin	*5/37*	Old Light[c]
Hampton, South	William Parsons	*12/40*	Old Light[c]
Hampton Falls	Joseph Whipple	*5/21*	Old Light[c]
Hudson	Nathaniel Merrill[b]	25/29	Old Light
Kensington	Jeremiah Fogg	30/33	Old Light[c]
Kingston, East	Peter Coffin	20/39	Old Light[c]
Londonderry	William Davidson[b]	(U. Edinburgh)	Presbyterian/ Old Light
Plaistow	James Cushing	*7/49*	Old Light
Rye	Samuel Parsons	*8/33*	Old Light
Salem	Abner Bayley	21/31	Old Light

Sources: Names, churches, religious preferences, and ranks compiled from Clifford Shipton, *Sibley's Harvard Graduates: Biographical Sketches of Those Who Attended Harvard College,* 17 vols. (1933-75); probable origins come from Henry Guppy, *Homes of Family Names in Great Britain* (1890); names of signers compiled from Joseph Tracy, *The Great Awakening: A History of the Revival of Religion in the Time of Edwards and Whitefield* (1842), 299-301.

a. Numbers in italic indicate those who graduated in the upper half of their classes.
b. Probable origins or high surname frequency in the Northwest.
c. Signed anti-Whitefield statement.

In 1766 the Hampton church and town called as successor a native of Boston who was a tutor at Harvard. He received a good salary and an elegant new house. He was an Arminian, and the New Light was put aside despite the grumbling of a few Cotton loyalists. Thus the colony's oldest church ended its religious deviation and was brought into conformity with its East Anglian roots, its Old Light neighbors in the area of the original Hampton grant, and eastern New Hampshire generally. The transformation from Congregationalism to Unitarianism came early to the Hampton church.[6]

Cotton's church at Hampton was exceptional; between Watertown and eastern New Hampshire were many towns along the north shore of Massachusetts, largely Old Light. In fact, there were relatively few signs of the Great Awakening in Middlesex and Essex counties (see table 8-3). Whitefield preached outdoors in most of these places in part because meetinghouses were denied him, but made few converts. Churches stood with their pastors and were not very receptive to Whitefield and his message, and the percentage of male converts actually

Table 8.3. Church Admissions on the North Shore, 1741–42

	Male	Female	Total	Percent Male	Percent Male Change
Watertown	23	38	61	37.7	-2.9
Hampton Falls, N.H.	12	29	41	29.3	-7.4
Beverly	8	24	32	25.0	-2.8
Amesbury	9	21	30	30.0	-11.3
Danvers (Salem Village)	12	18	30	40.0	-0.6
Salisbury, 1st	10	17	27	37.0	-1.9
Haverhill, 1st	3	15	18	16.7	-15.6

Sources: Watertown Records (1906), 4:180–83; Warren Brown, *History of Hampton Falls, N.H.* (1918), 2:83–84; "Beverly Church Records," *Essex Institute Historical Collections* 36 (1900): 307–10; Amesbury Church Records; *Confession . . . of Danvers First Church* (1879); "Records of the First Church at Salisbury, Massachusetts, 1687–1754," *Essex Institute Historical Collections* 16 (1879): 55–60; Haverhill First Church Records.

Note: The percent male change is calculated from the average percentage of men in the congregations between 1735 and 1740.

declined. Caleb Cushing of Salisbury complained in October 1742 about the "errors and frenzies" of the revival. The Cushings were in the forefront of anti-Whitefield activity and led many Essex County pastors to sign a remonstrance against him in 1744.[7]

Beverly, a stable agricultural community, exemplifies the conservatism of the region. Beverly completed its separation from Salem Town in 1668. Its original settlers were primarily from eastern Somerset and Dorset and showed distaste for Quakers early, for witches later, and for evangelicals in the Great Awakening because these groups posed a threat to Puritan orthodoxy and communal order. In the 1690s when townspeople were caught between deviant newcomers and an emerging mercantile elite in Salem Town, Beverly's first minister, John Hale, supported Pastor Parris of Salem Village and the executions of witches occurring there. The town was trapped in the middle, neither evangelical and sectarian nor mercantile and proto-Arminian, but, like Salem Village, disposed to defend community and orthodoxy. During the Great Awakening, only 25 percent of the new converts were male.[8]

For the churches of Essex County, the most important single event in making converts was not the Great Awakening but the Great Earthquake of 1727 (see table 8-4). In October of that year a great quake,

Table 8-4. Church Admissions in Essex County

	1727–28	1741–42
Haverhill	226	18
Newbury, West	147	32
Newbury	133	39
Newburyport	113	158
Salisbury, 2d	113	65
Salisbury, 1st	104	26
Groveland	98	30
Bradford	66	16
Danvers (Salem Village)	53	30

Source: Contributions to the Ecclesiastical History of Essex County, Massachusetts (1865), 248–50.

Note: The large gains at Newburyport during the Great Awakening were not long term for that church, however, because many defected afterward.

lasting almost two minutes, passed from northwest to southeast and was felt from the Kennebec to the Delaware. Houses rocked, rolled, and cracked; pewter fell off the shelves, stone walls fell down, and doors unlatched. People ran into the streets.[9]

Even parsons silent on Calvinist doctrines and suspicious of sudden conversions took advantage of fears that this earthquake engendered. These conservative clerics used fear, not directly by invoking original sin, but indirectly by God's wrath expressed in the earthquake, to gain members and hoped to persuade them to accept their view of faith and authority. In general, the admissions in Essex County were four times greater in 1725–30 than in 1740–45.[10] Evidence suggests, however, that these fears soon wore off since church gains were not sustained. The Great Earthquake also failed to improve the male percentage of converts. For these reasons, the quake of 1727 was less significant in altering religious and social attitudes and behavior in Old Light territory than the Great Awakening was in New Light territory.[11]

The Newbury vicinity was a partial exception to the predominant Old Light of the north shore. The town, named for Newbury in Berkshire, evidently harbored a New Light minority that became vocal. Pioneers of New England's Newbury were from four subregions of a triangle in Hampshire and Wiltshire. This part of England was undergoing rapid change in the seventeenth century with an increasingly free market for land. In New England, Newbury had open fields like Rowley, but they were much reduced when the town moved three miles inland in the 1640s. The drive for acquisition and consolidation was much stronger here, however, and there was more debt and real estate trading.

Orthodox Puritans from the river valleys of England predominated but a sectarian minority from the woodlands kept challenging them. Certain Puritan families—the Parker, Noyes, Dummer, and Woodbridge clans—prevailed among elections for selectmen and brought stratification with them, and some of the minority drifted away in the early years. The first clerics—Joseph Noyes, Thomas Parker, Samuel Woodbridge—did not hesitate to serve as selectmen and believed in hierarchy in religion. This meant a presbyterian polity with lax church admissions like the Church of England, open to all but the most scandalous. The woodlands minority dissented from this and as a result drifted away from the town. While many people seemed to agree on trading land, Newbury was never a religiously unified community like Hingham or Watertown. There was conflict in the 1670s and the differences smoldered, finally flaring up during the Great Awakening.[12]

Newbury had only one reported case of witchcraft, but that one was well known because Cotton Mather included it among his "remarkable providences." He believed that the household of William Morse was "disquieted by a daemon" in 1679. There were noises on the roof, bedsteads rising in the air, sticks and stones flying about, and a hog running loose inside the locked house. The occupants were pinched and scratched. Morse, an old shoemaker, blamed Caleb Powell for these occurrences, charging him with witchcraft. Powell was a sailor and an outsider in Newbury. He claimed knowledge of astrology and astronomy and had a reputation as a "cunning man." After studying mysterious happenings at the Morse house, he said he could resolve the matter by taking the grandson living there to consult a wise man. Morse let the boy go with Powell and the disturbances stopped, but he decided that Powell was in league with the Devil and brought charges. Like John Proctor in the more famous Salem episode, Powell counterattacked boldly, claiming that the grandson staged these "remarkable providences" for his unsuspecting grandparents. This counterattack worked and Powell was assessed court costs but acquitted. Powell did acknowledge that Francis Norwood of Gloucester, a Quaker, had instructed him in astrology. But then Elizabeth, Morse's wife, was charged. As a midwife she was vulnerable to such accusations. People had suspected her for some time and she was eventually convicted. After many delays, Governor Simon Bradstreet prevailed over the deputies and the sentence of execution was never carried out.[13]

Although all four of Newbury's ministers—Christopher Toppan, Thomas Barnard, John Lowell, and William Johnson—were Old Lights, Whitefield was able to arouse woodland folk in the community. A New Light minority—with Old Lights in the pulpits—made the situation ripe for itinerants, and some radicals did invade. Nathaniel Rogers, Daniel Rogers, and Samuel Buell occupied Lowell's meeting-house without consent; when they tried the same with Toppan, he repulsed them. In college Toppan had been the most rule-abiding student of his generation, a definite sign of piety, yet chose to oppose this evangelism head on. Instead of welcoming the Awakener as more diplomatic Old Lights did, Toppan called the revival a "delusion of Satan," labeling the aroused as "schemers" and "enthusiasts."[14] Toppan claimed he heard the voice of God directly encouraging him against the evagelists. While both New Lights and Old Lights had their paranoia, Toppan's behavior was extreme. His vocal opposition suggests that he was as divided as his community. He was Old Light in education but temperamentally New Light. The resulting internal conflict made him the most unreasonable and violent opposer in New England.[15]

Dissatisfaction with Toppan's nonevangelism was strong enough to result in a church council that recommended separation in 1744. When Toppan then defied opposition by choosing an Old Light colleague, withdrawals accelerated. Whitefield recommended Jonathan Parsons of Old Lyme, and this radical New Light came from Connecticut to Massachusetts and was ordained over a church organized in 1746. The new Separate church was located on the line between Newbury and Newburyport and attracted about one-third of its members from the churches of Toppan and Lowell. It chose to become the first Presbyterian church in Massachusetts to gain tax exemption from the Congregational establishment. George Whitefield was buried under this church building in 1770.[16]

Newburyport, at the west end of Newbury, was not incorporated as a separate town until 1764. During the revolutionary era it was an important center along the Merrimack River for West Indies trade, ship building, and lumber export. It had no agricultural hinterland and the mercantile class dominated, while many artisans were not qualified to vote. The Anglicans began church services in 1771, and clergy were appropriately conservative in later decades. The town supported the Federalists and attacked Jefferson as an infidel.

The revival was generally weak in the north shore area. Except for Newbury (and Rowley and Cape Ann), most people shared the neutral or Old Light views of their ministers and did not respond to the Great Awakening. In the pulpits, neutrals and Old Lights together outnumbered New Lights by six to one. In fact, after the revival, Arminians and those silent about Calvinist doctrine outnumbered the New Lights, and Arianism and Unitarianism would find fertile soil here in the second half of the eighteenth century.[17]

Boston

The case for Boston as a New Light town can best be made by citing the number and prominence of clergy supporting Whitefield and the revival: Benjamin Colman, William Cooper, Thomas Foxcroft, Joshua Gee, Thomas Prince, Joseph Sewall, Samuel Willard, and and the Scots-Irish John Moorhead. About half the Boston churches favored the Great Awakening but results varied (see table 8-5). At Old South where both pastors, Thomas Prince and Joseph Sewall, were effective advocates, the number of male converts did increase. Prince noted that more people came to see him after Whitefield's visit than after the earthquake. At Brattle Street Church, Benjamin Colman and William Cooper were sincere but genteel supporters who added sheep to the flock but lacked the Calvinistic vigor necessary to attract men. Colman's soft musical voice and proper accents were pleasing to women, and Cooper imitated him. This approach undoubtedly augured the romanticism and sentimentality so noticeable in some urban churches in the nineteenth century. This cultivation of feelings could later constitute an alternative—Transcendentalism-Spiritualism—to evangelism for a segment of the Saving Remnant.

At Boston's First Church ministers were divided. Charles Chauncy was silent early but by mid-1742 had become New England's most prolific antirevivalist. This nearly nullified the mild advocacy of his colleague, Thomas Foxcroft. Admission records confirm this by indicating a slight increase in the percentage of male converts but fewer converts overall than after the earthquake. New Brick Church did not respond much to either event. The Old South was the only church where the proportion of men rose.[18]

Table 8-5. Church Admissions in Boston

	1727	1741–42
Brattle		
Male	28	40
Female	51	89
First Church		
Male	12	8
Female	35	15
New Brick		
Male	0	10
Female	0	15
Old North		
Male	17	2
Female	51	15
Old South		
Male	21	44
Female	45	53

Source: Cowing, "Sex and Preaching," 633.

Yet Boston was where demand for soul liberty had aroused emotions and caused division in the beginning. Anne Hutchinson's antinomianism appealed to folk from Lincoln and her challenge of authority attracted commercial people chaffing under magistrates' restrictions. The town had also maintained its pioneer tradition of voluntary pastoral contributions, thereby keeping ministers responsive to hearers. Many worshippers had some sympathy with the revival and would not want to hear it condemned too strongly. Whitefield and other revivalists were well received. The Great Awakener drew 4,000 people to Brattle Street and 20,000 to Boston Common. When James Davenport, Gilbert Tennent, and Andrew Croswell followed up, there was some social radicalism in their messages. These New Lights were harsher than the Awakener, arraigning the powerful and undermining deference. The revival may have been transient but it did give new importance to the oral culture of the people and indicated a protodemocratic spirit that anticipated the Revolution.

Andrew Croswell, one of these New Lights, was a native of Massachusetts and a Harvard graduate but was ministering to Groton Second (Ledyard) Church in eastern Connecticut Colony when the Great Awakening arrived. In the excitement, his objections to singing were "sung away." Like Wesley, Whitefield, and, later, Wilberforce, he found frequent singing was an antidote for despondency. He encouraged lay exhortation and itinerated in Massachusetts and Connecticut in defiance of the law. He was censorious toward less aroused colleagues, and urged people to separate from unawakened clerics. His excessive behavior rivaled that of Davenport and his recantation of revival excesses was only halfhearted. Croswell moved from eastern Connecticut to Boston in 1746, settling over Eleventh Church, a flock of persons who had withdrawn from other churches. From this pulpit he would maintain a thirty-nine-year crusade against Arminianism in Boston and at Harvard College. His English origins were in the same region (Derby-Worcester) as James Davenport. And long after Davenport had faded from the scene, Croswell championed and perfected extreme New Light ideas, trying to make Boston and eastern New England uncomfortable for Old Lights.

After his conversion in 1736 at age twenty-seven, Croswell saw Christianity as joyful and rejected the trope of a painful pilgrimage in this world. He opposed preparation and the struggle for assurance; he favored instantaneous conversion and offered a God of comfort to relieve religious anxiety. Where works were "preached up, there was wickedness" while grace and goodness were correlated. For him the Awakening was holy, a second Reformation. Therefore he went back beyond Puritan thinkers to the Reformers—Luther, Zwingli, Beza. Among contemporaries, he found some kinship with the Erskines in Scotland and William Romaine and Martin Madan, Anglican Evangelicals in England.

Croswell's long tenure at the Eleventh Church (1746–85) gave Boston a direct link between the radical religion of the Great Awakening and the radical politics of the Revolution. But at the hub, where synods had met to banish Roger Williams and Anne Hutchinson, this critic of orthodox clergy was widely mocked for theatrical evangelism and did not find the resonance for his antinomian ideas that he might have had in eastern Connecticut or the Plymouth Colony. Attacked early for "enthusiasm" and later for "errors," Croswell stayed with evangelism, the religion of his origins. During the Revolution, he looked beyond Boston and took heart from the New Light Stir in northwestern New England and the revival in Nova Scotia.[19]

Croswell reflected the religious diversity that began when English authorities pressured the Puritans to permit a Baptist church in the 1660s. These early Baptists were Arminian, quietistic, and obscure. In addition, Sir Edmund Andros, royal governor of the Dominion of New England, started an Anglican chapel service in 1686. Anglicanism soon spread beyond families of English officials and gained fashion and status. At the end of the century, some liberals founded Brattle Street Church. This new congregation competed with Anglicans for the patronage of the genteel, abandoned public relation, and permitted extended reading from scriptures, a practice Puritans had once condemned as "popery." The mounting religious diversity and consequent tolerance in Boston weakened pressure to belong to any church at all. By the time of the Great Awakening in 1740, the lone Baptist church had a learned minister and its members had gained respectability. Jeremiah Condy was a Harvard graduate and native of Boston. He shared the strong Arminianism of England's General Baptists and its milder form in eastern Massachusetts. During the revival a New Light minority found his Old Light preaching dull and sought a separation.[20]

Charles Chauncy, minister in Boston, better represented the feelings of the congregations than did Condy or Croswell. He was the quintessential Ramistic Puritan, truly disturbed and offended by the emotion, spontaneity, and disorder the Great Awakening brought. He could not believe the converts had genuinely become "new creatures" and was on the lookout for backsliders. His antirevival tracts quickly made Boston the publishing center for Old Light material. Many prominent clergy who settled in eastern Massachusetts were natives of Boston, but few preached the New Light.[21]

Some prominent Bostonians, especially lawyers, were much more inclined to side with Chauncy than Edwards. If their antecedents were Southeastern, neither oratory nor guilt could bring them into the evangelical fold. By nature reserved and not disposed to activism, they were content to subscribe to Chauncy's *Seasonable Thoughts* and, if church members, vote to keep the New Light away from their own congregations. And some sons of clergy forsook theology for more lucrative careers available in the vicinity in the eighteenth century. Among lay opponents there were a few with Northwest surnames. These graduates, influenced no doubt by their professional colleagues or Boston residence, had drifted away from evangelical roots far enough to resist the revival, although they might prove vulnerable if it got too close.

The origins of Boston's inhabitants were broadly split, like those of its counterpart, London, with over 60 percent from the Southeast and a large Northwest minority. And like the English metropolis, Boston from its beginnings was a social *entrepôt* with many people passing through, moving out, or moving back.[22] As the hub of New England, Boston provided headquarters and printing presses for New Lights, Old Lights, and others. If New Lights commanded more attention in 1741, this was offset by the strong influence of opposers, lay as well as clerical. Therefore Boston should be viewed as neutral ground, an interesting mixture of revival advocates and critics.

The South Shore

Firstcomers on the south shore of the Massachusetts Bay Colony had come largely from the Southeast. Dorchester had a large Northwest minority. East Anglians had a majority in Roxbury, Dedham, and Hingham. Many settlers of Weymouth were from Dorset or eastern Somerset. In Scituate, at the northern tip of Plymouth Colony, Kentish people predominated; it is included here because of its cultural affinity with the south shore. Table 8-6 indicates that only 10 percent of the settlers were from the Northwest with another 17 percent from the Southeast, but with Northwest surnames.

Table 8-6. Probable Origins of Settlers of South Shore Towns

	Southeast	Southeast (Northwest Surnames)	Northwest	Total	Percent Northwest
Braintree	21	4	3	28	10.7
Dedham	24	1	3	28	10.7
Dorchester	21	11	13	45	28.0
Hingham and Hull	69	8	4	81	4.9
Roxbury	34	17	2	53	3.7
Scituate	29	5	3	37	8.1
Weymouth	15	5	1	21	4.7

Sources: Calculated from Banks, *Topographical Dictionary*, Holmes, *Ancestral Heads*, and Guppy, *Homes*.

At the northern edge of this district, Dorchester called Richard Mather, father of Increase and grandfather of Cotton, and first of this Lancashire clan in the colonies. He was a millennialist and strict congregationalist who looked with admiration on Davenport's settlement at New Haven. To combat indifference, Mather sought to use the Half-Way Covenant to keep children and baptized adults under the watch and care of the church. There was a mass covenant renewal after King Philip's War, and the church began to grow. Except for this renewal in 1677, however, most neophytes joined the church in the traditional manner, without owning the covenant. Reluctance to accept the Half-Way Covenant was never overcome and, although adopted at a fairly early date, never really became an integral part of the Dorchester polity.[23] The church recovered from the low period of 1650–77, but showed no signs of retaining any of the evangelical impulses of its first minister.

Dorchester had the largest Northwest minority on the south shore and during the Great Awakening the Old Light minister was openly challenged. Samuel Bird, a native of the town, called the pastor a "dumb dog" for not preaching original sin and publicly prayed for his conversion or removal from the pulpit. Bird had been expelled from Harvard for leaving his classes without permission to follow an itinerant preacher. New Lights tried to ordain him at Dunstable (Nashua) in southeastern New Hampshire but Old Lights denied him the ministerial salary. His New Light friend John Cleaveland of Chebacco had the connections to get Bird the pulpit in New Haven's White Haven Church, a more congenial place for his views.[24]

Between Braintree and Dorchester at the southern edge of Boston, the Northwest minority was larger and the New Light sentiment more visible. Braintree, childhood home of John Adams in the 1740s, was tranquil during the revival, however. The future president heard about the French and got his knowledge of contemporary affairs from John Hancock, a highly clerical Old Light there. Hancock warned that the new Anglican outpost in Quincy was a Trojan horse, posing a religious and social threat to the Congregational establishment.[25]

When Hancock died in 1744, the church unanimously chose Lemuel Briant, a native of Scituate, after only a two-week trial. Briant was annoyed by the aggressiveness of New Lights and challenged their claim that without conversion "all our righteousness is a filthy rag." While private criticism of this evangelical view was fairly common in this Old

Light town, when Briant called New Lights "fiery bigots" from the pulpit of liberal Jonathan Mayhew in Boston, this got the attention of New Light clergy. They sought to embarrass him by being charitable and tolerant, suggesting that he was the bigot denying the right of private judgment. The ensuing exchanges caused Braintree's church leaders to explore their pastor's theology. He was certainly too liberal and outspoken for this orthodox town, being not only Arminian but Arian, having recommended John Taylor, the Arian English writer, to his flock.

In pondering Briant's case, church elders consulted John Adams, by this time a Harvard student, who sympathized with Briant, calling him the only really enlightened person in town. Yet Adams conceded that Briant was "too jocular and liberal, too light and gay, if not immoral."[26] Briant had boasted that his congregation backed him, but support weakened during the long controversy. Finally in 1753 a committee of the church, headed by Colonel Josiah Quincy, sustained Briant, granting him the right to catechize only those parts of scriptures he still believed in and letting him recommend Taylor's book to church members so they could make up their own minds about the divinity of Christ. This generous decision, from a committee that represented the liberal majority of the church, came too late to save Briant, however. His wife had fled and his health was broken, so he resigned, dying not long afterward.

In nearby Weymouth, William Smith, pastor and friend of Gay at Hingham, had carried his church through the Great Awakening without stir or controversy. Smith had married into the Quincys of Northamptonshire, who had become the old family in this district, and none of them had shown any sympathy for evangelism.[27] Most people of the region had little history of that kind of emotionalism, and itinerants that visited lacked educational and social standing. As a result, the New Light was a genuine option only for a minority here, while most were left with orthodox Congregationalism, Arminianism, or the combination of Arminianism and episcopacy of the Church of England. After the Revolution, many would be ready to go beyond a quiet Arminianism to Arianism and Unitarianism, following the trend Gay set in Hingham.

A focus on several generations of the Tompson family will illustrate how those from the Northwest handled their faith in territory that became religiously unsympathetic. William Tompson came to New England in 1637 after preaching in Winwick, Lancashire, and was Braintree's first minister. He was a native of that northern county, an

Oxford graduate, and a powerful preacher. In his writings he usually collaborated with Richard Mather of Dorchester. Tompson made a long missionary tour of Virginia in 1642–43, an early date for a New England divine to show such interest. He made some converts but his wife's death and a decline in piety that set in shortly afterward may have affected him unduly. He fell out of the light and, as Cotton Mather phrased it, "into the Devil's bathtub." A black melancholia rendered him unable to perform his ministerial duties. Neighboring ministers and churches prayed for him and after seven years, the spell lifted and he died in peace. Mather was sympathetic with this sick soul because he believed that God had a controversy with New England that made its religious leaders especially vulnerable to "splenetic maladies." It was his realization that even saints could become sinners when "the humours vitiated" and "Satan insinuates himself and takes possession" that caused Mather's reservations about spectral evidence and compacts with the Devil in the Salem witchcraft cases.

Benjamin Tompson, William's son, was born in the Quincy section of Braintree in 1665. After college, he taught school and practiced "physick," but his distinction came as New England's first native poet. Modern critics have praised him for using local material and depicting real American Indians rather than European conceptions of them. Although his lamentations of the loss of the "golden times" of pioneer days were conventional for a poet who heard jeremiads from the pulpit, this does not necessarily mean that his rejection of materialism was insincere. Edward, son of Benjamin and grandson of William, was the schoolmaster who preached irregularly in the west end of Newbury before moving to Plymouth. With him the locus of the family, like that of others of Northwest origin, shifted away from eastern Massachusetts.

William, great-grandson and namesake of the first Tompson, was ordained pastor at Blue Point (Scarsborough) in the Maine District. He became friends with Thomas Smith of Falmouth and joined him in prayers against irreligion, epidemics, and Quakers. He signed the East York Association statement against Arminianism and antinomianism as well as the pro-revival testimonial of 1743. Whitefield preached from Tompson's Scarsborough pulpit three times in 1745. William's son became minister at Standish, Maine.[28]

Thus the Northwest tendencies toward irregular and evangelical preaching, missionary work, poetry, and pastoralism ran through four generations of the Tompson family from Lancashire to Plymouth and

Maine, centers of New Light. The Tompsons moved away from eastern Massachusetts, not the sustenance of the invisible world. Their kind of piety caused them to be invited to and, more importantly, accept settlement in areas of Northwest predominance that would respond warmly to the New Light in the 1740s.

Among those who remained along the south shore from East Anglian Hingham to Kentish Scituate, the Great Awakening was quite mild. At South Weymouth, where a church had been organized in 1723, James Bayley was a "rather quiet" New Light, signing the Whitefield testimonials of 1743 and 1745.

The Chauncy family was associated with early Scituate. The first Charles Chauncy moved from Ware, Hertfordshire, to Plymouth and then Scituate and after thirteen years became president of Harvard College in Cambridge. He was a strong-willed cleric who opposed baptizing infants but showed little evangelical tendencies. Chauncys were prominent in Massachusetts and Connecticut but none succumbed to the New Light in the colonial era.

Response to the revival was particularly weak at Scituate (see table 8-7). Because the majority of pioneers were from Kent on the south coast of England and the Northwest minority was small, this place was naturally unresponsive to evangelism.[29] The pastor of First Church, Shearjashub Bourne, was born on Cape Cod. Clifford Shipton called him cautious and obscure. He introduced the Half-Way Covenant and subscribed to Chauncy's *Seasonable Thoughts* but remained unchallenged throughout the revival. Bourne obviously had no need to be vociferous in articulating the Old Light position. In 1754 David Barnes received a unanimous call and was settled at Second Church (Norwell). Rational and laconic in speech, he avoided controversy and was one of the first Unitarians in Massachusetts. Scituate, with a population of only 3,700 in 1830, had two Unitarian churches.[30]

Lack of support for the Great Awakening in this region can also be demonstrated by analyzing its Harvard graduates. Between 1690 and 1745, forty-four graduated from Harvard, seventeen became ministers, but only one, Nicholas Loring, became a New Light and he moved to Maine.[31] While Old Light was notable along the south shore, there were some signs of New Light dissent in most towns, especially Dorchester and Roxbury, but rational religion was the norm for pastors and church members along this coast and this area would be a major spawning ground for Unitarianism.[32]

Table 8-7. Church Admissions in Scituate

Admissions	First Church	Second Church
1735–41		
Male	4	9
Female	10	12
Total	14	21
Average per year	2.0	3.0
Percent male	35.0	42.9
1742–45		
Male	10	14
Female	29	37
Total	39	51
Average per year	9.8	12.8
Percent male	25.6	27.4
Percent male change	-9.4	-15.5

Sources: "Records of the First Church of Scituate," *Mayflower Descendant* 11 (1909): 138-41; "Records of the Second Church of Scituate (Norwell)," *New England Historical and Genealogical Register* 58 (1904): 82-84. More than two out of three Scituate pioneers were from the Southeast; of the remainder, only one in twelve came from the Northwest; the others had Northwest surnames. See Banks, *Topographical,* and Holmes, *Ancestral Heads.*

Cape Cod

Barnstable County on Cape Cod differed in religiosity from eastern Massachusetts and Plymouth County. The majority of settlers had come from the Southeast, but only 15 percent were from East Anglia. Therefore, the cape was basically nonevangelical yet less presbyterian and more sectarian than the eastern Bay Colony (see table 8-8). By 1650 its character was beginning to take shape but later settlers, including some Northwest folk relocating from places like Hingham, would add to its religious pluralism.

At the end of the seventeenth century, Nathaniel Stone was ordained over Harwich First Church. Influential from the beginning, he was largely successful in setting the clerical tone on the cape. His father had arrived in Massachusetts from Essex in 1635. He was born in Watertown and one of the Hobarts of Hingham had prepared him for college. He believed in strict church discipline and rejected arguments for

Table 8-8. Church Admissions on Cape Cod, 1741–45

Church	Founded	Religion	Admissions per Year
Truro	1709	Old Light	15.4
Falmouth	1708	Old Light	14.6
Barnstable	1725	Old Light	11.0
Sandwich, 2d	1735	New Light	8.8
Harwich, 1st (Brewster)	1700	Old Light	7.6
Barnstable, West	1639	New Light	7.4
Sandwich, 1st	1638	Old Light	6.2
Yarmouth, East (Dennis)	1727	Old Light	5.6

Source: John Michael Bumsted, "The Pilgrims' Progress: The Ecclesiastical History of the Old Colony, 1620–1775" (Ph.D. diss., Brown University, 1965), 438.

Note: The average number of admissions per year was 9.6.

congregational autonomy. Stone represented the nonevangelical presbyterianism of East Anglia, but unlike the Hobarts of eastern Massachusetts, found himself in an area of somewhat more religious diversity, an atmosphere less conducive to deference and ecclesiastical order. The spread of settlers and the lax parish system made the cape vulnerable to discontents, divisions, and even separations. During the glacial age, rationalist leaders of Barnstable County therefore felt threatened by a rising tide of indifference, immorality, and sectarianism, and this was fueled to a minor degree by evangelical folk from the Northwest.

In 1718 Stone challenged the qualifications of Samuel Osborn, about to be settled as minister at Eastham. The Harwich pastor called Osborn a stranger who was ignorant, unorthodox, and immoral. Osborn had come to the colonies from Ireland in 1707 and had been preaching on Martha's Vineyard and the cape for over a decade. He had no letters of recommendation but claimed to be a graduate of Glasgow. His answers to examining ministers suggest that he may have leaned toward free will; he had been charged with fathering an illegitimate child on Martha's Vineyard. Stone explained that in opposing Osborn, he was upholding law, scripture, and the New England way. Despite Stone's efforts, however, most people proved reluctant to challenge publicly the settling of Osborn. Rowland Cotton of Sandwich had befriended Osborn and he, together with the clerics of Falmouth and Plymouth, proceeded to ordain Osborn. Stone was persistent, however, in dating permissiveness on the cape from the acceptance of Osborn. He blamed decline of family government, "wicked" practices, and sexual "unclean-ness" of young people on the presence of this Irishman among the cape clergy. Stone's church at Harwich responded only mildly to the Great Awakening, probably because of his strong attitude.

The first separation on the cape was different from those in New Light territory. Clerics who supported the separation at Sandwich in 1735 lat-er took an Old Light stance during the Great Awakening. Those defect-ing were objecting to the "premature" birth of the minister's child. The leader of the disaffected, Francis Worcester—of a Buckingham family—had trouble holding his followers even during the peak years of the re-vival. His grandson was an early Unitarian. Future New Lights could be more tolerant of an early baby and believed that desertion of a minister for that reason was unfair. Some persons from Chatham and Harwich came together, under the leadership of Joshua Nickerson, for meetings. A smaller number split off and drifted over to the Baptists. Nathan Ewer led a third group of Separates, but when he finally left the area, his group joined the Baptists. Separates on the cape may have been more inclined toward congregationalism than their ministers, but their feelings did not lead to evangelism. Scattered population and the low proportion of East Anglians gave Old Lights, and New Lights, only a precarious hold here, which left Cape Cod mixed in religious character, but mainly neutral.[33]

Thus the coastline was Old Light wherever the Southeasterners were dominant from Rye to Scituate; this was the seedbed for Unitarianism after 1800. Boston, the hub, had prominent leaders on both sides while Cape Cod was mixed. The Northwest people, like the Hutchinsonians earlier, moved away, up to northern New England, down to Plymouth and Rhode Island, or westward into the interior.

Notes

1. Harry S. Stout, *The New England Soul: Preaching and Religious Culture in Colonial New England* (1986), 218–22; George W. Harper, "Clericalism and Revival: The Great Awakening in Boston as a Pastoral Phenomenon," *New England Quarterly* 57 (1984): 554–66.

2. David Grayson Allen, *In English Ways: The Movement of Societies and Transferral of English Local Law and Custom to Massachusetts Bay, 1600–1690* (1981), 119–60. Perhaps the most familiar surname in Watertown to modern readers is Coolidge of Cambridgeshire.

3. Compiled from Clifford Shipton, *Sibley's Harvard Graduates: Biograph-ical Sketches of Those Who Attended Harvard College*, 17 vols. (1933–75), 6:412–14, and William B. Sprague, *Annals of the American Pulpit* (1865).

4. In Hampton, East Anglians comprised 70 percent of the population. Rachel Fuller and Isabella Towle were tried for witchcraft, and Eunice Cole was tried three times in 1656, 1673, and 1680. Although the records are incomplete, all five cases probably resulted in acquittal. See John P. Demos, *Entertaining Satan: Witchcraft and the Culture of Early New England* (1982), 318–21, 404, 406, 407. Thus Hampton is yet another instance of a link between Southeast (specifically East Anglian) settlers and prosecutions for witchcraft.

5. Joseph Dow, *The History of the Town of Hampton, New Hampshire from Its Settlement in 1638 to 1892* (1893), 402.

6. The Half-Way Covenant was already in use here in January 1667. See ibid., 359, 395–418.

7. The following pastors signed the anti-Whitefield statement: William Balch of Groveland, Edward Barnard of Haverhill, Thomas Barnard of Newbury, Caleb Cushing of West Boxford, William Johnson of Newbury, John Lowell of Newburyport, Elisha Odlin of Amesbury, Joseph Parsons of Bradford, and Samuel Webster of Salisbury's Second Church. See Joseph Tracy, *The Great Awakening: A History of the Revival of Religion in the Time of Edwards and Whitefield* (1842), 344–54.

8. Richard M. Gildrie, *Salem, Massachusetts: A Covenant Community* (1975), 118–19, 125–29, 131, 148.

9. W. B. Trask, "The Great Earthquake of 1727," *New England Historical and Genealogical Register* 14 (1860): 205; Alan Heimert, *Religion and the American Mind: From the Great Awakening to the Revolution* (1966), 68–75; William D. Andrews, "The Literature of the 1727 New England Earthquake," *Early American Literature* 7 (1973): 281–94.

10. *Contributions to the Ecclesiastical History of Essex County, Massachusetts* (1865), 248–50.

11. Cedric B. Cowing, "Sex and Preaching in the Great Awakening," *American Quarterly* 20 (1968): 626–27.

12. Allen, *In English Ways*, 82–116.

13. Demos, *Entertaining Satan*, 132–52; Richard Godbeer, *Devil's Dominion: Magic and Religion in Early New England* (1992), 196.

14. Shipton, *Harvard Graduates*, 4:116–17. Toppan thanked God for saving him from injury when his horse fell. He claimed the Devil threw a mist over his eyes and those of his horse. Joshua Coffin described Toppan as "partially deranged." See *Sketches of the History of Newbury* (1845), 367–77.

15. The Toppans were from Calbridge in Yorkshire's West Riding. See Herbert Tappan, "The English Ancestry of the Toppan or Tappan Family of Newbury," *New England Historical and Genealogical Register* 33 (1879): 66–68.

16. Clarence C. Goen, *Revivalism and Separatism: Strict Congregationalists and Separate Baptists* (1962), 100–101. An estimated two out of three permanent settlers came from the Southeast, especially Wiltshire and Hampshire.

Of the remainder, only one in twelve were from the Northwest; the rest were from the Southeast but had names with a high frequency in the Northwest. Calculated from Allen, *In English Ways*, 261–68; Charles E. Banks, *Topographical Dictionary*, ed. E. E. Brownell (1937); and Frank Holmes, *The Directory of Ancestral Heads of New England Families, 1620–1700* (1964 ed.).

17. Calculated from Shipton, *Harvard Graduates*, for the area north of Boston.

18. Cowing, "Sex and Preaching," 632–33.

19. Edwin S. Gaustad, *Great Awakening in New England* (1957), 56–59; Gary B. Nash, *The Urban Crucible: Social Change, Political Consciousness, and the Origins of the American Revolution* (1979), 198–232; Leigh Eric Schmidt, "A Second and Glorious Reformation: The New Light Extremism of Andrew Croswell," *William and Mary Quarterly* 43 (1986): 214–44. See also Clarke Garrett, *Spirit Possession and Popular Religion: From the Camisards to the Shakers* (1987), 114–15. Andrew's relative was converted during the Great Awakening. He became an itinerant preacher who often "experienced quickening influences of the Divine Spirit" while reading religious works. See *Sketches of the Life and Extracts from the Journals, and Other Writings, of the Late Joseph Croswell* (1809), 14–40.

20. William G. McLoughlin, *New England Dissent, 1630–1833* (1971), 1:49–53, 422, 318–19. The Condy (or Candy) surname derived from Hampshire, Wiltshire, and eastern Somerset, the cradle of latitudinarianism in the West Country east of the cultural divide. See Henry Guppy, *Homes of Family Names in Great Britain* (1890), 465.

21. Edward M. Griffin, *Old Brick: Charles Chauncy of Boston, 1705–1787* (1980), 54–74. Benjamin Franklin of Philadelphia was Boston-born and a definite Old Light. He befriended Whitefield but could not share his theology or feel his evangelical fervor. He was self-taught, but received honorary degrees from Harvard and Yale. Franklin's parents had come to Boston from Northamptonshire in 1673, during the Restoration. Banks, *Topographical*, 126.

22. Origins of Boston's early settlers are estimated from Banks, *Topographical*, Holmes, *Ancestral Heads*, and Guppy, *Homes*. For Boston's laity, see Shipton, *Harvard Graduates*.

23. Robert G. Pope, *Half-Way Covenant: Church Membership in Puritan New England* (1969), 226–31.

24. John Warner Barber, *Historical Collections of Every Town in Massachusetts* (1840), 526–27.

25. Catherine D. Bowen, *John Adams and the American Revolution* (1950), 27–29, 33–36.

26. Conrad Wright, *Beginnings of Unitarianism* (1955), 67–72, 78–81.

27. Most clerics named Smith favored the New Lights; the Weymouth minister was an exception. Samuel Quincy assisted Alexander Garden in

Charleston, South Carolina. He was a Boston-born missionary from the Society for the Propagation of the Gospel in Foreign Parts and "one of the most effective of southern Anglican preachers who directly opposed the Great Awakening," emphasizing "the reasonable quality of Christianity" and regeneration. See S. Charles Bolton, *Southern Anglicanism: the Church of England in Colonial South Carolina* (1982), 92–93. An excerpt from Samuel Quincy's arguments is included in Alan Heimert and Perry Miller, eds., *The Great Awakening: Documents Illustrating the Crisis and Its Consequences* (1967), 481–89. The Quincys came to Boston from Northamptonshire. See Banks, *Topographical,* 125.

28. Frederick Chase, "The Rev. William Tompson," *New England Historical and Genealogical Register* 15 (1861): 112–16.

29. Sprague, *Annals,* 1:110–14; Robert J. Wilson III, *The Benevolent Deity: Ebenezer Gay and the Rise of Rational Religion in New England, 1696–1787* (1984), 102–6.

30. Calculated from Shipton, *Harvard Graduates.*

31. Wilson, *Benevolent Deity,* 83–85, 102–6.

32. Shipton, *Harvard Graduates,* 4:79–82; John M. Bumsted, "A Caution to Erring Christians: Ecclesiastical Disorder on Cape Cod, 1717 to 1738," *William and Mary Quarterly* 28 (1971): 413–38; Gustavus S. Paine, "Ungodly Carriage on Cape Cod," *New England Quarterly* 25 (1952), 181–98.

33. Except for the Plymouth hinterland discussed in chap. 6, the Old Colony shared these characteristics with the cape, as did Rhode Island in its early days, with less than 30 percent deriving from the Northwest. By the time of the Great Awakening, many of these were Arminian sectarians—Quakers and Baptists—who were nonevangelical and suspicious of, or relatively immune to, the revival message. With Inner Light, they did not need New Light. Westerly, next to the Connecticut border, was an exception. The Reverend Joseph Park, a missionary in Westerly, went to nearby Stonington, Connecticut, and was converted by Gilbert Tennent. When itinerants brought the revival over to Rhode Island, Park helped them. In 1743, despite the opposition of some Baptists, he was ordained in Westerly over a Congregational church that included American Indian converts. See *Christian History* 1 (1743): 201. Park's immigrant ancestor, Robert, came to Boston from Preston, Lancashire, in 1630. See Banks, *Topographical,* 88. Westerly was in the "Narragansett country" that both Connecticut and Rhode Island claimed; the borderline was not finally established until 1728. See Robert J. Taylor, *Colonial Connecticut: A History* (1979), 56–59.

Chapter Nine

The Old Light Persists:
The Connecticut River Valley

Colonists from Massachusetts Bay founded Connecticut Colony in 1636. From Dorchester, Watertown, and Newton they moved a hundred miles down the Great Trail to settle Hartford, Wethersfield, and Windsor on the west bank of the Connecticut River. Crowding in some Massachusetts towns that had been laid out too close together without anticipating need for grazing land gave economic impetus for migration. But for the leader, Thomas Hooker, differences in religion were paramount. At the time of the decision to move, John Cotton and Anne Hutchinson's antinomian faction were temporarily in the ascendant and Hooker openly resisted the elevation of faith over works this group represented. Since Hooker could not compete with Cotton or Anne Hutchinson in charisma and his followers lacked land, removal to fertile Connecticut seemed to be the answer.[1]

These pioneers had come largely from the Southeast, and almost a third were from East Anglia (see table 9-1). Only five of the sixty-eight were from the Northwest and another dozen had Northwest surnames. The second group did contain some families that would later feel the New Light: Edwards, Lord, Reynolds, and Steel. As the two cultural groups sorted themselves out on the Connecticut River, some people from the Northwest moved again, thereby reducing this minority still further. Some went up the river into western Massachusetts, others down to New Haven or Long Island or across into eastern Connecticut.

At the very beginning of Connecticut's settlement there was some

Table 9-1. Probable Origins of the Connecticut Pioneers

	Hartford	Wethersfield	Windsor
East Anglia	16	2	4
Other Southeast	11	6	12
Southeast, Northwest surnames	6	1	5
Northwest	—	3	2
Total	33	12	23

Source: Compiled from Charles E. Banks, *Topographical Dictionary,* ed. E. E. Brownell (1937).

coercion. At Windsor emigrants from Massachusetts simply seized a trading post and land that the Plymouth Colony had started in 1633 to challenge Dutch traders. They later offered compensation, but Plymouth did not regard it as adequate and was resentful.[2] Thus Southeast people began colonization of Connecticut by displacing some first settlers, many from the West Country. This sorting out would eventually leave those from the Southeast with predominant influence on the west bank of the river from Hartford down to the sound and from Stratford along the shoreline to the New York border.

Thomas Hooker, leader of the exodus, settled in Hartford and made that town the intellectual capital of the region. He was a prolific writer and continued to develop his theory of preparation for grace, begun in England. He believed that baptism carried considerable efficacy, especially for children. Infants, he taught, lacked inherent grace yet had "a portion of grace" and "relative holiness," thanks to assistance from the Spirit of God. To Calvin conversion had been an enigma, and Cotton held that people were helpless to achieve it on their own, but Hooker emphasized a recognizable sequence of events and the role of the will in coming to God. Preparation was, in fact, absolutely necessary to salvation but should be done in a mood of anticipation, not fear. In admitting persons to church, he did not demand that they recount specifics or even steps in preparation but assumed that by the time they came forward with "a Hope toward God," conversion had already occurred. He stressed preparation and assumed that gradualism in conversion was normative.

Hooker actually diverged from Puritan manuals, changing his sermons for the sake of his system of preparation. He was a Ramist who came to see his sermons as efficacious in their own right because they relied on principles of "right reason." While agreeing with Calvin that humanity had fallen from grace, Hooker seemed to argue that faith engendered election and not the reverse. Hooker's views on conversion reflected a tendency to reduce the harshness of election doctrine and set a pattern of church admissions that has been called "judicial charity" and caused some to describe his Connecticut settlement as a "Valley of Democracy" compared with the Massachusetts Bay Colony.[3]

Thus Hooker and his party from the Southeast planted seeds of rational religion on the west bank of the Connecticut River and this outlook gradually prevailed in later decades. He also proved effective in advocating congregationalism. Yet after his death, divisions over polity quickly came to light, with East Anglians pushing presbyterianism as they had in Hingham. Deliberations over the Half-Way Covenant sharpened discussion of polity between 1650 and 1670. Presbyterians seemed ready to combine a strong minister and elders with an admission standard that deemphasized public relation of conversion further, requiring only good moral character and a promise to abide by church discipline. While other rationalists could compromise on adherence to church rules—Hooker's standard of "judicial charity" was generous— they did want to stay close to the congregationalism of Hooker, so dissension persisted.

These forces became personalized in the conflict between John Haynes and Joseph Whiting in the 1660s. Both young men were residents of Hartford but had different views of church polity. Haynes was the successor to Samuel Stone, who had defined elders in a historic phrase as "a speaking aristocracy in the face of a silent democracy." He was an East Anglian who advocated presbyterianism and gained the support of 80 percent of church members, most of whom had Southeast origins. Haynes led the town in gravitating toward the Old Light. Joseph Whiting formed a second church in Hartford in 1670 for the minority, thirty-one families. He was son of the Reverend John Whiting of Lincoln and drew his inspiration from John Davenport and New Haven Colony. A strict congregationalist, his chief concern was purity.[4] Yet religious rationalism and political conservatism predominated and persisted into the nineteenth century. The Hartford Wits ridiculed Jeffersonian Democracy and the Hartford Convention of 1814 explored the possibility of New England's gaining autonomy or even seceding because the rest of the United States was less orthodox and commercial.

In Wethersfield, the presbyterian polity also triumphed within a few decades. Early in the settlement a group—largely from the Northwest—dissented from this drift and, attracted by Davenport's strict congregationalism, moved down into the New Haven jurisdiction along Long Island Sound. The conservatism of remaining inhabitants then prevailed easily. Church and town called Gershom Bulkeley, knowing that he had not been ordained at Norwich because his presbyterianism had caused "uneasiness" there. Bulkeley built on the tendencies of his predecessors in Wethersfield. By 1667 a majority of the church favored a broad admissions policy. Bulkeley added 350 church members (in a town of 600), moving as far as he could toward inclusiveness. He went beyond the Half-Way Covenant but Wethersfield was much more receptive to his ideas than Norwich had been. Thus settlers from the Southeast set a pattern for presbyterianism in Wethersfield.

In Windsor in the 1640s, less than one person in three was a communicant. John Warham saw the Half-Way Covenant as the answer to reviving his church and endorsed it in 1657, the first pastor in Connecticut to do so. With it the church prospered immediately but Warham developed doubts and abandoned the covenant in 1664, causing a crisis. The church had become dependent on this liberalization and didn't want to restore public relation. Few sided with Warham and when the time came for choosing an assistant, the contest was between a moderate and a thorough presbyterian, Nathan Chauncy and John Woodbridge. Chauncy won and Windsor settled on a polity that was broad but stopped short of real presbyterianism. In Windsor, Warham's doubts about purity were not widely shared, and an early tendency to strict congregationalism was easily overcome.

Down the river at Killingworth, 40 percent of the people had no church connection. John Woodbridge, unable to obtain the pulpit in Windsor, settled there and sought to gain members by eliminating public relation and examining candidates for church membership himself. Within a few years he had overcome doubters and opened the church to almost all inhabitants while transferring power from the congregation to the elders and himself. Neighboring Guilford and Saybrook, still under some New Haven influence, didn't like this trend but were powerless to stop it.[5] By the early eighteenth century, central Connecticut had settled into an informal presbyterianism and therefore could accept the Saybrook Platform without too much opposition. Some potential opponents had voted earlier with their feet, moving down the river or away from the cultural influence of Hartford and Wethersfield.

In Connecticut witchcraft prosecutions were concentrated in the districts where Southeasterners predominated (see table 9-2). The original towns on the Connecticut River, Farmington, and Fairfield on the western coastline produced four-fifths of the witch cases and all eleven of the executions, most occurring between 1647 and 1663. These were years of drastic changes in the home country—Civil War, execution of Charles I, Cromwell's dictatorship, the prospect of King Jesus in a Fifth Monarchy, and finally the Restoration of Charles II and the Church of England. Some of this religio-political confusion no doubt reached New England and contributed to the witch accusations of the time.

Of the three original towns, Hartford had ten cases, the largest outbreak. This was appropriate because it was the capital, but it was also the place with the highest concentration of East Anglian inhabitants. Many of the cases arose in 1662, the year Connecticut received its royal charter after some years of political uncertainty; this bears some similarity to the situation in Massachusetts in 1692. That same year a synod recommended the Half-Way Covenant for churches in New England and Charles II ejected two thousand nonconforming divines from their livings in his realm, replacing them with those loyal to Anglicanism and the Crown.

Two of the eleven persons executed in Connecticut were male, one from Hartford, the other from Wethersfield. To Windsor goes the distinction of producing the first death for witchcraft in New England:

Table 9-2. Witchcraft in Old Light Connecticut

Town	Cases	Executed	Persons Executed	Date
Hartford	10	3	Mary Sanford; Nathaniel Greensmith; Rebecca Greensmith	1662
Fairfield	6	2	Goodwife Bassett; Goodwife Knapp	1651; 1653
Wethersfield	3	3	Mary Johnson; John Carrington; Joan Carrington	1648 1651
Windsor	2	2	Alice Young; Lydia Gilbert	1647; 1651
Farmington	1	1	Mary Barnes	1663
Saybrook	3			
Stamford	1			
Stratford	1			

Source: Frederick C. Drake, "Witchcraft in the American Colonies, 1647-1662," *American Quarterly* 20 (1968): 698-708.

Alice Young in 1647. On the western coastline, Fairfield was the center of witch prosecutions. Roger Ludlow, who had moved from Windsor to found Fairfield in 1639, was assiduous in consolidating power to defend settlers from the Dutch and in prosecuting witches. Despite New England's reputation for leniency toward those confessing to witchcraft, in Connecticut some convicted witches were executed after they had confessed.[6] Authorities were severe in these parts, even compared with Salem—twenty-seven cases, eleven executions.

These towns reacted mildly to the Great Awakening, with church statistics suggesting the region was predominantly Old Light (see tables 9-3 and 9-4). The Frontier Revival (1734–36), sweeping down the river from Northampton, affected many communities in eastern Connecticut but had only moderate effects in Hartford and Wethersfield. Despite Whitefield's visit to Hartford in October 1740, at the height of the revival in 1742, only one man and three women joined the church. Yet that was the year Hartford was the scene of the tumultuous trial of James Davenport. After he was charged with religious disorder in several Connecticut towns, the General Assembly decided that he was

Table 9-3. Church Admissions in Original Connecticut Towns

	Wethersfield	Hartford
1735–39		
Male	8	12
Female	8	21
Total	16	33
Average per year	3.2	6.6
Percent male	50.0	36.4
1740–44		
Male	25	13
Female	57	26
Total	82	39
Average per year	16.4	7.8
Percent male	30.5	33.3
Percent male change	-19.5	-3.1

Source: Calculated from church records at Connecticut State Library, Hartford, Conn. Membership numbers include those admitted in full communion only.

"disturbed in his rational faculties" and leniently ordered him to return to his flock on Long Island. Although there was some momentary sentiment for Davenport in Hartford, neither his trial nor any other event caused a schism in the town.

The preponderant Old Light of the original three towns can be demonstrated in other ways. None of the pastors signed the Whitefield testimonial in 1743. Of the nineteen men who grew up in these places and were active as ministers by 1741, only five were New Lights. Nor did the revival seem to inspire a desire for education at Yale. There were 176 Yale graduates between 1741 and 1748; Hartford contributed 5, while Wethersfield and Windsor had only 2 each. This compares with 15 from New Haven town (site of the college), 10 from Stratford, 10 from Lebanon, 8 from Norwich, 6 from Lyme, and 3 from Canterbury—all except Stratford were in New Light territory.[7] Whatever measure is used—reports of religious excitement, male percentages of converts, or learned clergy produced—Hartford and Wethersfield can

Table 9-4. Church Admissions in Central Connecticut, 1740–44

	Added per Year	Percent Male	Percent Male Change	Religion of Minister[a]
Middletown	22.8	48.2	+15.5	*Old Light*
Wethersfield	16.4	30.5	-29.5	*New Light*
East Hampton	12.2	32.8	—	Neutral
Cromwell	11.2	42.8	—	Neutral
Hartford	11.2	35.7	-14.3	*Old Light*
Meriden	10.4	42.3	+1.7	Old Light
Portland	7.6	36.8	-4.4	Neutral
Killingworth	5.8	40.7	—	Neutral
Old Saybrook	5.8	41.4	—	*Old Light*
Bloomfield	5.6	42.5	—	Neutral
Haddam, East	4.8	41.7	+6.5	Neutral
Branford	4.2	42.8	+4.2	New Light
New Hartford	4.2	42.9	—	*Old Light*
Average	9.7	39.4	-1.7	

Source: Calculated from church records at Connecticut State Library. Membership numbers include those admitted in full communion only.

Note: The percent male change is calculated from the average percentage of men in the congregations between 1735 and 1739. For the Old Light region of Connecticut, see map 2.

a. Affiliations in italic indicate ministers who graduated in the upper half of their classes.

be considered relatively weak in responding to evangelism and Windsor was little better.

Branford, although Old Light, seems to have begun with evangelical tendencies. This town on the sound was further from Hartford than Killingworth and right next to Davenport's New Haven. It was settled in the 1640s by people from Wethersfield and elsewhere, some of whom preferred the saintly congregationalism of Davenport and New Haven Colony. Abraham Pierson brought his flock from Long Island to Branford for this reason. As minister from 1647 to 1667, he vowed to preserve the true church against the corrupt state and worked with Davenport in preserving New Haven from the mounting influence of Connecticut, with its broad church admissions policy. When Connecticut finally absorbed New Haven Colony and Branford's strict congregationalism was threatened, Pierson led a party to settle along the Passaic River in New Jersey. More than half the town departed with him to found Newark. Pierson was a godly, learned man of status who was the first to translate the Bible into the local American Indian language and used Cotton's "Moses His Judicials" to draw up laws for the experiment at Newark. He exemplified the otherworldliness of Yorkshire and he married the daughter of John Wheelwright who had pioneered antinomianism in northern New England. Pierson's estate included four hundred forty volumes, and his namesake became first rector of Yale in 1701.

Departure of this large party of westering saints for Newark in 1667 left Branford with a more conservative remainder. Northwest people tended to follow Pierson to New Jersey, and those from the Southeast tended to stay put. Thus Branford began to diverge religiously from nearby New Haven and lean a bit in the direction of orthodox Killingworth. By the time the churches of Connecticut agreed to adopt the Saybrook Platform in 1708, a presbyterian spirit had crept in. Pastor Samuel Russell was a strong advocate of the Saybrook scheme, but respect for Branford's original polity kept the church from formally adopting that platform although its elders participated in meetings of the Saybrook association. In the early eighteenth century, Branford became a prosperous port rivaling New Haven, but its church life under Russell was dormant and without "sprinkles."[8]

Philemon Robbins, a native of Massachusetts and grandson of a Scottish cleric, was settled as Russell's successor in 1733. A Harvard graduate, he was also an energetic, fervent preacher and New Light leader in the Great Awakening yet failed to move his own flock. Although James Davenport paid a visit in 1741, this did not help, and Robbins still could not reach men in the community at the height of the revival (see table 9-5).[9] Robbins's frustration in this, as well as his fervor, explains the determination with which he sought other hearers despite his critics and the law against itineracy. He began preaching to Baptists at Wallingford, where ten families had been listening to itinerants since 1735 because of the nonevangelism of the pastor, Samuel Whittlesey.

Table 9-5. Church Admissions in Branford

	1735–40	1741–42
Male	14	4
Female	26	14
Total	40	18
Average per year	6.7	9.0
Percent male	35.0	22.2
Percent male change		-12.8

Source: Calculated from Branford Church Records, Branford

After the Great Awakening, a long controversy ensued in the Branford church over Robbins's outside preaching. He finally gained some security when members agreed with him that censures of councils of the association were not binding on the church because it had never formally agreed to the Saybrook Platform.[10] He could rally them to congregationalism but not to the New Light, yet he remained popular enough to retain his pulpit and serve for a long time, training young men for the ministry. His son, Chandler, was the pastor who sustained the New Light in Plymouth late in the eighteenth century.

More typical of central Connecticut, of course, were prominent and respected Old Light and neutral ministers (see table 9-6). Of these thirty-four, half ranked in the upper half of their classes and only eight had Northwest surnames; of the six New Light pastors, five had Northwest surnames, two ranked high, and one had no college degree. As the revival wound down, these few New Light ministers had even less success in attracting new members. Robbins failed to touch his own flock, so he preached to Baptists in Wallingford. Cleaveland was ineffective in Haddam. Only Lockwood gave continuity, but he tried to avoid controversy. As a result, his admissions went up, but the percentage of male converts plummeted.

After the Great Awakening, the two men most successful in sustaining the New Light in this Old Light territory were from Massachusetts. James Sproat had come to Yale from Middleborough in Plymouth County, a locality of particular evangelical and Separate fervor in the 1740s. As a Yale senior, he listened to Gilbert Tennent in New Haven and was converted by his pungent preaching. Sproat was ordained over Guilford's Fourth Church and proved to be eloquent and zealous. When Tennent died, however, Sproat moved to the Second Presbyterian Church in Philadelphia in 1768 to replace him.[11]

Table 9-6. Ministers in Central Connecticut, 1741–44

Town	Minister	Rank[a]	Religion of Minister
Amity (Woodbridge)	Benjamin Woodbridge	*3/21*	Old Light
Bloomfield (Wintonbury)	Hezekiah Bissell	12/16	Neutral
Branford	Philemon Robbins[b]	18/28H	New Light
Branford, North	Jonathan Merrick[b]	7/9	Old Light
Centerbrook	Abraham Nott[b]	9/10	Old Light
Chester	Jared Harrison[b]	16/19	Neutral
Cromwell	Edward Eells	*9/39*H	Neutral
Durham	Nathaniel Chauncy	1/1	Old Light
Eastbury	Nehemiah Brainerd	*4/23*	New Light
	Isaac Chalker	11/12	Neutral
East Haven	Jacob Hemingway	3/3	Old Light
Farmington	Samuel Whitman	6/10H	Old Light
Glastonbury	Ashbel Woodbridge	*2/17*	Neutral
Guilford	Thomas Ruggles, Jr.	*3/11*	Old Light
Guilford, East (Madison)	Jonathan Todd[b]	16/23	Old Light
Guilford, 4th	James Sproat[b]	*10/23*	New Light
Guilford, North	Samuel Russell	*1/2*	Neutral
Haddam, East	Stephen Hosmer	*6/12*	Neutral
Haddam, 1st	Aaron Cleaveland[b]	34/40H	New Light
Haddam, Middle (Chatham)	Benjamin Bowers[b]	33/39H	Old Light
Hartford, 1st	Daniel Wadsworth[b]	*9/23*	Old Light
Hartford, 2d (South)	Elnathan Whitman	*3/23*	Old Light
Hartford, 3d (East)	Samuel Woodbridge	18/19H	Old Light

Hartford, 4th (West)	Benjamin Colton	*1/2*	Old Light
Kensington	William Burnham	*5/14H*	Neutral
Killingworth (Clinton)	Jared Eliot	*1/3*	Old Light
Killingworth, North	William Seward	9/14	Neutral
Meriden	Theophilus Hall	6/10	Old Light
Middletown	William Russell	*2/9*	Old Light
Middletown, Separate	Ebenezer Frothingham[b]	—	New Light
Newington	Simon Backus[b]	17/17	Neutral
North Haven	Isaac Stiles	7/8	Old Light
Old Saybrook	William Hart	*9/23*	Old Light
Portland	Moses Bartlett	18/18	Neutral
Rocky Hill (Stepney)	Daniel Russell	*3/17*	Neutral
Wallingford	Samuel Whittlesey	*3/6*	Old Light
Westbrook (Pochaug)	William Worthington[b]	2/3	Old Light
Wethersfield	James Lockwood[b]	13/24	New Light
Windsor	Jonathan Marsh	*7/24H*	Old Light

Sources: Names, churches, and religious preferences compiled from Franklin B. Dexter, *Biographical Sketches of the Graduates of Yale College* (1885–1919) and Clifford Shipton, *Sibley's Harvard Graduates: Biographical Sketches of Those Who Attended Harvard College,* 17 vols. (1933–75); probable origins come from Henry Guppy, *Homes of Family Names in Great Britain* (1890); ranks compiled from Dexter, *Yale Graduates,* and Shipton, *Harvard Graduates.*

H = Harvard graduate.

a. Numbers in italic indicate those who graduated in the upper half of their classes.
b. Probable origins or high surname frequency in the Northwest.

The second man, Ebenezer Frothingham, was settled over a Separate church in Wethersfield in 1747, one of the few the revival produced in central Connecticut. This church was gathered from people who had fallen away from several congregations and therefore met with little acrimony. Some members migrated to New York in 1754 and the rest took the church to Middletown, where it became regular with Frothingham presiding until 1788. Ebenezer was the great-grandson of William Frothingham of Yorkshire, who came to Massachusetts in Winthrop's fleet and supported Anne Hutchinson in 1636. Although lacking higher education, he proved an influential exponent of Separatism. His defense of individual conscience and congregational autonomy was brilliant and drew bitter responses, notably from Moses Bartlett of nearby Portland, who defended the Saybrook Platform. Frothingham also took a strong position on assurance. He maintained that Christians who doubted their salvation could not perform their duties to God and humanity, pray in good faith, or help the needy in Christ. Of course the orthodox saw this as dangerous antinomianism but Frothingham's views were well-stated echoes of John Cotton and Anne Hutchinson and show him as reflecting the persistent otherworldliness of the British Northwest.[12]

Despite the conspicuous New Light that Sproat and Frothingham brought in, evangelism was quite weak in this central region. New Lights held only one in six of the pulpits and comprised one in five of ministers born in the region. Homegrown Old Lights settled and predominated, and half of them ranked high in their college placings. The people in these towns evidently called as pastors men who were not only familiar to them but were also orthodox. These clergy went along with the revival in the beginning, but soon turned into opposers. Church members must have been largely satisfied with this because there were so few dismissals or separations and little dissent. While many were no doubt favorable to evangelism, religious and social leaders were conservative and checked its impact. This pattern of presbyterianism and nonevangelism in the midseventeenth century had spread quietly down the river to the sound and was sustained through the Great Awakening. Members were content in their orthodoxy and there was no discernible drift to Arianism or Unitarianism later in the century.

The Separate movement was weak in these parts of Connecticut. There were far fewer separations, more that were only temporary, and fewer that moved beyond Separate status and became Baptist. While there may have been sizeable New Light minorities in some parishes, they evidently did not have the leadership, status, and determination to erect successful New Light churches outside the tax-supported Congregational establishment. Therefore in Old Light–neutral areas—the western Connecticut coastline, the Connecticut River valley, as well as eastern Massachusetts and Cape Cod—only sixteen permanent New Light Baptist churches can be connected with the separatism of the Great Awakening. There were six times as many in New Light territory. The relative lack of Separate churches differentiated Old Light from New Light districts for a long time afterward, from the First Great Awakening to the Second.

Charles M. Andrews, Yale's historian of the region, described Connecticut as "the most conventionally Puritan of all the settlements in New England."[13] This was actually true only for the central part because the religious character of the original towns was shaped from the outset, like that of eastern Massachusetts, by Ramistic Puritans from the

Southeast. It was strengthened and confirmed by a continual exodus of Northwest people, an acquiescence in extended clerical authority in the seventeenth century, and relative coolness to the Great Awakening in the eighteenth century.

Upper Connecticut Valley

The pioneers of western Massachusetts came in groups up the Connecticut River from Hartford, Wethersfield, and Windsor to the north-central part of the colony. They had originated in the Southeast, especially East Anglia; their cultural affinity was with towns on the river, not eastern Connecticut, and therefore were closer to the Hingham than the Rowley model.

William Pynchon made the first settlement in 1636 at Agawam and renamed it Springfield after his English birthplace in Essex. A gentleman already wealthy from New England's fur trade, he moved to the valley to get closer to the pelts. Some years later Pynchon turned to religious speculation, writing *The Meritorious Price of Our Redemption*, a rationalist deviation from Calvinism, published in London. In it he accepted limited atonement but rejected the imputation theory of original sin as unjust. How could obedience to God be required of people without the help of faith? He also denied that Christ had borne the wrath of God or suffered the pains of Hell. Pynchon was no Hales or Hobbes, but this prominent trader and magistrate, although a layman, combined the study of scriptures with an Arminian tendency.[14] The book was suppressed in New England, but his efforts suggest that a pioneer in the American wilderness could move with those in Southeast England to modify Calvinism. Massachusetts authorities burned his book and demanded recantation. He recanted in part but departed for East Anglia in 1652, never to return, and continued his religious ruminations.

Pynchon's power passed to his son, John, an entrepreneur like his father, who inherited large tracts of the best farmlands. He was as dominant in public life as in private enterprise so just about everyone in the valley was dependent on him in one way or another. Other pioneer families did not challenge his power, but complemented him in his role. Pynchon hegemony remained intact until the Glorious Revolution in 1688.

In the valley, the first people from the British Northwest were indentured servants, some prisoners John Pynchon brought from Scotland. Religiously unawakened, they chafed at Puritan mores and were not inclined to give Pynchon and the oligarchy much deference. The first from the Northwest to get attention, however, were more notorious than prominent. Mary Lewis, a Welshwoman formerly married to a Catholic, was charged with witchcraft and involved her second husband, Hugh Parsons, in the matter. Ultimately the General Court in Boston had her executed for murdering her child. Northwest people continued to move into the area and some with status would emerge. In 1679 inhabitants took oaths of allegiance and some of them can be documented as emigrants from the Northwest; if those with high frequency surnames from that zone are added, the total is almost one-third of the population.[15]

None of these Northwesterners could challenge John Pynchon, however. Because of his position in the valley, Pynchon was persuaded to support the Dominion of New England, James II's autocratic scheme for New England, and to recruit men who would render loyal military service to Andros, its hated royal governor. When the Glorious Revolution engulfed England and the Dominion regime collapsed in New England, Pynchon suffered somewhat from the backlash against Andros. Sgt. James King (from western Devon), a proprietor with some status, led the militia in a short revolt against officers. Pynchon felt a loss of respect and realized he had to reckon with the sergeant; after this, he would have to persuade, not coerce the people.[16]

Some of his power spread to other prosperous entrepreneurs—the River Gods—including Solomon Stoddard. Stoddard's reform, the open communion system begun in the 1670s, was visible and controversial by the 1690s. By emphasizing ministerial power and exerting presbyterian control of clerics through the Hampshire Association he organized, Stoddard remained in harmony with Pynchon and the other River Gods. But his system also provided for revivalism within this framework, which appealed to the Northwest minority. He provided a Scottish solution—a combination of the presbyterianism of the lowlands and the evangelism of the highlands—a Calvinistic compromise that was viable with the changing mixture of people on this frontier. Although he may have been a public presbyterian, Stoddard was a private maverick. His compromise may have been compatible with the River Gods and the mixture of settlers, but he became dissatisfied. Paul Lucas believes that in the last decade of his life, Stoddard actually concentrated on his evangelism and techniques for reaching people.[17]

The year 1729 was a turning point in Anglo-American religion. In Britain John Wesley became leader of the Holy Club at Oxford, giving birth to the Methodist-Evangelical movement; in Massachusetts, Cotton Mather died just before the evangelism and pietism he prayed for revived religion among the saints of New England; and in the valley, Stoddard passed away, leaving a large void in the religio-political life of Hampshire County. The religious equilibrium that Stoddard and the merchant families had created was lost, and religious differences that had been largely latent became overt. At Sunderland, the minister advanced some "new notions" about original sin and free will. At Northfield the pastor was criticized for harboring doubts about Calvinism as well as neglecting his flock.

These differences were most obvious and significant, however, in the valley's oldest town, Springfield, where William Pynchon had engaged in anti-Calvinist speculation in pioneer days. In 1734 church leaders and the community insisted on calling Robert Breck as minister in the face of opposition from the Hampshire Association. Extended controversy followed, and with the help of some Boston ministers, Breck was settled. He did not conceal his Arminian views and moved to implement them by persuading the church to adopt the Half-Way Covenant and abolish public relation.

Breck and his supporters prevailed in Springfield even though the Frontier Revival had awakened the people of Northampton at this same time.[18] This revival was the evangelical response to the religious void left in 1729 and the upsurge of local Arminianism. Jonathan Edwards reacted by making extraordinary efforts to arouse his flock in Northampton. At Hatfield, William Williams, a 1683 Harvard graduate, rivaled Stoddard in his evangelical influence. His sons, Elisha, rector of Yale, and Solomon, pastor of Lebanon, were highly visible members of the Saving Remnant. Revivalism was divisive in the region but after considering the results, Edwards's colleagues in six towns—Hatfield, Longmeadow, Westfield, West Springfield, Suffield, and Enfield—endorsed it in 1738.[19] Yet opposers grew into an Old Light alliance following Whitefield's arrival in 1740.

Whitefield made the long trek west to meet Jonathan Edwards in Northampton and was extravagant in praising him: "I have not seen his fellow in all New England." Down the river at Suffield, Whitefield encountered a minister who claimed that a pastor need not be converted to preach Christianity. Whitefield blamed the deceased Stoddard for encouraging this view and took sharp issue, citing Gilbert Tennent's sermon "The Dangers of an Unconverted Ministry." By his account, the Awakener was well received, yet the New Lights did not make great headway in the region (see table 9-7).[20]

Table 9-7. Ministers in Hampshire County, 1743

Town	Minister[a]	Religion of Minister
Amherst	David Parsons[a]	New Light
Bernardstown	John Norton	Old Light
Brimfield	James Bridgham	Old Light
Cold Spring	Edward Billing[a]	New Light
Deerfield	Jonathan Ashley[a]	Old Light
Enfield	Peter Reynolds[a]	New Light
Hadley	Chester Williams[a]	Regular Light
Hatfield	Timothy Woodbridge	New Light
Longmeadow	Stephen Williams[a]	New Light
New Salem	Samuel Kendall[a]	Regular Light
Northfield	Benjamin Doolittle[a]	Old Light
Northampton	Jonathan Edwards[a]	New Light
Palmer	John Harvey	Presbyterian
Pelham	Robert Abercrombie[a]	Presbyterian
Road Town	Abraham Hill	Regular Light
Sheffield	Jonathan Hubbard	Old Light
Somers	Samuel Allis	New Light
Southampton	Jonathan Judd	Neutral
South Hadley	John Woodbridge	New Light
Springfield	Robert Breck	Old Light
Springfield, Baptist	Edward Upham	Old Light
Stockbridge	John Sergeant	Old Light
Suffield	Ebenezer Gay	Old Light
Sunderland	William Rand	Old Light
Westfield	John Ballantine[a]	Regular Light
West Springfield	Samuel Hopkins[a]	Regular Light
Wilbraham	Noah Merrick[a]	Old Light

Sources: Adapted from Gregory H. Nobles, *Divisions throughout the Whole: Politics and Society in Hampshire County, Massachusetts, 1740-1775* (1983), 190-91, and supplemented with information from Shipton, *Harvard Graduates*, and Dexter, *Yale Graduates*. Distinctions between neutrals come from David Harlan, *The Clergy and the Great Awakening in New England* (1980), 4, 5.

Note: Three towns, Enfield, Somers, and Suffield, left Hampshire County and Massachusetts, joining Connecticut in the 1740s.

a. Probable origins or high surname frequency in the Northwest.

In the summer of 1743, county clerical opinion favored the Old Light. While eight clerics signed the testimonial favoring Whitefield and the revival, twelve subscribed to Chauncy's *Seasonable Thoughts*. Chester Williams did both and six others did not go on record. Two years later when the issue was the advisability of a second Whitefield tour, fifteen of the ministers were against it.[21] Of course, there was much more pro-revivalism than these numbers can indicate, especially in the vacant pulpits itinerants visited. And even though ministers may have been opposed to evangelism, some members of the congregations responded. Religious conflicts were more complex here than in many regions in New England, thanks to the influence of Stoddard and Edwards, but New Light ministers remained in a minority while their opponents were relatively successful in containing the emotions the Great Awakening aroused.

Among pastors of Northwest stock born in the valley, some New Lights were highly visible. Edward Billing was a descendant of Richard Billing, one of the very few original proprietors of Hadley from the Northwest (western Devon). He is remembered for his support of Jonathan Edwards in 1750. The Parsons family, also from western Devon, were linked with witchcraft early and revivalism later. Jonathan was the ardent pastor of Lyme later invited to lead a new church in Newburyport. David Parsons, whose father had been born in Northampton, became the New Light pastor in Amherst. The prolific Dickinsons of Hadley produced two New Light clerics active in New Jersey. Solomon Stoddard had come west to the valley in 1670 and his son, Anthony, got spectacular revival results in Woodbury, Connecticut. Jonathan Edwards's son, born in the area in 1745, would follow his father in religion. The most noteworthy strand of this Saving Remnant were the Williamses, who were closely related to the Mathers, Cottons, as well as Stoddards. Despite differences some of them had with Edwards, five of six Williams clerics born in the upper valley were prominent New Lights there or in Connecticut.

In comparison, the region's families produced only a few Old Light ministers, and no pastors came from the Pynchon family. Two Marshes—Jonathan and Elisha—came from Hadley. Jonathan Hubbard and Isaac Chauncy were from Hatfield. The Old Light leaders came from outside the valley.[22]

Jonathan Edwards discovered their power after the Great Awakening when he decided to drop the system of open communion he had inherited from Stoddard. Revivalism had left too much complacency and too many backsliders in its wake, so Edwards reluctantly concluded that he had to abandon the Half-Way Covenant and open communion system and require visible sainthood for admission. He knew this proposal would arouse much opposition, but hoped he would be able to explain his new thinking to his people.

He made his fateful decision to change this church policy in 1744 but did not have to reveal it until five years later when someone finally applied to join. It became the subject of heated discussions, and Edwards discovered that resistance to this radical New Light concept was greater than he had anticipated. His congregation feared that Edwards alone planned to decide who the saved were and the gap between pastor and members on this fundamental question was so wide that a regional church council was called to resolve the conflict. The admissions issue was complicated by other conflicts with his congregation and friction with the county elite. John Stoddard, the chief River God, had been his protector, but following his death in 1748, the pastor became more vulnerable to the accumulated grievances of his people.

A church council convened in 1750 to settle matters between Edwards and his flock. Edwards was allowed to name some members to the council and chose two reliable New Lights from outside the county, David Hall of Sutton and William Hobby of Reading.[23] With the lay delegates, they contributed four votes to his cause. In Hampshire County, he got two votes from Pelham, the small Scots-Irish town in the eastern hills. And at Edwards's insistence, Edward Billing attended and supported him, but his church in Cold Spring opposed this, sending no delegate. Edwards got two more votes from Enfield, one of the border towns that had become part of Connecticut, giving him a total of nine votes, but support for the New Light theologian and his reform was on the periphery. Ten opposing votes came from the ministers and delegates from Springfield, Hadley, Hatfield, Sunderland, and Sheffield, towns tilting against the New Light. The council voted to dismiss Edwards, ten to nine.

Edwards had to move from Northampton to the frontier, but a strong New Light region did finally appear in western Massachusetts following the French and Indian War. A new county, Berkshire, was created from the western half of Hampshire, and evangelicals, including many Baptists of Northwest origin, swarmed into it. Their fervor began the New Light Stir, which ran concurrently with the American Revolution and fostered patriotic sentiment.[24]

In sum, the upper Connecticut River valley, because of the character of settlers, was predisposed to the Old Light and this was still evident in the middle of the eighteenth century. Despite the influx of settlers with Northwest antecedents, Stoddard's "harvest," and Edwards's Frontier Revival and theological reputation, some prominent Old Lights were able in the 1740s to counter the surge of New Light. Compared with eastern Massachusetts, the valley did have more revivalism and "divisions throughout the whole." It is clear, nevertheless, that the oldest part of Hampshire County—the towns along the river above Suffield and Enfield—had enough anti-revivalism to be consistent with their origins and sustain an Old Light majority of clergy. It was outsiders, arriving late in the hill country, a more favorable terrain, who built a strong New Light region in western Massachusetts.

The Western Connecticut Coastline

Fairfield, on the coastline, actually exceeded Hartford as a beacon of Old Light. Settlers from Windsor, supplemented by some from Watertown and Concord in Massachusetts, founded the town in 1639 and the population was predominantly from the Southeast. Fairfield had been under the jurisdiction of Connecticut rather than New Haven, until the two colonies amalgamated in 1662.

At the time of the Great Awakening, Fairfield's minister was Noah Hobart, settled in 1733. Born and raised in Hingham, he was grandson of the first minister there, Peter Hobart. Like descendants of that clergyman and most Hingham natives, Hobart leaned toward the Old Light. Because the people seemed religiously indifferent, Hobart felt the need to defend orthodoxy—the New England way or, more precisely, the Hingham way—quite vociferously. He pressed the case for the Saybrook Platform as the polity God sanctified and also warned would-be defectors of the dangers of the Anglican version of Arminian theology.[25]

The low male percentage of admissions, 24.3, suggests that Hobart, like some Boston ministers, had to compete with Anglicans for men of affairs as church members and there were not enough to go around. Whitefield passed through the area in 1740, but no details of the reaction in Fairfield were reported. No doubt this reflects the nature of the population, the dampening effects of pastor Hobart, an able Old Light, as well as those of an Anglican minister in the vicinity, since there is no mention of impatient New Lights who wanted to separate. If there were post-awakening defectors, they would go to the Church of England.

At nearby Stratford, religious conditions were much the same. A group of Anglican tradespeople sought their own church from the beginning. Yet despite this favorable atmosphere for Anglicanism—or perhaps because of it—Stratford's long-settled minister of the Standing Order, Hezekiah Gould, took a markedly New Light stance and was a Whitefield supporter willing to sign his name. Gould may have had some effect on his parishioners, because the church at Stratford had a larger percentage of male converts than its neighbors.

The religious mood of this stretch of the coastline was not reflected, however, in either the Old Light of Hobart or the New Light of Gould but rather in the nonevangelism of the population. Anglican missionaries from New York had been recruiting here since the 1720s. Revivalism was not noticeable along this coastline from Stratford to the New York border. The Congregational churches had low admissions, and low, declining numbers of men. Among the seventeen ministers, eight remained neutral, four were Anglican, one was Old Light, another was an Old Light converted to Anglicanism, and only three were New Lights (see tables 9-8 and 9-9). All of the New Lights and Anglicans had Northwest roots; one of the eight others did.

Compared with New Light territory, evangelism was weak along the coast. Separatism was clearly not an attractive option for the orthodox

Table 9-8. Church Admissions in Coastal Connecticut, 1740–44

	Average per Year	Percent Male	Percent Male Change	Religion of Minister[a]
Fairfield-Green Hill	9.0	33.3	-14.5	*Neutral*
Stratford	8.4	38.0	-1.2	*New Light*
Fairfield	7.4	24.3	-9.0	Old Light
Trumbull (North Stratford)	4.6	21.4	-14.6	*Neutral*
Average	7.4	29.3	-9.8	

Sources: Calculated from records at the Connecticut State Library, Hartford, Conn. Compiled from Shipton, *Harvard Graduates,* and Dexter, *Yale Graduates.*

Note: The percent male change is calculated from the average percentage of men in the congregations between 1735 and 1739. On his first visit, Whitefield had little success at Stratford and few hearers at Fairfield and Norwalk; there was a little more response at Stamford. Tracy, *Great Awakening,* 103.

a. Affiliations in italic indicate ministers who graduated in the upper half of their classes.

inhabitants of this region; instead, some chose Anglicanism—liturgical or metaphysical—as an alternative to revivalism. The most influential of these converts was Samuel Johnson, who left Congregationalism to join the Church of England in 1722.

Johnson was a perfectionist who liked scholarship and showed early proficiency in Hebrew, then considered a sign of a prospective minister. He absorbed knowledge voraciously and while at Yale was inclined to sketch out philosophical systems of knowledge and the universe. He wanted to know everything, and exposure to the Enlightenment in the library whetted his appetite. Erudite Anglican authorities he found there won him over to the view that when Puritan ministers ordained each other in the absence of a bishop, the continuity of apostolic succession was broken, making the Congregational churches not true churches in

Table 9-9. Ministers in Coastal Connecticut, 1741–44

Church	Minister	Rank[b]	Religion of Minister
Bridgeport (Stratfield)	Samuel Cooke[a]	4/6	New Light
Darien (Middlesex)	Moses Mather[a]	6/10	Neutral
Fairfield	Noah Hobart	*16/39H*	Old Light
	Henry Caner[a]	14/20	Anglican
Green Farms	Daniel Buckingham	*12/24*	Neutral
Greenfield	John Goodsell	16/18	Neutral
Greenwich, 1st	Ephriam Bostwick	15/17	Neutral
Greenwich, West	Abraham Todd[a]	8/10	Neutral
New Canaan	Robert Silliman	*9/24*	Neutral
Norwalk	Moses Dickinson[a]	5/5	New Light
	Richard Caner[a]	17/19	Anglican
Stamford	Ebenezer Wright	*8/18*	Neutral
Stamford and Greenwich	Ebenezer Dibble[a]	12/14	Anglican
Stanwich	Benjamin Strong[a]	14/14	Neutral
Stratford	Hezekiah Gould[a]	*3/27H*	New Light
	Samuel Johnson[a]	8/9	Anglican
Trumbull (North Stratford)	Richardson Miner[a]	*10/23*	Old Light/ Anglican

Sources: Names, churches, and religious preferences compiled from Dexter, *Yale Graduates,* and Shipton, *Harvard Graduates;* probable origins come from Guppy, *Homes.*

H = Harvard graduate.

a. Probable origins or high surname frequency in the Northwest.
b. Numbers in italic indicate ministers who graduated in the upper half of their classes.

the eyes of God. At the Yale commencement in 1722 Johnson along with two other tutors and Rector Timothy Cutler announced their support for episcopacy and their intentions to sail to England to receive Anglican orders. Yale authorities were shocked by these defections and quickly adopted a faculty loyalty oath to discourage them in the future. They did not completely succeed, however; the college produced a trickle of students who followed Cutler and Johnson. After receiving his orders Johnson returned to the colonies to become the first missionary to Connecticut from the Society for the Propagation of the Gospel in Foreign Parts (SPG). Afterward, he spent most of his life operating from his Anglican post at Stratford.

This apostasy grew from within Yale's walls but stemmed from the characters of Johnson and the other dissidents. Johnson longed for status, unity, and comprehensive learning and was dissatisfed by the outdated curriculum at Yale. His perfectionism and awe of metropolitan scholarship made him favorably inclined toward the Church of England and its tradition.

Under attack from the deism and skepticism unleashed during the Glorious Revolution and stung by the ridicule of the Enlightenment intelligentsia, the church had weakened considerably. Immorality and corruption in public life increased. Johnson came to believe that the problems of the Church of England—the absence of ecclesiastical reform and the lack of a bishop in the colonies—were the consequences of this skepticism, corruption, and failure of nerve in the homeland.

As a young convert to Anglicanism, Johnson knew he would have to operate outside Connecticut's Standing Order and seek converts from a population brought up to fear bishops and resent the aristocratic ways of the Church of England (see table 9-10). Despite his difficulties, he was not tempted by latitudinarianism or rationalism. Governor Francis Burnet of New York made his large library available in the hope of pulling the neophyte in that direction, but Johnson recoiled at this challenge to his cosmology. He declared that articles of faith could not be treated as subjects for philosophical inquiry and reasoning. Instead, he embraced both reason and revelation, asserting that our souls are made free by accepting the clearest truths and rejecting soaring speculations.

George Berkeley, the dean of Derry, arrived in New England in 1729 at just the right time to affect Johnson. Berkeley was an idealist and his belief that God is omnipresent and people are constantly dependent on

Table 9-10. Connecticut Converts to Anglicanism, to 1740

Name	Class	Rank	Birthplace	Probable Origin
Arnold, Jonathan	1723	7/11	Haddam	(Warwick, 30)
Beach, John	1721	13/14	Stratford	(Cheshire, 27)
Dean, Barzillai	1737	24/24	Groton	western Somerset
Dibble, Ebenezer	1734	12/14	Stamford	western Somerset
Johnson, Samuel	1714	8/9	Guilford	Yorkshire
Lamson, Joseph	1740	14/20	Stratford	Durham
Punderson, Ebenezer	1733	15/23	New Haven	Yorkshire
Seabury, Samuel	1724	28/39H	Groton	western Somerset
Thompson, Ebenezer	1733	16/16	New Haven	(Durham, 148)
Watkins, Hezekiah	1737	21/24	Stratford	(Hereford,193)

Sources: Vos, "The Great Awakening," 314-330; Clarence C. Goen, *Revivalism and Separatism: Strict Congregationalists and Separate Baptists* (1962), 116-18; John J. Ellis III, "Anglicanism in Connecticut, 1725-1750: The Converson of the Missionaries," *New England Quarterly* 44 (1971): 66-81; Guppy, *Homes.*

Note: Surname frequency per 10,000 from Guppy, *Homes,* appears in parentheses.

H = Harvard graduate.

him was just what Johnson's nature craved. The notion that abstract ideas originated in the mind of God and religious teachers were divine philosophers bolstered Johnson's view of himself as a missionary to New England. Johnson felt an immediate affinity with this learned man because Berkeley's ideas fit his needs yet bore the imprimatur of an Anglican dean. He had found a British thinker with some contemporary theological and philosophical standing. Embracing Berkeley's immaterialism gave Johnson a way of rising above provincial and dormant Calvinism and accepting Anglicanism without surrendering his otherworldliness to the latitudinarians. It was the Church of England's episcopal polity that originally attracted him, but Johnson also found within its ranks a divine philosophy that met his continuing need for theocentric cosmology.[26]

Skepticism continued to be fashionable among intellectuals, however, and as Johnson slipped into middle age, Berkeley's immaterialism was evidently not enough to sustain him. Suddenly in 1757, he became infatuated with the ideas of John Hutchinson, a self-educated Yorkshireman. Hutchinson had gained fame (or notoriety) earlier for his *Moses His Principia* (1724), challenging Newton by finding basic scientific truths in his own translation of the Old Testament. Duncan Forbes, a

Scottish lawyer, had recommended Hutchinson, and after reading the twelve volumes, Johnson described the author as a "prodigious genius" and his writings as "the only right system of philosophy." While Johnson's attraction to this "scripture philosophy" may be seen as an extension of his early, emotional attachment to Hebrew, it also suggests how desperate he had become in resisting the rationalist tide. This belated endorsement of Hutchinson has hurt Johnson's standing as a philosopher with some scholars of the 1930s, Herbert Schneider and Theodore Hornberger, who call him medieval, anti-scientific, pathetic, and cranky. Thus Johnson assimilated the Enlightenment early in life, but rejected its materialist urban milieu and found solace in Berkeley, Hutchinson, and a pastoral setting, refusing to yield the other world.[27]

Johnson needed a way to express his otherworldliness. The reverence for learning in his home, the complacent legalism of central Connecticut's Congregationalists during the glacial age, and the Anglican books in the Yale library tilted him consciously toward the Church of England, but he remained vulnerable to evangelism. When the Great Awakening came, Anglicans generally tried to make their chapels arks of safety from fervor, and Johnson conformed by decrying the "wild enthusiasm" of the revivalists. He discovered, however, that he was physically susceptible to the revivalists' spoken words despite his education and training. Much to his embarrassment, this Anglican intellectual "suffered surprising convulsions and involuntary agitation," reactions mistakenly attributed only to unchurched farmers stricken by the New Light.[28]

The key to Johnson's persistent otherworldliness and vulnerability to the revivalists lies primarily in his English antecedents. Robert, the first emigrant from this family, was in Ezekiel Rogers's company from Yorkshire, settling in Rowley in 1638 before moving to New Haven. This Northwest heritage was reinforced on the other side of the family; Samuel's mother was Ann Sage, granddaughter of David Sage, who came from Wales to Middletown in 1650. Even Johnson's wife, Charity Floyd of Long Island, was of Welsh stock.[29]

Johnson's predisposition to otherworldliness was reinforced by his association with other converts in Connecticut as well as SPG missionaries from Britain, who also had Northwest backgrounds. Compared with the Congregationalists, these prospective Anglicans were ranked quite low in their classes at Yale. It has been conjectured that the defectors may have resented, at least unconsciously, such low placings and sought to circumvent the system by joining the Church of England to gain some status, autonomy, and revenge. Certainly Samuel Johnson succeeded in this and managed to influence other young men of similar origins and similar social status to follow him.[30]

The parts of New England settled from the English Southeast followed that region in moving toward rationalism in the 1640s. In the oldest towns of Salem, Hartford, Wethersfield, Windsor, and Fairfield, Puritanism became legalistic and this led to some executions for witchcraft in the seventeenth century. This rationalistic, nonevangelical trend continued in the eighteenth century, paralleling developments in the home country. In the English Southeast, Independents and Particular Baptists clung to their Calvinist orthodoxy, but Presbyterians and General Baptists moved to Arminianism and latitudinarianism, bringing them closer to the Church of England. In New England, central Connecticut, with its Southeast heritage, was orthodox during the Great Awakening, while eastern Massachusetts was tilting toward Arminianism. Both regions were Old Light, certainly not immune but relatively cool toward the Great Awakening. The Old Light and neutral ministers together outnumbered New Lights four to one.

The typical minister of the Old Light elite—those ranking in the upper half of their classes—was the son or grandson of a minister, raised in an Old Light district or in Boston, and settled near home.[31] Early exposure to New Light preaching and theology and intermarriage or expedient settlement in New Light territory might dilute or submerge this tendency toward orthodoxy or rationalism. A few clerics in the elite had to accept settlement elsewhere and compromised with their new communities, becoming prudent neutrals instead of outspoken opponents to evangelism. At bottom, however, was ancestry and the religious ethos of the region or community where the person was raised.

By focusing on the clergy of New England, it is possible to summarize and confirm the connection between British origins and response to the Great Awakening. Old Light leadership in the eighteenth century came largely from East Anglia and the cloth towns of the Southeast (see appendixes E and F). East Anglians had begun the drift toward rationalism before the Civil War and this increased after the Glorious Revolution. Settlers from the region continuing on this course reacted against the Great Awakening and, in most cases, became ardent opponents.

Clergy deriving from the rest of the Southeast reveal a pattern similar to those of East Anglia. Most were Old Lights and some families from this part of England—Chauncy, Clap, Stiles, Mayhew, and Gay—contributed "once-born" liberals, the pioneers of Arminian and Unitarian tendencies in New England.[32] Many Southeasterners in the colonies took the opportunity to serve God in other callings—trade and the law—instead of the ministry. In this the colonists were paralleling the sectionalism of Britain and reflecting the trend toward rational religion emerging in the Southeast from the time of Hales, Hobbes, and Hooker. They also were paralleling mainline dissenters of England who had recoiled from the religious chaos of the Civil War, accommodated to the Age of Reason, and did not readily respond to efforts of Whitefield and Wesley in the eighteenth century.

Clergy with Northwest origins provide a marked contrast to those of East Anglia and the Southeast. They were New Lights who supported the Great Awakening overwhelmingly. This group contributed intellectual leaders as well as lively itinerants to the cause, including Whitefield himself. An interesting additional category are ministers whose forebears had emigrated from East Anglia, or elsewhere in the Southeast, but had surnames with a high frequency of occurrence in the

Table 9-11. Religion and Probable Origins of the Clergy in the Great Awakening

	Southeast	Northwest	Total	Percent Northwest
Old Light Elite	48	12	60	20.0
Saving Remnant	18	51	69	73.9

Probable Origins	Old Light	Neutral	New Light	Total	Percent New Light
East Anglia	54	3	15	72	20.8
Other Southeast	76	8	42	126	33.3
Northwest	31	8	99	138	71.7
Southeast, Northwest surname	9	1	35	45	77.8

Sources: Shipton, *Harvard Graduates;* Dexter, *Yale Graduates;* Banks, *Topographical;* Holmes, *Ancestral Heads;* Guppy, *Homes.*

Northwest. They were probably catalysts for the Puritan religiosity that preceded New England settlement, but research is needed on their antecedents.[33] The Rogers, Backus, and Cleaveland families stood out in this group as opponents of legalistic Puritanism and crusaders for soul liberty. With roots in the Northwest, but emigrating from East Anglia, they may have had a particular call to come out from that cradle of orthodoxy and pioneer in the wilderness Zion.

A final compilation of known religious preferences of ministers active during the Great Awakening demonstrates that their probable origins were a good indicator of their religious affiliation (see table 9-11). More than seven out of ten ministers linked to the Northwest warmed to the New Light. In contrast, those with Southeast ties leaned toward the Old Light in almost the same numbers. Clearly, despite their education and social status, the ministers followed the path of their ancestors and sections in the homeland.[34]

Notes

1. Isabel M. Calder, "John Cotton and the New Haven Colony," *New England Quarterly* 12 (1939): 82–94.

2. John A. Goodwin, *The Pilgrim Republic: An Historical View of the Colony of New Plymouth* (1879; rpt., 1970), 391–96.

3. Norman Pettit, *The Heart Prepared: Grace and Conversion in Puritan Spiritual Life* (1966), 89–101. Alfred Habegger, "Preparing the Soul for Christ: The Contrasting Sermon Forms of John Cotton and Thomas Hooker," *American Literature* 41 (1969): 342–54; David L. Parker, "Petrus Ramus and the Puritans: The 'Logic' of Preparationist Conversion Doctrine," *Early American Literature* 8 (1974): 140–62.

4. Edwin P. Parker, *The History of the Second Church of Christ in Hartford* (1892), 13–48; Paul Lucas, *Valley of Discord: Church and Society along the Connecticut River, 1636–1725* (1976), 43–71.

5. Robert G. Pope, *The Half-Way Covenant: Church Membership in Puritan New England* (1969), 102–14.

6. John M. Taylor, *The Witchcraft Delusion in Colonial Connecticut, 1647–1697* (1908), 35–44, 142–57.

7. Stephen Nissenbaum, ed., *The Great Awakening at Yale College* (1972), 254–58.

8. J. Rupert Simonds, *A History of the First Church and Society of Branford, Connecticut, 1644–1919* (1919), 19–65.

9. "Little permanent fruit was produced." Timothy P. Gillett, *The Past and Present in the Secular and Religious History of the Congregational Church and*

Society of Branford: A Semi-Centennial Discourse (1858), 13. Benjamin Trumbull, *The Complete History of Connecticut, Civil and Ecclesiastical* (1818), 2:160.

10. Simonds, *Branford,* 68–111.

11. William B. Sprague, *Annals of the American Pulpit* (1865), 3:125–29. The first Sproat arrived in Scituate early from Kent. The surname, however, was northern and had some variations: Sproate, Sprott, Sprotte, Sprout. The locus for the Sproat variation was Preston, Lancashire. See Charles W. Bardsley, *Dictionary of English and Welsh Names* (1967 ed.), 709.

12. Clarence C. Goen, *Revivalism and Separatism: Strict Congregationalists and Separate Baptists* (1962), 44–45, 86, 126–36, 152–56, 161–63, 171–72. The first Frothingham, William, from Yorkshire's East Riding, was in Anne Hutchinson's support group, but publicly acknowledged his error. See Charles E. Banks, *Topographical Dictionary,* ed. E. E. Brownell (1937), 187; Emery Battis, *Saints and Sectaries: Anne Hutchinson and the Antinomian Controversy in Massachusetts Bay Colony* (1962), 313. In the nineteenth century, the Frothingham surname became more prominent. Octavius, seventh in line from William and a contemporary of Ralph Waldo Emerson, wrote a history of Transcendentalism. In early nineteenth-century New England, some of the Saving Remnant preserved their kind of religiosity by drawing on German Pietism and becoming Transcendentalists.

13. Charles M. Andrews, *Our Earliest Colonial Settlements* (1933), 114.

14. Philip F. Gura, *A Glimpse of Sion's Glory: Puritan Radicalism in New England, 1620–1660* (1984), 304–22; Stephen Innes, *Labor in a New Land: Economy and Society in Seventeenth Century Springfield* (1983), 14–16.

15. "'The Inhabitants of Springfield,' Their Oaths of 1679." *New England Historical and Genealogical Register* 5 (1851): 82–84.

16. Carl Bridenbaugh, ed., *The Pynchon Papers: Letters of John Pynchon, 1654–1700* (1982), 1:198–201; Innes, *New Land,* 159–61.

17. Lucas, *Valley of Discord,* 196–202. See also Edward J. Cleveland, comp., "The King Family of Suffield," *New England Historical and Genealogical Register* 46 (1892): 370–74.

18. Gregory H. Nobles, *Divisions throughout the Whole: Politics and Society in Hampshire County, Massachusetts, 1740–1775* (1983), 38–44; Mary Catherine Foster believes that "Frontier Revival" is a misnomer—suggesting "Connecticut Valley Revival" instead—because the awakening of 1734–35 did not reach into the hills and did not affect the Elbows (Palmer) or Cold Spring, the actual frontier. See "Hampshire County, Massachusetts, 1729–1754: A Covenant Society in Transition" (Ph.D. diss., University of Michigan, 1967), 92–100.

19. Foster, "Hampshire County," 97–98. Philip F. Gura, "Sowing the Harvest: William Williams and the Great Awakening," *Journal of Presbyterian History* 56 (1978): 326–41.

20. George Whitefield, *Whitefield's Journals* (1960 ed.), 477–78.

21. Abercrombie of Pelham supported Edwards in the dismissal proceeding in 1750. See Nobles, *Divisions*, 71.

22. Billing provided an account of the revival at Cold Spring in *Christian History* 1 (1743): 178–80. Valley birthplaces and religious inclinations are drawn from Clifford Shipton, *Sibley's Harvard Graduates: Biographical Sketches of Those Who Attended Harvard College,* 17 vols. (1933–75); Franklin B. Dexter, *Biographical Sketches of the Graduates of Yale College* (1885–1919); and Nobles, *Divisions*.

23. The son of Ann Paddy and John Hobby, a wealthy sea captain, William was pompous in the pulpit until Whitefield converted him. He was born and bred in Boston, unusual for an ardent, high-ranking New Light. He retained his civility, but did publish a minority report on Edwards's dismissal. Hobby maintained a New Light outpost at Reading in eastern Massachusetts, but the church chose a liberal successor in 1765, against his recommendation. The surname was peculiar to Herefordshire in the West. See Shipton, *Harvard Graduates,* 7:530–37; Henry Guppy, *Homes of Family Names in Great Britain* (1890), 502.

24. Nobles, *Divisions*, 85–90.

25. Shipton, *Harvard Graduates*, 359–67.

26. Peter N. Carroll, *The Other Samuel Johnson: A Psychohistory of Early New England* (1978), 96–129, 138–46. And Johnson was impressed that his mentor, Berkeley, who had become Bishop of Cloyne in Ireland, took Hutchinson very seriously in his final work, *Siris.* See Herbert Leventhal, *In the Shadow of the Enlightenment: Occultism and Renaissance Science in Eighteenth-Century America* (1976), 180–89. Thus conservative reaction to the Enlightenment came from otherworldly thinkers on the geographical periphery—i.e., Yorkshire, Scotland, Ireland, and Connecticut.

27. John J. Ellis III, *The New England Mind in Transition: Samuel Johnson of Connecticut, 1696–1772* (1973), 227–31; Herbert Schneider and Carol Schneider, "Samuel Johnson, President of King's College: A Note on the Relation of Science and Religion in Provincial America," *New England Quarterly* 8 (1935): 378–97. Jonathan Edwards had followed a similar path in rejecting materialism. After absorbing the Enlightenment in the Yale library, he reverted to the Calvinism of his father, a Connecticut pastor. Perry Miller made a sophisticated defense of Edwards against the charge of medievalism but his claim for Edwards's modernity was challenged from the outset. According to James Hoopes, one of the more recent critics, Edwards's intentions were not modern. The "new sense" he developed from Locke was not primarily an effort to bring theology in line with the Englishman's empirical psychology. Instead Edwards used Lockean terminology "to draw the fangs of empiricism by ridding it of its materialist assumptions." Edwards looks like he belongs with

Roger Williams and Samuel Johnson; this trio with Northwest roots, despite their intellectuality, did not yield their otherworldliness. See "Jonathan Edwards' Religious Psychology," *Journal of American History* 69 (1983): 849–65.

28. Carroll, *Johnson,* 185.

29. Ibid., 76–77, 80; Frank Holmes, *Directory of the Ancestral Heads of New England Families, 1620–1700* (1964 ed.), ccviii.

30. Cedric B. Cowing, *The Great Awakening and the American Revolution* (1971), 28–29.

31. For members of the Old Light elite see appendix C.

32. For the probable origins of ministers from East Anglia see appendix E. For the probable origins of ministers from the rest of the Southeast see appendix F. The clerics in the Barnard, Cushing, Hobart, and Marsh families did not show evangelical sympathies in the colonial period.

33. For members of the upper half of the clerical Saving Remnant, see appendix D; for clerics with Northwest origins, see appendix G; for those with Southeast origins but Northwest surnames, see appendix H.

34. Calculated from Banks, *Topographical;* Holmes, *Ancestral Heads;* and Guppy, *Homes.* After the Great Awakening, learned ministers in New England were quite evenly divided according to their origins, but the birthrate of the New Light clergy was almost 40 percent higher than that of the Old Light. Harry Stout assumes this was because of birth control among the latter. See "The Great Awakening in New England Reconsidered: The New England Clergy as a Case Study," *Journal of Social History* 4 (1974): 37.

Looking toward
the Future

A division in religiosity in England antedated settlement of New England. It was intensified by the spread of the textile industry from the Low Countries to East Anglia and the West Country and by the Reformation. A new rationalism was emerging in Southeast England while the Northwest retained its potential for evangelism and pietism. Using data on ancestry and religious responses of clergy and communities in New England, a cultural dividing line can be drawn across the homeland from the Wash to Exeter, via Bristol. Of course, beyond this line in the Northwest were some outposts of Southeast sympathy, such as Manchester and the English colony in Pembroke, Wales. On the other hand, southeast of the line, there were outposts of evangelical-pietistic influence in London, Norwich, the Isles of Ely and Wight, and some wealds and fens. Nevertheless, this line has proved essential in considering predispositions toward New and Old Light religion in New England.

The settlement pattern of New England took shape by the 1660s and immigration slowed to a trickle; later, some Scots-Irish folk settled on the frontier after 1718. Those arriving early reflected fairly accurately the religious sectionalism of the home population at that time: three-quarters of them were from the Southeast, one-quarter from the Northwest. The Great Migration of 1630–40, when fifteen to twenty thousand came, was notable for its high concentration of Ramistic Puritans. The covenant Calvinism of the Puritan Southeast pioneers contained seeds of rationalism that would develop in parallel with the home country, with some variations. The Puritan contingent was primarily pushed by conditions at home rather than pulled by prospects in the colonies. Once in New England, they did move around, but not as much as the others, and were more likely to return home after the Civil War started. In comparison, Northwest folk were more likely to remain in New England and moved around twice as much in the early years, often withdrawing from places where others were dominant and resettling with others from the Northwest. From the beginning, New England was not homogeneous in religion. Those who have stressed differences between the Pilgrims of Plymouth and the Puritans of Massachusetts Bay have been on the right track. One kind of New Englander was pastoral and westering, the other, more sedentary and mercantile. The first tended to be evangelical and devotional, the second, theological and orthodox or, later, liberal. These differences were latent much of the time but came to the surface in religious crises and movements for reform.

The rationalism of Puritans from East Anglia was reflected in New England once the excitement of exodus and settlement subsided. This Ramism and concurrent spiritual declension became more evident with the end of Puritan rule in England. As early as 1636, Anne Hutchinson had warned against creeping formalism at Massachusetts Bay but it grew anyway; jeremiads and a reforming synod could not stem the tide. Among settlers in New England, overt presbyterianism and a Ramism that was becoming covert Arminianism were undermining religious vitality. In England the Glorious Revolution and consequent purge of pious leaders of the High Church party strengthened these tendencies. In New England, when communal values eroded, Cotton Mather and his followers fell back on family religion but indifference and toleration increased. Prominent men founded the liberal Brattle Street Church in Boston that did not require public relation and permitted dumb reading. There were signs of this laxity on both sides of the Atlantic. In England, Dissenter clergy at Salters Hall defeated subscription to Calvinist tenets in 1719, and the right of ministers to private judgment accelerated heterodoxy and decline in church attendance in the Southeast.

The histories of Rowley and Hingham, coastal towns in Massachusetts, illustrate the persistence of the two religious orientations from initial settlement to the Great Awakening. While the rational presbyterianism of the English Southeast was evident in Hingham from the outset, Rowley maintained its religious disposition, responding strongly to the first awakening in the 1740s and sustaining the evangelical spirit of the Northwest into the nineteenth century. The histories of these two towns suggest that when colonial settlements were not invaded by large organized groups of a different religious persuasion, those settlements tended to retain their views.

Prosecutions for witchcraft in seventeenth-century New England were concentrated in places where Southeast immigrants established control, such as Salem, Hartford, Fairfield, and Hampton. The leaders, orthodox Calvinists, sought to use law to combat the upsurge of orality, spontaneity, and heterodoxy that appeared to them as superstition and the work of the Devil. Their draconian measures were not effective for long, however, in slowing the power of the Northwest minority that was increasing with new settlements. The witch accusations of New England ran parallel to those in Europe. In places where Calvinism was strong—parts of Scotland and Switzerland—the authorities took those invoking occult powers to court, alleging direct links with Satan.[1]

With the Great Awakening, this growing minority was ready to take center stage, to reach out to new places and seek majority status. Religious differences, perennial but latent, finally came into full view. The revival brought pressure to bear on clergy and laity to choose between two paths, New Light and Old Light. Some managed to remain neutral and others—the Regular Lights—tried to stay in the middle or were contradictory or changed sides as fervor and arguments shifted. But in New England, those with Northwest roots were naturally drawn to New Light ministers and leaders, a Saving Remnant that rekindled old fires. Those from the Southeast, after welcoming Whitefield the first time, gravitated to the Old Light position, following leaders who feared enthusiasm and disorder. The Church of England, a small minority in New England, gained refugees from religious controversy and turbulence. Anglicans could offer the umbrella of a middle way, latitudinarianism for rationalists but ritual and metaphysics for a much smaller number of the mystically inclined.

The frontier was conducive to evangelical and sectarian religion from the beginning and became more so in the eighteenth and nineteenth centuries. People with pastoral roots could escape the mundane complexity of larger towns and continue or resume westering, the restless pursuit of soul liberty and the kingdom to come. Each "sprinkling" or "downpour" of evangelism produced persons who wanted to come out and separate from the world. And the dislocations of colonial wars—resistance to involvement as well as postwar migrations—contributed to populating the frontier.

In the eighteenth century, however, Frederick Jackson Turner's frontier thesis could apply to Britain as well as to the colonies. As the population grew in frontier areas and towns of both places after 1740, so did partisans of the New Light and New Birth. On both sides of the Atlantic, people with pastoral histories found itinerants of evangelical and pietistic Protestantism tuned to their feelings, temperament, and situation. This was evident in the Methodist-Evangelical Revival as well as the Great Awakening.

Revivalism was not strictly a frontier phenomenon confined to district edges or new lands opening up. It occurred also in long-settled towns and regions where the ethos of original Northwest settlers continued to prevail. With the right population mix, evangelism could be almost urban. Thus Rowley, Portsmouth, Gloucester, Plymouth, Norwich, and New Haven—older communities on the coast of New England—responded warmly to the Great Awakening. In England the centers of Methodism, Newcastle and Bristol, were old but expanding towns, the latter having passed Norwich to become England's second largest.

In New England, New Light clerics, like their Old Light counterparts, had a share of good collegiate education and social standing at Harvard and Yale and came from families that had settled in the colonies early. While New Lights had some well-born leaders and sympathizers, they also attracted many less well-educated converts who managed to gain pulpits without high collegiate standing, but this was true of Old Lights as well. The difference was origins in the British Isles in the seventeenth century. If they descended from the 25 percent who had emigrated from the Northwest or from the 10 to 15 percent in the Southeast with Northwest surnames, they were likely to sympathize with calls for a New Birth coming from Whitefield, Edwards, Davenport, and Wheelock. If they descended from those arriving from the Southeast between 1630 and 1640, they tried to ride out the revival and check enthusiasm without offending their flocks. Of course, an Old Light in Old Light territory or Boston could speak freely and arraign revivalists for excesses and irregularities, but the best weapons of the critics were printed pamphlets.

Surviving statistics from the churches in eighteenth-century New England indicate the differences between New Light and Old Light churches. In the former, membership gains came in cycles with a higher percentage of male converts at the top of the cycle. The Word of New Lights, spoken and sung, stirred some American Indians and made many converts among the small black population. Men were attracted early in life instead of treating church membership as an obligation that went with marriage, family, property, and public office. Because many were young, single, and unpropertied, some have discounted the importance of such converts, but these new adherents brought energy and idealism to the cause. They would gain friends and experience by participating in church affairs and were a force for reform. Later in life, a pastor could often recall them to their early commitment even if they had fallen away. And their early conversion could also lead them to leave the vicinity of their extended families and move to new lands. While the Great Awakening drew New Lights in various colonies together, it could also loosen bonds not only of orthodoxy, but also of community. Social mobility was enhanced. In distinctly Old Light communities, on the other hand, converts were fewer or disproportionately female and fewer controversies and permanent separations ensued from the effects of the Great Awakening. The revival's contribution to reform was correspondingly less in these places.

The Great Awakening undermined religious monopoly, reduced clericalism, and gave people a greater voice and choice in their faith. The eighteenth-century revival corresponded with the surge of laissez-faire ideas in the Anglo-American economic world. Colonials had learned to appreciate free trade and wanted individual decisions to determine supply and demand, prices in the marketplace; they also liked the political corollary, consent of the governed. And as they became free to choose their religious creeds and disciplines, they also came to dislike state-supported religion. The thirteen colonies were the laboratory for the Enlightenment of western Europe, and experimental religion was a natural concomitant of economic and political experiments.

Pastoral religion, emphasizing conversion and itineracy, was endemic on the British periphery. It built self-confidence, making many people "protestant" and providing the emotional seedbed for the Country or Real Whig ideology of natural rights and republicanism. In New England, and in the colonies generally, New Lights lent the power of their religion—orality, religiosity, and ethnicity—to Real Whig arguments against monarchy and for liberty, and these had much more influence in the colonies than in Britain.

Evangelical Protestantism reached its national apogee later, in the 1830s, during the Second Great Awakening, a level of religious fervor not attained since.[2] In the North, the Saving Remnant, invoking the higher law and Spirit of '76, went on to play a large role in antislave agitation and pushed a reluctant nation into freeing the slaves and re-forming itself in other ways. After Reconstruction and a trough in the moral reform cycle, cultural differences among descendants of New England would continue in the North.

After the First Great Awakening, revivalism slowly gained power in the South. The origins of up-country southerners in Virginia and the Carolinas were quite similar to those of the New Light regions of New England, and this frontier was even more conducive to evangelism—Calvinist and Arminian. The southern backcountry reached its religious apogee later, and because immigrants from Europe avoided the region in the nineteenth century, religion did not change there as much as in the North. Therefore, in seeking heirs of New England's New Light, one should look south of the Ohio River and west below the 36–30° latitude as well as to the Midwest, the Yankee Heartland that received so many settlers from New England.

America offers a variety of religious experiences and has extolled these choices as consonant with republican freedom. Of these, evangelism has proved to be the most adaptive and innovative—as the tags New Light, New Side, New School, and Neo-Evangelical suggest—and the mode of "Americanization" for many immigrants. Evangelism has continued to be the characteristic way of relating to this modernity.

In the years after World War II the lifestyles of Americans fragmented noticeably, further enhancing choices. People now want religion that is accessible, portable, and personal and with "hot" experiences; they still want soul liberty. While some mainline denominations have been puzzled by these tendencies, evangelicals have thrived and so—to a lesser extent—have their smaller, apolitical sectarian partners. Martin Marty thinks evangelicals have finally burst the bounds of the Old South, moving out from their base much like Catholics did from northern cities a generation earlier. He has noted that demographic trends favor this group; "the real power and greater share in American destiny will probably emerge from the course southern evangelicals will take."[3]

Some data from a "revisit" to "Middletown" is relevant here. The sociologists Robert Lynd and Helen Lynd conducted their famous first study of the town (Muncie, Indiana) in 1924. A social science team returned in 1978 to focus on religion and changes over two generations. They found basic beliefs about the same but religious life much less chauvinistic, puritanical, and theological—more tolerant and ecumenical than the Lynds had reported. They could not confirm any obvious signs of "secularization." Their findings pointed in the other direction, toward more marriages in church, more churches per capita, and, especially, better attendance and giving.[4] By 1978 a mild decline in mainline churches of northern origin was discernible, however, as was an increase in "southern religion." The team demonstrated that evangelical religion remained popular in modern "Middletown" and, by implication, hearty in the Midwest.

But what of a Saving Remnant—can a similar group, a modern "mystical elite" still be found amidst the many tables and charts of this community study? The best indicator is the Devotional Index the team constructed. It shows the relationship between private devotions, basic beliefs, and time and money donated. If the educational standard used to define the clerical Saving Remnant in the colonial period is applied, the result is that 30 percent of those with college degrees score high on the Devotional Index. This remnant can be described as more pietistic than evangelical, more optimistic than somber, more involved and sympathetic to religious revitalization than not, and still seekers, but less influential than those in nineteenth-century America.[5] Muncie lies north of the Ohio River and is now a small city with a regional university. The authors note that it actually falls a bit below national norms of religious activity; this large percentage of pious believers suggests that this moderate evangelism will continue to expand. It should be safe to infer that southward in the Sunbelt, this kind of remnant continues to comprise a significant fraction of those with some college education.[6]

Religious beliefs, according to George Gallup, are surprisingly durable and have remained about the same since the 1940s despite wars and the civil rights movement. As a result, he predicts for the 1990s some increase in both spiritual and community concerns, but with a continuing decline in members of the mainline denominations. Gallup suspects that "any increase in educational levels is very likely to lead to an increase in church membership and attendance," but people want a larger role for laity. Distrust of institutions continues, and interest in religion and church attendance remain cyclical; 49 percent of the Baby Boomers, now raising families, expect to participate in church activities more often in the coming years. The churches' perceived attitudes toward sex have kept many young people away, but they view their absence as temporary. Most likely to return to the fold, according to the Gallup polls, are people under thirty, African Americans, Hispanics, Baptists, Southern Baptists, and southerners generally. The United States has become more pluralistic and less specifically Protestant, but that a consistent one-third of Americans still have "breakthrough" religious experiences is, Gallup claims, "the most significant survey results ever uncovered."[7]

Tendencies toward New Light religiosity (evangelical-pietistic-transcendental) and Old Light (orthodox-rationalist-liberal) can be traced back from the Great Awakening to England before the first American settlements; this has been indicated for New England. Spiritual restlessness, sectionalism, and the frontier antedated the Plymouth Colony and Massachusetts Bay. Nevertheless, Frederick Jackson Turner was right in emphasizing these elements in shaping American character. He was wrong, or at least premature, in supposing in 1893 that the frontier was gone and that characteristics he admired would soon disappear in urban America; they both have thrived. The religion of pastoral people has proved popular, adaptable, and, where dominant, still capable of attracting new believers of different origins. Religion and ethnicity have always been major forces in American life and politics. Although in the twentieth century religion has become more private than earlier, the quest of American people for soul liberty for themselves and others has not been exhausted. We now describe this tendency by speaking of "self-determination," "choice," and "empowerment." The large fraction of the population historically inclined to religious influence and their willingness to vote and hold office has given the United States much vitality and unpredictability. Americans continue to measure religion pragmatically, the New Lights by its power to move them, the Old Lights by the power to attract converts and dollars. This tension is still discernible in religion, politics, and foreign policy as the twenty-first century approaches.

Notes

1. Christina Larner, *Enemies of God: The Witch-Hunt in Scotland* (1981), 171–74, 194–99. The Scottish lowland near Edinburgh was another enclave of Calvinistic nonevangelism in the Northwest.

2. Nathan O. Hatch believes that protagonists of the Second Great Awakening have not been given their due. Historians have emphasized social control and overlooked or downplayed influence in the early republic of these successors to eighteenth-century New Lights, especially their populism, Methodism, sectarianism, entrepreneurialism, religious music, and press. See *The Democratization of American Christianity* (1989), 220–26.

3. Martin E. Marty, "Introduction," in *Varieties of Southern Evangelism*, ed. Martin Marty and David E. Harrell (1981), ix–xii; Edwin S. Gaustad, "Regionalism in American Religion," in *Religion in the South*, ed. Charles R. Wilson (1985), 156; see also Wade C. Roof and William McKinney, *American Mainline Religion: Its Changing Shape in the Future* (1987), 126–38; and Martin E. Marty, *Religion and the Republic: The American Circumstance* (1987), 270–86.

4. The sociologist Robert Bellah and his researchers have reached a similar finding in their interviews. "Religious individualism is, in many ways, appropriate in our kind of society. It is no more going away than secular individualism. Ours is a society that requires people to be strong and independent." See Robert Bellah, Richard Madsen, William M. Sullivan, Ann Swidler, and Steven M. Tipton, *Habits of the Heart: Individualism and Commitment in American Life* (1985), 247.

5. The Bellah team found that "mysticism is probably the commonest form of religion" among those they interviewed, and "is found most often among prosperous well educated people, perhaps one reason why it flourishes in an affluent society." Some of these people remain outside organized religion. Ibid., 246, 247.

6. Theodore Caplow, Howard M. Bahr, Bruce A. Chadwick, Reuben Hill, and Margaret Holmes Williamson, *All Faithful People: Change and Continuity in Middletown's Religion* (1983), 148–62, 327–32. Examining the Lynds' data, they find some indicators of religious decline between 1890 and 1935 when the Lynds reexamined the town.

7. George Gallup, Jr., and Jim Castelli, *The People's Religion: American Faith in the 90's* (1989), 251–65, quotations from 258 and 252.

Appendix A: Methodology

Very many of the probable origins of surnames cited here come from Charles E. Banks's *Topographical Dictionary.* He in turn cites a great variety of sources from his research over the years. E. E. Brownell took over the work on Banks's death and finally published the dictionary in 1937. In editing, Brownell made some errors, which has caused scholars to describe the work as "flawed," though still useful. Despite the criticisms lodged against it, I have found Banks's work essential for illustrating the general patterns I discuss and thus have cited him frequently. Where possible I have checked his data against other such works by Frank Holmes, Charles Bardsley, Thomas Savage, John Farmer, Robert Pope, Sybil Noyes, and R. R. Hinman and corrected what to me seemed obvious errors. The result is that what I call "probable origins" actually vary from "highly" to "quite" likely.

Experience with the evidence has also convinced me that Henry Guppy's *Homes of Family Names in Great Britain* (1890) is also useful and is therefore cited frequently. While most people in Britain were more mobile from an earlier date than we have supposed—especially artisans and laborers—Guppy indicated that the yeoman class was the most stable and least likely to move about. Therefore their locations in the nineteenth century provide a good indication of their origins of even two centuries earlier. Guppy showed where these surnames were by county, yet listed only those with a frequency of 7 per 10,000 and above. If Guppy did not list a surname at all in the northern or western counties, I have presumed it to be of Southeast origin, unless a reliable source indicates otherwise.

In cases where a name appears frequently in a number of counties on both sides of the cultural line, the surname has been classified as Northwest if two of three of the highest frequencies are in that zone or if the larger of only two frequencies appeared in the Northwest.

I have found that very often surname frequency has been a better clue to religious inclination and behavior than the actual place the emigrant departed from in sailing to New England. Some Southeast counties, especially Norfolk in East Anglia, had a number of emigrants whose names had a high frequency in the Northwest. In fact, these people made up over 10 percent of the population in the Southeast in general and probably 40 percent of the London metropolis. Despite their county of emigration, they behaved religiously much like those from the Northwest.

If the county the emigrant came from is definitely known, I have listed it; if the county is unknown, but listed by Guppy, I have shown that frequency; in some cases, both are shown side by side. In chapter 3, I supplied only the surname frequencies listed by Guppy for the accused wizards because they revealed more about the origins of these people than did the actual counties of emigration.

The data on origins has been carefully checked but readers should recognize, of course, that the possibilities for error and omission are considerable. I have consistently used "probable" to remind people of this. Small errors should not detract from the arguments put forth in this book because they are broadly based and certainly do not depend upon any single, or small group of, surnames. This is a pioneer effort, and much more research is needed to amplify, modify, and supplement what is presented here.

Appendix B: Harvard Graduates from Rowley and Hingham, to 1765

Name	Class	Occupation
Rowley		
Thomas Mighill	1663	minister, South Scituate
Samuel Shepard, Jr.	1685	minister, New Jersey
George Phillips	1686	minister, Long Island
Spencer Bennett (Phips)	1703	gentleman
Samuel Payson	1716	assistant pastor
Jedidiah Jewett	1726	minister, Rowley
David Jewett	1736	minister, New London (Montville), Conn.
Thomas Hibbert	1748	minister, Amesbury
Dummer Jewett	1752	merchant
Jacob Bailey	1755	minister, Anglican missionary in Maine
Joseph Pearson	1758	secretary, New Hampshire Colony
Phineas Adams	1762	minister, West Haverhill
Thomas Lancaster	1764	minister, Scarsborough, Maine
Jonathan Searle	1764	minister, Mason, N.H.
Jonathan Searle	1765	minister, Salisbury, N.H.
Hingham		
Jeremiah Hobart	1650	minister
Joshua Hobart	1650	minister
Gershom Hobart	1667	minister, Groton
Japhet Hobart	1667	doctor
Nehemiah Hobart	1667	minister, Newton
Jeremiah Cushing	1676	minister, Scituate
Jedidiah Andrews	1695	minister, Philadelphia
Peter Cutler	1698	doctor
Jonathan Cushing	1712	minister, Dover, N.H.
Adam Cushing	1714	landholder, officeholder
Job Cushing	1714	minister, Shrewsbury
Nehemiah Hobart	1714	minister, Cohasset
Samuel Thaxter	1714	gentleman
Isaac Lincoln	1722	schoolmaster, Hingham
Isaiah Lewis	1723	minister, Wellfleet
Noah Hobart	1724	minister, Fairfield
Jeremiah Chubbock	1725	doctor

Appendix B, continued.

Name	Class	Occupation
Thomas Gill	1725	farmer, militia captain
Joseph Lewes	1725	schoolmaster, merchant
Ezekiel Hersey	1728	doctor
Thomas Lewes	1728	trader, farmer
James Lewes	1731	schoolmaster, Marshfield
Daniel Lewes	1734	lawyer
Samuel Gay	1740	doctor
John Thaxter	1741	farmer
Samuel Thaxter	1743	trader
Samuel French	1748	schoolmaster
Benjamin Lincoln	1749	farmer, general
Bela Lincoln	1754	doctor

Source: Clifford Shipton, *Sibley's Harvard Graduates: Biographical Sketches of Those Who Attended Harvard College,* 17 vols. (1933–75).

Appendix C: The Old Light Elite

Name	Rank	Birthplace	Parish	Probable Origin[a]
Angier, John	2/21	Watertown	Bridgewater, 3d	Essex
Avery, Ephraim	13/37	Truro	Brooklyn, Conn.	Berkshire
Balch, William	19/40	Beverly	Bradford	Dorset
Barnard, Edward	11/31	North Andover	Haverhill	Essex
Barnard, John	2/10	North Andover	Andover	Essex
Barnard, Thomas	8/29	Boston	West Newbury	Essex
Bowes, Nicholas	17/49	Boston	Bedford	—
Breck, Robert	5/33	Marlborough	Springfield	(Manchester)
Briant, Lemuel	11/32	Scituate	Quincy	Kent
Bridgham, James	17/34	Boston	Brimfield	Suffolk
Byles, Mather	13/49	Boston	Boston	Hampshire
Callender, J. (Baptist)	14/42	Boston	Newport, R.I.	(Durham, 24)[a]
Chauncy, Charles	3/7	Boston	Boston	Hertfordshire
Colton, Benjamin	1/2Y	Longmeadow	Hartford, Conn., 4th	Warwick[a]
Cushing, James	7/49	Salisbury	Plaistow, N.H.	Norfolk
Cushing, John	9/28	Salisbury	West Boxford	Norfolk
Devotion, Ebenezer, Jr.	10/23	Suffield	Scotland, Conn.	(France)
Eliot, Jacob	3/35	Guilford	Lebanon, 3d	Essex
Eliot, Jared	1/3Y	Guilford	Killingworth, Conn.	Essex
Emery, Stephen	9/33	Wells, Maine	Chatham	Hampshire
Fiske, Samuel	4/13	Braintree	Salem	Suffolk

Appendix C, continued

Name	Rank	Birthplace	Parish	Probable Origin[a]
Gardner, Joseph	11/29	Boston	Newport, R.I.	(Warwick, 45)[a]
Gookin, Nathaniel	5/37	Hampton	Northampton, N.H.	Kent
Hall, Samuel	1/3Y	Wallingford	Cheshire, Conn.	Kent
Hancock, John	8/27	Lexington	Braintree	(Derby, 30)[a]
Hart, William	9/23Y	Old Saybrook	Madison, Conn.	Essex
Hobart, Noah	16/40	Hingham	Fairfield, Conn.	Norfolk
Johnson, William	17/37	West Newbury	Newbury, 2d	(Cambridgeshire, 100)
Marsh, Jonathan	7/24Y	Windsor, Conn.	New Hartford, Conn.	Suffolk
Mayhew, Jonathan	8/33	Martha's Vineyard	Boston	Wiltshire
Merrick, Noah	5/13	West Springfield	Wilbraham	Wales[a]
Moody, John	15/37	Byfield	Newmarket	(Hampshire, 15)
Odlin, Elisha	8/37	Exeter, N.H.	Amesbury	Lincoln[a]
Odlin, Woodbridge	7/36	Exeter, N.H.	Exeter, N.H.	Lincoln[a]
Parsons, Joseph	9/21	Lebanon, Conn.	Bradford	(Wiltshire, 80)
Parsons, Samuel	8/33	Boston	Rye, N.H.	(Wiltshire, 80)
Parsons, William	12/40	Boston	Southampton, N.H.	(Wiltshire, 80)
Porter, Samuel	15/33	Hadley	Sherborn	Essex
Rogers, Daniel, II	5/49	Ipswich	Littleton	Essex (Shropshire, 65)[a]
Rossiter, Asher	8/17Y	Guilford, Conn.	Preston, Conn.	Dorset
Ruggles, Thomas	3/11Y	Guilford, Conn.	Guilford, Conn.	Essex
Russell, William	2/9Y	Middletown, Conn.	Middletown, Conn.	(Cambridgeshire, 50)
Smith, William	21/49	Charlestown	Weymouth	(Worcester, 300)[a]
Sparhawk, John	4/37	Bristol	Salem, 1st	Essex
Stone, Nathan	11/34	Brewster	Southborough	Essex

Stone, Nathaniel	10/22	Watertown	Harwich	Essex
Townsend, Jonathan	9/28	Needham	Medfield	Suffolk
Walter, Nathaniel	6/28	Ireland	West Roxbury	Ireland[a]
Webster, Elisha	6/15Y	Hartford	Canaan, Conn.	Norfolk
Webster, Samuel	12/40	Bradford	Salisbury, 2d	Norfolk
Whipple, Joseph	5/21	Hamilton	Hampton Falls, N.H.	Essex
Whitman, Elnathan	3/23Y	Farmington, Conn.	Hartford, Conn., 2d	Buckinghamshire
Whittlesey, Samuel	3/6Y	Saybrook	Wallingford, Conn.	Cambridgeshire
Whittlesey, Samuel, Jr.	4/17Y	Wallingford	Milford, Conn.	Cambridgeshire
Williams, Wareham	6/27	Deerfield	Waltham	(Wales)[a]
Wingate, Paine	16/43	Hampton, N.H.	Amesbury	Bedfordshire
Woodbridge, Ashbel	2/17Y	Hartford	Glastonbury, Conn.	Wiltshire
Woodbridge, Benjamin	3/21Y	West Springfield	Amity, Conn.	Wiltshire

Sources: Charles E. Banks, *Topographical Dictionary*, ed. E. E. Brownell (1937); Henry Guppy, *Homes of Family Names in Great Britain* (1890).

Note: Surname frequency from Henry Guppy, *Homes of Family Names in Great Britain* (1890), appears in parentheses. Other probable origins are from Banks, *Topographical*. Only ministers who ranked in the top half of their classes are included here.

Y = Yale graduate.

a. Those with origins in the Northwest.

Appendix D: The Saving Remnant Elite

Name	Rank	Parish	Probable Origin[a]
Abbot, Hull	10/21	Charlestown	(Dorset, 20)[a]
Bradstreet, Benjamin	15/49	Gloucester, 4th	Lincoln
Bradstreet, Simon	4/16	New London, Conn.	Lincoln
Bradstreet, Simon	11/49	Marblehead	Lincoln
Brainerd, Nehemiah	4/23Y	Eastbury, Conn.	Essex (France)[a]
Buell, Samuel	7/20Y	East Hampton, Long Island	Huntingdonshire (France)[a]
Bull, Nehemiah	5/11Y	Westfield	Surrey (Wales)
Checkley, Samuel	3/20	Boston	Northamptonshire[a]
Cheever, Ames	5/19	Manchester	Kent (France)[a]
Colman, Benjamin	3/8	Boston	Essex[a]
Cooper, Samuel	3/40	Boston, Brattle St.	(Hampshire)[a]
Cooper, William	2/20	Boston, Brattle St.	(Hampshire)[a]
Cotton, John	7/33	Halifax	Derby
Cotton, John	4/14	Newton	Derby
Cotton, Josiah	8/32	Providence, R.I.	Derby
Cotton, Ward	7/28	Hampton, N.H.	Derby
Crocker, Josiah	11/37	Taunton	western Devon
Davenport, James	2/23Y	Southold, Long Island	Warwick
Edwards, Jonathan	4/8	Northampton	London (Wales)
Edwards, Timothy	7/23	East Windsor	London (Wales)
Foxcroft, Thomas	1/11	Boston	Yorkshire
Gee, Joshua	8/17	Boston	western Devon
Gilman, Nicholas	14/40	Durham, N.H.	Essex (Staffordshire, 18)
Gould, Hezekiah	3/27Y	Stratford, Conn.	(Dorset, 31, Staffordshire, 30
Graham, John, Jr.	6/21Y	West Suffield	Scotland
Griswold, George	1/5Y	East Lyme, Conn.	Warwick
Hale, John	2/21	Ashford, Conn.	Hertfordshire (Monmouthshire, 28)
Hobby, William	10/49	Reading	(Hereford, 14)
Hopkins, Samuel	6/23Y	Great Barrington	western Devon
Horton, Simon	4/13Y	Southold, Long Island	South Leicester (western Devon)
Jewett, David	13/31	Montville, Conn.	Yorkshire
Judson, David	5/15Y	Newton, Conn.	Yorkshire
Leavitt, Dudley (Separate)	13/32	Stratham, N.H.	Dorset[a]

Leonard, Silas	9/19Y	Goshen, N.Y.	Staffordshire (Wales)
Lord, Benjamin	4/9Y	Norwich, Conn.	Essex (Lancashire, 42)
Lord, Hezekiah	2/5Y	Griswold, Conn.	Essex (Lancashire, 42)
Lord, Joseph	12/34	Pequoiag (Athol)	Essex (Lancashire, 42)
Mather, Nathaniel	1/3Y	Jamesport, Long Island	Lancashire
Parsons, David	12/28	Hadley	(Wiltshire, 80)[a]
Pemberton, Ebenezer	8/38	New York, N.Y.	Essex (Lancashire, 8)
Pierson, John	1/3Y	Woodbridge, N.J.	Yorkshire
Pike, James	24/49	Somersworth, N.H.	western Somerset
Porter, Samuel	15/33	Sherborn	Hampshire (Oxfordshire, 35)[a]
Prince, Thomas	6/19	Boston	Berkshire (Staffordshire, 20)
Prince, Thomas, Jr.[b]	1/23	Boston	Berkshire (Staffordshire, 20)
Rogers, Daniel I	4/49	Exeter, N.H.	Essex (Shropshire, 65)
Rogers, John	2/9	Ipswich	Essex (Shropshire, 65)
Rogers, John	2/32	Gloucester, 4th	Essex (Shropshire, 65)
Rogers, John	5/12	Kittery (Eliot)	Essex (Shropshire, 65)
Rogers, Nathaniel	6/31	Ipswich	Essex (Shropshire, 65)
Ruggles, Benjamin	1/14Y	Lakeville	Suffolk (France)[a]
Sewall, Joseph	1/19	Boston	Warwick
Smith, Josiah	22/49	Charleston, S.C.	(Worcester, 300)
Smith, Thomas	4/21	Falmouth	(Worcester, 300)
Sproat, James	10/20Y	Guilford, 4th	Kent (Lancashire)
Stoddard, Anthony	2/14Y	Woodbury, Conn.	London (Staffordshire)
Thacher, Peter	3/7	Middleborough	Wiltshire[a]
Thacher, Roland	12/39	Wareham	Wiltshire[a]
Treat, Richard	2/9Y	Abington, Pa.	western Somerset
Tucke, John	17/43	Gosport, N.H.	(Wiltshire, 16)[a]
Walley, John	4/34Y	South Ipswich	(Cheshire, 17)
Weld, Habijah	18/42	Attleborough	Suffolk[a]
White, John	7/15	Gloucester	(Devon, 90, Wiltshire, 86)[a]
Wigglesworth, Samuel	3/19	Ipswich Hamlet	Yorkshire
Willard, Samuel	7/43	Winter Harbor	Kent[a]
Williams, Chester	5/24Y	Hadley	(Wales)
Williams, Solomon	7/27	Lebanon, Conn.	(Wales)
Williams, Stephen	3/6	Longmeadow	(Wales)
Wise, Jeremiah	6/15	South Berwick	(Yorkshire, 18; Cornwall, 8)
Woodbridge, John	5/23Y	South Hadley	Wiltshire[a]
Woodbridge, Timothy	7/23Y	Hatfield	Wiltshire[a]

Sources: Banks, *Topographical;* Guppy, *Homes.*

Note: Surname frequency from Guppy, *Homes,* appears in parentheses. Other probable origins are from

Banks, *Topographical.* Only ministers who ranked in the top half of their classes are included here.

Y = Yale graduate.

a. Those with origins in the Southeast.

b. Never settled as a minister.

Appendix E: Clergy Active in the Great Awakening with East Anglian Origins

Name	Probable Origin	Religion
Allis, Samuel	Essex	New Light
Andrews, Jedidiah	Suffolk	Old Light
Angier, John	Essex	Old Light
Barnard, Edward	Essex	Old Light
Barnard, John	Essex	Old Light
Barnard, Thomas	Essex	Old Light
Barratt, Samuel	Norfolk	Old Light
Bass, Benjamin	Essex	Old Light
Bass, John	Essex	Old Light
Brainerd, David	Essex (France)	New Light
Brainerd, Nehemiah	Essex (France)	New Light
Bridgham, James	Suffolk	Old Light
Burr, Aaron	Essex	Regular Light
Burr, Isaac	Essex	Old Light
Case, Benajah	Norfolk	New Light
Chase, Stephen	Essex	Old Light
Cheney, Thomas	Essex (France)	New Light
Collins, Timothy	Essex	Old Light
Colman, Benjamin	Norfolk	New Light
Cowell, David	Essex	Old Light
Cushing, Caleb	Norfolk	Old Light
Cushing, James	Norfolk	Old Light
Cushing, Job	Norfolk	Old Light
Cushing, John	Norfolk	Old Light
Cushing, John	Norfolk	Old Light
Cushing, Jonathan	Norfolk	Old Light
Cushing, Mathew	Norfolk .	Old Light
Dwight, Josiah	Essex	Old Light
Eliot, Andrew	Essex	Regular Light
Eliot, Jacob	Essex	Old Light
Eliot, Jared	Essex	Old Light
Fiske, John	Suffolk	New Light
Fiske, Samuel	Suffolk	Old Light
Fitch, Jabez	Essex	New Light
Flagg, Ebenezer	Norfolk	Old Light
Fuller, David	Norfolk	Old Light

Appendix E, continued.

Name	Probable Origin	Religion
Hart, William	Essex	Old Light
Hobart, Noah	Norfolk	Old Light
Hovey, John	Essex (France)	New Light
Hovey, Ivory	Essex (France)	New Light
Hubbard, Jonathan	Suffolk	Old Light
Marsh, Cyrus	Suffolk	Old Light
Marsh, Edmund	Suffolk	Old Light
Marsh, Elisha	Suffolk	Old Light
Marsh, Jonathan	Suffolk	Old Light
Marsh, Jonathan	Suffolk	Old Light
Payson, Philip	Norfolk	Old Light
Prentice, John	Essex	Old Light
Prentice, Joshua	Essex	Old Light
Prentice, Solomon	Essex	New Light
Prentice, Thomas	Essex	New Light
Ruggles, Benjamin	Essex (France)	New Light
Ruggles, Thomas	Essex (France)	Old Light
Rust, Henry	Norfolk	Old Light
Salter, Richard	Suffolk	Old Light
Sparhawk, John	Essex	Old Light
Stearns, David	Suffolk	Old Light
Stone, Nathan	Essex	Old Light
Stone, Nathaniel	Essex	Old Light
Townsend, Jonathan	Suffolk	Old Light
Townsend, Jonathan, Jr.	Suffolk	Old Light
Townsend, Solomon	Suffolk	Old Light
Tucke, John	Suffolk	New Light
Tufts, Joshua	Norfolk	Regular Light
Turner, David	Essex	Old Light
Waller, Timothy	Norfolk	Old Light
Webster, Elisha	Norfolk	Old Light
Wester, Samuel	Norfolk	Old Light
Weld, Habijah	Suffolk	New Light
Weld, Thomas	Suffolk	Old Light
Whipple, Joseph	Essex	Old Light
Winthrop, John, IV	Suffolk	Old Light
Youngs, David	(Norfolk 26; Suffolk, 14)	New Light

Sources: Banks, *Topographical;* Guppy, *Homes.*

Note: Surname frequency from Guppy, *Homes,* appears in parentheses. Other probable origins are from Banks, *Topographical.* Less than one in four were New Lights.

Appendix F: Clergy Active in the Great Awakening with Other Southeast Origins

Name	Probable Origin	Religion
Adams, Eliphalet	(Buckinghamshire, 50; eastern Devon, 42; Shropshire, 38)	Regular Light
Adams, Joseph	(Buckinghamshire, 50; eastern Devon, 42; Shropshire, 38)	New Light
Avery, Ephraim	(Sussex, 18; Buckinghamshire, 12)	Old Light
Avery, Joseph	(Sussex, 18; Buckinghamshire, 12)	Regular Light
Bacheller, Stephen	—	Old Light
Bacon, Jacob	(Essex, 21; Leicestershire and Rutland, 20)	Old Light
Balch, Thomas	Dorset and eastern Somerset	New Light
Balch, William	Dorset and eastern Somerset	Old Light
Bartlett, Moses	(Dorset, 73; Oxfordshire, 35)	Old Light
Blunt, John	(Cambridgeshire, 29; Leicestershire and Rutland, 21; Northamptonshire, 15)	New Light
Boardman, Daniel	Oxfordshire	Old Light
Bourne, Shearjashub	(Wiltshire, 22; Shropshire, 22; Sussex, 21)	Old Light
Bucknam, Nathan	—	Old Light
Buell, Samuel	Huntingdonshire (France)	New Light
Burt, John	Wiltshire	Old Light
Cabot, Marston	Channel Islands (France)	Regular Light
Carpenter, Ezra	(Wiltshire, 30; Somerset, 27)	Old Light
Champney, James	(France)	Old Light
Chauncy, Charles	Hertfordshire	Old Light
Chauncy, Nathaniel	Hertfordshire	Old Light
Checkley, Samuel	(Oxfordshire, 35; Buckinghamshire, 18)	New Light
Cheever, Ames	Kent (France)	New Light
Chipman, John	Dorset	New Light
Clap, Supply	eastern Somerset	Old Light
Clark, Peter	(Buckinghamshire, 150; Leicestershire and Rutland)	Old Light
Cogswell, James	Wiltshire	Old Light
Conant, Sylvanus	eastern Devon	New Light

Appendix F, continued.

Name	Probable Origin	Religion
Condy, Jeremiah	(Somerset, 29; Hampshire, 21; Wiltshire, 13)	Baptist
Cooke, Samuel	(Northamptonshire, 65; Gloucester, 60; Suffolk, 62)	Old Light
Cooke, Samuel	(Northamptonshire, 65; Gloucester, 60; Suffolk, 62)	New Light
Cooke, William	(Northamptonshire, 65; Gloucester, 60; Suffolk, 62)	Old Light
Cooper, Samuel	(Hampshire, 70; Leicestershire and Rutland, 64)	Old Light
Cooper, William	(Hampshire, 70; Leicestershire and Rutland, 64)	New Light
Curtis, Jeremiah	(Buckinghamshire, 60; Dorset, 30)	Old Light
Curtis, Philip	(Buckinghamshire, 60; Dorset, 30)	Old Light
Devotion, Ebenezer	(France)	New Light
Devotion, Ebenezer, Jr.	(France)	Old Light
Dexter, Samuel	Buckinghamshire	New Light
Diman, James	—	New Light
Dwight, Josiah	(Buckinghamshire, 20)	Old Light
Eells, Nathaniel	Hertfordshire	Old Light
Eells, Nathaniel	Hertfordshire	Regular Light
Ellis, Jonathan	(Devonshire, 43; Cambridgeshire, 38; Essex, 27)	Old Light
Elmer, Daniel	Northamptonshire	Old Light
Emery, Stephen	Hampshire	Old Light
Fessenden, Benjamin	Kent	Old Light
Fogg, Ebenezer	London (Kent)	Old Light
Fowle, John	(Kent, 15)	Regular Light
Frink, Thomas	—	Old Light
Gardner, John	(Warwick, 45; Essex, 33; Northamptonshire, 30)	Old Light
Gardner, Joseph	(Warwick, 45; Essex, 33; Northamptonshire, 30)	Old Light
Gay, Ebenezer	(Wiltshire, 31; Hampshire, 14)	Old Light
Gay, Ebenezer	(Wiltshire, 31; Hampshire, 14)	Old Light
Goddard, David	(Berkshire, 55; Dorset, 31)	New Light
Gookin, Nathaniel	Kent	Old Light
Goss, Thomas	(Buckinghamshire, 20)	Old Light
Gray, Ellis	(Northumberland, 26; Hertfordshire, 30; Dorset, 20)	Regular Light
Hall, Samuel	Kent	Old Light
Hall, Theophilus	Kent	Old Light

Hall, Willard	Kent	Old Light
Harrington, Timothy	—	Old Light
Haven, Elias	—	New Light
Heminway, Jacob	—	Old Light
Heminway, Phineas	—	New Light
Henchman, Nathaniel	—	Old Light
Johnson, Jacob	(Cambridgeshire, 100; Northumberland, 96; Leicestershire and Rutland, 94)	New Light
Johnson, William	(Cambridgeshire, 100; Northumberland, 96; Leicestershire and Rutland, 94)	Old Light
Judd, Jonathan	(Hampshire, 30; Bedford, 15)	New Light
Judd, Reuben	(Hampshire, 30; Bedford, 15)	Regular Light
Kent, Elisha	Hampshire	New Light
Leavitt, Dudley	(Kent, 18; Sussex, 17)	New Light
Lewes, Daniel	Kent (Sussex)	Old Light
Lewes, Isaiah	Kent (Sussex)	Old Light
Lombard, Solomon	Dorset	Old Light
Loring, Israel	(France)	Old Light
Loring, Nicholas	(France)	New Light
Lovett, Joseph	(Leicestershire and Rutland, 25; Hampshire, 12)	Old Light
Main, Amos	(Northamptonshire, 15)	New Light
Mayhew, Jonathan	Wiltshire	Old Light
Mellen, John	(Holland)	Old Light
Messinger, Henry	(Northamptonshire, 25)	New Light
Mills, Gideon	Holland	New Light
Mills, Jedidiah	Holland	New Light
Mills, Ebenezer	Holland	New Light
Moody, John	(Hampshire, 15)	Old Light
Moody, Samuel	(Hampshire, 15)	New Light
Morse, Ebenezer	(Wiltshire, 22)	Old Light
Nightingale, Samuel	(Lancashire, 16; Sussex, 14; Surrey, 8)	Old Light
Norton, John	Hertfordshire	Old Light
Noyes, Joseph	Wiltshire	Old Light
Parkman, Ebenezer	eastern Devon	New Light
Peabody, Oliver	Leicester	New Light
Pomeroy, Benjamin	eastern Somerset	New Light
Porter, Samuel	Hampshire	New Light
Porter, John	Hampshire	New Light
Putnam, Daniel	Buckinghamshire	New Light
Rand, William	—	Old Light
Rice, Caleb	Hertfordshire	Old Light
Rossiter, Asher	Dorset	Old Light
Russell, Daniel	(Cambridgeshire, 50; Sussex, 40)	Old Light

Appendix F, continued.

Name	Probable Origin	Religion
Russell, William	(Cambridgeshire, 50; Sussex, 40)	Old Light
Silliman, Robert	(Italy, Holland)	Old Light
Skinner, Thomas	Sussex	Old Light
Stevens, Phineas	Oxfordshire	Old Light
Stiles, Abel	Bedford	Old Light
Stiles, Isaac	Bedford	Old Light
Thacher, Peter	Wiltshire	New Light
Thacher, Roland	Wiltshire	New Light
Torrey, Joseph	eastern Somerset	Old Light
Upham, Edward	Dorset	Baptist
Veazie, Samuel	Rutland	New Light
Vinal, William	Sussex	Old Light
Warren, John	(Dorset, 46; Cambridgeshire, 24)	New Light
Webb, Benjamin	Wiltshire	Old Light
Webb, John	Wiltshire	New Light
Welsteed, William	—	Regular Light
White, Ebenezer	(Devon, 90; Wiltshire, 86; Dorset, 85)	New Light
White, Ebenezer	(Devon, 90; Wiltshire, 86; Dorset, 85)	Old Light
White, John	(Devon, 90; Wiltshire, 86; Dorset, 85)	New Light
White, Stephen	(Devon, 90; Wiltshire, 86; Dorset, 85)	New Light
White, Thomas	(Devon, 90; Wiltshire, 86; Dorset, 85)	Old Light
Whitman, Elnathan	Buckinghamshire	Old Light
Whitman, Samuel	Buckinghamshire	Old Light
Whitman, Thomas	Buckinghamshire	Old Light
Whittlesey, Samuel	Cambridgeshire	Old Light
Whittlesey, Samuel, Jr.	Cambridgeshire	Old Light
Willard, Samuel	Kent	New Light
Wingate, Paine	Bedfordshire	Old Light
Woodbridge, Benjamin	Wiltshire	Old Light
Woodbridge, John	Wiltshire	New Light
Woodbridge, Samuel	Wiltshire	Old Light
Woodbridge, Timothy	Wiltshire	New Light

Sources: Banks, *Topographical;* Guppy, *Homes.*

Note: Surname frequency from Guppy, *Homes,* appears in parentheses. Other probable origins are from Banks, *Topographical.* Those from the Southeast but with Northwest surnames are not included here. See appendix H. Despite the Old Light of the prominent Chauncy family, clerics with French names tilted toward the New Light. Perhaps some derived from the Christian Heartland, the pious belt stretching across France, mentioned in chap. 1.

Appendix G: Clergy Active in the Great Awakening with Northwest Origins

Name	Probable Origin	Religion
Abbot, Hull	western Devon	New Light
Allen, Benjamin	western Devon (Barnstaple, Braunton)	New Light
Allen, Timothy	western Devon (Barnstaple, Braunton)	New Light
Allen, William	western Devon (Barnstaple, Braunton)	New Light
Ashley, Jonathan	(Shropshire, 12)	Old Light
Ballantine, John	Scotland	Regular Light
Barker, Nehemiah	Yorkshire	New Light
Bayley, Abner	(Hampshire, 81; Staffordshire, 60; Gloucester, 43)	Old Light
Bayley, James	(Hampshire, 81; Staffordshire, 60; Gloucester, 43)	New Light
Bellamy, Joseph	(Lincoln, 18; Nottinghamshire, 16)	New Light
Billing, Edward	western Somerset	New Light
Billing, Richard	western Somerset	New Light
Bliss, Daniel	western Devon	New Light
Bradstreet, Benjamin	Lincoln	New Light
Bradstreet, Simon	Lincoln	New Light
Bradstreet, Simon	Lincoln	New Light
Bridge, Ebenezer	(Lancashire, 20; Derby, 7)	Old Light
Brown, Samuel	(Northumberland, 123; Durham, 116)	Old Light
Byram, Elias	Nottinghamshire	New Light
Campbell, Othneil	Scotland	New Light
Canfield, Thomas	Yorkshire	New Light
Coffin, Peter	western Devon	Old Light
Caulkins, Hugh[a]	Wales	New Light
Coit, James	Wales	Old Light
Colton, Benjamin	Warwick	Old Light
Cotton, John	Derby	New Light
Cotton, John	Derby	New Light
Cotton, Joseph	Derby	New Light
Cotton, Ward	Derby	New Light
Crocker, Joseph	western Devon	New Light
Crocker, Josiah	western Devon	New Light
Croswell, Andrew	(Worcester, 18; Derby, 7)	New Light
Davenport, James	Warwick	New Light

Appendix G, continued.

Name	Probable Origin	Religion
Davidson, William	Scotland	Presbyterian
Davis, Joseph	(Worcester, 85, Gloucester, 80)	Old Light
Dickinson, Jonathan	Northumberland	New Light
Dickinson, Moses	Northumberland	New Light
Doolittle, Benjamin	Worcester	Old Light
Dorr, James	Derby	New Light
Dunbar, Samuel	Scotland	Regular Light
Dunster, Isaiah	Lancashire	New Light
Eaton, Joshua	Worcester	New Light
Emerson, Daniel	Durham, Lincoln	New Light
Emerson, John	Durham, Lincoln	New Light
Emerson, Joseph	Durham, Lincoln	New Light
Fish, Joseph	Lancashire	New Light
Foxcroft, Thomas	Yorkshire	New Light
Frost, Amariah	western Devon	New Light
Frothingham, Ebenezer[a]	Yorkshire	New Light
Gaylord, William	western Somerset (France)	New Light
Gee, Joshua	western Devon	New Light
Graham, John	Scotland	New Light
Graham, John, Jr.	Scotland	New Light
Griswold, George	Warwick	New Light
Hancock, John	Derby	New Light
Hancock, John	Derby	Old Light
Heaton, Stephen	(Lancashire and West Riding; Yorkshire, 21)	Old Light
Hill, Abraham	(Gloucester, 73; Somerset, 70)	Regular Light
Hill, Samuel	(Gloucester, 73; Somerset, 70)	New Light
Hobby, William	(Hereford, 14)	New Light
Hopkins, Samuel	Shropshire	New Light
Hopkins, Samuel	Shropshire	Regular Light
Hyde, Jedidiah[a]	Worcester	New Light
Jefferds, Samuel	Scotland	New Light
Jewett, David,	Yorkshire	New Light
Jewett, Jedidiah	Yorkshire	New Light
Johnes, Timothy	western Somerset	New Light
Judson, David	Yorkshire	New Light
Kendall, Samuel	(Leicester and Rutland, 26; Cumberland and Westmorland, 25; Yorkshire, 17)	Regular Light
Leavenworth, Mark	Wales	New Light
Lee, Jonathan	(Nottinghamshire, 50; Northumberland, 48; Durham, 44)	New Light

Leonard, Nathaniel	Staffordshire	New Light
Leonard, Silas	Staffordshire	New Light
Little, Ephraim	(Cumberland and Westmorland, 80; Northumberland, 30)	Old Light
Lowell, John	Worcester	Regular Light
Maccarty, Thaddeus	Ireland	New Light
McGregore, David[a]	Ireland	Presbyterian/ New Light
Mather, James	Lancashire	New Light
Mather, Nathaniel	Lancashire	New Light
Meacham, Joseph	Derby	New Light
Merrick, Jonathan	(Hereford, 17; Shropshire, 12)	Old Light
Merrick, Noah	(Hereford, 17; Shropshire, 12)	Old Light
Moorhead, John	Ireland	Presbyterian/ New Light
Moseley, Samuel	Lancashire	New Light
Newell, Samuel	(Cheshire, 9)	New Light
Niles, Samuel	Wales	Regular Light
Nott, Abraham	(Hereford, 54; Worcester, 22; Hertfordshire, 18)	Old Light
Odlin, Elisha	Lincoln	Old Light
Odlin, Woodbridge	Lincoln	Old Light
Owen, John	Wales	New Light
Park, Joseph	Lancashire	New Light
Perkins, Daniel	(South Wales and Warwick, 30; Monmouthshire, 25)	Regular Light
Pickering, Theophilus	Warwick	Old Light
Pierson, John	Yorkshire	New Light
Pike, James	western Somerset	New Light
Prescott, Benjamin	Yorkshire	Old Light
Roberts, Nathaniel	(North Wales, 500; South Wales, 110)	New Light
Rowland, Daniel	Cheshire	New Light
Seccombe, Joseph	(Cornwall, 8)	New Light
Sewall, Joseph	Warwick	New Light
Shaw, John	Yorkshire	New Light
Shurtleff, William	Yorkshire	New Light
Smith, Aaron	(Worcester, 300)	Old Light
Smith, Josiah	(Worcester, 300)	New Light
Smith, Thomas	(Worcester, 300)	New Light
Smith, Thomas	(Worcester, 300)	New Light
Smith, William	(Worcester, 300)	Old Light
Strong, Nathaniel	Wales	New Light
Swan, Josiah	(Northumberland, 17)	Old Light
Taylor, John	(Warwick, 140; Lancashire, 135)	Old Light
Tobey, Samuel	Wales	New Light
Todd, Abraham	Yorkshire	New Light
Todd, Jonathan	Yorkshire	Old Light

Appendix G, continued.

Name	Probable Origin	Religion
Todd, Samuel	Yorkshire	New Light
Tompson, William	Lancashire	New Light
Treat, Richard	western Somerset	New Light
Trumbull, John	Northumberland	Old Light
Turell, Ebenezer	western Devon	Regular Light
Wales, Atherton	Yorkshire	New Light
Wales, Eleazer	Yorkshire	New Light
Wales, John	Yorkshire	New Light
Walker, Timothy	(Durham, 110; Nottinghamshire, 90)	Old Light
Walter, Nathaniel	Ireland	Old Light
Wheelock, Eleazar	Shropshire	New Light
Whiting, John	Lincoln	New Light
Wigglesworth, Samuel	Yorkshire	New Light
Wight, Jabez	Lincoln	New Light
Wight, John	Lincoln	New Light
Wilkins, Daniel	Wales	New Light
Williams, Chester	Wales	New Light
Williams, Eleazar	Wales	New Light
Williams, Jeremiah	Wales	New Light
Williams, Solomon	Wales	New Light
Williams, Stephen	Wales	New Light
Williams, Warham	Wales	Old Light
Williams, William	Wales	Old Light
Willys, Henry	Warwick	New Light
Wilmot, William	Derby	New Light
Wise, Jeremiah	Cornwall	New Light
Worthington, William	(Cheshire, 38; Lancashire, 13; Nottinghamshire, 11)	Old Light

Sources: Banks, *Topographical;* Guppy, *Homes; New England Historical and Genealogical Register* 68 (1914): 77; Charles W. Bardsley, *Dictionary of English and Welsh Names* (1967 ed.).

Note: Surname frequency from Guppy, *Homes,* appears in parentheses. Other probable origins are from Banks, *Topographical.* Less than one in four were Old Lights.

a. Did not attend college.

Appendix H: Clergy Active in the Great Awakening from the Southeast but with Northwest Surnames

Name	Banks-Holmes Probable Origin	Guppy/Other Probable Origin	Religion
Emigrated from East Anglia			
Appleton, Nathaniel	Suffolk	(Yorkshire, 12; Lancashire, 8)	Regular Light
Backus, Isaac[a]	Norfolk	Yorkshire (Cumberland and Westmorland, 25)	Baptist/
			New Light
Barber, Jonathan	Suffolk	(Cheshire, 62; Gloucester, 27)	New Light
Baxter, Joseph	Norfolk	(Lincoln and Yorkshire, 9)	Old Light
Chandler, James	Suffolk	(Gloucester, 46; Hampshire, 25)	New Light
Chandler, Samuel	Suffolk	(Gloucester, 46; Hampshire, 25)	New Light
Cleaveland, Aaron	Suffolk	Yorkshire	New Light
Cleaveland, John[b]	Suffolk	Yorkshire	New Light
Gilman, Nicholas	Norfolk	(Staffordshire, 18; Derby, 13)	New Light
Greenwood, John	Norfolk	(West Riding, Yorkshire, 80)	Old Light
Lockwood, James	Suffolk	(Yorkshire, 15; Lincoln, 13)	New Light
Lord, Benjamin	Essex	(Lancashire, 42; Suffolk, 26)	New Light
Lord, Hezekiah	Essex	(Lancashire, 42; Suffolk, 26)	New Light
Lord, Joseph	Essex	(Lancashire, 42; Suffolk, 26)	New Light
Merrill, Isaac	Suffolk	(Worcester, 18, West Riding, Yorkshire, 15)	New Light
Merrill, Moses	Suffolk	(Worcester, 18, West Riding, Yorkshire, 15)	New Light
Merrill, Nathaniel	Suffolk	(Worcester, 18, West Riding, Yorkshire, 15)	Old Light
Pemberton, Ebenezer	Essex	(Lancashire, 8)	New Light

Appendix H, continued.

Name	Banks-Holmes Probable Origin	Guppy/Other Probable Origin	Religion
Phillips, Samuel	Norfolk	(South Wales, 150)	Old Light
Reynolds, Peter	Suffolk	(Shropshire and Wiltshire, 31; Cornwall, 30)	New Light
Rogers, Daniel	Essex	(Shropshire and Hereford, 65; Cornwall, 55)	Old Light
Rogers, Daniel	Essex	(Shropshire and Hereford, 65; Cornwall, 55)	Old Light
Rogers, John	Essex	(Shropshire and Hereford, 65; Cornwall, 55)	New Light
Rogers, John	Essex	(Shropshire and Hereford, 65; Cornwall, 55)	New Light
Rogers, Nathaniel	Essex	(Shropshire and Hereford, 65; Cornwall, 55)	New Light
Steel, Stephen	Essex	(Cumberland and Westmorland, 60; Strafford-shire, 26)	New Light
Toppan, Abraham	Norfolk	Yorkshire	Old Light
Toppan, Christopher	Norfolk	Yorkshire	Old Light

Emigrated from Other Southeast Counties

Name	Banks-Holmes Probable Origin	Guppy/Other Probable Origin	Religion
Boardman, Daniel	Oxford	(Lancashire, 17; Lincoln, 8)	Old Light
Bull, Nehemiah	Westfield	Surrey (Wales)	New Light
Edwards, Jonathan	London	(Shropshire, 210; Wales, 140)	New Light
Edwards, Timothy	London	(Shropshire, 210; Wales, 140)	New Light
Gould, Ebenezer	Hertfordshire, Buckinghamshire	(Dorset, 31; Staffordshire, 30; Derby, 25)	New Light
Gould, Hezekiah	Hertfordshire, Buckinghamshire	(Dorset, 31; Staffordshire, 30; Derby, 25)	New Light
Hale, John	Hertfordshire	(Monmouthshire, 28; Gloucester, 24)	New Light
Hale, Moses	Hertfordshire	(Monmouthshire, 28; Gloucester, 24)	New Light
Horton, Simon	South Leicester	(Warwick and Devon, 20; Worcester, 18)	New Light

Humphreys, Daniel	Dorset	(North Wales, 75; Shropshire, 30)	New Light
Kirkland, Daniel	Buckinghamshire	(Nottinghamshire, 12; Derby, 7)	New Light
Parker, Jonathan	Wiltshire	(West Riding, Yorkshire, 60; Northumberland, 48)	New Light
Parker, Thomas	Wiltshire	(West Riding, Yorkshire, 60; Northumberland, 48)	Old Light
Prince, Thomas	London	(Staffordshire, 20; Derby, 17)	New Light
Robbins, Philemon	South Leicester	(Warwick, 13; Hertfordshire, 12)	New Light
Sproat, James	Kent	(Lancashire)	New Light
Stoddard, Anthony	London	(Staffordshire and Scotland, 10)	New Light
Symmes, Timothy	Kent	(Wiltshire, 35; Derby, 34; Gloucester)	New Light

---

Sources: Banks, *Topographical;* Frank Holmes, *Directory of Ancient Heads of New England Families, 1620–1700* (1964 ed.); and Guppy, *Homes.*

Note: Surname frequency from Guppy, *Homes,* appears in parentheses. Other probable origins are from Banks, *Topographical.* Of the forty-five in this category, thirty-five were New Lights, nine were Old Lights, and one was a Regular Light.

a. Did not attend college.

b. John Cleaveland and his brother, Elisha, were expelled from Yale in 1744. John received his degree many years later. Christopher M. Jedrey, *The World of John Cleveland: Family Life in Eighteenth-Century New England* (1979), 40, 167.

Index

CEDRIC B. COWING is a professor of history at the University of Hawaii at Manoa. He is the author of *Populists, Plungers, and Progressives* and *The Great Awakening and the American Revolution* and the editor of *The American Revolution: Its Meaning to Asians and Americans.*